Neuro-Fuzzy Architectures and Hybrid Learning

Studies in Fuzziness and Soft Computing

Editor-in-chief
Prof. Janusz Kacprzyk
Systems Research Institute
Polish Academy of Sciences
ul. Newelska 6
01-447 Warsaw, Poland
E-mail: kacprzyk@ibspan.waw.pl
http://www.springer.de/cgi-bin/search_book.pl?series=2941

Danuta Rutkowska

Neuro-Fuzzy Architectures and Hybrid Learning

With 102 Figures
and 3 Tables

Physica-Verlag

A Springer-Verlag Company

Professor Danuta Rutkowska
Technical University of Czestochowa
Department of Computer Engineering
Armii Krajowej 36
42-200 Czestochowa
Poland
drutko@kik.pcz.czest.pl

ISSN 1434-9922
ISBN 978-3-7908-2500-8   e-ISBN 978-3-7908-1802-4

Cataloging-in-Publication Data applied for
Die Deutsche Bibliothek – CIP-Einheitsaufnahme
Rutkowska, Danuta: Neuro-fuzzy architectures and hybrid learning / Danuta Rut-
kowska. – Heidelberg; New York: Physica-Verl., 2002
     (Studies in fuzziness and soft computing; Vol. 85)

Physica-Verlag Heidelberg New York
a member of BertelsmannSpringer Science+Business Media GmbH

© Physica-Verlag Heidelberg 2010
Printed in Germany

Hardcover Design: Erich Kirchner, Heidelberg

This book is dedicated to the memory of the late Professor Ernest Czogała whose contribution and inspiration to develop the implication-based neuro-fuzzy systems should be greatly acknowledged. His final book entitled "Fuzzy and Neuro-Fuzzy Intelligent Systems" is closely related to the subject of this book.

This work is also dedicated to Professor Lotfi A. Zadeh known as the "Father of Fuzzy Logic", who laid the foundations of fuzzy sets and systems, and whose outstanding scientific activity is still appreciated and admired by all. His ideas and writings have shaped and inspired the contents of this book.

Foreword

The advent of the computer age has set in motion a profound shift in our perception of science – its structure, its aims and its evolution. Traditionally, the principal domains of science were, and are, considered to be mathematics, physics, chemistry, biology, astronomy and related disciplines. But today, and to an increasing extent, scientific progress is being driven by a quest for machine intelligence – for systems which possess a high MIQ (Machine IQ) and can perform a wide variety of physical and mental tasks with minimal human intervention.

The role model for intelligent systems is the human mind. The influence of the human mind as a role model is clearly visible in the methodologies which have emerged, mainly during the past two decades, for the conception, design and utilization of intelligent systems. At the center of these methodologies are fuzzy logic (FL); neurocomputing (NC); evolutionary computing (EC); probabilistic computing (PC); chaotic computing (CC); and machine learning (ML). Collectively, these methodologies constitute what is called soft computing (SC). In this perspective, soft computing is basically a coalition of methodologies which collectively provide a body of concepts and techniques for automation of reasoning and decision-making in an environment of imprecision, uncertainty and partial truth.

There are two facets of soft computing which are of basic importance. First, the constituent methodologies of SC are, for the most part, complementary rather than competitive. And second, the SC methodologies are synergistic in the sense that, in general, better results can be achieved when they are used in combination, rather than in a stand-alone mode. At this juncture, a combination which has highest visibility is that of neuro-fuzzy systems. But other combinations, such as neuro-genetic systems, fuzzy-genetic systems, and neuro-fuzzy-genetic systems are growing in visibility and importance. It is logical to expect that eventually almost all high MIQ systems will be of hybrid type.

This is the backdrop against which the publication of Professor Danuta Rutkowska's work,"Neuro-Fuzzy Architectures and Hybrid Learning," or NFAHL for short, should be viewed. Professor Rutkowska is one of the leading contributors to the theory of neuro-fuzzy systems and her expertise is reflected in the organization of NFAHL, the choice of subject matter and the high quality of exposition.

Historically, the first paper to consider a facet of neuro-fuzzy systems was that of S.C. Lee and E.T. Lee, published in 1974. Subsequently, important contributions were made by Butnariu, Chorayan, Rocha and Kosko. But the theory of neuro-fuzzy systems as we know it today, owes much to the pioneering work of H. Takagi and I. Hayashi at Matsushita, in the late eighties, which won them the basic patent on systems with neuro-fuzzy architecture.

A key issue which is highlighted with keen insight in NFAHL is that of parameter adjustment in fuzzy systems using neural network techniques and, reciprocally, parameter adjustment in neural networks using fuzzy if-then rules. Furthermore, parameter adjustment in both neural and fuzzy systems can be carried out through the use of genetic algorithms. The extensive coverage of this basic issue in Professor Rutkowska's work is one of its many outstanding features.

In my view, the natural starting point for parameter adjustment in both fuzzy and neural systems is multistage dynamic programming. However, the curse of dimensionality forces resort to gradient methods, which lead to backpropagation in the context of neural networks, and similar techniques for fuzzy systems which were developed by Takagi-Sugeno, Lin, Jang, Wang and others. A closely related technique is that of radial basis functions, which has been developed independently in the contexts of both neural networks and fuzzy systems.

In both neural network theory and fuzzy systems theory there is a widely held misconception centering on the concept of universal approximation. Specifically, in neural network theory it is accepted without question that any continuous function on a compact domain can be approximated arbitrarily closely by a multilayer neural network. The same is believed to be true for the class of additive fuzzy systems, from which a conclusion is drawn that there is an equivalence between neural networks and fuzzy systems.

What is not widely recognized is that universal approximation is valid only if the function which is approximated is known. Thus, if one starts with a black box which contains a function which satisfies the conditions of the approximation theorem, but is not known a priori, it is not possible to guarantee that it approximates to the function in the box to a given epsilon.

The universal approximation theorem is merely a point of tangency between the theories of neural networks and fuzzy systems. The agendas of the two theories are quite different, which explains why the two theories are complementary and synergistic, rather than competitive in nature. The highly insightful treatment of the synergism of neural network theory, fuzzy systems theory and genetic algorithm is a major contribution of Professor Rutkowska's work.

As was alluded to already, as we move farther into the age of machine intelligence and automated reasoning, what is likely to happen is that most high MIQ (Machine IQ) systems will be of hybrid type, employing a combination of methodologies of soft computing – and especially neurocomputing, fuzzy logic and evolutionary computing – to achieve superior performance. In this perspective, Professor Rutkowska's work lays the groundwork for the conception, design and utilization of such systems.

Professor Rutkowska has authored a book which is an outstanding contribution to our understanding and our knowledge of systems which have the capability to learn from experience. Dr. Rutkowska and the publisher, Physica-Verlag, deserve our thanks and plaudits.

Lotfi A.Zadeh
Berkeley, CA
May 7, 2001

Professor in the Graduate School, Computer Science Division
Department of Electrical Engineering and Computer Sciences
University of California
Berkeley, CA 94720 -1776
Director, Berkeley Initiative in Soft Computing (BISC)

Contents

1
Introduction

The initial idea behind writing this book was to present the new neuro-fuzzy architectures and the novel hybrid learning algorithms, developed as results of research into implication-based neuro-fuzzy systems and learning methods. These research projects were conducted in the Department of Computer Engineering, Technical University of Czestochowa, Poland, and supervised by the author of this book. Some of the conclusions have been published in papers contributed by the author, as well as Dr. Robert Nowicki and Dr. Artur Starczewski, who are the author's former Ph.D. students. Their Ph.D. dissertations [366], [479] were prepared on the basis of the above mentioned research.

However, it became clear that the scope of this book should go far beyond the initial idea of its contents. It was obvious that the book ought to provide much more information, not only concentrate on the subject of the research into implication-based neuro-fuzzy systems and hybrid learning, but also exhibit a wider view within the general framework of computational (or artificial) intelligence.

In addition to the first idea, concerning the above mentioned research, the intention was to incorporate some results from the author's other papers and books on neuro-fuzzy systems and intelligent systems. The main reason for this was that these books [434], [420] have been published in Polish, and are not accessible to many interested readers. Therefore, there are parts in this book referring to those in Polish. However, in fact, only a few sections have such references. Generally speaking, the subject of this book pertains to intelligent systems, and the research, mentioned above, can be treated as a tiny portion in this realm.

It is easy to notice that the title of this book - "Neuro-Fuzzy Architectures and Hybrid Learning" - is strictly related to the research corresponding to the findings presented in [366], [479], and in the researcher's papers. However, as explained in Chapter 7, the results concerning both directions of the research, i.e. *neuro-fuzzy architectures* and *hybrid learning*, combined together, constitute a special case of *Intelligent Computational Systems*, described in [420]. Thus the object of this book could be expressed as follows: **Neuro-Fuzzy Architectures + Hybrid Learning = Intelligent Systems**.

Chapter 7 also clarifies the difference between intelligent systems in the sense of *computational* and *artificial intelligence*. Since this book addresses intelligent systems, some information about *expert systems*, is included in this chapter. In addition, the latest research concerning *perception-based systems,* developed by Prof. Lotfi A. Zadeh, is also presented, with reference to intelligent systems. This research was preceded by his work on *computing with words*, and earlier on *calculus of fuzzy rules*. All these problems, as well as related issues on *granulation* and *fuzzy graphs*, introduced by Prof. Zadeh, are depicted in this book. Moreover, the basic knowledge of *fuzzy sets* and *fuzzy logic*, from the earliest papers of Prof. Zadeh, is provided in Chapter 2. In the same chapter, *fuzzy systems* are described in detail.

Since *neuro-fuzzy* systems, which are combinations of *fuzzy systems* and *neural networks*, are one of the key subjects of this book, a section on neural networks has been included in Chapter 3. It mainly contains information about the types of networks which are used in the neuro-fuzzy systems presented in this book and which influence the hybrid learning procedures. The difference between *fuzzy neural networks* and *fuzzy inference neural networks* is also explained in this chapter, within the framework of neuro-fuzzy systems.

Neuro-fuzzy architectures are described in Chapters 4 and 5. They refer, respectively, to the well-known and most often applied Mamdani approach, and the logical approach which is employed very seldom. The latest results concerning these architectures, mentioned at the beginning, are included mainly in Chapter 5. However, the former chapter also contains some novel results.

Chapter 6 is devoted to *hybrid learning*. It consists of sections on *gradient, genetic*, and *clustering algorithms*, as well as combinations of these. In this chapter, the new algorithms proposed in [479] are also presented. Moreover, other methods introduced to generate fuzzy IF-THEN rules are outlined.

Research combining *fuzzy systems* (FSs), *neural networks* (NNs), and *genetic algorithms* (GAs) has grown rapidly in recent years. Earlier, these methods had been developed independently. Now, they are considered within the framework of *Soft Computing*, and the trend is to employ them jointly to create intelligent systems. Thus the contents of this book may be viewed as the application of *soft computing methods* in the area of *artificial* (or *computational*) *intelligence*.

Many researchers contributed to the current results in the field related to the contents of this book. The long list of reference includes their names associated with the publications cited in the book. Professor L.A. Zadeh, who is known as the " *Father of Fuzzy Logic*", and the pioneers who initiated research into neural networks, and genetic algorithms, are mentioned with regard to their publications. The outstanding contributions of Prof. E. Ruspini and Prof. J. Bezdek to *fuzzy clustering*, which is a very important method employed in hybrid learning, should also be emphasized. However, a number of researchers who made significant contributions to neuro-fuzzy and intelligent systems, are not cited in this book, since it is impossible to refer to all of them. The interested reader can find the related papers and books in other bibliography lists.

The author would like to especially acknowledge the contribution of Prof. E. Czogała to fuzzy and neuro-fuzzy systems, in particular the logical approach. His book, entitled "*Fuzzy and Neuro-Fuzzy Intelligent Systems*" [101], with Prof J. Łeski as co-author, was published recently. It was Prof. Czogała's final book. The contents are closely related to this book. The work of Prof. Czogała was an inspiration to the research resulting in this book. Therefore, the author dedicates her book to Prof. Ernest Czogała.

There are more persons whose important contributions to the contents of this book should be acknowledged. One of them, with reference to neural networks, is Prof. Ryszard Tadeusiewicz, who can be called the "*Father of Neural Networks*" in Poland. He is the author of many books on neural networks (see e.g. [490]), as well as a large number of papers. He is one of the founders of the Polish Neural Network Society, and currently is the Vice-President of this Society. He is also one of the initiators of the Conference on Neural Networks and Their Applications, which has changed its name, and is known as the Conference on Neural Networks and Soft Computing.

There are many people whom the author would like to thank for their help, encouragement, and understanding. Presented below is a special acknowledgment.

Acknowledgments.
As the author, I would like to express my sincere gratitude to Prof. Janusz Kacprzyk, the Editor of the book series "Studies in Fuzziness and Soft Computing", for his encouragement to publish the book.

I greatly appreciate the discussions with Prof. Lotfi A. Zadeh concerning this book. His comments and suggestions have improved its contents.

I also thank Dr. Robert Nowicki for his help in the process of preparing the final form of this book.

The words of special thankfulness are directed to my husband for creating a supportive environment for writing the book, and to my children for tolerating my absence at home.

Finally, I would like to thank the Committee for Scientific Research in Poland for the financial support (Project No. 7 T11A 017 20).

2
Description of Fuzzy Inference Systems

Approximate reasoning, based on fuzzy sets and fuzzy logic, has been successfully employed in fuzzy inference systems. These systems are used in many practical applications, mainly as fuzzy controllers, but also as other knowledge-based systems such as expert systems, fuzzy classifiers and so on. Fuzzy systems have been recently combined with neural networks and genetic algorithms to create different kinds of neuro-fuzzy systems and intelligent systems. This chapter presents an overview of fuzzy sets, approximate reasoning, and fuzzy systems.

2.1 Fuzzy Sets

This section deals with the fundamentals of fuzzy sets introduced by Zadeh [559] in 1965. The concept of fuzzy sets can be viewed as a generalization of ordinary (crisp) sets. The theory of fuzzy sets and the foundations of fuzzy logic were developed by Zadeh based on the traditional set theory and classical logic, respectively. The literature on the fuzzy set theory as well as the fuzzy logic includes e.g. the books [246], [353], [253], [112], [102], [234], [235], [259], [583].

2.1.1 Basic Definitions

Starting from the concept of a fuzzy set, proposed by Zadeh, basic definitions concerning fuzzy sets are presented in this section, including a fuzzy set of type 2. The *extension principle*, which plays an important role in the fuzzy set theory, is also depicted. First, a fuzzy set is defined as follows [559]:

Definition 1 *Let X be a space of points (objects), with a generic element of X denoted by x. A fuzzy set A in X is characterized by a membership function $\mu_A(x)$ which associates with each point x a real number in the interval $[0,1]$ representing the grade of membership of x in A*

$$A = \{(x, \mu_A(x)); x \in X\} \tag{2.1}$$

where

$$\mu_A(x) : X \to [0,1] \tag{2.2}$$

The nearer the value of $\mu_A(x)$ to unity, the higher the grade of membership of x in A. If $\mu_A(x) = 1$, then x fully belongs to A. If $\mu_A(x) = 0$, then x does not belong to A. Space X is called the universe of discourse.

A fuzzy set A is completely determined by the set of pairs (2.1). When the universe of discourse is a finite set, that is $X = \{x_1, \dots, x_n\}$, a fuzzy set A can be represented as

$$A = \sum_{i=1}^{n} \mu_A(x_i)/x_i = \mu_A(x_1)/x_1 + \cdots + \mu_A(x_n)/x_n \tag{2.3}$$

or equivalently

$$A = \sum_{i=1}^{n} \frac{\mu_A(x_i)}{x_i} = \frac{\mu_A(x_1)}{x_1} + \cdots + \frac{\mu_A(x_n)}{x_n} \tag{2.4}$$

When the universe of discourse X is not finite, a fuzzy set A can be expressed as

$$A = \int_X \mu_A(x)/x \tag{2.5}$$

or

$$A = \int_X \frac{\mu_A(x)}{x} \tag{2.6}$$

respectively. Symbols $\sum$, $+$, $\int$ in formulas (2.3)-(2.6) refer to set union rather than to arithmetic summation. Similarly, there is not any arithmetic division in these formulas. This symbolic notation is employed in order to connect an element and its membership value. The former notation, used in Equations (2.3) and (2.5), has been suggested by Zadeh as corresponding to the similar notations applied, e.g. in veristic sets (see the example of *ethnicity* in Section 7.4, page 223). However, the latter, used in Equations (2.4) and (2.6), is more convenient to employ in fuzzy relations described in Sections 2.1.3 and 2.1.4.

Figure 2.1 shows examples of two membership functions which characterize fuzzy sets A and B in the universe of discourse $X = \mathbf{R}$, that is the real line. The membership function illustrated in Fig. 2.2 represents a fuzzy set in the universe of discourse $X = \mathbf{R}^2$. In this case each point x in X is a vector $\mathbf{x} = [x_1, x_2] \subset \mathbf{R}^2$ with the associated membership grade in the interval $[0, 1]$. Although the same notation is applied, the components x_1, x_2 of the vector $\mathbf{x}$ should be distinguished from the points $x_1, x_2, \ldots, x_n \in X$ in Equations (2.3) and (2.4).

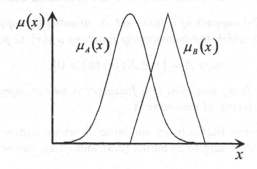

FIGURE 2.1. Examples of membership functions in $\mathbf{R}$

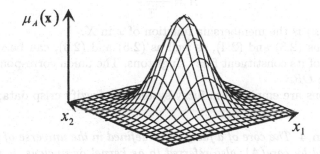

FIGURE 2.2. An example of membership functions in $\mathbf{R}^2$

Since a fuzzy set is completely determined by its membership function, it is possible to simplify the notation by using $A(x)$ instead of $\mu_A(x)$, unless it is necessary to distinguish between a fuzzy set and its membership function. Thus the membership functions μ_A and μ_B portrayed in Fig. 2.1 are denoted as fuzzy sets A and B in Fig. 2.6. This simpler notation becomes more often applied in the literature and is suggested to use. However, in this book the original notation for a membership function, introduced in Definition 1, is mostly employed. In spite of being less compact, this notation clearly points out that operations on fuzzy relations (Section 2.1.4) as well as fuzzy implications (Section 2.3.4) refer to membership functions. The simpler notation is convenient to apply in the neuro-fuzzy architectures, whose a general form is portrayed in Fig. 3.10, in Section 3.3. In this case, the elements of the first layer represent fuzzy sets but, in fact, they realize their membership functions.

Different shapes of membership functions can be used in various applications. Gaussian and triangular, as well as trapezoidal membership functions, are most often employed in fuzzy systems.

Other definitions concerning fuzzy sets are presented below.

Definition 2 *The support of a fuzzy set A, denoted by supp A, is the set of points in X at which the membership function $\mu_A(x)$ is positive*

$$supp\ A = \{x \in X; \mu_A(x) > 0\} \tag{2.7}$$

Definition 3 *A fuzzy singleton is a fuzzy set A whose support is a single point x in the universe of discourse X.*

It should be noted that a fuzzy singleton A whose support is a point x can be written, according to formulas (2.3) and (2.4), respectively, as

$$A = \mu_A(x)/x \tag{2.8}$$

and equivalently

$$A = \frac{\mu_A(x)}{x} \tag{2.9}$$

where $\mu_A(x)$ is the membership function of x in X.

Equations (2.3) and (2.4), as well as (2.5) and (2.6), can be viewed as the union of its constituent fuzzy singletons. The union corresponds to the connective *OR*.

Singletons are employed in fuzzy systems to fuzzify crisp data; see Section 2.3.1.

Definition 4 *The core of a fuzzy set A defined in the universe of discourse X, denoted by core(A), also referred to as kernel or nucleus, is the set of points in X at which the membership function $\mu_A(x)$ equals 1, that is*

$$core(A) = \{x \in X; \mu_A(x) = 1\} \tag{2.10}$$

Definition 5 *The height of a fuzzy set A defined in the universe of discourse X, denoted by hgt(A), is the maximal value of its membership function $\mu_A(x)$, that is*

$$hgt(A) = \sup_{x \in X} \mu_A(x) \tag{2.11}$$

Definition 6 *A fuzzy set A is called a normal fuzzy set if and only if the maximal value of its membership function equals 1, which means that* $hgt(A) = 1$.

If a fuzzy set is not normal, it can be normalized by altering all the membership values in proportion (dividing by the height of this fuzzy set) so as to make the largest value 1.

Definition 7 *A fuzzy set A defined in the universe of discourse X is an empty set, denoted* $A = \varnothing$, *if and only if its membership function* $\mu_A(x) = 0$ *for all* $x \in X$.

Definition 8 *A fuzzy set A defined in the universe of discourse X, which we shall assume to be a real Euclidean N-dimensional space, is convex if and only if*

$$\mu_A\left(\lambda x_1 + (1 - \lambda)\, x_2\right) \geqslant \min\left[\mu_A\left(x_1\right), \mu_A\left(x_2\right)\right] \qquad (2.12)$$

for all x_1 *and* x_2 *in X and all* λ *in* $[0, 1]$.

The fuzzy sets represented by the membership functions depicted in Figs. 2.1 and 2.2 are convex fuzzy sets. Examples of non-convex fuzzy sets will be shown in Fig. 2.6, in Section 2.1.2.

Definition 9 *A fuzzy set A is a fuzzy number if the universe of discourse X is* **R** *and the following criteria are fulfilled: the fuzzy set A is convex, normal, the membership function of the fuzzy set* $\mu_A(x)$ *is piecewise continuous, and the core of the fuzzy set consists of one value only.*

The fuzzy sets illustrated in Fig. 2.1 are examples of fuzzy numbers.

Definition 10 *A fuzzy set A is a fuzzy interval if the universe of discourse X is* **R** *and the following criteria are fulfilled: the fuzzy set A is convex, normal, and the membership function of the fuzzy set* $\mu_A(x)$ *is piecewise continuous.*

It should be noted that a fuzzy interval is a fuzzy set with the same criteria as those defined for fuzzy numbers, but with the exception that the core is no longer restricted to one point only. For both fuzzy numbers and fuzzy intervals the universe of discourse is the real line **R**. Thus fuzzy numbers and fuzzy intervals are special cases of fuzzy sets.

Sometimes fuzzy intervals are treated as fuzzy numbers, for example trapezoidal membership functions. A triangular fuzzy number is a special case of such an interval.

Fuzzy numbers play an important role as input and output values of fuzzy systems (see Section 2.3).

Definition 11 *Two fuzzy sets A and B are equal, written as* $A = B$, *if and only if their membership functions are equal, that is* $\mu_A(x) = \mu_B(x)$ *for all x in the universe of discourse X.*

Presented below is the definition of α-cuts, also called α-level sets of a fuzzy set A, proposed by Zadeh [560], [567].

Definition 12 *The crisp (non-fuzzy) set of elements that belong to the fuzzy set A in X at least to the degree of α is called an α-level set (or α-cut) and defined by*

$$A_\alpha = \{x \in X : \ \mu_A(x) \geqslant \alpha\} \qquad\qquad \forall \alpha \in [0,1] \qquad (2.13)$$

If the condition $\mu_A(x) \geqslant \alpha$ in (2.13) is replaced by $\mu_A(x) > \alpha$, the set A_α will be called a *strong α-level set,* or a *strong α-cut.* Figure 2.3 shows a graphical interpretation of α-cuts in $X = \mathbf{R}$; for different α-levels: $\alpha_1, \alpha_2, \alpha_3, \alpha_4$. It is easy to notice that

$$\alpha_1 > \alpha_2 > \alpha_3 > \alpha_4 \Longrightarrow A_{\alpha_1} \subset A_{\alpha_2} \subset A_{\alpha_3} \subset A_{\alpha_4}$$

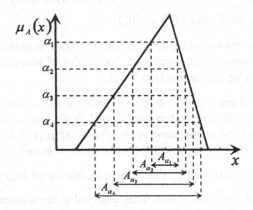

FIGURE 2.3. Illustration of α-level sets (α-cuts)

The α-cuts make it possible to exhibit elements $x \in X$ that typically belong to a fuzzy set A; with membership values which are greater than a certain threshold $\alpha \in [0,1]$. The concept of α-cuts was applied in [404] to the algebra of level fuzzy sets. Taking into account only the most significant parts of fuzzy set *supports* (see Definition 2), computation time as well as computer memory size was saved in many practical applications. Now α-cuts are also employed in fuzzy arithmetic, for example with reference to fuzzy neural networks [56], [141].

As an alternative to Definition 8, we may say that a fuzzy set A in the n-dimensional Euclidean vector space $\mathbf{R}^n$ is *convex* if and only if each of its α-cuts is a convex set [259]. Figure 2.4 portrays a convex fuzzy set in $\mathbf{R}^2$ expressed by its α-cuts.

In [567] Zadeh introduced the *extension principle.* It can also be found in [559] in an implicit form. Further work concerning this principle was

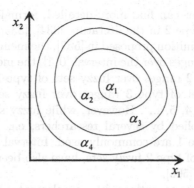

FIGURE 2.4. Illustration of α-cuts of a convex fuzzy set in $\mathbf{R}^2$

presented in [541]. The extension principle is very important for fuzzy set theory. It provides a general method for extending crisp mathematical concepts to a fuzzy framework. Suppose that f is a function that maps points in space X to points in space Y, that is

$$f : X \rightarrow Y \qquad (2.14)$$

and A is a fuzzy subset of X expressed by Equation (2.4). Then, the extension principle asserts that

$$f(A) = \sum_{i=1}^{n} \frac{\mu_A(x_i)}{f(x_i)} = \frac{\mu_A(x_1)}{f(x_1)} + \cdots + \frac{\mu_A(x_n)}{f(x_n)} \qquad (2.15)$$

If more than one element of X is mapped by f to the same element $y \in Y$, then the maximum of the membership grades of these elements in the fuzzy set A is chosen as the membership grade for y in $f(A)$. If no element $x \in X$ is mapped to y, then the membership grade of y in $f(A)$ is zero.

According to Definition 1, a fuzzy set is characterized by a membership function which associates with each point (member of the fuzzy set) its grade of membership, expressed by a real number in the interval $[0,1]$. In this case, the membership grades are precise numbers. However, there are situations where uncertainty can exist about the membership grades themselves. Therefore, the concept of a type 2 fuzzy set, as well as higher type fuzzy sets, was introduced by Zadeh [567]. In this context, the fuzzy sets presented in this chapter, and in the whole book, refer to type 1 fuzzy sets, but we call them, simply, fuzzy sets. A type 1 fuzzy set is a special case of a type 2 fuzzy set. The definition formulated in [334] states the following:

Definition 13 *A fuzzy set of type 2 is defined by a fuzzy membership function, the grade (that is, fuzzy grade) of which is a fuzzy set in the unit interval* $[0,1]$, *rather than a point in* $[0,1]$.

The interested reader can find more detailed, formal explanations concerning fuzzy sets of type 2 in the literature [334], [335], [231], [445].

According to the definition proposed in [567], the membership function of a fuzzy set of type 1 ranges over the interval $[0, 1]$, the membership function of a fuzzy set of type 2 ranges over fuzzy sets of type 1, the membership function of a fuzzy set of type 3 ranges over fuzzy sets of type 2, etc., for fuzzy sets of type 4, 5, ... However, while fuzzy sets of type 2 have been studied and applied by several researchers, e.g. [540], [240], [511], only fuzzy sets of type 1 are commonly used. Interval type 2 sets, which are the simplest kind of type 2 fuzzy sets, have also been considered in the literature [186], [152], [505].

In Section 2.1.2, basic operations, i.e. complementation, union, intersection, etc., on fuzzy sets (of type 1) are presented. To define such operations for fuzzy sets of type 2, it is natural to make use of the extension principle and interval-valued membership functions; see [567]. More details concerning operations on type 2 fuzzy sets can be found in [237].

2.1.2   Operations on Fuzzy Sets

The original theory of fuzzy sets was formulated in terms of the complement, union, and intersection operators, defined as generalizations of the corresponding operators for crisp (non-fuzzy) sets.

First, the definition of the *complement* operation, proposed by Zadeh [559], is presented for a fuzzy set A in the universe of discourse X.

Definition 14 *The complement of a fuzzy set A, denoted by $\widetilde{A}$, is defined by*

$$\mu_{\widetilde{A}}(x) = 1 - \mu_A(x) \tag{2.16}$$

for all $x \in X$.

The complement of the fuzzy set A is specified by a function

$$c: \quad [0, 1] \rightarrow [0, 1] \tag{2.17}$$

which assigns a value $c(\mu_A(x))$, according to Equation (2.16), to each membership grade $\mu_A(x)$. This assigned value is interpreted as the membership grade of the element x in the fuzzy set corresponding to the negation of the concept represented by the fuzzy set A. For example, if A is a fuzzy set of tall men, the complement of this fuzzy set is the fuzzy set of men who are not tall. Obviously, there are many elements that can have some non-zero degree of membership in both the fuzzy set and its complement [259].

The function c must satisfy at least the two following requirements in order to represent the complement operation [259]:

- $c(0) = 1$ and $c(1) = 0$, which means that c behaves as the ordinary complement for crisp sets (*boundary conditions*)

- For all $a, b \in [0,1]$, if $a < b$, then $c(a) \geqslant c(b)$, where a and b represent degrees of membership. This means that c is *monotonic non-increasing* function.

Many functions fulfil these requirements; see e.g. [258]. However, the complement (2.16) is most often applied. Figure 2.5 illustrates this operation, assuming that A is a normal fuzzy set (Definition 6).

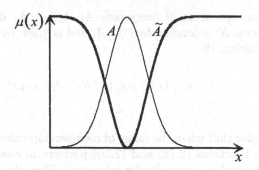

FIGURE 2.5. Complement operation according to Definition 14

The classical union and intersection operations of ordinary subsets of X have also been extended for fuzzy sets and the following definitions have been proposed by Zadeh [559].

Definition 15 *The union of two fuzzy sets A and B with respective membership functions $\mu_A(x)$ and $\mu_B(x)$ is a fuzzy set denoted by $A \cup B$ whose membership function is given by*

$$\mu_{A \cup B}(x) = \max\left[\mu_A(x), \mu_B(x)\right] \qquad \forall x \in X \qquad (2.18)$$

or, in abbreviated form

$$\mu_{A \cup B}(x) = \mu_A(x) \vee \mu_B(x) \qquad (2.19)$$

Definition 16 *The intersection of two fuzzy sets A and B with respective membership functions $\mu_A(x)$ and $\mu_B(x)$ is a fuzzy set denoted by $A \cap B$ whose membership function is given by*

$$\mu_{A \cap B}(x) = \min\left[\mu_A(x), \mu_B(x)\right] \qquad \forall x \in X \qquad (2.20)$$

or, in abbreviated form

$$\mu_{A \cap B}(x) = \mu_A(x) \wedge \mu_B(x) \qquad (2.21)$$

The union and intersection operations have the associative property, which means that $A \cup (B \cup C) = (A \cup B) \cup C$ and $A \cap (B \cap C) = (A \cap B) \cap C$ for fuzzy sets A, B, C in X.

The union operation of fuzzy sets $A_1, A_2 \ldots, A_n$ defined in the universe of discourse X is denoted by $\cup_{i=1}^{n} A_i$ and is given by the following extension of Definition 15

$$\mu_{A_1 \cup A_2 \ldots \cup A_n}(x) = \mu_{A_1}(x) \vee \mu_{A_2}(x) \vee \cdots \vee \mu_{A_n}(x) \qquad (2.22)$$

for all x in X.

The intersection operation of fuzzy sets $A_1, A_2 \ldots, A_n$ defined in the universe of discourse X is denoted by $\cap_{i=1}^{n} A_i$ and is given by the following extension of Definition 16

$$\mu_{A_1 \cap A_2 \ldots \cap A_n}(x) = \mu_{A_1}(x) \wedge \mu_{A_2}(x) \wedge \cdots \wedge \mu_{A_n}(x) \qquad (2.23)$$

for all x in X.

It is easy to notice that when the range of membership values is restricted to the set $\{0, 1\}$, functions (2.18) and (2.20) perform in exactly the same way as the corresponding operators for crisp sets. Thus the union and intersection of fuzzy sets, defined by these formulas, are clear generalizations of the union and intersection operators of crisp sets. Definitions 14, 15, 16 constitute a consistent framework for the theory of fuzzy sets, formulated by Zadeh [559]. This theory is usually referred to as *possibility theory* and the operators defined by formulas (2.16), (2.18), (2.20) are called *standard operations* of fuzzy set theory [259]. The standard operations, however, are not the only possible way to extend classical set theory consistently to fuzzy set theory. Zadeh and other authors have suggested alternative or additional definitions concerning the operations on fuzzy sets. Different fuzzy negation functions have been studied by many researchers (see e.g. [307], [371], [538], [109]). However, as mentioned before, the standard fuzzy negation (2.16) is most often used in various applications.

A general class of intersection operators for fuzzy sets is defined by so-called *triangular norms* or *T-norms*, and a general class of union operators is defined, analogously, by *S-norms* (*T-conorms*). Triangular norms were introduced by Schweizer and Sklar [458], [459] to model distances in probabilistic metric spaces. These functions are extensively applied in fuzzy sets theory as logical connective *AND*, which represents the intersection operator [7]. Similarly, the *S-norms* are widely employed to model logical connective *OR*, which represents the union operator. The triangular norms and *T*-conorms can be characterized as follows [112], [383], [583], [141], [519].

Definition 17 *A triangular norm T is a function of two arguments*

$$T: \quad [0, 1] \times [0, 1] \to [0, 1] \qquad (2.24)$$

which satisfies the following conditions for $a, b, c, d \in [0, 1]$

$$Monotonicity: T(a, b) \leqslant T(c, d) ; a \leqslant c; b \leqslant d \qquad (2.25)$$

$$Commutativity: T(a, b) = T(b, a) \qquad (2.26)$$

$$Associativity: T(T(a, b), c) = T(a, T(b, c)) \qquad (2.27)$$

$$Boundary\ conditions: T(a, 0) = 0; \quad T(a, 1) = a \qquad (2.28)$$

Moreover, every triangular norm fulfils the following inequality

$$T_w(a, b) \leqslant T(a, b) \leqslant \min(a, b) \qquad (2.29)$$

where

$$T_w(a, b) = \begin{cases} a & \text{if} & b = 1 \\ b & \text{if} & a = 1 \\ 0 & \text{if} & a, b \neq 1 \end{cases} \qquad (2.30)$$

The T-norm, depicted in Definition 17, will also be denoted as

$$T(a, b) = a \overset{T}{*} b \qquad (2.31)$$

Definition 18 *An S-norm is a function of two arguments*

$$S: \ [0, 1] \times [0, 1] \to [0, 1] \qquad (2.32)$$

which satisfies the following conditions for $a, b, c, d \in [0, 1]$

$$Monotonicity: S(a, b) \leqslant S(c, d) ; a \leqslant c; b \leqslant d \qquad (2.33)$$

$$Commutativity: S(a, b) = S(b, a) \qquad (2.34)$$

$$Associativity: S(S(a, b), c) = S(a, S(b, c)) \qquad (2.35)$$

$$Boundary\ conditions: S(a, 0) = a; \quad S(a, 1) = 1 \qquad (2.36)$$

Moreover, every S-norm fulfils the following inequality

$$\max(a, b) \leqslant S(a, b) \leqslant S_w(a, b) \qquad (2.37)$$

where

$$S_w(a, b) = \begin{cases} a & \text{if} & b = 0 \\ b & \text{if} & a = 0 \\ 0 & \text{if} & a, b \neq 0 \end{cases} \qquad (2.38)$$

The S-norm, depicted in Definition 18, will also be denoted as

$$S(a, b) = a \overset{S}{*} b \qquad (2.39)$$

The T-norms and T-conorms are related in the sense of logical duality. Any T-conorm (S-norm) can be derived from a T-norm through the following formula [6]

$$T(a,b) = 1 - S(1-a, 1-b) \qquad (2.40)$$

which is related to the De Morgan law in set theory.

The basic examples of T-norms and S-norms, most frequently used as AND and OR connectives in fuzzy logic, are presented in Table 2.1. The first row of the table illustrates the T-norm and S-norm applied by Zadeh [559] as the intersection and union operations on fuzzy sets, respectively. The second and last rows contain so-called algebraic and bounded T-norms and the corresponding S-norms. The S-norms are T-conorms in the sense of duality. The algebraic and bounded operators are also known by the names probability and Łukasiewicz, respectively [222].

TABLE 2.1. Basic examples of triangular norms

Name	T-norm	S-norm
Zadeh	$\min(a,b)$	$\max(a,b)$
Algebraic	ab	$a+b-ab$
Bounded	$\max(a+b-1,0)$	$\min(a+b,1)$

Many other examples of T-norms and S-norms can be found in the literature (see e.g.[383], [583], [260], [141], [101]). The interested reader can be also refer to [258], [358].

Figure 2.6 portrays intersection and union operations on two fuzzy sets A and B with Gaussian and triangular membership functions, $\mu_A(x)$ and $\mu_B(x)$, respectively, based on the T-norm and S-norm operators depicted in Table 2.1. The operations introduced by Zadeh are illustrated in Figs. 2.6 (a) and (b). Operations based on algebraic and bounded T-norms and S-norms are shown in Figs. 2.6 (e) and (f), respectively.

It should be noted that the fuzzy sets $A \cap B$ presented in Figs. 2.6 (a) and (c), as well as the fuzzy set $A \cup B$ shown in Fig. 2.6 (f) are convex fuzzy sets, according to Definition 8. The fuzzy set $A \cap B$ depicted in Fig. 2.6 (c) and the fuzzy sets $A \cup B$ illustrated in Figs. 2.6 (b) and (d) are examples of non-convex fuzzy sets.

All T-norms and S-norms can be extended through associativity to $n > 2$ arguments, a_i, for $i = 1, \ldots, n$, and denoted as follows

$$T(a_1, a_2, \ldots, a_n) = a_1 \overset{T}{*} a_2 \overset{T}{*} \cdots \overset{T}{*} a_n = \overset{n}{\underset{i=1}{\mathbf{T}}} a_i \qquad (2.41)$$

and

$$S(a_1, a_2, \ldots, a_n) = a_1 \overset{S}{*} a_2 \overset{S}{*} \cdots \overset{S}{*} a_n = \overset{n}{\underset{i=1}{\mathbf{S}}} a_i \qquad (2.42)$$

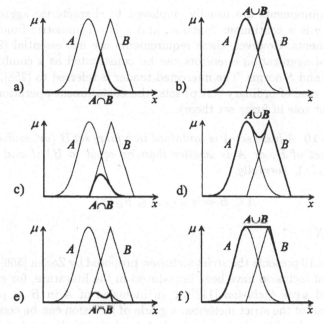

FIGURE 2.6. Intersection and union operations: a) $A \cap B$ defined by Equation (2.20); b) $A \cup B$ defined by Equation (2.18); c) $A \cap B$ based on algebraic T-norm; d) $A \cup B$ based on algebraic S-norm; e) $A \cap B$ based on bounded T-norm; f) $A \cup B$ based on bounded S-norm

T-norms satisfy the basic properties of the intersection operator, while S-norms fulfil the properties of the union operator. These properties are: *monotonicity, commutativity, associativity,* and *boundary conditions.*

Since the values of the membership functions are real numbers in the interval $[0, 1]$, T-norms and S-norms are considered to be the most general intersection and union operators of fuzzy sets, respectively.

The fuzzy union and intersection operations presented by Equations (2.22) and (2.23), respectively, as well as other S-norms and T-norms, are examples of aggregation operations on fuzzy sets, generally defined by a function

$$g: \quad [0,1]^n \rightarrow [0,1] \qquad (2.43)$$

for some $n \geqslant 2$. When this function is applied to n fuzzy sets $A_1, A_2 \ldots, A_n$ in X, it produces an aggregated fuzzy set $\underline{A}$ by operating on the membership grades of each $x \in X$ in the aggregated sets. Thus

$$\mu_{\underline{A}}(x) = g\left(\mu_{A_1}(x), \mu_{A_2}(x), \ldots, \mu_{A_n}(x)\right) \qquad (2.44)$$

for each $x \in X$. In order to qualify as an aggregation function, g must satisfy the boundary conditions, that is $g(0, 0, \ldots, 0) = 0$ and $g(1, 1, \ldots, 1) = 1$, and be monotonic nondecreasing in all its arguments. In addition, the following requirements are usually employed to characterize aggregation operations: g is a continuous function, and g is a symmetric function in all its arguments. However, these requirements are not essential [259]. A large class of aggregation operators can be constructed as a combination of T-norms and S-norms. The interested reader is referred to [258], [50].

As in the case of ordinary (crisp) sets, the containment operation plays an important role in fuzzy set theory.

Definition 19 *A fuzzy set A is contained in a fuzzy set B (or, equivalently, A is a subset of B, or A is smaller than or equal to B) if and only if $\mu_A(x) \leqslant \mu_B(x)$. Formally,*

$$A \subset B \Longleftrightarrow \mu_A(x) \leqslant \mu_B(x) \tag{2.45}$$

for all $x \in X$.

Definition 19 presents the *strict inclusion* proposed by Zadeh [559]. Other definitions of inclusion have been introduced in the literature, for example the so-called *weak inclusion* [112] or an inclusion of A in B at point x, where instead of the strict inclusion, a grade of inclusion can be considered [383]. The grade of the inclusion equals 1 in the case of complete (strict) inclusion.

Now let us consider other kinds of operations on fuzzy sets that are of use in the representation of linguistic hedges [287], [562], [563]. Hedges are linguistic modifiers which can be used to modify the meaning of fuzzy sets (see Section 2.2.3). Two operations, called *concentration* and *dilation*, yield new fuzzy sets with suppressed or elevated grades of membership.

Definition 20 *The concentration of a fuzzy set A in X, denoted by $CON(A)$, is defined by*

$$\mu_{CON(A)}(x) = (\mu_A(x))^2 \tag{2.46}$$

for all $x \in X$.

Definition 21 *The dilation of a fuzzy set A in X, denoted by $DIL(A)$, is defined by*

$$\mu_{DIL(A)}(x) = (\mu_A(x))^{0.5} \tag{2.47}$$

for all $x \in X$.

The effect of *dilation* is the opposite of that of *concentration*. Other similar operations can be found in the literature, e.g. [563]. The concentration and dilation operations defined by Equations (2.46) and (2.47), respectively, are illustrated in Fig. 2.7.

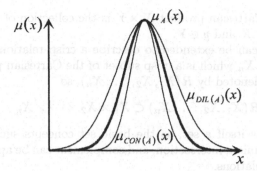

FIGURE 2.7. Concentration and dilation operations

2.1.3 Fuzzy Relations

In Sections 2.1.1 and 2.1.2 only fuzzy sets with membership functions of one variable have been considered. However, fuzzy sets can be extended to have higher dimensional membership functions. These multi-dimensional fuzzy sets are normally referred to as *fuzzy relations* [222]. The concept of fuzzy relations was introduced by Zadeh [559] as a natural extension of the concept of crisp relations. Both kinds of relations are based on the definition of the *Cartesian product*.

Definition 22 *The Cartesian product of two crisp sets X and Y, denoted by $X \times Y$, is the crisp set of all ordered pairs such that the first element in each pair is a member of X and the second element is a member of Y. Formally,*

$$X \times Y = \{(x,y) ; x \in X \ and \ y \in Y\} \tag{2.48}$$

The Cartesian product of n crisp sets $X_1, X_2, \ldots, X_n$, denoted by $X_1 \times X_2 \times \cdots \times X_n$, is the following generalization of formula (2.48)

$$X_1 \times X_2 \times \cdots \times X_n = \{(x_1, x_2, \ldots, x_n) ; x_i \in X_i \ for \ i = 1, 2, \ldots, n \} \tag{2.49}$$

A crisp relation represents the presence or absence of association, interaction, or interconnectedness between the elements of two or more crisp sets [259].

Definition 23 *A crisp relation among crisp sets X and Y is a crisp subset of the Cartesian product $X \times Y$. It is denoted by $R(X,Y)$. Thus*

$$R(X,Y) \subset X \times Y \tag{2.50}$$

Ordinarily, a relation is defined as a set of ordered pairs, e.g. the set of all ordered pairs of real numbers x and y such that $x \leqslant y$. It should be noted that the Cartesian product $X \times Y$ is the collection of ordered pairs (x, y), where $x \in X$ and $y \in Y$.

Definition 23 can be extended to describe a crisp relation among crisp sets $X_1, X_2, \ldots, X_n$ which is a crisp subset of the Cartesian product $X_1 \times X_2 \times \cdots \times X_n$, denoted by $R(X_1, X_2, \ldots, X_n)$, so

$$R(X_1, X_2, \ldots, X_n) \subset X_1 \times X_2 \times \cdots \times X_n \tag{2.51}$$

The relation is itself a set, so the basic set concepts such as containment or subset, union, intersection, and complement can be applied without modifying the relations.

The concept of crisp relations can be generalized to allow for various degrees or strengths of relation or interaction between elements. Degrees of association can be represented by membership grades in a *fuzzy relation* in the same way as degrees of set membership are represented in fuzzy sets.

Definition 24 *A fuzzy relation R from a crisp set X to a crisp set Y is a fuzzy subset of the Cartesian product $X \times Y$. Formally,*

$$R = \int_{X \times Y} \frac{\mu_R(x, y)}{(x, y)} \tag{2.52}$$

where $x \in X$, $y \in Y$, and $\mu_R(x, y)$ is a membership function of fuzzy set R.

Let us compare formulas (2.52) and (2.6). As mentioned earlier, a fuzzy relation can be viewed as a multi-dimensional fuzzy set. Equation (2.52) expresses the two-dimensional fuzzy set defined over the universe of discourse $X \times Y$. For a finite universe of discourse, it can be presented in the form of Equation (2.4). Of course, the fuzzy relation can be expressed according to Equations (2.5) and (2.3), respectively, instead of formulas (2.6) and (2.4). However, the notation used in Equation (2.52) is more convenient for the multi-dimensional case, especially for presenting the operations on fuzzy relations in Section 2.1.4. It is obvious that the general form of Equations (2.1) and (2.2), for the point (x, y) in $X \times Y$ with the membership function $\mu_R(x, y)$, also expresses the fuzzy relation (2.52).

A relation matrix is very useful to represent the fuzzy relation in the case of a finite universe of discourse. The elements of the matrix are values of the membership function. These elements correspond to the pairs (x, y), where $x \in X$ and $y \in Y$.

More generally, a fuzzy relation R among crisp sets $X_1, X_2, \ldots, X_n$ is a fuzzy subset of the Cartesian product $X_1 \times X_2 \times \cdots \times X_n$; so Definition 24 can be extended as follows

$$R = \int_{X_1 \times X_2 \times \cdots \times X_n} \frac{\mu_R(x_1, x_2, \ldots, x_n)}{(x_1, x_2, \ldots, x_n)} \tag{2.53}$$

where $x_i \in X_i$, for $i = 1, 2, \ldots, n$, and $\mu_R(x_1, x_2, \ldots, x_n)$ is a membership function of fuzzy set R.

Thus a fuzzy relation is a fuzzy set defined on the Cartesian product of crisp sets $X_1 \times X_2 \times \cdots \times X_n$, where tuples $(x_1, x_2, \ldots, x_n)$ may have varying degrees of membership within the relation. The membership grades, represented by values in the interval $[0, 1]$, indicate the strength of the relation between the elements of the tuple.

Any relation (crisp or fuzzy) between two sets X and Y is known as a *binary relation.*

Analogously to the Cartesian product of crisp sets, the Cartesian product of fuzzy sets has been defined in fuzzy set theory.

Definition 25 *The Cartesian product of two fuzzy sets A and B in the universe of discourse X and Y, respectively, is denoted by $A \times B$ and defined by use of their membership functions $\mu_A(x)$ and $\mu_B(y)$ as follows*

$$\mu_{A \times B}(x, y) = \min\left[\mu_A(x), \mu_B(y)\right] = \mu_A(x) \wedge \mu_B(y) \tag{2.54}$$

or

$$\mu_{A \times B}(x, y) = \mu_A(x) \; \mu_B(y) \tag{2.55}$$

for all $x \in X$ and $y \in Y$.

Thus the Cartesian product $A \times B$ is a fuzzy set in the universe of discourse $X \times Y$, which is the Cartesian product of the crisp sets X, Y, defined by formula (2.48), with the membership functions (2.54) or (2.55). In other words, the Cartesian product $A \times B$ is a fuzzy set of ordered pairs (x, y), $x \in X$, $y \in Y$, with the grade of membership of (x, y) in $X \times Y$ given by Equations (2.54) or (2.55). In this sense, $A \times B$ is a fuzzy relation from X to Y; an example can be found in [563]. It is easy to notice that when A and B are non-fuzzy (crisp) sets then the fuzzy set $A \times B$ reduces to the conventional Cartesian product of crisp sets.

The following extension of Definition 25 is used to present the Cartesian product of n fuzzy sets. The Cartesian product of fuzzy sets $A_1, A_2, \ldots, A_n$ in $X_1, X_2, \ldots, X_n$, respectively, denoted by $A_1 \times A_2 \times \cdots \times A_n$ is defined by use of their membership functions $\mu_{A_1}(x_1)$, $\mu_{A_2}(x_2)$, $\ldots$, $\mu_{A_n}(x_n)$ as follows

$$\mu_{A_1 \times A_2 \times \cdots \times A_n}(x_1, x_2, \ldots, x_n) = \mu_{A_1}(x_1) \wedge \mu_{A_2}(x_2) \wedge \ldots \wedge \mu_{A_n}(x_n) \tag{2.56}$$

or

$$\mu_{A_1 \times A_2 \times \cdots \times A_n}(x_1, x_2, \ldots, x_n) = \mu_{A_1}(x_1) \; \mu_{A_2}(x_2) \ldots \mu_{A_n}(x_n) \tag{2.57}$$

for all $x_1 \in X_1$, $x_2 \in X_2, \ldots, x_n \in X_n$.

Example 1 *Let $A_1, \ldots, A_n$ be fuzzy sets in the universes of discourse $X_1, \ldots, X_n = \mathbf{R}$, characterized by Gaussian membership functions*

$$\mu_{A_i}(x_i) = \exp\left[-\left(\frac{x_i - \overline{x}_i}{\sigma}\right)^2\right] \tag{2.58}$$

for $i = 1, \ldots, n$. Figure 2.8 shows the Gaussian membership function (2.58). According to formulas (2.57) and (2.58), the Cartesian product of the fuzzy sets $A_1, \ldots, A_n$, in the universe of discourse $X_1 \times \cdots \times X_n = \mathbf{R}^n$, is a fuzzy set $A_1 \times \cdots \times A_n$ with the following membership function

$$\mu_{A_1 \times \cdots \times A_n}(x_1, \ldots, x_n) = \prod_{i=1}^{n} \mu_{A_i}(x_i)$$

$$= \exp\left[-\left(\frac{\sum_{i=1}^{n}(x_i - \bar{x}_i)^2}{\sigma^2}\right)\right]$$

$$= \exp\left[-\frac{(\mathbf{x} - \bar{\mathbf{x}})^T (\mathbf{x} - \bar{\mathbf{x}})}{\sigma^2}\right] \qquad (2.59)$$

where $\mathbf{x} = [x_1, \ldots, x_n]^T \in X_1 \times \cdots \times X_n = \mathbf{R}^n$, and $\bar{x}_1, \ldots, \bar{x}_n$, which constitutes the vector $\bar{\mathbf{x}} = [\bar{x}_1, \ldots, \bar{x}_n]^T \in X_1 \times \cdots \times X_n = \mathbf{R}^n$, are centers of the Gaussian membership functions, while σ is a parameter defining the width of the membership functions (see Fig. 2.8). In the case of two fuzzy sets A_1, A_2, that is, for $n = 2$, the membership function $\mu_{A_1 \times A_2}(x_1, x_2)$, given by Equation (2.59), looks like that in Fig. 2.2, where $A = A_1 \times A_2$, and $\mathbf{x} = [x_1, x_2]^T$.

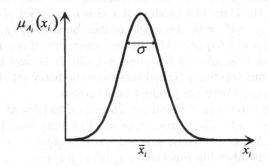

FIGURE 2.8. Gaussian membership function

Example 2   *Let A_1, A_2 be fuzzy sets in the universes of discourse $X_1, X_2 = \mathbf{R}$, characterized by Gaussian membership functions (2.58). Figure 2.9 illustrates the Cartesian product $A_1 \times A_2$ defined by minimum operation, i.e. Equations (2.54) and (2.56); $\mathbf{x} = [x_1, x_2]^T$, where $x_1, x_2 \in \mathbf{R}$.*

2.1.4   Operations on Fuzzy Relations

As described in Section 2.1.3, fuzzy relations are fuzzy sets in product spaces. Fuzzy relations in different product spaces can be combined with

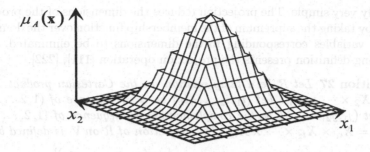

FIGURE 2.9. Cartesian product defined by minimum

each other by a *composition* operation. Various kinds of composition operations have been suggested [583], though these differ in their results and also with respect to their mathematical properties. The max-min composition (or the sup-min composition), proposed by Zadeh [560], [563], has become the best known and the most frequently used one.

Definition 26 *If R is a relation from X to Y and P is a relation from Y to Z, then the composition of R and P is a fuzzy relation denoted by R∘P and defined by*

$$R \circ P = \int_{X \times Z} \frac{\sup_{y \in Y} \left[\min \left[\mu_R (x,y), \mu_P (y,z) \right] \right]}{(x, z)} \tag{2.60}$$

where $x \in X$, $y \in Y$, $z \in Z$, and $\mu_R (x,y)$, $\mu_P (y,z)$ are membership functions of R and P, respectively.

If the domains of the variables x, y, and z are finite sets, then symbol $\int$ in Equation (2.60) is replaced by symbol $\sum$, according to formulas (2.4), (2.6), and *sup* is replaced by *max*. In this case we have the max-min composition instead of the sup-min composition described by Equation (2.60). Max-product composition was defined by Zadeh [560] in the same way as the max-min composition of R and P in Definition 26, except that *min* is replaced by the arithmetic product.

The sup-min composition given by formula (2.60) can be generalized by taking any other kinds of T-norm (see Section 2.1.2) instead of *min* operation [222].

It was mentioned in Section 2.1.3 that since relations are sets, operations such as containment, union, intersection, and complement can be applied to relations. It is very easy to use these operations on fuzzy relations defined on the same Cartesian product space. However, it is not possible to apply these operations directly to fuzzy relations defined on different product spaces. Therefore, two very important operations on fuzzy relations, called *projection* and *cylindrical extension*, have been introduced by Zadeh [566], [567]. The whole definition of projection seems quite complicated, but is actually very simple. The projection reduces the dimensions of the product space by taking the supremum of the membership function over the domains of the variables corresponding to the dimensions to be eliminated. The following definition presents the projection operation [111], [222].

Definition 27 *Let R be a fuzzy relation on the Cartesian product* $X = X_1 \times X_2 \times \cdots \times X_n$. *Let* $(i_1, i_2, \ldots, i_k)$ *be a subsequence of* $(1, 2, \ldots, n)$ *and let* $(j_1, j_2, \ldots, j_l)$ *be the complementary subsequence of* $(1, 2, \ldots, n)$. *Let* $V = X_{i_1} \times X_{i_2} \times \cdots \times X_{i_k}$. *The projection of R on V is defined by*

$$proj\,(R; V) = \int_V \frac{\sup_{x_{j_1}, x_{j_2}, \ldots, x_{j_l}} [\mu_R\,(x_1, x_2, \ldots, x_n)]}{(x_{i_1}, x_{i_2}, \ldots, x_{i_k})} \tag{2.61}$$

where $\mu_R\,(x_1, x_2, \ldots, x_n)$ *is the membership function of fuzzy relation R.*

Definition 27 is much simpler in the case of binary relations. Let R be defined on $Y \times Z$. Then

$$proj\,(R; Z) = \int_Z \frac{\sup_y [\mu_R\,(y, z)]}{z} \tag{2.62}$$

where $y \in Y$, $z \in Z$, and $\mu_R\,(y, z)$ is the membership function of R. The projection operation (2.62) brings a binary relation to a fuzzy set (unary relation).

The projection operation is almost always used in combination with the cylindrical extension operation, which is more or less the opposite of the projection, by extending fuzzy sets to binary fuzzy relations and binary relations to ternary relations, etc. The cylindrical extension basically works as follows. Let C be a fuzzy set defined on Y, and let R be a fuzzy relation defined on $Y \times Z$. In this case it is not possible to take the intersection of C and R, but if the universe of discourse of C is extended to $Y \times Z$, it becomes possible. The following definition presents the cylindrical extension operation.

Definition 28 *Let* $X = X_1 \times X_2 \times \cdots \times X_n$ *and let Q be a fuzzy relation on* $V = X_{i_1} \times X_{i_2} \times \cdots \times X_{i_k}$, *where* $(i_1, i_2, \ldots, i_k)$ *is a subsequence of* $(1, 2, \ldots, n)$. *The cylindrical extension of Q to the Cartesian product space X is defined by*

$$ce\,(Q; X) = \int_X \frac{\mu_Q\,(x_{i_1}, x_{i_2}, \ldots, x_{i_k})}{(x_1, x_2, \ldots, x_n)} \tag{2.63}$$

where $\mu_Q\,(x_{i_1}, x_{i_2}, \ldots, x_{i_k})$ *is the membership function of fuzzy relation Q.*

In the case of binary relations, Definition 28 is much simpler. Let C be a fuzzy set defined on Y. The cylindrical extension of C on $Y \times Z$ is the set of all tuples $(y, z) \in Y \times Z$ with the membership $\mu_C\,(y)$, that is

$$ce\,(C; Y \times Z) = \int_{Y \times Z} \frac{\mu_C\,(y)}{(y, z)} \tag{2.64}$$

It is easy to see that the projection and cylindrical extension operations play an important role in the composition of fuzzy relations (Definition 26).

The composition of a fuzzy set and a fuzzy relation is a special case of the operation presented in Definition 26. It is a combination of cylindrical extension and projection [111], [222].

Definition 29 *Let A be a fuzzy set defined on X and R be a fuzzy relation defined on X × Y. Then the composition of A and R resulting in a fuzzy set B defined on Z is given by*

$$B = A \circ R = proj\left(\left(ce\left(A; X \times Y\right) \cap R\right); Y\right) \tag{2.65}$$

According to Definition 26 the composition of the fuzzy set and the fuzzy relation presented in Definition 29 is expressed as follows

$$B = A \circ R = \int_Y \frac{\sup_{x \in X}\left[\min\left[\mu_A\left(x\right), \mu_R\left(x, y\right)\right]\right]}{y} \tag{2.66}$$

or in the general case the membership function of fuzzy set B is given by

$$\mu_B\left(y\right) = \sup_{x \in X}\left[\mu_A\left(x\right) \overset{T}{*} \mu_R\left(x, y\right)\right] \tag{2.67}$$

where $\overset{T}{*}$ can be any type of T-norm (not necessarily *min*).

The composition of the fuzzy set A and fuzzy relation R, defined by Equation (2.65), is illustrated in Fig. 2.10. The fuzzy set A and the fuzzy relation R are presented in Figs. 2.10 (a) and (c), respectively. Figure 2.10 (b) portrays the cylindrical extension of A on X to Cartesian product $X \times Y$. Figure 2.10 (d) shows the union of the cylindrical extension $ce\left(A\right)$ and fuzzy relation R. The result of the composition $A \circ R$, defined as the projection of $ce\left(A\right) \cap R$ on Y, is depicted in Fig. 2.10 (e).

2.2 Approximate Reasoning

Reasoning with fuzzy logic is not exact but rather approximate. Based on fuzzy premises and fuzzy implications, fuzzy conclusions are inferred. This kind of fuzzy inference has been applied in fuzzy controllers and other fuzzy systems. It should be noticed that much human reasoning is performed by use of fuzzy concepts. Approximate reasoning is thus suitable for intelligent systems, which try to imitate human intelligence.

2.2.1 Compositional Rule of Inference

In [563] Zadeh introduced the compositional rule of inference, which plays the most important role in approximate reasoning. *Fuzzy conditional statements* in the form: IF A THEN B, denoted for short by $A \Longrightarrow B$, with the

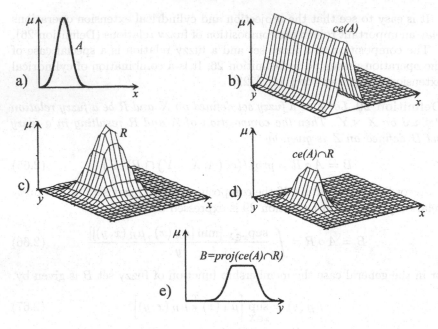

FIGURE 2.10. Illustration of the composition of fuzzy set A in X and fuzzy relation R in $X \times Y$

fuzzy sets A (antecedent) and B (consequent), were considered as fuzzy relations. The basic rule of inference in classical logic, i.e. *modus ponens*, was generalized in [567] and viewed as a special case of the compositional rule of inference.

The *generalized modus ponens*, defined in [567], can be depicted as follows

premise	A'
implication	$A \Longrightarrow B$
conclusion	$A' \circ (A \Longrightarrow B)$

(2.68)

where A', A, B are fuzzy sets. The above statement differs from the traditional *modus ponens* because fuzzy sets are used instead of propositional variables and A' is different from A. The well known rule of inference in classical logic, based on *modus ponens*, is: IF A is true (premise) and A implies B (implication), then B is true (conclusion). According to the *generalized modus ponens*, the conclusion inferred based on the premise A' (fuzzy set) and the implication $A \Longrightarrow B$ (fuzzy relation) differs from B and is obtained as the composition of A' and $A \Longrightarrow B$. Thus the *compositional rule of inference* leads to the *generalized modus ponens*. Since A' is a fuzzy set and $A \Longrightarrow B$ is a fuzzy relation, the conclusion is determined by use of

Definition 29. In this case, symbols A and B in Equations (2.65), (2.66), (2.67) should be replaced by A' and B', respectively.

It is worth remembering that in classical propositional calculus, the expression IF A THEN B, where A and B are propositional variables, is written as $A \Longrightarrow B$, with the implication $\Longrightarrow$ regarded as a connective which is defined by the following truth table [202], [563]

$$\begin{array}{|c|c||c|}
\hline
A & B & A \Longrightarrow B \\
\hline
1 & 1 & 1 \\
\hline
1 & 0 & 0 \\
\hline
0 & 1 & 1 \\
\hline
0 & 0 & 1 \\
\hline
\end{array} \tag{2.69}$$

The propositional expressions $A \Longrightarrow B$ and $\tilde{A} \vee B$, where the latter means NOT A OR B, have the identical truth table (2.69), so the latter represents the implication. The fuzzy implication called Boolean, binary, Kleene-Dienes, or Dienes-Rescher, has been defined based on this expression.

2.2.2 Implications

The *compositional rule of inference*, which can be considered to be a special case of the *generalized modus ponens*, presented in Section 2.2.1, is of major importance in *approximate reasoning*. The inference based on this rule depends on the implication $A \Longrightarrow B$. Various implication functions have been widely studied by many authors with reference to the implication relation existing in the *generalized modus ponens* rule (see e.g. [501], [311], [92]). Presented below is the definition of an implication function [501].

Definition 30 *A continuous function*

$$I: \quad [0,1] \times [0,1] \to [0,1] \tag{2.70}$$

is an implication function iff $\forall \ a, a', b, b', c \ \epsilon [0,1]$ *verifies the following properties*

$$P1: \quad If \ a \leqslant a' \ then \ I(a,b) \geqslant I(a',b) \tag{2.71}$$
$$P2: \quad If \ b \leqslant b' \ then \ I(a,b) \leqslant I(a,b') \tag{2.72}$$
$$P3: \quad I(0,a) = 1 \tag{2.73}$$
$$P4: \quad I(1,a) = a \tag{2.74}$$
$$P5: \quad I(a, I(b,c)) = I(b, I(a,c)) \tag{2.75}$$

Properties P3, P4, and P5 are called falsity, neutrality, and exchange principles, respectively. The well known symbol iff stands for if and only if.

TABLE 2.2. Basic examples of implication functions

Name	Implication
Kleene-Dienes	$\max(1 - a, b)$
Łukasiewicz	$\min(1, 1 - a + b)$
Zadeh	$\max(1 - a, \min(a, b))$
Reichenbach	$1 - a + ab$
Goguen	$\begin{cases} \min\left(1, \frac{b}{a}\right) & \text{if} \quad a \neq 0 \\ 1 & \text{otherwise} \end{cases}$
Gödel	$\begin{cases} 1 & \text{if} \quad a \leqslant b \\ b & \text{otherwise} \end{cases}$
Dubois-Prade	$\begin{cases} 1 - a & \text{if} \quad b = 0 \\ b & \text{if} \quad a = 1 \\ 1 & \text{otherwise} \end{cases}$

Table 2.2 illustrates basic examples of implication functions. It is easy to show that the implications listed in the table satisfy conditions (2.71)-(2.75). The first implication, called Kleene-Dienes, as well as Dienes-Rescher, Boolean, or binary, implication corresponds to the propositional expression $\widetilde{A} \vee B$, where $\widetilde{A}$ denotes negation of A. This expression fulfills truth table (2.69), so it represents the well known implication in classical logic.

Implications studied in the literature are classified in the following groups [92]:

- *Strong implications* (S-implications)

- *Residual implications* (R-implications)

- *Quantum mechanics implications* (QM-implications)

Strong implications correspond to the definition of an implication in classical Boolean logic, that is, expressed as $A \Longrightarrow B \equiv \widetilde{A} \vee B$. The Kleene-Dienes implication is a typical example of the implications belonging to this group. Others are the Reichenbach and Dubois-Prade implications.

Residual implications are obtained by residuation of a continuous T-norm. The Łukasiewicz, Goguen, and Gödel implications are examples of these. However, the Łukasiewicz implication belongs to both the *strong implication* and *residual implication* groups.

Quantum mechanics implications correspond to the definition of implication in Quantum logic, that is, expressed as $A \Longrightarrow B \equiv \widetilde{A} \vee (A \wedge B)$. The Zadeh implication is an example of the QM-implications.

Many others, not belonging to any of these well defined groups, have been introduced in the literature on fuzzy logic in order to be employed as implication operators [336], [255], [68], [93], [92]. Different implications are also considered in [113].

2.2.3   Linguistic Variables

The concept of linguistic variables was introduced by Zadeh [563], [567] to provide a basis for *approximate reasoning*. In [567], apart from a formal definition, the author described this concept in the following way: "By a *linguistic variable* we mean a variable whose values are words or sentences in a natural or artificial language. For example *Age* is a linguistic variable if its values are linguistic rather than numerical, i.e., *young, not young, very young, quite young, old, not very old and not very young, etc., rather than 20, 21, 22, 23, ...* " The author also explained: " The motivation for the use of words or sentences rather than numbers is that linguistic characterizations are, in general, less specific than numerical ones. For example, in speaking of age, when we say *John is young*, we are less precise than when we say *John is 25*. In this sense, the label *young* may be regarded as a *linguistic value* of the variable *Age*, with the understanding that it plays the same role as the numerical value 25 but is less precise and hence less informative." However, "by providing a basis for *approximate reasoning*, that is a mode of reasoning which is not exact nor very inexact, such logic may offer a more realistic framework for human reasoning than the traditional two-valued logic." The last sentence refers to *fuzzy logic*, proposed by Zadeh: "Treating *Truth* as a linguistic variable with values such as *true, very true, completely true, not very true, untrue,* etc. leads to what is called *fuzzy logic.*" Fuzzy logic is an extension of multivalued logic in which the truth values are linguistic variables.

In Section 2.2.1 the *compositional rule of inference* uses the implication $A \Longrightarrow B$, treated as a fuzzy relation, which corresponds to the *fuzzy conditional statement* IF A THEN B. Typical examples of the statement of this kind are [563]:

$$\text{IF } large \text{ THEN } small \qquad (2.76)$$

$$\text{IF } slippery \text{ THEN } dangerous \qquad (2.77)$$

which can be treated as abbreviations of the following statements

$$\text{IF } a \text{ is } large \text{ THEN } b \text{ is } small \qquad (2.78)$$

$$\text{IF } the\ road \text{ is } slippery \text{ THEN } driving \text{ is } dangerous \qquad (2.79)$$

In the above statements A is interpreted as a fuzzy predicate (fuzzy set), which may be viewed as the equivalent of the membership function of the fuzzy set A. In these examples, *large* and *slippery* are labels of the fuzzy set A, *small* and *dangerous* are labels of the fuzzy set B. The first two statements of the form IF A THEN B are the abbreviations of the statement IF x is A THEN y is B, where x and y are linguistic variables.

In statement (2.78) the names of the linguistic variables x and y are a and b, while in statement (2.79) these names are *the road* and *driving*, respectively. The values of the linguistic variables a and b, in statement (2.78), are *large* and *small*, respectively. The values of the linguistic variables *the road* and *driving*, in statement (2.79), are *slippery* and *dangerous*, respectively.

The propositions x is A, y is B, of the antecedent and consequent parts of the IF-THEN statement may be read as x has property A, and y has property B, where A and B are names of fuzzy subsets of the universes of discourse X and Y, respectively.

The concept of *linguistic variables* plays a pivotal role in fuzzy logic, as a stepping-stone to the concept of *fuzzy rules* [563]; see also Section 2.2.4. Fuzzy rules provide an alternative method of characterization when the dependencies are imprecise or when a high degree of precision is not required. They have been widely employed in various practical applications, especially in fuzzy controllers. The IF-THEN statements (2.78) and (2.79) can be treated as examples of fuzzy rules.

As we have seen, the *linguistic variables* can take words, which are usually labels of fuzzy sets, as their values. Of course, values of the *linguistic variables* can be either words or numbers. A real (crisp) number can be treated as a special case of a fuzzy set (fuzzy number) with its *support* equal to this crisp number (see Definitions 9 and 2); such a fuzzy set is called a *singleton* (see Definition 3).

The formal definition of the *linguistic variables* proposed by Zadeh [567] was formulated as follows.

Definition 31 *A linguistic variable is characterized by a quintuple*

$$(\ell, \Im(\ell), U, G, M)$$

in which ℓ is the name of the variable; $\Im(\ell)$ is the term-set of ℓ, that is, the collection of its linguistic values; U is a universe of discourse; G is a syntactic rule which generates the terms in $\Im(\ell)$; and M is a semantic rule which associates each linguistic value with its meaning, i.e. a fuzzy subset of U.

In [567] the author explained that a *linguistic variable* is *structured* in the sense that it is associated with two rules: a *syntactic rule* and a *semantic rule*. The former specifies the manner in which the linguistic values in the term-set of the variable may be generated. With regard to this rule, our usual assumption will be that the terms in the term-set of the variable are generated by a context-free grammar. The latter one is a *semantic rule* which specifies a procedure for computing the meaning of any given linguistic value. In this connection, we observe that a typical value of a linguistic variable, e.g., *not very young and not very old*, involves what might be called the *primary* terms, e.g., *young* and *old*, whose meaning is both subjective and context-dependent. We assume that the meaning of such terms is specified *a priori*. In addition to the primary terms, a linguistic value may involve connectives such as *and, or, either, neither*, etc.; the negation *not*; and the hedges such as *very, highly, more or less, completely, quite, fairly, extremely, somewhat, etc.* The connectives, the hedges and the negation may be treated as operators which modify the meaning of their operands in a specified, context-independent fashion.

The negation *not*, the connectives *and* and *or*, as well as the hedges, and other terms which enter into the representation of the values of linguistic variables may be viewed as labels of various operations defined in a fuzzy subset of the universe of discourse. These operations are *complement, intersection, union, concentration, dilation,* etc. (see Section 2.1.2). Examples which illustrate computation of the meaning of values of a linguistic variable are presented in [563].

As an example, let us consider a linguistic variable named *Age*. In this case, according to Definition 31, $\ell = Age$, with the universe of discourse $U = [0, 100]$ that is the interval of 0 to 100 years. Values of this linguistic variable might be: *young, very young, not very young, more or less old, very old*, etc. These values constitute the term-set $\Im(\ell)$ of $\ell = Age$, i.e. $\Im(Age) - V_1 + V_2 + \cdots$, where $V_1 -$ *young*, $V_2 -$ *very young*, ... A particular V, that is, a name generated by G, is called a *term*. If it is necessary to make it clear that $\Im$ is generated by a grammar G, then $\Im$ will be written as $\Im(G)$. The meaning $M(V)$, of a term V, is usually used interchangeably with V, although according to Definition 31, V is distinct from $M(V)$. When we say that the term *young* is a value of *Age*, it should be understood that the actual value is $M(V_1)$ and that V_1 is merely the name of the value [567]. Figure 2.11 illustrates the values of the linguistic variable *Age*. The hedges *very* and *more or less* are realized by means of *concentration* and *dilation* operations, respectively (see Definitions 20 and 21). For example, applying the linguistic hedge *very* to the fuzzy set labeled as *young*, we obtain a new fuzzy set representing the concept of *very young* persons. The negation operation (Definition 14) is employed in order to get the value *not very young*, treated as the complement of *very young*.

The linguistic hedge *very* can be also realized by a so-called *shifted* hedge instead of the *concentration* operator which is an example of a class of *powered* hedges. Combinations of both types of hedges are possible, too. Figure 2.12 portrays two values of the linguistic variable *Age*, namely *old* and *very old*, where the former is the same as in Fig. 2.11 but the latter is obtained from the *old* value by use of the *shifted* hedge operator. Thus, the *very old* value is represented by a membership function which equals one starting from a greater crisp value of *Age* than the membership function which corresponds to the *old* value. Concerning *Age*, this kind of representation of the hedge is more suitable that the *concentration* operator. For example, if the hedge *very old* is realized by the *concentration* operator, a person of 80 will be treated as *very old* (with the membership function equaled to one), as well as *old* (with the same membership value). However,

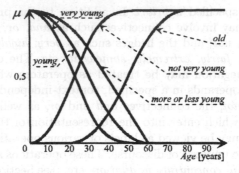

FIGURE 2.11. Values of the linguistic variable *Age*

if the hedge *very old* is realized by the *shifted* operator, the same person will be considered as *old* (with the membership function equaled to one) but as *very old* with the membership function less than one. Of course, the linguistic values of *Age*, shown in Figs. 2.11 and 2.12, should be viewed as examples, especially the linguistic hedges. Everybody can propose slightly different shapes of the membership functions which would represent the linguistic values of *Age*.

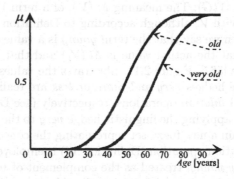

FIGURE 2.12. Linguistic values: *old* and *very old*

With reference to the linguistic hedges (linguistic modifiers) the following hedges are distinguished in the literature [222]: *powered* hedges, *shifted* hedges, and *scaled* hedges.

The *powered* hedges [583] modify the membership function $\mu_A(x)$ of a fuzzy set A in X by using the exponent

$$\mu_{hedge(A)}(x) = (\mu_A(x))^p \tag{2.80}$$

for all $x \in X$, and $p > 0$. Depending on the exponent value, the modifier realizes a concentration $(p > 1)$ or dilation $(p < 1)$ of the fuzzy set A. If

$p = 1$, operation (2.80) does not cause any modification. The *concentration* and *dilation* operators, presented in Definitions 20 and 21, are special cases of the *powered* hedges, where $p = 2$ and $p = 0.5$, respectively. The former is usually interpreted as *very* and the latter one as *more or less*. Powered hedges are characterized by the fact that the *support* and *core* (see Definitions 2 and 4) of a modified fuzzy set are not changed by these operations, since the membership values equal 0 and 1 are not changed by an exponent operation with the value $p > 0$.

The *shifted* hedges [287] shift the original membership function to the left or right along the universe of discourse. They are defined by

$$\mu_{hedge(A)}(x) = \mu_A(x - r) \tag{2.81}$$

where r denotes the magnitude of the shift. The value of r can be positive as well as negative. In [392] the *shifted* hedges have been applied in order to modify a trapezoidal shaped membership function. In this case a positive value of r shifted the left side of the membership function and a negative value of r shifted the right side, so the fuzzy set was concentrated, resulting in the linguistic hedge *very*. In a similar way, by an inverse operation, dilation of a fuzzy set can be realized, for example, to represent the linguistic hedge *more or less*.

As mentioned before, *powered* hedges and *shifted* hedges can be combined to perform the following operation [101]

$$\mu_{hedge(A)}(x) = (\mu_A(x - r))^p \tag{2.82}$$

for all $x \in X$, and $p > 0$, where r denotes the magnitude of the shift.

The *scaled* hedges have been defined in order to combine the advantageous features of the *powered* hedges and the *shifted* hedges. The general form of the function proposed as this kind of modifier is

$$\mu_{hedge(A)}(x) = \mu_A(c(x - r_A) + r_A) = \mu_A(cx + (1 - c)r_A) \tag{2.83}$$

where c is a scaling factor and r_A is a reference point for the modified fuzzy set A. The same values which are usually chosen for the exponent p, when the *powered* hedges are employed, can serve as the values of the scaling factor c. Thus, we choose $c = 2$ for the linguistic modifier *very*, and $c = 0.5$ for the linguistic hedge *more or less*. The reference point, r_A, is a characteristic point of the fuzzy set A, for instance, the center of the *core* of the membership function. The *scaled* modifiers preserve the original shape of the basic membership function. An example can be found in [222].

From the point of view described in [562], a hedge may be regarded as an operator which transforms the fuzzy set representing the meaning of a linguistic variable into the fuzzy set representing the meaning of the transformed fuzzy set. The hedges allow a larger set of values to be generated for a linguistic variable from a small collection of primary terms.

2.2.4 Calculus of Fuzzy Rules

The concept of a linguistic variable, described in Section 2.2.3, was a stepping-stone to the concept of a fuzzy IF-THEN rule, introduced in [563]. Fuzzy rules and their manipulation refer to the so-called *calculus of fuzzy rules* [574], the largely self-contained part of fuzzy logic, often used in practical applications. The concept of a fuzzy rule is very important in situations when the dependencies described by these rules are imprecise or a high degree of precision is not required. For example, let us assume now that x and y are real-valued variables, whose dependency function f is coarsely described in words by the following fuzzy rules

IF x is *very small* THEN y is *large*

IF x is *small* THEN y is *medium*

IF x is *medium* THEN y is *small*   (2.84)

IF x is *large* THEN y is *medium*

IF x is *very large* THEN y is *large*

where *small* and *large* are linguistic values of x and y. It is easy to notice that the same function can be represented by a different number of rules that are similar to the collection (2.84). The more linguistic values are distinguished the less is the coarseness of the dependency expressed by function f. It will be illustrated in the next section (see Fig. 2.16).

Fuzzy rules may be classified as *categorical* or *qualified* [574]. The former ones are widely used in control and industrial applications. A basic type of these rules has the form

IF x_1 is A_1 AND ... AND x_n is A_n
THEN y_1 is B_1 AND ... AND y_m is B_m (2.85)

where $A_1, \ldots, A_n$ and $B_1, \ldots, B_m$ are labels of the linguistic values of $x_1, \ldots, x_n$ and $y_1, \ldots, y_m$, respectively. The following rule is an example of the categorical type of rules expressed by formula (2.85)

IF *Temperature* is *high* AND *Pressure* is *low*
THEN *Volume* is *high*   (2.86)

The qualified rules, as the name suggests, contain one or more qualifications. Examples of this type of rules might be

IF x is A THEN y is B unless x is C

$$\text{IF } x \text{ is } A \ \text{ THEN } (y \text{ is } B) \text{ is likely}$$

$$\text{IF } x \text{ is } A \ \text{ THEN } ((y \text{ is } B) \text{ is very true })$$
$$\text{usually } (\text{IF } x \text{ is } A \ \text{ THEN } y \text{ is } B)$$

In the above examples, there are instances of a rule with exceptions, as well as probability-qualification, truth-qualification, usuality-qualification.

Qualified rules, especially probability-qualified rules, play an important role in knowledge-based and expert systems. These kinds of rules are not usually employed in fuzzy control and industrial applications. Generally, we can say that it is much more difficult to deal with qualified rules than with the categorical ones.

A significant part of the calculus of fuzzy rules refers to the semantics of the rules. One aspect of semantics that is essential in the application of fuzzy logic concerns the concept of a fuzzy graph, presented in the next section. There are two separate issues with regard to the semantics of fuzzy rules: the meaning of a single rule and the meaning of a collection of rules. The meaning of an elementary categorical rule of the form

$$\text{IF } x \text{ is } A \ \text{ THEN } y \text{ is } B \tag{2.87}$$

can be defined in two distinct ways. In practical applications of fuzzy logic, the following way is predominant

$$\text{IF } x \text{ is } A \ \text{ THEN } y \text{ is } B \ \rightarrow \ (x, y) \text{ is } A \times B \tag{2.88}$$

where the arrow stands for "translates into" and $A \times B$ denotes the Cartesian product of fuzzy sets A and B; see Definition 25. In this expression, the Cartesian product $A \times B$ plays the role of a fuzzy constraint on the joint variable (x, y). Therefore, this way of interpretating the fuzzy IF-THEN rule is called a *joint constraint* interpretation.

Another way of interpretating the rule in the form of Equation (2.87) is as an instance of a genuine logical implication (see Section 2.2.2). The meaning of rule (2.87), in the case of the Lukasiewicz implication (see Table 2.2), can be expressed as follows

$$\text{IF } x \text{ is } A \ \text{ THEN } y \text{ is } B \ \rightarrow \ (x \mid y) \text{ is } ce\left(\widetilde{A}\right) \oplus ce\left(B\right) \tag{2.89}$$

where $x \mid y$ denotes "y conditioned on x"; the complement of A is denoted as $\widetilde{A}$, and $ce\left(\widetilde{A}\right)$, $ce\left(B\right)$ are cylindrical extensions of $\widetilde{A}$, B, respectively; to the Cartesian product of X, Y, assuming that $(x, y) \in X \times Y$, see Definition 28; symbol $\oplus$ in Equation (2.89) is explained as follows, with reference to the Lukasiewicz implication

$$\mu_{ce(\widetilde{A}) \oplus ce(B)}(x, y) = \min\left(1, 1 - \mu_A(x) + \mu_B(y)\right) \tag{2.90}$$

This interpretation of the fuzzy IF-THEN rule is called a *conditional constraint* interpretation.

The elementary rule (2.87) has been chosen for simplicity. Of course, the joint and conditional constraint interpretations of the rule (2.87) can be extended to rule (2.85). The conditional constraint interpretation may be explained, analogously, for other genuine implications presented in Table 2.2.

Now, let us consider a collection of fuzzy IF-THEN rules, also in the simple form (2.87), that is

$$\text{\textbf{IF } } x \text{ is } A^k \text{ \textbf{THEN} } y \text{ is } B^k \quad \text{for } k = 1, \dots, N \qquad (2.91)$$

where N is the number of rules.

If the joint constraint interpretation is used for each rule (2.91), then the constraints associated with the rules are combined disjunctively. Thus, the meaning of the collection of rules, for $k = 1, \dots, N$, is expressed as

$$\text{\textbf{IF } } x \text{ is } A^k \text{ \textbf{THEN} } y \text{ is } B^k \rightarrow (x, y) \text{ is } \sum_{k=1}^{N} A^k \times B^k \qquad (2.92)$$

where the summation denotes disjunction.

Formula (2.92) can be easily illustrated using the concept of a fuzzy graph, presented in the next section. The Cartesian products $A^k \times B^k$, for $k = 1, \dots, N$, may be treated as fuzzy points of the fuzzy graph and the graph may be viewed as a disjunctive superposition of the fuzzy points.

If the conditional constraint interpretation is applied for each rule (2.91), then the constraints associated with the rules are combined conjunctively. In this case, the meaning of the collection of rules, for $k = 1, \dots, N$, is formulated as follows

$$\text{\textbf{IF } } x \text{ is } A^k \text{ \textbf{THEN} } y \text{ is } B^k \rightarrow (x \mid y) \text{ is } \bigwedge_{k=1}^{N} \left(ce \left(\widetilde{A^k} \right) \oplus ce \left(B^k \right) \right) \qquad (2.93)$$

on the assumption that the Łukasiewicz implication is used.

The fact that the fuzzy IF-THEN rules can be interpreted in two distinct ways has created some confusion, especially in the literature on fuzzy control. This is explained in [574]. The problem is that the Cartesian product violates some of the basic conditions which a genuine implication must fulfil. In Section 2.3 two different approaches to fuzzy systems are considered: the Mamdani approach and the logical approach. The former employs the joint constraint interpretation of the rules, while the latter applies the conditional constraint interpretation.

According to [574], one of the most basic problems in the calculus of fuzzy rules is the following: Given a collection of fuzzy IF-THEN rules (2.91), what is the value of y corresponding to x is A, where A need not be equal to any A^k, $k = 1, \dots, N$? This is a problem of interpolation. The solution can be obtained, making use of the compositional rule of inference

(Section 2.2.1), based on Definition 29. The inference may be illustrated by means of the concept of a fuzzy graph [574]. It is much easier to find the solution for the joint constraint interpretation of the rules. This is the reason why this way of rule interpretation is employed in most practical applications of fuzzy logic. However, the conditional constraint interpretation of the rules is suitable for many tasks, especially in expert systems.

2.2.5 Granulation and Fuzzy Graphs

Linguistic variables, described in Section 2.2.3, are concomitant with the concept of *granulation* [569], [574], [576], [577]. As the author explained in [574], granulation, in fuzzy logic, involves a grouping of objects into fuzzy granules, with a granule being a clump of objects drawn together by similarity. In effect, granulation may be viewed as a form of fuzzy quantization, which in turn may be seen as an instance of fuzzy data compression. We can also say that quantization (non-fuzzy) is crisp granulation (see Section 3.1.9). In this case the granules are not fuzzy. In order to illustrate the difference, let us consider quantization (granulation) of domains X and Y of variables x and y, respectively, according to rules (2.84). Let us assume that these variables take real values in $[0, x_{\max}]$ and $[0, y_{\max}]$, respectively. The values of variables x are granulated to obtain five values: *very small, small, medium, large, very large*, but for variable y there are only three values: *small, medium, large* (see Figs. 2.13 and 2.14). Thus, values of a *linguistic variable* may be treated as *granules* whose labels are the linguistic values of the variable.

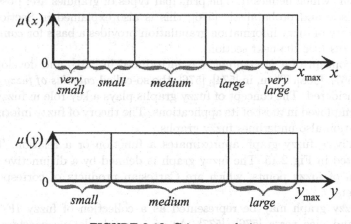

FIGURE 2.13. Crisp granulation

Models of information granulation in which the granules are crisp play an important role in many methods and approaches. However, crisp granulation does not reflect the fact that humans usually incorporate fuzzy

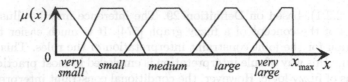

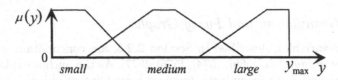

FIGURE 2.14. Fuzzy granulation

granulation when they granulate and manipulate information. Thus the theory of fuzzy information granulation is inspired by human reasoning which is fuzzy rather than crisp. The foundation of this theory comes from the concept of linguistic variables and fuzzy IF-THEN rules. The machinery of fuzzy information granulation plays an important role in the applications of fuzzy logic. In fact, it underlies most of the successes of fuzzy logic in dealing with real-world problems.

The foundations of the theory of fuzzy information granulation are mathematical in nature. The departure point of this theory is the concept of generalized constraint [572]. A granule is characterized by a generalized constraint which defines it. The principal types of granules are: possibilistic, veristic and probabilistic [576]; this is also explained in Section 7.4. The theory of fuzzy information granulation provides a basis for *computing with words* (see the next section).

The concept of a *fuzzy graph* was introduced in [561], and developed in [564], [567], [568]. Then, in [574], [576], the so-called *calculus of fuzzy graphs* was considered. The concept of fuzzy graphs plays a key role in fuzzy logic and is employed in most of its applications. The theory of fuzzy information granulation also underlines fuzzy graphs.

Usually, a fuzzy graph approximates a function or a relation. This is illustrated in Fig. 2.15. The fuzzy graph is defined by a disjunctive superposition of fuzzy points, which are Cartesian products of corresponding fuzzy sets.

A fuzzy graph may be represented as a collection of fuzzy IF-THEN rules, and vice versa [576], [577]. As an example, let us consider fuzzy rules (2.84) and notice that these rules and the fuzzy graph illustrated in Fig. 2.16 mutually correspond to each other. The fuzzy rules constitute the coarse description of the dependency given by function f, and Fig. 2.16 shows the fuzzy graph of function f. This function is approximated by the fuzzy graph. This graph has been portrayed based on fuzzy granulation of

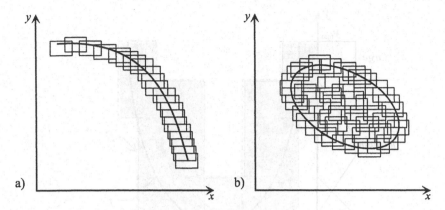

FIGURE 2.15. Approximate representations of: a) functions, b) relations; by fuzzy graphs

the domains of variables x and y, depicted in Fig. 2.14. These granules are the linguistic values in the rules (2.84).

As mentioned in Section 2.2.4, a fuzzy graph can illustrate the meaning of a collection of fuzzy IF-THEN rules (2.91), expressed in the form of Equation (2.92), for $k = 1, \dots, N$. This fuzzy graph portrays the relation, corresponding to the collection of the rules, as a disjunctive representation of the fuzzy points that are Cartesian products of fuzzy sets. This fuzzy graph is similar to that shown in Fig. 2.16. However, in this case, the linguistic values of x, y are A^k, B^k, respectively, for $k = 1, \dots, N$. In addition, the shape of the function that describes the relation may be different and it depends on the fuzzy sets A^k, B^k.

According to [577], an expression of the form $A^k \times B^k$, where A^k, B^k are linguistic values (words), can be referred to as a *Cartesian granule*. In this sense, the fuzzy graph, considered above, may be viewed as a disjunction of Cartesian granules. Generally, a word is assumed to be a label of a fuzzy granule. In this sense, values of a linguistic variable can be treated as granules whose labels are the linguistic values of the variable. Thus, the calculus of fuzzy graphs, with the theory of fuzzy information granulation, leads to the concept of *computing with words*, described in the next section.

Representations of an n-ary fuzzy graph in two equivalent forms: (a) as a collection of fuzzy IF-THEN rules; and (b) as a disjunctive combination of Cartesian products, constitute the basis of the calculus of fuzzy graphs. The problems whose solution can be considered are similar to the tasks known in the standard calculi. A simple example is the problem of maximization of a fuzzy graph. This can be solved by employing the technique of α-cuts (see Definition 12). The solution, in the form of a fuzzy set, is presented in [576]. Another is a problem of finding the intersection of two fuzzy graphs [574]. This is related to the problem of interpolation, mentioned in Sec-

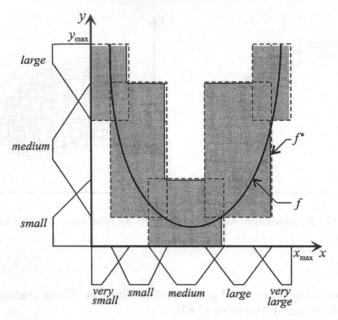

FIGURE 2.16. Fuzzy rules (2.84) represented by a fuzzy graph

tion 2.2.4. Strictly speaking, the interpolation task may be interpreted as that of finding the intersection of fuzzy graphs.

Figure 2.17 illustrates the definition of the intersection of fuzzy graphs $F \cap G$, assuming that F and G are fuzzy graphs of the form

$$F: \quad \sum_{j} A_j \times B_j$$

$$G: \quad \sum_{k} C_k \times D_k$$

where $A_j \times B_j$ and $C_k \times D_k$ are Cartesian products of fuzzy sets A_j, B_j, C_k, D_k, respectively, and the summations denote disjunction. The intersection of the fuzzy graphs F and G is expressed as

$$F \cap G = \quad \sum_{j,k} (A_j \cap C_k) \times (B_j \cap D_k)$$

Of course, the intersection $F \cap G$ is a fuzzy graph, given as a disjunctive representation of the fuzzy points that are Cartesian products of fuzzy sets $(A_j \cap C_k)$ and $(B_j \cap D_k)$.

It was mentioned in Section 2.2.4 that the inference process based on the compositional rule of inference may be illustrated by means of the concept

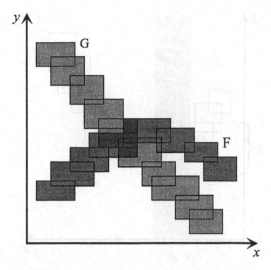

FIGURE 2.17. Intersection of fuzzy graphs

of a fuzzy graph. Figure 2.10 shows the process of inference for only one individual rule (fuzzy relation). This rule can be treated as a fuzzy point on the fuzzy graph that represents a collection of rules (in the form of fuzzy points). The inference process based on the collection of rules can be portrayed as the intersection of this fuzzy graph and the cylindrical extension of the fuzzy set A, defined on X, to $X \times Y$. Then, the projection (see Definition 27) of the graph intersection on Y gives the inferred output fuzzy set in Y. This is illustrated in Fig. 2.18.

It is interesting to observe the result for the above mentioned interpolation problem, presented in [574]. The case of the conditional constraint interpretation of the fuzzy IF-THEN rules is considered, with the assumption that the fuzzy set A is a singleton (see Definition 3). Using the definition of the intersection of fuzzy graphs, the same result has been obtained as that presented in the seminal paper by Mamdani and Assilian [310]; see also Sections 2.3.2 and 2.3.3.

Other problems of the calculus of fuzzy graphs, for example "what is the integral of a fuzzy graph?" or "what are the roots of a fuzzy graph?" fall, according to [576], within the realm of computing with words.

2.2.6 Computing with Words

The calculus of fuzzy graphs is a cornerstone of *computing with words* (CW), which involves manipulation of words rather than numbers. As a methodology, introduced by Zadeh [574], [575], [577], CW is a derivative of fuzzy logic. It is a methodology for computing and reasoning which is close to human intuition, and can thus be applied in Artificial Intelligence.

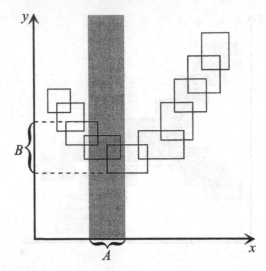

FIGURE 2.18. Illustration of the inference process as intersection of fuzzy graphs

The so-called *computational theory of perceptions* (CTP) was developed by Zadeh [578], [579], based on the methodology of CW; see Section 7.4, in Chapter 7.

As mentioned in Section 2.2.5, one concept which plays a pivotal role in CW is that of a granule. A fuzzy granule is a fuzzy set of points drawn together by similarity. A word may be atomic, e.g. *young*, or composite – for example *not very young* – treated as a label of a fuzzy granule.

In CW, a granule *g*, which is the denotation of a word, *w*, is viewed as a fuzzy constraint on a variable. A key role in CW is played by fuzzy constraint propagation from premises to conclusions. A basic assumption in CW is that information is conveyed by constraining the values of variables. Moreover, information is assumed to consist of a collection of propositions expressed in a natural or synthetic language. Such propositions, typically, play the role of linguistic characterization of perceptions (see Section 7.4).

Let I denote information and $p_1, \ldots, p_n$ be propositions, so the information can be represented as a collection of propositions, thus

$$I = \{p_1, \ldots, p_n\}$$

with each proposition in the collection denoting a constraint on a variable. In CW, the constraints can take a variety of forms.

Examples of these propositions may be "Jim is tall" , "Thomas is 15", with the constrained variables *Jim's height* and *Thomas' age*, respectively. The constraints can be expressed as

$$Height \ (Jim) \ \text{is tall}$$

$$Age \ (Thomas) = 15$$

Both of these propositions may be viewed as linguistic characterizations of perception. The linguistic value "tall" is the label of a granule "tall" (for simplicity the same symbol is used for a word and its denotation). The fuzzy set "tall" plays the role of a fuzzy constraint on the *height* of *Jim*. This is an example of a disjunctive (possibilistic) constraint; see Section 7.4. The latter is an equality constraint. However, 15 can be treated as the label of a granule "15" which may represent a fuzzy number (about 15). This is thus a fuzzy constraint on the *age* of *Thomas*, that might also be viewed as a possibilistic constraint, so the equality symbol can be replaced by "is".

Other examples of such propositions, like "Most students are young", "Carol lives near Mary", are considered in [574], [577].

The following basic generic problem is posed in CW. From the initial data set, which is a collection of propositions expressed in a natural language, we wish to infer the answer to a query, both of these formulated in a natural language. A few tasks of CW, with reference to this basic problem, have been proposed in [577]. One of them refers to a function described in words by fuzzy IF-THEN rules, similar to that expressed by formula (2.84). These rules may be viewed as a linguistic representation of a perception of this function. What this implies is that the function is approximated by a fuzzy graph (see Section 2.2.5, Fig. 2.16). In this example, the initial data set consists of the collection of rules. The query is: What is the maximum value of the function described by these rules? This problem was mentioned in Section 2.2.5; the solution is presented in [576]. Another task, formulated in [577], with regard to CW, also refers to fuzzy IF-THEN rules in a similar form, and to fuzzy graphs.

Concerning the examples, mentioned above, in linguistic characterizations of variables and their dependencies, words – which may be viewed as a form of fuzzy granulation – serve as values of variables and play the role of fuzzy constraints.

In CW, there are two core issues. First is the question: How can the fuzzy constraints which are implicit in propositions expressed in a natural language be made explicit? This is the issue of representation of fuzzy constraints. Second is the question of how fuzzy constraints can be propagated from premises to conclusions. These issues are addressed in [577]; see also Section 7.4.

2.3 Fuzzy Systems

The concepts of fuzzy sets and fuzzy logic have been used in fuzzy systems [561], [563]. Most of them are rule-based fuzzy systems, in which relationships between variables are represented by fuzzy IF-THEN rules. These kind of systems have been successfully applied, mainly as fuzzy controllers. During the 1980s and 1990s, fuzzy theory was extensively employed in a wide range of consumer products in Japan [184], [493]. The most notable and spectacular examples of fuzzy system applications are an automatic train controller and a helicopter controller. Some introductory information about fuzzy control and fuzzy controllers can be found e.g. in [484], [289]. Some industrial applications of fuzzy control are presented in [485]. In the literature, there are many books and papers on theoretical as well as practical aspects of fuzzy control; see e.g. [403], [288], [112], [24], [111], [383], [513], [96], [281], [224], [554], [356], [357], [16], [378], [508], [393]. However, rule-based fuzzy systems can also be employed to solve other problems, for instance, pattern classification tasks, e.g. [365], and function approximation, e.g. [274]. This section deals with fundamentals of rule-based fuzzy logic systems.

2.3.1 Rule-Based Fuzzy Logic Systems

The name *fuzzy logic systems* refers to the systems which incorporate fuzzy logic. Figure 2.19 shows the general structure of a fuzzy logic system, which is a knowledge-based system.

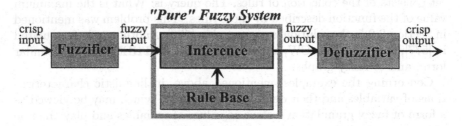

FIGURE 2.19. General structure of a fuzzy logic system

The main part of the system depicted in Fig. 2.19 constitutes a so-called *"pure" fuzzy system*, composed of the *inference engine* and the *fuzzy rule base*. The inference engine performs an inference process by use of approximate reasoning (see Section 2.2). The fuzzy rule base is the knowledge base, which consists of a collection of fuzzy IF-THEN rules. The *"pure" fuzzy system* realizes a mapping from input fuzzy sets to output fuzzy sets. A *fuzzifier* and a *defuzzifier* are used in order to obtain a system with crisp (non-fuzzy) inputs and crisp outputs. This is necessary in most engineering systems where the inputs and outputs are real-valued variables.

Let us start from the most essential part of the fuzzy logic system, i.e. the *"pure" fuzzy system*. It realizes a mapping from the input fuzzy sets to the output fuzzy sets. This mapping is conducted by the inference engine, based on the collection of fuzzy IF-THEN rules.

The rule base consists of rules in the following form

$$R^{(k)} : \textbf{IF } x_1 \text{ is } A_1^k \text{ AND } x_2 \text{ is } A_2^k \text{ AND } \ldots \text{ AND } x_n \text{ is } A_n^k$$
$$\textbf{THEN } y \text{ is } B^k \tag{2.94}$$

for $k = 1, \ldots, N$, where $x_1, \ldots, x_n$, and y are linguistic variables, corresponding to input and output, respectively. According to Definition 31, $x_1, \ldots, x_n$, and y are the symbolic names of linguistic variables, which can take their values from the term-sets of the linguistic values. In this case, $A_1^k, \ldots, A_n^k$, and B^k are elements of the term-sets. The semantic function, M, in Definition 31, gives a meaning (interpretation) of a linguistic value, that is a fuzzy set (or its membership function) defined over the appropriate universe of discourse. It was mentioned, in Section 2.2.3, that the linguistic terms and their meanings were usually interchangeable.

Now let us explain the inference process. Two types of approximate reasoning are employed in fuzzy inference systems: FITA - *first inference then aggregation*, and FATI - *first aggregation then inference* [56], [101]. In the former method, firstly the inference is performed based on each individual rule, then the aggregation of the inferred fuzzy sets is applied. This method is often called *individual-rule based inference* [111]. In the latter one, also called *composition based inference* [111], at first the aggregation of the rules is employed. Then, the output fuzzy set is inferred as a composition of the global (aggregated) rule and the input fuzzy set. Aggregation of the rules is usually realized by aggregation of the relation matrices which represent the rules (see e.g. [56], [442]). This corresponds to the aggregation of rules via union operation, for example. In the FITA inference, each rule in the fuzzy rule base determines an output fuzzy set, and after that the fuzzy sets are aggregated via union operation (or others). The FITA and FATI types of inference are also called *local* and *global* inference, respectively (see [222]). In both methods, the inference is conducted based on the *compositional rule of inference* (see Section 2.2.1).

The following formula expresses the compositional rule of inference applied to an individual rule

$$\overline{B}^k = A' \circ \left(A^k \rightarrow B^k \right) \tag{2.95}$$

where A' is an input fuzzy set, $A^k \rightarrow B^k$ represents the rule $R^{(k)}$ in the form of Equation (2.94), and $\overline{B}^k$ is the output fuzzy set inferred on the basis of A' and $A^k \rightarrow B^k$.

Formula (2.95) realizes the composition of fuzzy set A' and fuzzy relation $A^k \rightarrow B^k$, according to Definition 29. Hence, from Equation (2.67), formula (2.95) takes the following form, known as the *sup-star composition*

$$\mu_{\overline{B}^k}(y) = \sup_{\mathbf{x} \in \mathbf{X}} \left[\mu_{A'}(\mathbf{x}) \overset{T}{*} \mu_{A^k \rightarrow B^k}(\mathbf{x}, y) \right] \tag{2.96}$$

where $\mu_{A'}$, $\mu_{A^k \to B^k}$, and $\mu_{\overline{B}^k}$ are membership functions of fuzzy sets A', $A^k \to B^k$, and $\overline{B}^k$, respectively, $\mathbf{x} = [x_1, \dots, x_n]^T \in X_1 \times \cdots \times X_n = \mathbf{X}$, and $y \in Y$, assuming that $X_1, \dots, X_n$ and Y are universes of discourse of fuzzy sets $A_1^k, \dots, A_n^k$, and B^k, respectively, the $\overset{T}{*}$ operation can be any type of the T-norm (see Section 2.1.2).

It should be noted that $A^k \to B^k$, which corresponds to the IF-THEN rule (2.94), where $A^k = A_1^k \times \cdots \times A_n^k$, is interpreted as a fuzzy relation (see Section 2.1.3). It was mentioned in Section 2.1.3 that the Cartesian product of fuzzy sets (see Definition 25) was a fuzzy relation. In Section 2.2.2, various implication functions are presented. When their arguments are membership functions, they are referred as fuzzy implications (see Section 2.3.4). The fuzzy implications are also fuzzy relations. Both kinds of fuzzy relations can be used in fuzzy systems. The former is applied in the so-called Mamdani approach, and the latter in the logical approach. These fuzzy systems are described in the next sections.

The fuzzy logic system under consideration is the multi-input, single output (MISO) system. It can be easily extended a to multi-input, multi-output (MIMO) system. The inference method is the FITA. If the FATI inference is employed, the $A^k \to B^k$ in Equation (2.95) will be replaced by the global, i.e. aggregated rule, and instead of the fuzzy set $\overline{B}^k$, the overall fuzzy set B' will be inferred.

The fuzzifier and the defuzzifier are added to the "pure" fuzzy logic system in order to use this system in engineering applications, where the inputs and outputs are real-valued variables [513]. The fuzzifier maps crisp points in $\mathbf{X}$ to fuzzy sets in $\mathbf{X}$, and the defuzzifier maps fuzzy sets in Y to crisp points in Y.

Let $\overline{\mathbf{x}} = [\overline{x}_1, \dots, \overline{x}_n]^T$ is a crisp point in $\mathbf{X} = X_1 \times \cdots \times X_n$. The fuzzifier that is most often employed in fuzzy systems is the *singleton* fuzzifier, characterized by the following membership function

$$\mu_{A'}(\mathbf{x}) = \begin{cases} 1 & \text{if} \quad \mathbf{x} = \overline{\mathbf{x}} \\ 0 & \text{if} \quad \mathbf{x} \neq \overline{\mathbf{x}} \end{cases} \tag{2.97}$$

The fuzzy set A' represented by Equation (2.97) is called a *fuzzy singleton* (see Definition 3). The fuzzifier characterized by the membership function that equals 1 for $\mathbf{x} = \overline{\mathbf{x}}$ and decreases from 1 as $\mathbf{x}$ moves away from $\overline{\mathbf{x}}$ is called a *non-singleton* fuzzifier. An example of the *non-singleton* fuzzifier is a fuzzy set A' with the Gaussian membership function

$$\mu_{A'}(\mathbf{x}) = \exp\left(\frac{(\mathbf{x} - \overline{\mathbf{x}})^T (\mathbf{x} - \overline{\mathbf{x}})}{\sigma^2}\right) \tag{2.98}$$

where σ is a parameter which corresponds to the *width* of the Gaussian function.

The fuzzy set represented by the membership function (2.98) is a fuzzy number, according to Definition 9, assuming that $\mathbf{X} = \mathbf{R}$; see Fig. 2.8. For $\mathbf{X} = \mathbf{R}^2$, membership function (2.98) looks similar to that in Fig. 2.2.

The *non-singleton* fuzzifier is very seldom applied in fuzzy systems. However, it might be useful if the inputs are corrupted by noise.

Although the same symbol $\mathbf{x} = [x_1, \dots, x_n]^T$ denotes linguistic variables in the rule base (2.94) as well as the crisp (real-valued) input variables in Equations (2.97) and (2.98), these can be easily distinguished, if necessary. Similarly, the symbol T denotes transposition of the vector, as well as the T-norm operator (in Section 2.1.2 and others).

The defuzzifier performs a mapping from the inferred fuzzy sets $\overline{B}^k$ or B' in Y to a crisp point $\overline{y}$ in Y. There are many defuzzification methods [111], [178]. The best known is the *center-of-area* (COA), also called the *center-of-gravity* (COG) method. In the continuous case, it is defined by

$$\overline{y} = \frac{\int_Y y\ \mu_{B'}(y)\ dy}{\int_Y \mu_{B'}(y)\ dy} \qquad (2.99)$$

In the discrete case, this method takes the following form

$$\overline{y} = \frac{\sum_{j=1}^m y_j\ \mu_{B'}(y_j)}{\sum_{j=1}^m \mu_{B'}(y_j)} \qquad (2.100)$$

where y_j, for $j = 1, \dots, m$, are discrete points in Y.

This method, in the continuous case, determines the center of the area below the combined membership functions.

If the fuzzy system B' is created as the union of all fuzzy sets $\overline{B}^k$, for $k = 1, \dots, N$, then Equations (2.99) and (2.100) can be presented as follows, respectively

$$\overline{y} = \frac{\int_Y y \max_{1 \leqslant k \leqslant N} \left\{ \mu_{\overline{B}^k}(y) \right\}\ dy}{\int_Y \max_{1 \leqslant k \leqslant N} \left\{ \mu_{\overline{B}^k}(y) \right\}\ dy} \qquad (2.101)$$

and

$$\overline{y} = \frac{\sum_{j=1}^m y_j \max_{1 \leqslant k \leqslant N} \left\{ \mu_{\overline{B}^k}(y_j) \right\}}{\sum_{j=1}^m \max_{1 \leqslant k \leqslant N} \left\{ \mu_{\overline{B}^k}(y_j) \right\}} \qquad (2.102)$$

It should be noted that these forms of the COA defuzzification method avoid computation on B'. The maximum operation in formulas (2.101) and (2.102) corresponds to the union of fuzzy sets $\overline{B}^k$, realized as the aggregation by use of the S-norm (see Section 2.1.2).

Another defuzzification method, is *center-of-sums* (COS) defuzzification. This method is similar to the COA but faster. Instead of the maximum operation in Equations (2.101) and (2.102) it employs the sum of $\overline{B}^k$, for $k = 1, \ldots, N$. This method can thus be represented by the following formulas, in the continuous and discrete case, respectively

$$\overline{y} = \frac{\int_Y y \sum_{k=1}^N \mu_{\overline{B}^k}(y) \, dy}{\int_Y \sum_{k=1}^N \mu_{\overline{B}^k}(y) \, dy} \qquad (2.103)$$

and

$$\overline{y} = \frac{\sum_{j=1}^m y_j \sum_{k=1}^N \mu_{\overline{B}^k}(y)}{\sum_{j=1}^m \sum_{k=1}^N \mu_{\overline{B}^k}(y)} \qquad (2.104)$$

where y_j, for $j = 1, \ldots, m$, are discrete points in Y.

In this method the overlapping areas of the combined membership functions are taken into consideration. Moreover, this method is faster than the COA, so it has been used quite often.

It should be noted that there are some fuzzy systems which claim to have employed the *center-of-gravity* defuzzification, but which actually applied the *center-of-sums* method [111].

A simple and very quick method is *height* defuzzification. The computation of the algorithm concerns the fuzzy sets $\overline{B}^k$, inferred by the individual rules. Neither the support nor shape of the membership function $\mu_{\overline{B}^k}$ plays the role in this method. Only *centers* of the membership functions, i.e. the points with the largest membership values are important. This method takes the peak value of each membership function $\mu_{\overline{B}^k}$, for $k = 1, \ldots, N$, and creates the weighted, with respect to the *height* (see Definition 5) of the fuzzy sets $\overline{B}^k$, sum of these peak values. Formally, this method can be described by the following equation

$$\overline{y} = \frac{\sum_{k=1}^N \overline{y}^k \, \mu_{\overline{B}^k}(\overline{y}^k)}{\sum_{k=1}^N \mu_{\overline{B}^k}(\overline{y}^k)} \qquad (2.105)$$

where $\overline{y}^k$ is the peak point of the membership function $\mu_{\overline{B}^k}$.

The defuzzification method expressed by formula (2.105) is also known as the *center average* (CA) defuzzification. This method can be determined from the discrete version of the COA defuzzification method. In this case, the peak values $\overline{y}^k$, for $k = 1, \ldots, N$, are the same as the *centers* of the membership functions μ_{B^k}, defined as the points in Y such that

$$\mu_{B^k}(\overline{y}^k) = \max_y \{\mu_{B^k}(y)\} \qquad (2.106)$$

since the fuzzy sets $\overline{B}^k$, inferred in a fuzzy logic system, are usually clipped or scaled forms of the fuzzy sets B^k.

As a special case of the discrete version of COA defuzzification (2.100), the following method can be used

$$\bar{y} = \frac{\sum_{k=1}^{N} \bar{y}^k \, \mu_{B'}\left(\bar{y}^k\right)}{\sum_{k=1}^{N} \mu_{B'}\left(\bar{y}^k\right)} \tag{2.107}$$

where $\bar{y}^k$, for $k = 1, \ldots, N$, which are discrete points in Y, satisfy condition (2.106).

Some other defuzzification methods are presented in [111].

Apart from fuzzy logic systems with a fuzzifier and a defuzzifier, the Takagi-Sugeno type of fuzzy systems [494] have also been successfully employed in many practical applications. These systems use a rule base with the same antecedents (IF parts) of the rules as depicted in formula (2.94), but with different consequents (THEN parts) of the IF-THEN rules. The consequent (conclusion) parts of the rules, in the Takagi-Sugeno systems, do not contain fuzzy sets. They have a functional form that is a linear combination of input variables. Therefore these systems do not need defuzzifiers.

2.3.2 The Mamdani and Logical Approaches to Fuzzy Inference

The Mamdani approach refers to the work of Mamdani and Assilian [310]. They interpreted the fuzzy IF-THEN rules as implications, defined as the Cartesian product. As a matter of fact, what they called implications were not actually implications in a logical sense (see Section 2.2.2). In this case, the fuzzy rules are viewed in terms of a function defined by a number of different samples.

Although the fuzzy systems based on IF-THEN rules, according to the Mamdani approach, are also called fuzzy logic systems, they refer to *fuzzy logic* in a broad sense, i.e. understood as using fuzzy sets. In this sense, which is that most generally employed nowadays, fuzzy logic is almost synonymous with the theory of fuzzy sets.

Fuzzy logic systems employing implications in a logical sense, as the interpretation of IF-THEN rules, refer to fuzzy logic in a narrow sense, i.e. the extension of classical logic. These systems are considered with reference to the logical approach to fuzzy inference.

Let us consider the fuzzy logic system described in Section 2.3.1, with the rule base expressed by formula (2.94), which can also be presented in the following form

$$R^{(k)} : \textbf{IF } \mathbf{x} \textbf{ is } A^k \textbf{ THEN } y \textbf{ is } B^k \tag{2.108}$$

where $\mathbf{x} = [x_1, \ldots, x_n]^T \in \mathbf{X} \subset \mathbf{R}^n$, and $y \in Y \subset \mathbf{R}$, are linguistic variables corresponding to the input and output of the system, $A^k = A_1^k \times \cdots \times A_n^k$

and B^k are fuzzy sets characterized by the membership functions $\mu_{A^k}(\mathbf{x})$ and $\mu_{B^k}(y)$, respectively, for $k = 1, \dots, N$.

If $x_1, \dots, x_n$ are independent variables, then the rule base (2.108) takes the form (2.94). Fuzzy IF-THEN rules (2.108) or (2.94) are interpreted as fuzzy relations (see Definition 24) and the inference process is performed as the approximate reasoning, according to the compositional rule of inference (see Section 2.3.1). The output fuzzy sets $\overline{B}^k$ are inferred by individual rules $R^{(k)}$, for $k = 1, \dots, N$, according to formula (2.95), so these fuzzy sets are characterized by the membership functions expressed by Equation (2.96).

Using the Mamdani approach, the fuzzy relation $A^k \to B^k$ which corresponds to the rule $R^{(k)}$ is represented by the T-norm (see Table 2.1), usually minimum or product (i.e. the Zadeh or algebraic T-norms, respectively). Moreover, the aggregation is realized by the S-norm, usually maximum operation (see Table 2.1). This means that the overall output fuzzy set B' is obtained by the union operation

$$B' = \bigcup_{k=1}^{N} \overline{B}^k \qquad (2.109)$$

for $k = 1, \dots, N$, and the membership function of B' is expressed by

$$\mu_{B'}(y) = \mathop{\mathbf{S}}_{k=1}^{N} \mu_{\overline{B}^k}(y) \qquad (2.110)$$

where $\mathbf{S}$ is the S-norm operator, generalized for more than two arguments (see Section 2.1.2), usually chosen as the maximum.

Presented above refers to the FITA type of fuzzy inference. Similarly, when the FATI type of inference is employed, the rule aggregation is realized by the union operation, so the global rule is given by the following formula

$$\Re = \bigcup_{k=1}^{N} R^{(k)} \qquad (2.111)$$

and the output fuzzy set B' is obtained, according to the compositional rule of inference, as follows

$$B' = A' \circ \Re \qquad (2.112)$$

According to Definition 29, the membership function of B', in this case, is expressed by the *sup-star composition*

$$\mu_{B'}(y) = \sup_{\mathbf{x} \in \mathbf{X}} \left[\mu_{A'}(\mathbf{x}) \overset{T}{*} \max_{1 \leqslant k \leqslant N} \{ \mu_{A^k \to B^k}(\mathbf{x}, y) \} \right] \qquad (2.113)$$

assuming that the maximum operator has been chosen as the S-norm, in order to perform the aggregation.

It is easy to show [289] that when the Mamdani approach is applied, the FITA and FATI types of the inference give the same result (the same output fuzzy set B').

Using the logical approach, the fuzzy relations $A^k \rightarrow B^k$, which correspond to the rules $R^{(k)}$, for $k = 1, \ldots, N$, are implications in a logical sense. In this case, the aggregation is realized by the intersection operation instead of the union, so the overall output fuzzy set B' is obtained according to the expression

$$B' = \bigcap_{k=1}^{N} \overline{B}^k \qquad (2.114)$$

for $k = 1, \ldots, N$, and the membership function of B' is computed by use of the T-norm instead of the S-norm, that is

$$\mu_{B'}(y) = \mathop{\mathbf{T}}_{k=1}^{N} \mu_{\overline{B}^k}(y) \qquad (2.115)$$

where $\mathbf{T}$ is the T-norm operator, generalized for more than two arguments (see Section 2.1.2), usually chosen as minimum or product operators.

This type of inference, presented above, refers to the FITA method. The rule aggregation, when the FATI type of the inference is employed, is realized by the intersection operation instead of the union, so the global rule is given by the following formula

$$\Re = \bigcap_{k=1}^{N} R^{(k)} \qquad (2.116)$$

and the output fuzzy set B' is obtained according to the compositional rule of inference (2.112).

It is important to emphasize that when the FATI type of the inference is applied, formula (2.113) is different. The maximum operator should be replaced by the minimum or product.

Using the logical approach, the FITA and FATI types of inference lead to different results (see e.g. [222]). In the case of fuzzy inputs (*non-singletons*), the results obtained by *local* inference (FITA) are less restrictive and less informative than the results inferred by the *global* (FATI) method [113], [222]. However, in the case of numerical inputs (*singletons*) the local inference does not cause worse results than the *global* inference.

The S-norm and T-norm operators, used in the Mamdani and logical approach, refer to the disjunction and conjunction, respectively, concerning the combinations of the constraints in Equations (2.92) and (2.93).

The Mamdani and logical approaches to fuzzy inference have been discussed in [113], [547], [222], [16], [101]. In [547], as well as in [127], the Mamdani and logical approach are also called the *constructive* and *destructive* approaches, respectively.

2.3.3   Fuzzy Systems Based on the Mamdani Approach

The fuzzy controller introduced by Assilian [13] and Mamdani [309], also described in [310], used the minimum operator as the T-norm which represented the fuzzy relations corresponding to the IF-THEN rules, the same operator for conjunction in the premises (antecedents) of the rules, and the maximum operator for the aggregation. Fuzzy rules employed in this controller had the following general form

$$R^{(k)} : \textbf{IF } x_1 \text{ is } A_1^k \textbf{ AND } x_2 \text{ is } A_2^k \textbf{ AND } \ldots \textbf{ AND } x_n \text{ is } A_n^k \textbf{ THEN}$$

$$y_1 \text{ is } B_1^k \textbf{ AND } y_2 \text{ is } B_2^k \textbf{ AND } \ldots \textbf{ AND } y_m \text{ is } B_m^k \qquad (2.117)$$

for $k = 1, \ldots, N$, with the linguistic variables $x_1, \ldots, x_n$, and $y_1, \ldots, y_m$, associated with the fuzzy sets $A_1^k, \ldots, A_n^k$, and $B_1^k, \ldots, B_m^k$, in the universes of discourse $X_1, \ldots, X_n \subset \mathbf{R}$, and $Y_1, \ldots, Y_m \subset \mathbf{R}$, respectively.

Formula (2.117) is an extension of the rule form (2.94) for the MIMO system. We can assume that the fuzzy sets are characterized by the membership functions $\mu_{A_1^k}(x_1), \ldots, \mu_{A_n^k}(x_n)$ and $\mu_{B_1^k}(y_1), \ldots, \mu_{B_m^k}(y_m)$, respectively, for $k = 1, \ldots, N$; moreover $\mathbf{x} = [x_1, \ldots, x_n]^T \epsilon \mathbf{X} \subset \mathbf{R}^n$, and $\mathbf{y} = [y_1, \ldots, y_m]^T \epsilon \mathbf{Y} \subset \mathbf{R}^m$, where $\mathbf{X} = X_1 \times \cdots \times X_n$, and $\mathbf{Y} = Y_1 \times \cdots \times Y_m$.

The rule base (2.117) can be presented in the form of Equation (2.108), where $A^k = A_1^k \times \cdots \times A_n^k$ and $B^k = B_1^k \times \cdots \times B_m^k$ are fuzzy sets characterized by the membership functions $\mu_{A^k}(\mathbf{x})$ and $\mu_{B^k}(\mathbf{y})$, respectively. However, it is sufficient to consider the MISO system, with rule base (2.94). The results obtained for this kind of fuzzy system can easily be extended to the MIMO system. Therefore, the fuzzy logic system with rule base (2.94) and its shorter version (2.108), for a single output, will be under consideration.

The fuzzy controller introduced by Assilian [13] and Mamdani [309] used the so-called *max-min* method of fuzzy inference. The minimum operation refers to the T-norm which represents the fuzzy relation corresponding to the IF-THEN rule. The maximum operation refers to the S-norm applied as the aggregation operator. The minimum operation has also been employed in order to realize the Cartesian product of the fuzzy sets in the antecedent part of the rule, i.e. to perform the conjunction in the premise of the rule.

The *max-min* inference is conducted as follows, according to the FITA method. The overall fuzzy set B' is obtained by formulas (2.109) and (2.110), where the S-norm is chosen as the *max* operator, i.e. as the aggregation of the fuzzy sets $\overline{B}^k$, for $k = 1, \ldots, N$, by the *max* operation

$$\mu_{B'}(y) = \max_{1 \leqslant k \leqslant N} \left\{ \mu_{\overline{B}^k}(y) \right\} \qquad (2.118)$$

The fuzzy set $\overline{B}^k$, inferred by the fuzzy relation $A^k \rightarrow B^k$, which corresponds to the IF-THEN rule $R^{(k)}$, is a composition of the input fuzzy set A' and the relation, i.e. $A' \circ (A^k \rightarrow B^k)$. According to Definition 29, the membership function of the fuzzy set $\overline{B}^k$ is given by Equation (2.96). If the *min* operator is chosen as the T-norm in this equation, it will take the following form

$$\mu_{\overline{B}^k}(y) = \sup_{\mathbf{x} \in \mathbf{X}} \left[\mu_{A'}(\mathbf{x}) \wedge \mu_{A^k \to B^k}(\mathbf{x}, y) \right] \qquad (2.119)$$

The *min* operator also realizes the fuzzy relation $A^k \to B^k$, so the membership function of the relation is given by

$$\mu_{A^k \to B^k}(\mathbf{x}, y) = \min \{ \mu_{A^k}(\mathbf{x}), \mu_{B^k}(y) \} = \mu_{A^k}(\mathbf{x}) \wedge \mu_{B^k}(y) \qquad (2.120)$$

Fuzzy sets A^k, as well as A' are defined in the universe of discourse $\mathbf{X} = X_1 \times \cdots \times X_n \subset \mathbf{R}^n$, as the Cartesian products $A_1^k \times \cdots \times A_n^k$ and $A_1' \times \cdots \times A_n'$, respectively, so from formulas (2.119) and (2.120) we have

$$\mu_{\overline{B}^k}(y) = \sup_{x_i} \left[\min \{ \mu_{A_1'}(x_1), \ldots, \mu_{A_n'}(x_n), \right. \\ \left. \mu_{A_1^k}(x_1), \ldots, \mu_{A_n^k}(x_n), \mu_{B^k}(y) \} \right] \qquad (2.121)$$

If the input fuzzy set A' is the singleton (the singleton fuzzifier), defined by Equation (2.97), then formula (2.119) will be simplified to

$$\mu_{\overline{B}^k}(y) = \mu_{A^k \to B^k}(\overline{\mathbf{x}}, y) \qquad (2.122)$$

and Equation (2.121) will be expressed as follows

$$\mu_{\overline{B}^k}(y) = \min \left\{ \mu_{A_1^k}(\overline{x}_1), \ldots, \mu_{A_n^k}(\overline{x}_n), \mu_{B^k}(y) \right\} \qquad (2.123)$$

where $\overline{\mathbf{x}} = [\overline{x}_1, \ldots, \overline{x}_n]^T$ is a crisp point in $\mathbf{X} = X_1 \times \cdots \times X_n \subset \mathbf{R}^n$.

Thus, from formulas (2.118) and (2.123), we obtain the *max-min* inference method in the form

$$\mu_{B'}(y) = \max_{1 \leqslant k \leqslant N} \left\{ \min \left\{ \mu_{A_1^k}(\overline{x}_1), \ldots, \mu_{A_n^k}(\overline{x}_n), \mu_{B^k}(y) \right\} \right\} \qquad (2.124)$$

Another method of inference, commonly applied in fuzzy control systems, is the *max-product* inference method, also called the *max-dot* method. Instead of the *min* operator, the *product* operator is used in this method in order to represent the fuzzy relation $A^k \to B^k$. Although the fuzzy relation realized by the product operator is not an implication in a logical sense, it is known in the literature as Larsen's implication [288]. Similarly, the fuzzy relation as the *min* operator, employed in the previous method, is known as Mamdani's implication.

In the *max-product* inference method either the *min* or the *product* operator is applied as the T-norm in Equation (2.96), as well as the Cartesian product to represent the conjunction in the rule premises (antecedents). However, it is usually assumed that the same operators are used for the sup-star composition, the Cartesian product, and the fuzzy relation. In this case, the *min* operator in formulas (2.119), (2.120), (2.121) must be replaced by the *product* operator. If the input fuzzy set A' is the single-ton, the *max-product* inference method will be expressed, analogously to Equation (2.124), as follows

$$\mu_{B'}(y) = \max_{1 \leqslant k \leqslant N} \left\{ \mu_{A_1^k}(\overline{x}_1) \cdots \mu_{A_n^k}(\overline{x}_n) \ \mu_{B^k}(y) \right\} \tag{2.125}$$

It is easy to determine similar formulas with reference to other combinations applied in both methods of inference.

Figures 2.21 and 2.22 illustrate the *max-min* and the *max-product* inference methods, assuming that only *max* and *min* operators are employed in the former method, and only *max* and *product* operators are used in the latter one. It should be noted that the membership functions of the fuzzy sets $\overline{B}^k$, inferred by the particular rules (fuzzy relations $A^k \rightarrow B^k$), for $k = 1, \ldots, N$, in the *max-min* inference method, are "clipped" versions of the membership functions of the conclusion fuzzy sets B^k. The membership functions of these fuzzy sets, inferred by the *max-product* method, are "scaled" forms of the membership functions of the conclusion fuzzy sets. This effect is shown in Figs. 2.21 and 2.22, respectively.

During the inference process, first of all the matching of input data and the rule premises is carried out. This step is illustrated, for crisp input data (singleton fuzzifier), in Fig. 2.20. It is assumed that there are two inputs which correspond to two linguistic variables in the antecedent parts of the rules; thus $n = 2$.

Two antecedent fuzzy sets A_1^k and A_2^k with Gaussian membership functions are shown in Fig. 2.20 (a). Crisp values $\overline{x}_1$ and $\overline{x}_2$ of the input vector $\overline{x}$ are marked and values of the membership functions in this points, $\mu_{A_1^k}(\overline{x}_1)$ and $\mu_{A_2^k}(\overline{x}_2)$, are indicated.

The conjunction in the rule antecedents, in the *max-min* and *max-product* inference methods, is represented by the Cartesian product of the fuzzy sets in the rule premises. In Fig. 2.20 (b) and (c) the Cartesian product $A_1^k \times A_2^k$ of the fuzzy sets A_1^k and A_2^k, realized by the *min* and *product* operators, respectively, are portrayed. The crisp point $\overline{x}$ and the corresponding values of the membership function of the Cartesian product in this point, $\mu_{A_1^k \times A_2^k}(\overline{x})$, denoted τ_k, where $\overline{x} = [\overline{x}_1, \overline{x}_2]^T$, are marked in the figures.

The value, τ_k, of the Cartesian product presented in Fig. 2.20 (b) is equal to $\mu_{A_1^k}(\overline{x}_1) \wedge \mu_{A_2^k}(\overline{x}_2)$, while the value $\tau_k = \mu_{A_1^k \times A_2^k}(\overline{x})$, for the Cartesian product depicted in Fig. 2.20 (c), is equal to $\mu_{A_1^k}(\overline{x}_1) \ \mu_{A_2^k}(\overline{x}_2)$. The matching of the crisp input $\overline{x}$ with the antecedents of each rule $R^{(k)}$, for $k = 1, \ldots, N$, is performed in this way. Different matching results are obtained as values of the membership function $\mu_{A_1^k \times A_2^k}(\overline{x})$ for each rule.

In the same way, the matching is conducted for more than two linguistic variables in the rule premises, but the Cartesian product of the fuzzy sets can not be graphically illustrated for $n > 2$. However, Fig. 2.20 (a) can be easily extended for the case of $n > 2$, and the Cartesian product of the fuzzy sets A_i^k, for $i = 1, \ldots, n$, can be easily computed.

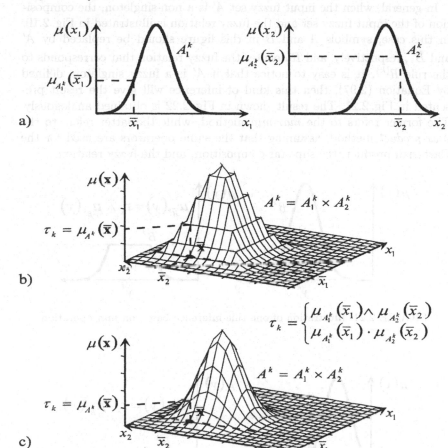

a)

b)

c)

FIGURE 2.20. Illustration of the first step of inference: matching of the crisp input data and the antecedent part of the rule

The value of the membership function of the Cartesian product in the point $\overline{\mathbf{x}}$, determined as shown in Fig. 2.20, and denoted τ_k, is used in order to perform the inference, according to the *max-min* or *max-product* method. Figure 2.21 portrays the inference conducted on the basis of Equation (2.123) for the *max-min* method. Figure 2.22 shows the inference for the *max-product* method, based on a similar formula, where the *min* operator is replaced by the *product* operator.

The inference is illustrated in Figs. 2.21 and 2.22 for one particular rule $R^{(k)}$, in the form (2.94). This kind of inference is part of the FITA method. The inference, for individual rules, is performed according to the compo-

sitional rule of inference, applying the composition of the input fuzzy set
(the singleton) and the fuzzy relation which represents the rule.

In general, when the input fuzzy set A' is a non-singleton, the composition of the input fuzzy set and the fuzzy relation is illustrated in Fig. 2.10.
In this case, symbols A and B in this figure should be replaced by A'
and $\overline{B}^k$, respectively, and R denotes the fuzzy relation that corresponds to
the rule $R^{(k)}$. It is easy to notice that if A' is a fuzzy singleton, defined
by Equation (2.97), then this kind of inference will give the result presented in Fig. 2.21. The result shown in Fig. 2.22 is obtained analogously.
The former refers to the *max-min* method, while the latter refers to the
max-product method, assuming that the same operators are used for the
Cartesian product, the sup-star composition, and the fuzzy relation.

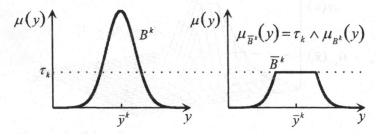

FIGURE 2.21. Illustration of one rule inference based on *min* operation

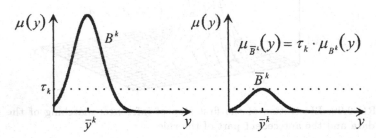

FIGURE 2.22. Illustration of one rule inference based on *product* operation

Figure 2.23 illustrates the FITA *max-min* inference method for each
rule in the rule base; assuming that $N = 3$. The inference for the first
rule in this figure is exactly the same as that presented in Fig. 2.21; the
others are similar. For three rules, in this example, three different fuzzy
sets $\overline{B}^k$ are inferred. Their membership functions are "clipped" versions of
the membership functions of fuzzy sets B^k, respectively. The overall output
fuzzy set B' is obtained by aggregation of the fuzzy sets $\overline{B}^k$, using the *max*
operator, according to Equation (2.118).

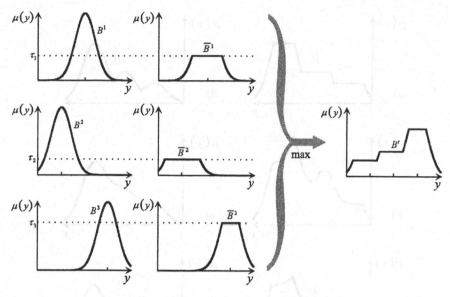

FIGURE 2.23. Illustration of *max-min* inference

An illustration analogous to that depicted in Fig. 2.23 can be presented for the FITA *max-product* inference method. However, in this case the inferred fuzzy sets $\overline{B}^k$ have membership functions which are "scaled" forms of the membership functions of the consequent fuzzy sets B^k. This is shown in Fig. 2.22. Thus, the overall output fuzzy set B', obtained by aggregation of the fuzzy sets $\overline{B}^k$, using the *max* operator, according to Equation (2.118), differs from the fuzzy set B' depicted in Fig. 2.23.

Usually the *max* operator is employed for the aggregation, but it is possible to apply other S-norms as the aggregation operators (see Table 2.1, Section 2.1.2). Figure 2.24 shows the output fuzzy set B', inferred by the method illustrated in Fig. 2.23, when three basic S-norms, listed in Table 2.1, are used. Figure 2.24 (a) repeats the same results which are obtained in Fig. 2.23. Figures 2.24 (b) and (c) present the analogical results for the algebraic and bounded S-norm, respectively. Figures 2.24 (d), (e), and (f) portray the output fuzzy set B', obtained when the fuzzy sets $\overline{B}^k$ are inferred using the FITA *max-product* inference method instead of the *max-min* method, and the aggregation by *max*, as well as the algebraic and bounded S-norm, respectively.

As can be seen, in Figs. 2.23 and 2.24, in the Mamdani approach, the overall output fuzzy set B' is constructed as a superposition of the output fuzzy sets $\overline{B}^k$, inferred by the individual rules $R^{(k)}$, for $k = 1, \dots, N$. Therefore, the Mamdani approach is also called the *constructive* approach [547], [127].

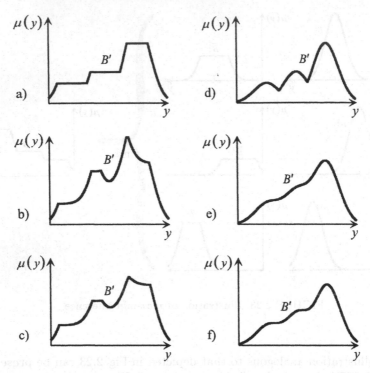

FIGURE 2.24. Output fuzzy sets obtained by inference based on *min* and *product* operations, respectively, and aggregation by different *S*-norms: a), d) max, b), e) algebraic, c), f) bounded.

It was mentioned in Section 2.3.2 that using the Mamdani approach both the FITA and FATI types of inference give the same result (the same output fuzzy set B'). It is worth adding that the equivalence of both methods was very important from a computational point of view. The FATI method requires more time and computer memory to perform the operation of composition and store the global rule than the FITA method which is an individual rule based inference [111].

The defuzzification methods applied in order to obtain crisp output from the inferred fuzzy sets are described in Section 2.3.1. As can be seen (Fig. 2.23), the *center average* defuzzification, defined by Equation (2.105), gives the same result as the special case of the *center-of-area* defuzzification, given by formula (2.107).

The following lemmas have been formulated in [513].

Lemma 1 *Fuzzy logic systems with the center average defuzzifier (2.105), min operation as fuzzy relation (2.120), min operation as Cartesian products*

$A_1^k \times \cdots \times A_n^k$, and singleton fuzzifier (2.97) are expressed as follows

$$\bar{y} = \frac{\sum_{k=1}^{N} \bar{y}^k \; min\left\{\mu_{A_1^k}(\bar{x}_1), \ldots, \mu_{A_n^k}(\bar{x}_n)\right\}}{\sum_{k=1}^{N} min\left\{\mu_{A_1^k}(\bar{x}_1), \ldots, \mu_{A_n^k}(\bar{x}_n)\right\}} \qquad (2.126)$$

where $\bar{y}^k$ satisfies condition (2.106) and we assume that fuzzy sets B^k, for $k = 1, \ldots, N$, are normal fuzzy sets (see Definition 6).

Lemma 2 *Fuzzy logic systems with the center average defuzzifier (2.105), product operation as fuzzy relation $A^k \to B^k$, product operation as Cartesian products $A_1^k \times \cdots \times A_n^k$, and singleton fuzzifier (2.97) are expressed as follows*

$$\bar{y} = \frac{\sum_{k=1}^{N} \bar{y}^k \; \prod_{i=1}^{n} \mu_{A_i^k}(\bar{x}_i)}{\sum_{k=1}^{N} \prod_{i=1}^{n} \mu_{A_i^k}(\bar{x}_i)} \qquad (2.127)$$

where $\bar{y}^k$ satisfies condition (2.106) and we assume that fuzzy sets B^k, for $k = 1, \ldots, N$, are normal fuzzy sets (see Definition 6).

Both lemmas can easily be proved, using Equations (2.105), (2.122). Then, formula (2.120) and the *min* operation as Cartesian products $A_1^k \times \cdots \times A_n^k$ must be applied in the case of Lemma 1. Analogously, the *product* operation as fuzzy relation $A^k \to B^k$, and *product* operation as Cartesian products $A_1^k \times \cdots \times A_n^k$ must be employed in the case of Lemma 2. The first lemma refers to the *max-min* inference method, while the second one corresponds to the *max-product* inference.

The inference processes are portrayed in Figs. 2.20 - 2.24, using Gaussian membership functions. Similar illustrations, with triangular membership functions, are often presented in the literature on fuzzy systems. Fuzzy sets with triangular membership functions were employed in the first fuzzy systems, introduced by Assilian [13] and Mamdani [309], and used in many practical applications. Examples of both Gaussian and triangular membership functions are depicted in Fig. 2.1.

Presented below is another lemma, formulated in [513], with Gaussian membership functions.

Lemma 3 *A fuzzy logic system with the center average defuzzifier (2.105), the product operation as fuzzy relation $A^k \to B^k$, product operation as Cartesian products $A_1^k \times \cdots \times A_n^k$, singleton fuzzifier (2.97), and Gaussian membership functions (2.58) with center and width parameters, respectively, σ_i^k and $\bar{x}_i^k$, and additional scaling parameter c_i^k is expressed as follows*

$$\bar{y} = \frac{\sum_{k=1}^{N} \bar{y}^k \; \prod_{i=1}^{n} c_i^k \exp\left[-\left(\frac{\bar{x}_i - \bar{x}_i^k}{\sigma_i^k}\right)^2\right]}{\sum_{k=1}^{N} \prod_{i=1}^{n} c_i^k \exp\left[-\left(\frac{\bar{x}_i - \bar{x}_i^k}{\sigma_i^k}\right)^2\right]} \qquad (2.128)$$

where $\bar{y}^k$ satisfy condition (2.106) and we assume that fuzzy sets B^k, for $k = 1, \ldots, N$, are normal fuzzy sets (see Definition 6).

In order to prove this lemma, just substitute the proper equation defining the Gaussian membership function into formula (2.127).

Assuming that $c_i^k = 1$, the following mathematical description of the system given by Equation (2.128) is obtained

$$\bar{y} = \frac{\sum_{k=1}^{N} \bar{y}^k \, \tau_k}{\sum_{k=1}^{N} \tau_k} \tag{2.129}$$

where

$$\tau_k = \prod_{i=1}^{n} \mu_{A_i^k} (\bar{x}_i) \tag{2.130}$$

and

$$\mu_{A_i^k} (\bar{x}_i) = \exp \left[- \left(\frac{\bar{x}_i - \bar{x}_i^k}{\sigma_i^k} \right)^2 \right] \tag{2.131}$$

Equation (2.130) represents the *antecedent matching degree* (see Figs. 2.20 - 2.23), also called the *degree of activation of rule* $R^{(k)}$. Equation (2.131) expresses the value of the Gaussian membership functions with *center* and *width* parameters, respectively, σ_i^k and $\bar{x}_i^k$, for the crisp input $\bar{x}_i$, where $i = 1, \ldots, n$, and $k = 1, \ldots, N$.

The fuzzy logic systems described by Equations (2.126) and (2.127) will be called *Mamdani systems* and *Larsen systems*, respectively. The former refer to Lemma 1 and use the *min* operation, applied in the fuzzy systems proposed by Mamdani [309], [310]. The latter refer to Lemma 2, and use the *product* operation, introduced to this kind of system, as a representation of the IF-THEN rules (*max-product* inference method), by Larsen [288]. In both systems the fuzzy sets in the antecedent and consequent parts of the rules can be of different types, including Gaussian and triangular. However, the Gaussian functions are very convenient, since they are expressed in the form of Equation (2.131).

2.3.4 Fuzzy Systems Based on the Logical Approach

It was mentioned in Section 2.3.2 that fuzzy systems based on the logical approach use the implications in a logical sense to represent the fuzzy IF-THEN rules (2.108). The genuine implications are presented in Section 2.2.2; see Table 2.2. The fuzzy systems described in Section 2.3.3, with the Mamdani approach to fuzzy inference, employed the *min* or *product* operations. In the former case, the membership function of the fuzzy relation $A^k \to B^k$, which corresponds to the fuzzy IF-THEN rule $R^{(k)}$, for

$k = 1, \ldots, N$, is given by Equation (2.120). In the latter case, it is expressed as a product of the membership functions $\mu_{A^k}(\mathbf{x})$ and $\mu_{B^k}(y)$, for the MISO system, where $\mathbf{x} = [x_1, \ldots, x_n]^T \in \mathbf{X} \subset \mathbf{R}^n$, and $y \in Y \subset \mathbf{R}$. When the inference of the fuzzy systems is based on the logical approach, the membership function of the fuzzy relation $A^k \to B^k$ is given according to the definition of the implication. For instance, if the Kleene-Dienes implication is employed, this membership function will be depicted as follows

$$\mu_{A^k \to B^k}(\mathbf{x}, y) = \max(1 - \mu_{A^k}(\mathbf{x}), \mu_{B^k}(y)) \qquad (2.132)$$

where $\mu_{A^k}(\mathbf{x})$ is the membership function of the fuzzy set $A^k = A_1^k \times \cdots \times A_n^k$. Using Definition 25, this membership function can be calculated based on Equation (2.56) or (2.57); hence

$$\mu_{A^k}(\mathbf{x}) = \left\{ \begin{array}{l} \min\left\{\mu_{A_1^k}(x_1), \ldots, \mu_{A_n^k}(x_n)\right\} \\ \mu_{A_1^k}(x_1) \cdots \mu_{A_n^k}(x_n) \end{array} \right. \qquad (2.133)$$

Just as in the case of the Mamdani approach, the fuzzy set $\overline{B}^k$ inferred by the fuzzy relation $A^k \to B^k$, which corresponds to the IF-THEN rule $R^{(k)}$, is a composition of the input fuzzy set A' and the relation. Thus $A' \circ (A^k \to B^k)$, and the membership function of the fuzzy set $\overline{B}^k$ is given by the *sup-star composition* (2.96). If the *min* or *product* operator is chosen as the T-norm in this equation, and the input fuzzy set A' is a fuzzy singleton, as defined by formula (2.97), then the membership function of the fuzzy set $\overline{B}^k$ will be expressed by Equation (2.122). Hence, from formula (2.132), we obtain

$$\mu_{\overline{B}^k}(y) = \max(1 - \mu_{A^k}(\overline{\mathbf{x}}), \mu_{B^k}(y)) \qquad (2.134)$$

where $\overline{\mathbf{x}} = [\overline{x}_1, \ldots, \overline{x}_n]^T$, and $\mu_{A^k}(\overline{\mathbf{x}})$ represents the *antecedent matching degree* which is calculated based on Equation (2.133); see Fig. 2.20.

In the same way as in the Mamdani approach, the value of the membership function $\mu_{A^k}(\overline{\mathbf{x}})$, denoted by τ_k, is determined as shown in Fig. 2.20 and used in order to perform the inference. Figure 2.25 portrays the inference for the individual rule $R^{(k)}$, according to Equation (2.134); $k = 1, \ldots, N$. In the figure $\widetilde{\tau}_k = 1 - \tau_k$.

Figure 2.26 illustrates the FITA inference method for each rule in the rule base; assuming that $N = 3$. The inference for the first rule in this figure is exactly the same as presented in Fig. 2.25; others are similar. For three rules, in this example, three different fuzzy sets $\overline{B}^k$ are inferred. Unlike in the case of the Mamdani approach, where the aggregation of the fuzzy sets $\overline{B}^k$ is realized by the S-norm operator, in the logical approach the aggregation is performed by the T-norm operator (see Section 2.3.2). In Fig. 2.26 the *min* operator has been chosen as the T-norm. Let us compare

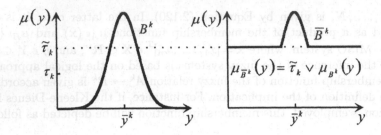

FIGURE 2.25. Illustration of one rule inference based on the Kleene-Dienes implication

the overall output fuzzy set B', obtained by the aggregation of the fuzzy sets $\overline{B}^k$ in Figs. 2.26 and 2.23, for the same consequent fuzzy sets B^k. Although the membership functions $\mu_{B'}(y)$ are different in both figures, we can see that both of them have the greater value in the *center* point of the membership function $\mu_{B^k}(y)$ for $k = 3$. It is clear in Fig. 2.23 that this rule has a higher *degree of activation* (*antecedent matching degree*). The overall output fuzzy set B', inferred using the aggregation by algebraic and bounded T-norm, possesses the same feature. Different fuzzy sets B', obtained by *min*, algebraic, and bounded T-norm, respectively, are shown in Figs. 2.27 (a), (b), and (c).

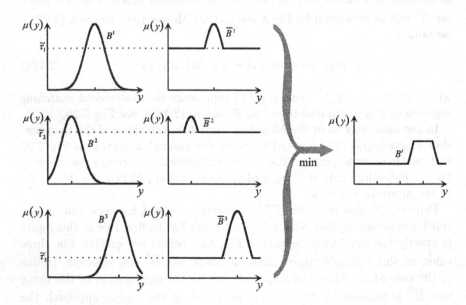

FIGURE 2.26. Illustration of inference based on the Kleene-Dienes implication

As can be seen, in Fig. 2.26, the overall output fuzzy set B', in the logical approach to fuzzy inference, is not constructed as the superposition of the output fuzzy sets $\overline{B}^k$, for $k = 1, \ldots, N$. In this case, the overall output fuzzy set B' is obtained by eliminating these solutions which are not accepted by the particular rules. Therefore, this approach is also called the *destructive* approach [547], [127].

If the Łukasiewicz implication (see Table 2.2) is used instead of the Kleene-Dienes one, the membership function of the fuzzy relation $A^k \rightarrow B^k$ will be expressed as follows

$$\mu_{A^k \rightarrow B^k}(\mathbf{x}, y) = \min\left(1, 1 - \mu_{A^k}(\mathbf{x}) + \mu_{B^k}(y)\right) \tag{2.135}$$

Thus, the fuzzy set $\overline{B}^k$, inferred by the fuzzy implication $A^k \rightarrow B^k$, assuming that the input fuzzy set A' is a fuzzy singleton, is given by

$$\mu_{\overline{B}^k}(y) = \min\left(1, 1 - \mu_{A^k}(\overline{\mathbf{x}}) + \mu_{B^k}(y)\right) \tag{2.136}$$

where $\overline{\mathbf{x}} = [\overline{x}_1, \ldots, \overline{x}_n]^T$, and $\mu_{A^k}(\overline{\mathbf{x}})$ represents the *antecedent matching degree* which is calculated based on Equation (2.133); see Fig. 2.20.

In this case, the overall output fuzzy sets B', as inferred using the aggregation by the *min*, algebraic, and bounded T-norm, respectively, for the same consequent fuzzy sets B^k, $k = 3$, as shown in Fig. 2.26, are depicted in Figs. 2.27 (d), (e), and (f).

Similarly, we can apply other implications, listed in Table 2.2, to represent the fuzzy IF-THEN rule $R^{(k)}$, for $k = 1, \ldots, N$. If the Zadeh or Reichenbach implication is employed, the fuzzy set $\overline{B}^k$, inferred by the fuzzy implication $A^k \rightarrow B^k$, assuming that the input fuzzy set A' is a fuzzy singleton, is given by the following formulas, respectively

$$\mu_{\overline{B}^k}(y) = \mu_{A^k \rightarrow B^k}(\overline{\mathbf{x}}, y) = \max\left(1 - \mu_{A^k}(\overline{\mathbf{x}}), \min\left(\mu_{A^k}(\overline{\mathbf{x}}), \mu_{B^k}(y)\right)\right) \tag{2.137}$$

for the Zadeh fuzzy implication, and

$$\mu_{\overline{B}^k}(y) = \mu_{A^k \rightarrow B^k}(\overline{\mathbf{x}}, y) = 1 - \mu_{A^k}(\overline{\mathbf{x}}) + \mu_{A^k}(\overline{\mathbf{x}})\,\mu_{B^k}(y) \tag{2.138}$$

for the Reichenbach fuzzy implication, where $\overline{\mathbf{x}} = [\overline{x}_1, \ldots, \overline{x}_n]^T$, and $\mu_{A^k}(\overline{\mathbf{x}})$ represents the *antecedent matching degree* which is calculated based on Equation (2.133); see Fig. 2.20.

The fuzzy implication in the following form

$$\mu_{A^k \rightarrow B^k}(\mathbf{x}, y) = \min\left\{1, 1 - \mu_{A^k}(\mathbf{x}) + \mu_{A^k}(\mathbf{x})\,\mu_{B^k}(y)\right\} \tag{2.139}$$

is called a *stochastic* (or *probabilistic*) implication [111], by analogy with the equality $P(B|A) = 1 - P(A)P(B)$, known in probability theory.

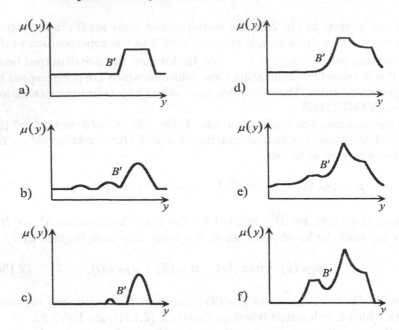

FIGURE 2.27. Output fuzzy sets obtained by inference based on the Kleene-Dienes and Łukasiewicz implications and aggregation by different T-norms: a), d) min, b), e) algebraic, c), f) bounded

Using the *stochastic* implication, and the singleton input fuzzy set, the fuzzy set $\overline{B}^k$, inferred by this implication, is expressed as follows

$$\mu_{\overline{B}^k}(y) = \min\{1, 1 - \mu_{A^k}(\overline{\mathbf{x}}) + \mu_{A^k}(\overline{\mathbf{x}}) \, \mu_{B^k}(y)\} \tag{2.140}$$

where $\overline{\mathbf{x}} = [\overline{x}_1, \ldots, \overline{x}_n]^T$, and $\mu_{A^k}(\overline{\mathbf{x}})$ represents the *antecedent matching degree* which is calculated based on Equation (2.133); see Fig. 2.20.

The overall output fuzzy sets B', obtained by the inference based on the Zadeh and *stochastic* implication, respectively, and the aggregation by the *min*, algebraic, and bounded T-norm, respectively, for the same consequent fuzzy sets B^k, $k = 3$, as shown in Fig. 2.26, are depicted in Fig. 2.28.

Similarly, we can obtain the membership functions of the overall output fuzzy set B', employing inference based on other implications, for example Goguen, Gödel, etc. The shapes of these functions may be different from these presented in Figs. 2.27 and 2.28. However, the crisp output values, calculated by use of the defuzzification methods, are more important than the shapes of the output fuzzy sets. In the case of the fuzzy systems described in this section the *center-of-area* (COA) method (see Section 2.3.1) is recommended for application to obtain the crisp value from the fuzzy set B'.

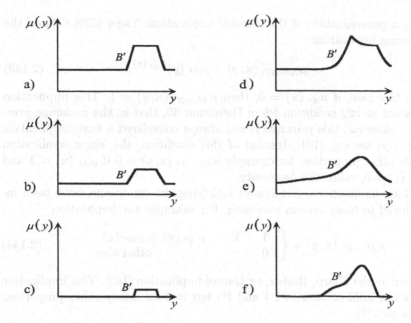

FIGURE 2.28. Output fuzzy sets obtained by inference based on the Zadeh and stochastic implications and aggregation by different T-norms: a), d) min, b), e) algebraic, c), f) bounded

Figures 2.27 and 2.28 illustrate the output fuzzy sets B', obtained by using different T-norms for the aggregation. However, the *min* operation is that most often applied. In the case of some fuzzy logic systems, this operation gives the same result, for example for systems based on the Kleene-Dienes and Zadeh implications; see Figs. 2.27 (a) and 2.28 (a). The same result is also inferred by systems based on the Fodor and Willmott fuzzy implications. These implications are defined by the following formulas, respectively

$$\mu_{A^k \to B^k}(\mathbf{x}, y) = \begin{cases} 1 & \text{if} \quad \mu_{A^k}(\mathbf{x}) \leqslant \mu_{B^k}(y) \\ \max(1 - \mu_{A^k}(\mathbf{x}), \mu_{B^k}(y)) & \text{otherwise} \end{cases} \quad (2.141)$$

and

$$\mu_{A^k \to B^k}(\mathbf{x}, y) = \min(\max(1 - \mu_{A^k}(\mathbf{x}), \mu_{B^k}(y)),$$
$$\max(\mu_{A^k}(\mathbf{x}), 1 - \mu_{B^k}(y),$$
$$\min(1 - \mu_{A^k}(\mathbf{x}), \mu_{B^k}(y)))) \quad (2.142)$$

The fuzzy implication given by Equation (2.141) was introduced by Fodor [129]; see also [100] and [101]. The fuzzy implication defined by Equation (2.142) was proposed by Willmott [533]. It is easy to check whether the implications satisfy the conditions P1-P5 in Definition 30; Section 2.2.2.

As a generalization of the classical implication, Yager [539] defined the following implication

$$\mu_{A^k \to B^k}(\mathbf{x}, y) = \mu_{B^k}(y)^{\mu_{A^k}(\mathbf{x})} \tag{2.143}$$

In this case, if $\mu_{A^k}(\mathbf{x}) = 0$, then $\mu_{A^k \to B^k}(\mathbf{x}, y) = 1$. This implication does not satisfy condition P5 in Definition 30, that is, the *exchange principle*. However, this principle is not always considered a basic implication property; see e.g. [101]. Instead of this condition, the Yager implication fulfils other properties, for example $\mu_{A^k \to B^k}(\mathbf{x}, y) = 0$ if $\mu_{A^k}(\mathbf{x}) = 1$ and $\mu_{B^k}(y) = 0$, called the *booleanity*.

Many implications, not always satisfying the conditions, have been introduced to fuzzy system reasoning. For example, the implication

$$\mu_{A^k \to B^k}(\mathbf{x}, y) = \begin{cases} 1 & \text{if} \quad \mu_{A^k}(\mathbf{x}) \leqslant \mu_{B^k}(y) \\ 0 & \text{otherwise} \end{cases} \tag{2.144}$$

known as the Sharp, Resher, or Gaines implication [143]. This implication does not fulfil conditions P4 and P5 but it does satisfy other properties; see e.g. [101].

The Goguen implication [149], for instance, fulfils the conditions P1-P5 in Definition 30 as well as the properties listed in [101]; in the same way as other genuine implications. The Goguen implication is defined as follows

$$\mu_{A^k \to B^k}(\mathbf{x}, y) = \begin{cases} \min\left(1, \frac{\mu_{B^k}(y)}{\mu_{A^k}(\mathbf{x})}\right) & \text{if} \quad \mu_{A^k}(\mathbf{x}) \neq 0 \\ 1 & \text{otherwise} \end{cases} \tag{2.145}$$

The Gödel implication is also a genuine implication (see Table 2.2); it is expressed by

$$\mu_{A^k \to B^k}(\mathbf{x}, y) = \begin{cases} 1 & \text{if} \quad \mu_{A^k}(\mathbf{x}) \leqslant \mu_{B^k}(y) \\ \mu_{B^k}(y) & \text{otherwise} \end{cases} \tag{2.146}$$

The last implication listed in Table 2.2 is defined by the following equation

$$\mu_{A^k \to B^k}(\mathbf{x}, y) = \begin{cases} 1 - \mu_{A^k}(\mathbf{x}) & \text{if} \quad \mu_{B^k}(y) = 0 \\ \mu_{B^k}(y) & \text{if} \quad \mu_{A^k}(\mathbf{x}) = 1 \\ 1 & \text{otherwise} \end{cases} \tag{2.147}$$

It is also an implication, according to Definition 30.

The fuzzy implications depicted in this section, as well as others presented in the literature, can be used to build implication-based fuzzy logic systems. For all of them the inference is conducted in the way illustrated in Fig. 2.26. Of course, different shaped membership functions can be applied, but the most often used are Gaussian or triangular ones. However, it is worth noting that for the system based on implication (2.147) triangular fuzzy sets are more suitable, because the Gaussian membership functions $\mu_{B^k}(y)$, for $k = 1, \ldots, N$, never equal zero. Figure 2.29 portrays the inference process based on implication (2.147), with triangular membership functions, and aggregation performed by the *min* operation.

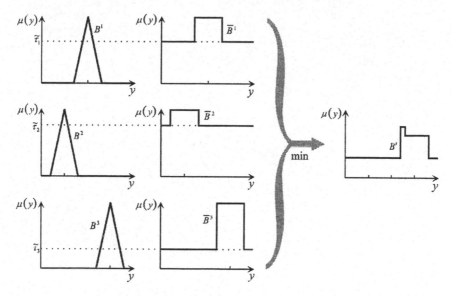

FIGURE 2.29. Illustration of inference based on the Dubois-Prade implication

Mathematical descriptions of implication based fuzzy systems, using the logical approach to fuzzy inference, can be determined, similar to those obtained for the Mamdani approach systems. However, in this case it is not possible to apply the *center average* defuzzification method, like in Lemmas 1 and 2. The mathematical formulas that describe the logical approach systems, based on the COA defuzzification method, are presented in Section 5.1, in Chapter 5.

Some theoretical aspects of employing various implication operators in fuzzy systems are considered in [113], [27]. However, it is not easy to select an appropriate implication, since the final output value of the system is not only determined by the implication operator but also by the aggregation and defuzzification methods. Therefore, many different combinations should be examined in order to choose the most suitable implication for a specific application of the fuzzy system.

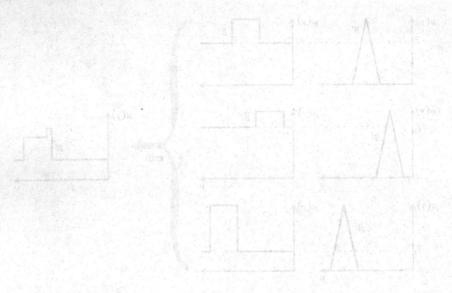

3
Neural Networks and Neuro-Fuzzy Systems

This chapter presents an overview of *neural networks* and *neuro-fuzzy systems*. The latter are a fusion of *neural networks* and *fuzzy* techniques, introduced in [293], initially developed in [66], [408], [87], and then in [167], [166], [491], [273], [169], [157], [228], [503], [270], and others. *Neuro-fuzzy systems* have been applied in many consumer products [492], [493]. They incorporate some merits of both *neural networks* and *fuzzy systems*. In the *neuro-fuzzy* combinations we distinguish *fuzzy neural networks* (see Section 3.2), obtained by introducing fuzziness directly into neural networks [169], and *fuzzy inference neural networks* (see Section 3.3), which are representations of *fuzzy systems* in the form of connectionist networks [513], similar to neural networks. Of course, different types of neuro-fuzzy systems can be found in the literature, e.g. [493], [300], [53], [162], [361], [243], [347], [582], [229], [223], [496], [244], [56], [141], [101].

3.1   Neural Networks

Artificial neural networks (called *neural networks*, for short) were inspired by the modelling of networks of natural (biological) neurons in a human brain. One motivation behind neural network research concerns a variety of problems that have proved to be very difficult to solve using conventional computers. Neural networks are connectionist architectures, composed of simple processing elements. They have interesting features, such as fault tolerance and the ability to generalize.

3.1.1   Model of an Artificial Neuron

An *artificial neuron*, also called a *processing element* (PE), or simply *neuron*, receives input values from other neurons or from an external input stimulus. These inputs are multiplied by corresponding connection *weights* and all these signals are added together. The output of the linear part of the neuron thus equals the weighted sum of the inputs. This output value is then transformed by a so-called *activation function* or *transfer function*, which is usually nonlinear. Figure 3.1 illustrates this model of an artificial neuron.

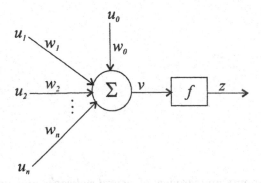

FIGURE 3.1. Model of an artificial neuron

The neuron model presented in Fig. 3.1 realizes nonlinear mapping from $\mathbf{R}^n$ to $[0,1]$, or $[-1,1]$. Formally, this mathematical model is expressed as follows

$$z = f\left(\sum_{i=1}^{n} w_i u_i - \vartheta\right) \tag{3.1}$$

where $u_1, \ldots, u_n$ are inputs of the neuron, ϑ denotes a *bias*, and $w_1, \ldots, w_n$ are connection *weights*, and z is the output of the neuron. The *bias* can be treated as a fixed input value $u_0 = -1$, that is multiplied by the *weight* $w_0 = \vartheta$. Thus, Equation (3.1) takes the following form

$$z = f\left(\sum_{i=0}^{n} w_i u_i\right) \tag{3.2}$$

or

$$z = f\left(\mathbf{u}^T \mathbf{w}\right) \tag{3.3}$$

where $\mathbf{u} = [u_0, u_1, \ldots, u_n]^T$ and $\mathbf{w} = [w_0, w_1, \ldots, w_n]^T$. This means that the neuron receives input vector $\mathbf{u}$ and produces scalar output z, according to formula (3.3). Various types of *activation (transfer) function* f can be chosen, depending on the characteristics of the applications. Some commonly used functions are

- *Step function*

$$f(v) = \begin{cases} 1 & \text{if} \quad v \geqslant 0 \\ 0 & \text{otherwise} \end{cases} \tag{3.4}$$

- *Hard limiter (threshold) function*

$$f(v) = sgn(v) = \begin{cases} 1 & \text{if} \quad v \geqslant 0 \\ -1 & \text{otherwise} \end{cases} \tag{3.5}$$

- *Ramp functions*

$$f(v) = \begin{cases} 1 & \text{if} \quad v > 1 \\ v & \text{if} \quad 0 \leqslant v \leqslant 1 \\ 0 & \text{if} \quad v < 0 \end{cases} \tag{3.6}$$

or

$$f(v) = \begin{cases} 1 & \text{if} \quad v > 1 \\ v & \text{if} \quad |v| \leqslant 1 \\ -1 & \text{if} \quad v < -1 \end{cases} \tag{3.7}$$

- *Sigmoidal function*

$$f(v) = \frac{1}{1 + e^{-\beta v}} \qquad \text{for} \quad \beta > 0 \tag{3.8}$$

- *Hyperbolic tangent function*

$$f(v) = tgh\left(\frac{\alpha v}{2}\right) = \frac{1 - e^{-\alpha v}}{1 + e^{-\alpha v}} \qquad \text{for} \quad \alpha > 0 \tag{3.9}$$

We can choose, for example, $\beta = 1$, and $\alpha = 1$ in Equations (3.8) and (3.9), respectively. It should be noted that the sigmoidal function defined by Equation (3.8) takes the form of the step function given by Equation (3.4) if $\beta \to \infty$. Similarly, the hyperbolic tangent function expressed by Equation (3.9) takes the form of the threshold function defined by Equation (3.5) if $\alpha \to \infty$.

The artificial neuron depicted in Fig. 3.1 is a model of a natural (biological) neuron, i.e. a nerve cell in the human brain. Inputs coming into the natural neuron are stimulation levels. The *weights* of the artificial neuron represent biological synaptic strengths in the natural neuron. Each input is multiplied by its corresponding synaptic *weight* and the result is fed into the body of the natural neuron. The cell body of the natural neuron is called a *soma*, and is a central part of the neuron. All natural neurons are constructed from the same basic parts: the cell body, *dendrites*, and an *axon*; see Fig. 3.2. The *dendrites* are located at the end of the cell body. There are a number of *dendrites*. They form so-called *dendritic trees*. The *axon* is the neuron's transmission line. Each nerve cell has precisely one *axon*. The joint between the end of the *axon* and another neuron or muscle is called a *synapse*. The *synapses* may be located either directly on the cell body or on the *dendrite*. The *synapses* allow a cell to influence the activity of other neurons. A neuron receives signals from the *synapses* and sends the output through the *axon*. The cell body generates nerve impulses, the *axon* transmits the generated neural activity to other neurons, or to muscle fibers, and the *dendrites* serve as receptors for signals from adjacent neurons, muscle or sensory organs, such as the eye, ear, or skin. Nerve signal transmission in the brain is of two types: chemical signals across the *synapses*, and electrical signals within the neuron. A nervous system consists of many natural neurons. There are approximately 1.5×10^{10} neurons of various types in the human brain. Each neuron receives signals through as many as 10^4 *synapses*. More information about natural neurons, as well as their mathematical models, can be found e.g. in [9].

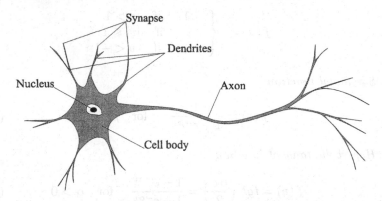

FIGURE 3.2. A natural neuron

The historically first neuron model was proposed by McCulloch and Pitts [317] in 1943. The model of operation of this neuron is very simple. The neuron responds to the activity of its synapses. If no inhibitory synapses are active, the neuron adds up its synaptic inputs and checks to see if the sum meets or exceeds its threshold. If it does, the neuron becomes active. If it does not, the neuron is inactive.

With reference to the *activation (transfer) functions* of the artificial neural networks, it is worth noticing that the *step function* defined by Equation (3.4) corresponds to the natural neuron performance: the nerve cell "fires" only if its activity (i.e. its membrane potential) exceeds a certain threshold [187]. Artificial neurons are not restricted to this condition. Thus, the *activation function* does not have to be the *step function*. Very similar to the natural model is the *threshold function* given by Equation (3.5). Since the output of the neuron should not decrease if the activity increases, the *activation function* must increase monotonely. The *sigmoidal function* and *hyperbolic tangent function* defined by Equations (3.8) and (3.9), respectively, are convenient to use in artificial neural networks, because they are differentiable functions.

3.1.2 Multi-Layer Perceptron

Natural neurons are the fundamental building blocks of nervous systems. Each neuron in the human brain has in the order of hundreds or thousands of connections to other neurons, making the total number around 10^{14} or 10^{15}. Connections play a very important role in neural networks.

The neuron model, introduced in 1943, started research on artificial neural networks. In the literature, other neuron models have also been considered.

Artificial neural networks are called *connectionist networks*. They are constructed using connections between the basic processing elements, i.e. artificial neurons. Neural networks organized in the form of *layers* are called *layered networks*. Two kinds of the networks are distinguished: *single-layer* and *multi-layer* neural networks.

Many different paradigms of artificial neural networks have been developed and applied since the late 1950s. The first artificial neural networks were known as the *Perceptron* and *Madaline*.

The *perceptron* was proposed by Rosenblatt [410] in 1958, or even earlier [409]. It was a device consisting of layers of neurons that received input signals from a sensory surface (*retina*); see e.g. [9], [125]. The perceptron was constructed from the so-called *threshold logic units*. These kind of elements are neurons in the form presented in Fig. 3.1, where the *activation function*, f, is the *threshold function* defined by Equation (3.5).

The single-layer perceptron has the ability to learn and recognize simple patterns [411]. The perceptron is trained by presenting a collection of patterns to its inputs, one at a time, and adjusting the weights until the desired output appears for each of them. The *perceptron convergence theorem* [411], [9], [584], [172], [302] says that the perceptron learning rule converges to a correct set of weights in a finite number of training steps. However, there is no statement in the proof of this theorem that indicates how many steps are required to train the network.

In 1959 Widrow [529], [530] introduced a device, called *Adaline*, which stands for *Adaptive linear neuron* or *Adaptive linear element*. It is a simple neural model, a basic building block of neural networks. The *Madaline* is a *Multi-Adaline* form of neural network. The *Adaline* has a linear output, i.e. without a threshold. Thus, the *Adaline* can be viewed as an artificial neuron model presented in Fig. 3.1, without the non-linear part, that is the function f block. The learning method of the *Adaline* is called the *Adaline learning rule* or the *Widrow-Hoff learning rule* [531]. It is also referred to as the *least mean square* (LMS) rule, since it converges in the mean square to the solution that corresponds to the LMS output error if all input patterns are of the same length [532].

Both networks, the *Perceptron* as well as the *Madaline*, are learning neural networks that use a type of learning rule called the *delta rule* [413]. This learning rule is a generalization of the perceptron training algorithm, introduced by Rosenblatt [411], to continuous inputs and outputs. For the simple (discrete) perceptron the outputs can take only 1 and -1 values. The delta rule is employed for single-layer feed-forward networks with continuous activation functions.

Rosenblatt and his co-workers assumed several layers of neurons, in the perceptron, with complex sets of interconnections between them. However, the perceptron with many feedback connections was too complicated for easy analysis. Almost all mathematical analysis of the perceptron have therefore referred to the simplified perceptron with only feed-forward connections. Different types of perceptrons are described in the literature. The original one had three layers of neurons: sensory units, associator units, and a response unit which formed an approximate model of the retina.

A multi-layer perceptron is much more powerful than a single-layer one. It has been proved that multi-layer networks have capabilities beyond those of a single layer; see e.g. [517], [584]. For instance, the well-known XOR problem can not be solved by the single-layer perceptron, because the XOR function (Exclusive-OR) is not linearly separable. However, it is known that multi-layer networks are not limited to the problems of linear separability. Two-layer perceptrons can solve the XOR example. A two-layer network can be constructed by cascading two single-layer ones.

The multi-layer perceptron is a feed-forward neural network obtained as a generalization of the single-layer perceptron, by connecting the single layers. Typically, the network consists of an *input layer*, one or more *hidden layers*, and an *output layer*. The input signal propagates through the network in a forward direction. The first hidden layer is fed from the input layer. The resulting outputs of this layer are in turn applied to the next hidden layer, and so on for the rest of the network. The output signals are obtained from the output neurons which constitute the output layer.

Figure 3.3 illustrates the neural network called a multi-layer perceptron (MLP). This network has two hidden layers, but it can easily be extended to MLP neural network with more hidden layers. The elements of the hidden layers and the output layer are neurons, presented in Fig. 3.1. They are also called *nodes* of the network. The number of neurons can be different in each layer. The network depicted in Fig. 3.3 has n inputs, and m outputs. In the hidden and output layers there are N_1, N_2, and m neurons, respectively. Four layers are marked in this figure but the input layer is indicated in a slightly different way (broken line). This network can be considered a three-layer perceptron, since the input layer does not contain neurons and does not change the input signals. However, in the literature, e.g. [134], [2], [348], a three-layer network can be found that has input and output layers, and only one hidden layer. In this book, as well as in many others, such a network is treated as a two-layer neural net, so the number of layers does not include the input layer. For simplicity, the crisp input and output in Fig. 3.3 are not marked by a dash (as used in Chapter 2), since here we do not need to distinguish between real variables and linguistic variables.

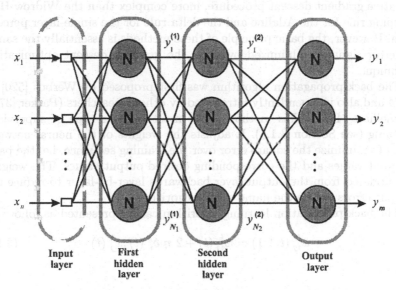

FIGURE 3.3. Architecture of a multi-layer perceptron

Single-hidden-layer neural networks are universal approximators and classifiers; see e.g. [165]. An MLP with one hidden layer can approximate any continuous function to any desired accuracy (subject to a sufficient number of neurons in the hidden layer). This statement expresses the theorem formulated in [99], as well as in others, e.g. [198], [142]. This is proved in [99] based on the Kolmogorov theorem [267]. The latter says that any real-valued continuous function defined on an n-dimensional cube can be represented as a sum of functions that have their arguments as sums of single-variable continuous functions. Thus, for any continuous function, there exists an MLP which can approximate it to any desired degree of accuracy if the continuous increasing functions are, for example, sigmoidal functions; see [243], for details. In [198], the Stone-Weierstrass theorem [94] has been used to prove that MLPs are universal approximators, and a different method was employed in [142]. The universal approximation theorem can be extended to classifier-type mappings [99]. Thus, a single-hidden-layer network with sigmoidal activation functions and a single linear output neuron is a universal classifier. This result has been confirmed empirically in several examples [201], see also [165].

3.1.3 Back-Propagation Learning Method

The best known and most often used method of learning, applied to feedforward multi-layer neural networks, is the back-propagation algorithm, also called *backward error propagation* or *backprop* (for short). It is an iterative gradient descent procedure, more complex than the Widrow-Hoff learning rule for the Adaline and the delta rule for the single-layer perceptron. However, the basic principle of these methods is essentially the same: an error signal is minimized by using the gradient descent optimization technique.

The back-propagation algorithm was first proposed by Werbos [520] in 1974 and also independently introduced by other researchers (Parker [375], Rumelhart [413]). This method is the most popular type of supervised learning (see Section 3.1.5). It adjusts the weights of the neural network so as to minimize the square error over the training sequence, i.e. the pairs of input values and the corresponding desired output values. The weights are updated from the output layer backwards layer-by-layer to reduce the output errors, hence the name of this algorithm.

The back-propagation learning algorithm can be presented as follows

$$w_{ij}^k (t + 1) = w_{ij}^k (t) + 2\,\eta\,\delta_i^k (t)\,\, x_j^k (t) \tag{3.10}$$

where

$$\delta_i^k (t) = \varepsilon_i^k (t)\,\, f'\left(s_i^k (t)\right) \tag{3.11}$$

$$\varepsilon_i^k (t) = \begin{cases} \widehat{y}_i^L (t) - y_i^L (t) & \text{for } k = L \\ \sum_{l=1}^{N_{k+1}} \delta_l^{k+1} (t)\, w_{li}^{k+1} (n) & \text{for } k = 1, \dots, L - 1 \end{cases} \tag{3.12}$$

$$y_i^k (t) = f\left(s_i^k (t)\right) \tag{3.13}$$

$$s_i^k (t) = \sum_{j=0}^{N_{k-1}} w_{ij}^k (t)\,\, x_j^k (t) \tag{3.14}$$

and w_{ij}^k denotes the weight of the i-th neuron in the k-th layer, referring to the j-th input, ε_i^k is the output of the linear part of the i-th neuron in the k-th layer, f is the activation function, $\widehat{y}_i^L$ is the desired output value (of the last layer), $t = 1, 2, \dots$, is a time instant, indicating a learning step,

η is called the *learning rate*, assuming that $\eta > 0$, input and output values of i-th neuron in the k-th layer are denoted by x_j^k and y_i^k, respectively; N_k is the number of neurons in the k-th layer, $k = 1, \ldots, L$.

The modified version of the back-propagation algorithm with the *momentum term* is expressed by the following formula [397], [88], instead of Equation (3.10)

$$w_{ij}^k (t + 1) = w_{ij}^k (t) + 2 \, \eta \, \varepsilon_i^k (t) \; f' \left(s_i^k (t) \right) \; x_j^k (t) + \alpha \left(w_{ij}^k (t) - w_{ij}^k (t - 1) \right) \tag{3.15}$$

As mentioned earlier, the back-propagation method minimizes the error criterion, as the delta rule does for the single-layer perceptron. The criterion is the squares of the differences between the actual and the desired output values summed over the output neurons and all pairs of input/output vectors, that is

$$Q(\mathbf{W}) = \sum_{i=1}^{N_L} \left(\widehat{y}_i^L - y_i^L \right)^2 \tag{3.16}$$

where $\mathbf{W}$ represents the set of all the weights in the network, y_i^L and $\widehat{y}_i^L$ are the network's actual and desired output values, respectively.

According to the delta rule, the formula for updating the weights of a single-layer perceptron can be presented as follows

$$\Delta w_{ij} = w_{ij} (t + 1) - w_{ij} (t) = - \eta \, \frac{\delta Q}{\delta w_{ij}} \tag{3.17}$$

where the index k is omitted since only one layer is considered; and Q is given by Equation (3.16), where index L can also be omitted in the case of a one-layer network.

It is very easy to determine the weight updating formulas, from Equation (3.17), for single-layer networks with linear neurons or for the single-layer perceptrons, with differentiable activation functions. The back-propagation method, for MLPs, leads to formula (3.10), which corresponds to the Equation (3.17) in the case of multi-layer networks.

The back-propagation learning method requires a *training sequence*, also called a *learning set*, which is used for training. After the learning process is complete a testing sequence is usually employed in order to assess the performance of the trained network. Both the learning and testing sequences contain input/output data pairs, that is, input patterns and corresponding desired output patterns. As mentioned earlier, back-propagation is a supervised algorithm, so the desired outputs are presented to the network.

The following steps describe the back-propagation learning method:

• Initialize (usually at random) all weights $\mathbf{W}$ to small values and set the learning rate η to a small positive value.

- Select, preferably at random, a pair from the training sequence (input and the corresponding desired output) and compute in a feed-forward direction the output values for each i-th neuron of the k-th layer, using Equations (3.14) and (3.13).

- Apply the values y_i^L, for $i = 1, \ldots, N_L$, obtained in the previous step, to compute the errors ε_i^L, which are the difference between the actual output values y_i^L and desired output values $\widehat{y}_i^L$; see Equation (3.12).

- Compute the delta quantities δ_i^L, for $i = 1, \ldots, N_L$, substituting the errors ε_i^L, obtained in the previous step, and the linear outputs s_i^L, determined by formula (3.14) in the second step, into Equation (3.11).

- Compute the values of the deltas for each of the preceding layers by back-propagating the errors using formulas (3.11) and (3.12) for all $i = 1, \ldots, N_L$ in each of the layers $k = 1, \ldots, L$.

- Update all weights w_{ij}^k according to Equation (3.10) for each layer $k = 1, \ldots, L$.

- Return to the second step and repeat the next steps for the newly selected training data pair until the total error has reached an acceptable level.

The back-propagation process, described above, is based on *incremental learning*, which means that the weights are updated after each presentation of the input data vector (input pattern). Another approach is to employ *batch learning*, where weights are modified only after all the patterns (all data vectors that constitute a finite learning sequence) have been presented to the network. The batch learning is formally expressed as the minimization of the following criterion

$$Q\left(\mathbf{W}\right) = \sum_{t=1}^{M} \sum_{i=1}^{N_L} \left(\widehat{y}_i^L\left(t\right) - y_i^L\left(t\right)\right)^2 \qquad (3.18)$$

instead of that given by Equation (3.16); see [165] for details.

The learning sequence is composed of the pairs $\{\mathbf{x}\left(t\right), \widehat{\mathbf{y}}\left(t\right)\}$, for $t = 1, \ldots, M$, where $\mathbf{x}$ and $\widehat{\mathbf{y}}$ are input and desired output vectors, respectively, so $\mathbf{x} = [x_1, \ldots, x_n]^T$ and $\widehat{\mathbf{y}} = [\widehat{y}_1, \ldots, \widehat{y}_m]^T$; see Fig. 3.3. This kind of learning corresponds to summing the right-hand sides of Equation (3.17) over all the patterns of the training set.

The presentation of every pair of the training sequence is called the *epoch*. The same training data can be presented many times to the network, during different epochs. The learning time from the initial weights can take hundreds of epochs – passes through the training set – to get good results. This depends on the problem to be solved, on the amount of learning data, and so on.

Batch learning, also called *off-line* updating [379], accumulates the errors over the whole learning sequence and performs the weight updating for a complete epoch, that is a complete pass through the training set. Errors for each pattern presentation are stored during the pass through the learning sequence. After an epoch of training, the error expressed by Equation (3.18) is computed and each weight is then modified according to the accumulated errors. To perform off-line training requires the whole learning sequence to be available prior to the start of the learning process.

Incremental learning, i.e. adjusting the weights after each pattern is presented rather than after each epoch, is a more commonly used method. However, in some cases, batch training may be more efficient. On the other hand, the requirement of having the whole learning sequence before starting the algorithm cannot always be met, for example in real-time control problems or adaptive signal equalization [532].

The back-propagation algorithm is based on the gradient descent optimization method, as shown above. This process of learning iteratively searches for a set of weights that minimize the error function over all pattern pairs. In conventional back-propagation, minimization takes place with respect to the mean square error (MSE). The MSE measure is given by $\frac{1}{M}Q(\mathbf{W})$, where $Q(\mathbf{W})$ is expressed by Equation (3.18). As well as the MSE error, other functions that measure the approximation error of the network can be defined. This kind of error measure, chosen for the back-propagation algorithm, should be a differentiable function and ought to tend toward zero as the collective differences between the desired and actual output patterns decrease over the entire training set [379].

One of the earliest applications of the back-propagation algorithm was to train the NETtalk system, implemented on a VAX computer. This system was designed by Sejnowski and Rosenberg [460], [461] to convert English text into speech. A feed-forward neural network was trained by the back-propagation method to pronounce a written text. The input to the neural network was a 203-dimensional binary vector that encoded a window of 7 consecutive characters (29 bits for each of the 7 characters, including punctuation marks). Thus, the input layer had 7 neural groups, each with 29 neurons (one for each character, i.e. letters of the alphabet, space, comma, and period). The input text (a first grade level conversation) was converted to sound for the outputs, using a commercial speech synthesis module. The hidden layer of the neural network was composed of 80 neurons. The output layer had 26 neurons that encoded phonemes and drove the speech synthesizer, which generated sounds associated with the input phonemes. The desired output was a phoneme code giving the pronunciation of the letter at the center of the input window. The network, which produced sounds as it was learning phonetic rules, sounded uncannily like a child learning to read aloud. The network learned the phonetic rules during two weeks of CPU time on the VAX computer. It was trained on 1024 words from a set of English phoneme exemplars, and was capable of intelligible speech after only 10 training cycles; but after 50 cycles it obtained an accuracy of 95 percent on the training data sequence. When the network was tested on a new text, it achieved generalization accuracy of 78 percent. The NETtalk system is often described in the literature on neural nets, e.g. [165], [355], [182].

The back-propagation method of neural network learning has been successfully applied to solve many difficult and diverse problems, such as pattern classification, function approximation, nonlinear system modeling, time-series prediction, image compression and reconstruction. In fact, the development of the back-propagation algorithm was one of the main reasons for the renewed interest in artificial neural networks, after the quiet (dark) research period caused by Misnky and Papert's publication [328] criticizing the perceptron. Some detailed information about the attack on the perceptrons can be found in [9]. Two of the reasons for the "quiet" years of the 1970s were the failure of single-layer perceptrons to be able to solve such simple problems as the XOR example, mentioned in Section 3.1.2, and the lack of a general method of training multi-layer neural networks.

The back-propagation training method also has some drawbacks. One of them is the fact that this algorithm, based on the steepest descent optimization technique, runs the risk of being trapped in a local optimum, while the method should find a globally optimal solution. Of course, it is undesirable for this algorithm to get stuck in a local minimum, especially if this is located far from the global one. In this case, it is necessary to repeat the learning process, starting from a different initial point (initial weight values). In order to eliminate this drawback, the back-propagation method is often preceded by a special technique to choose an appropriate starting point. In some applications, a hybrid approach that combines a genetic algorithm or a clustering method with the back-propagation learning is employed (see Chapter 6), to avoid the local-minimum problem.

3.1.4 RBF Networks

Radial Basis Function (RBF) neural networks can be implemented within the standard architecture of the feed-forward multi-layer network with an input layer, one hidden layer, and an output layer. The output nodes are linear neurons. The hidden layer nodes differ from the typical neuron. Instead of performing the weighted sum of the inputs (transformed by an activation function), they realize the radial basis functions. These kind of functions were applied in the early 1960s for interpolation [318], and probability density estimation [376], later [116]. In 1987 they were employed by Powell [402] for high-dimensional interpolation. The RBF functions, used within a neural network framework, were proposed independently in 1988 by Broomhead and Lowe [52], Lee and Kil [295], Niranjan and Fallside [362], and by Moody and Darken [340], [341]. The RBF networks were adopted by other researchers, and applied for specific tasks, like classification [406], modelling [84], control [451].

Different types of radial basis functions are considered in the literature, for example: the radial linear function, radial cubic function, thin plate spline function, multi-quadratic function, and shifted logarithm function [53]. The thin plate spline function and Gaussian function have the most interesting properties from the point of view of RBF neural network application. The former has been extensively used in the papers by Chen et al. [82], [83], [84]. The latter, i.e. the Gaussian function, is unique, as it is the only radial basis function which can be written as a product of univariate functions, in the following form

$$G_j\left(\mathbf{x}\right) = \exp\left[-\left(\frac{\|\mathbf{x} - \mu_j\|}{\sigma_j}\right)^2\right] = \prod_{i=1}^{n} \exp\left[-\left(\frac{x_i - \mu_{ji}}{\sigma_j}\right)^2\right] \qquad (3.19)$$

where $\|.\|$ is the Euclidean norm, $\mathbf{x} = [x_1, \dots, x_n]^T$ and $\mu_j = [\mu_{j1}, \dots, x_{jn}]^T$.

Therefore Gaussian functions are most often employed as the basis functions for hidden units of the RBF neural networks.

Figure 3.4 illustrates an RBF network with hidden units, i.e. elements of the hidden layer, denoted by $\mathbf{G}_j$, for $j = 1, \dots, r$. These elements realize the radial basis functions, usually given by Equation (3.19). The input vector $\mathbf{x} = [x_1, \dots, x_n]^T$ is a crisp-valued input. The components of the center vector $\mu_j = [\mu_{j1}, \dots, x_{jn}]^T$ of the radial basis Gaussian function are centers of the univariate Gaussian functions. All the hidden units simultaneously receive the n-dimensional real-valued input vector $\mathbf{x}$. Notice that the neural network weights are visible only in the output layer, not in the hidden layer.

The RBF network, in the contrast to the MLP, performs a local tuning of the network parameters. Each hidden unit, in order to obtain its output value, calculates the Euclidean distance between the input vector and the center of the radial basis function. Thus, the learning process and the performance of the network is based on the measure of how close the input is to the RBF centers. The MLP neural networks realize the global weight tuning, based on the back-propagation of the output error.

The output of the RBF network, given the input vector $\mathbf{x}$, is the m-dimensional, crisp (real)-valued vector $\mathbf{y} = [y_1, \dots, y_m]^T$ whose l-th component is expressed by

$$y_l = \sum_{j=1}^{r} w_{lj}\, G_j\left(\mathbf{x}\right) \qquad (3.20)$$

where $G_j\left(\mathbf{x}\right)$, for $j = 1, \dots, r$, are given by Equation (3.19).

Similarly to the Sections 3.1.2 and 3.1.3, for simplicity, the crisp input and output are not marked by a dash (used in Chapter 2), since here we do not need to distinguish between real variables and linguistic variables.

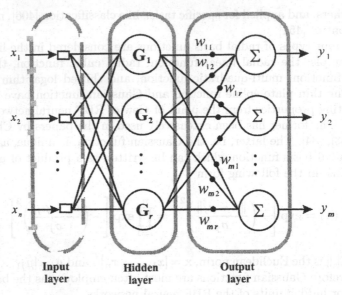

Input   **Hidden**   **Output**
layer   **layer**   **layer**

FIGURE 3.4. Architecture of RBF neural network

An RBF neural network can be trained by a supervised gradient-descent method, similar to the back-propagation algorithm [340], [398]. The Gaussian function is differentiable, so this method is suitable for tuning the parameters (centers and widths of the Gaussian functions), as well as the weights of the output layer. However, because of the local nature of the hidden units, other learning algorithms have been proposed. One of them is a hybrid approach that employs two different methods: one for tuning the parameters of the Gaussian functions and another for updating the weights of the output layer. Usually, this approach uses unsupervised learning of the center parameters and supervised learning (see Section 3.1.5) of the output-layer weights; without modifying the width parameters [340], [305]. Some details concerning these algorithms are presented, for example, in [165], [172].

It is worth mentioning the following conclusions, obtained by Wettschereck and Dietterich [524] from the comparison of the learning approaches, made for the NETtalk system (described in Section 3.1.3). Firstly: the RBF networks, with unsupervised learning of the centers and supervised learning of the output-layer weights, did not generalize nearly as well as the multi-layer perceptrons trained with the back-propagation algorithms. Secondly, generalized RBF networks, with supervised learning of the centers as well as the output-layer weights, were able to substantially exceed the generalization performance of the multi-layer perceptrons; see also [172].

The generalized RBF network differs from the network presented in Fig. 3.4 only because of a bias applied to the output neuron. This is done simply by setting one of its weights equal to the bias and treating the associated radial basis function as a constant equal to 1. The bias is illustrated in Fig. 3.1, where $u_0 = 1$, and w_0 takes the value of the bias. Of course, the linear neuron does not contain the function f.

Apart from the generalized RBF network, other modifications have also been proposed. For example, He and Lapedes [173] suggested using an RBF network that involves two hidden layers. In this network, the second hidden layer and the output layer are both linear, performing successive approximations of the functions of the first hidden layer; see also [172].

Moody and Darken [340] introduced a normalized RBF network. In this case the l-th component of the output vector $\mathbf{y}$ is expressed by

$$y_l = \sum_{j=1}^{r} w_{lj} \frac{G_j(\mathbf{x})}{\sum_{k=1}^{r} G_k(\mathbf{x})} = \frac{\sum_{j=1}^{r} w_{lj} G_j(\mathbf{x})}{\sum_{k=1}^{r} G_k(\mathbf{x})} \qquad (3.21)$$

This means that the unweighted sum of all the hidden-unit outputs equals 1, so the RBF network realizes a *partition to unity*, which is a desired mathematical property in function decomposition/approximation [523]. The normalization leads to "smoothness" regularization [165].

It should be noted that the network described by Equation (3.21) can be presented in the form shown in Fig. 3.5.

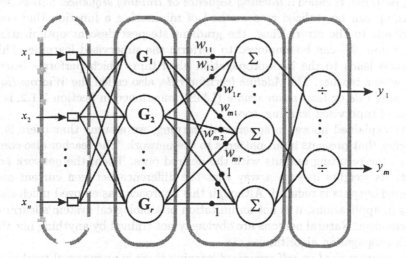

FIGURE 3.5. Architecture of a normalized RBF network

RBF neural networks, similarly to the multi-layer perceptrons, are universal approximators. The RBF approximation theorem (see e.g. [286]) can be derived immediately from the classic Stone-Weierstrass theorem [94].

The universality of RBF networks has also been proved, as described by Park and Sandberg [374]. It is not surprising therefore to find that always exists an RBF network capable of accurately mimicking a given MLP neural network, and vice versa [172].

3.1.5 Supervised and Unsupervised Learning

The ability to learn is one of the most important features of neural networks. Learning in an artificial neural network usually takes place by an adaptive process of weight modification, known as a *learning algorithm* or *learning rule*. The learning process can be seen as an optimization task, or, more precisely, as a "search" within a multidimensional parameter (weight) space for a solution, which gradually optimizes a prespecified objective (criterion) function [165]. There are number of different learning rules. The back-propagation learning method presented in Section 3.1.3 is one of the most popular learning algorithms, belonging to the group of *supervised* learning rules.

In supervised learning, also called *learning with a teacher*, it is assumed that the learning process is supervised by a teacher who provides the network with a sequence of input-output examples. In addition, error correction is conducted by the external teacher. The error expresses the difference between the actual and desired response of the network to a given input pattern. The sequence of examples, i.e. pairs of input and desired output patterns, is called a *learning sequence* or *training sequence*. Supervised learning can be realized as a method of minimizing a function that corresponds to the error. Thus, the gradient steepest descent optimization algorithm [98] can be employed to perform the supervised learning. This method leads to the back-propagation algorithm, which performs learning with a teacher. The *Adaline learning rule*, also called the *Widrow-Hoff learning rule* or *least mean square* (LMS), mentioned in Section 3.1.2, is a form of supervised learning, too.

As explained above, in supervised learning, we assume that there is a teacher that presents input patterns to the network. The teacher also compares the resulting outputs with the desired ones. Then, the network adjusts its weights in such a way that the difference between current and desired outputs is reduced. Although this approach has enjoyed much success in applications, it is not an imitation of a biological system's learning mechanism. Natural neurons are obviously not trained by anything like the back-propagation algorithm.

In *unsupervised* or *self-organized* learning there is no external teacher to supervise the learning process. Therefore, it is also called *learning without a teacher*, but this terminology is not the most appropriate [584]. In this type of learning, no specific examples are provided to the network. The desired response is not known, so explicit error information cannot be used to improve network behavior. Since no information is available concerning cor-

rectness or incorrectness of responses, the learning process must somehow
be accomplished based on observations of responses to inputs that we have
very little or no knowledge about. Using no supervision from any teacher,
neural networks with unsupervised learning adapt their weights and verify
the results based only on the input patterns. Because no desired output
is displayed during the learning process, the results are unpredictable as
regards firing patterns of specific neurons. However, the network develops
emergent properties of the learning patterns through a self-organization
process. For example, input patterns may be classified according to their
similarity, so that similar patterns activate the same neuron (see e.g. [517]).

The technique of unsupervised learning is often applied to perform clustering (see Section 6.3, in Chapter 6) as the unsupervised classification of
objects without providing information about the actual classes. This kind
of learning corresponds to the minimal *a priori* information available. The
self-organizing algorithm presented in Section 3.1.8 is an example of unsupervised clustering.

It is worth mentioning that in addition to the supervised and unsupervised learning approaches, so-called *reinforcement learning* is also considered in the literature; see e.g. [165], [177], [182], [273], [379]. In this
kind of learning, the network is given input data but is not supplied with
the desired outputs. Instead, it is occasionally provided a "performance
score" that tells it how well it has worked since the last time it received
such "evaluative" teacher response. In the extreme case, this information
(from a teacher) only says whether the output produced by the network
represents a right or wrong answer. This learning approach differs from
supervised learning, because in the latter the teacher delivers the "correct
answer". Reinforcement learning rules may be viewed as stochastic search
techniques that attempt to maximize the probability of positive external
reinforcement for a given learning sequence. The idea that the network
outputs can be reinforced to increase the probability of producing desired
responses comes from the reinforcement defined in [472]. Positive and negative reinforcement have been considered as forms of reward or punishment.
This approach imitates behavioral responses in a natural environment.

3.1.6 Competitive Learning

To perform unsupervised learning a *competitive learning rule* may be employed. For example, a neural network composed of two layers can be used.
The first layer may be called the input layer, and the second one – the competitive layer. The input layer receives the available data. The competitive
layer contains neurons that compete with each other in order to respond
to the input data. The network, in its simplest form, works in accordance
with a *winner takes all* (WTA) strategy. The neuron that wins the compe-
tition is active (fired), others are turned off. For details, see e.g. [172], [165],
[584]. Figure 3.6 illustrates this kind of learning rule. Each output neuron

is a *linear neuron*, which is represented by the model shown in Fig. 3.1, but without the non-linear activation function f. These neurons thus produce their output values by computing the weighted sum of their input values

$$y_j = \sum_{i=1}^{n} w_{ji} x_i = \mathbf{w}_j^T \mathbf{x} \qquad (3.22)$$

where $\mathbf{x} = [x_1, \ldots, x_n]^T$, and $\mathbf{w}_j = [w_{j1}, \ldots, w_{jn}]^T$, for $j = 1, \ldots, c$.

The neuron that has the maximum response due to input $\mathbf{x}$ is called the *winner* or *winning neuron*. In Fig. 3.6, the winning output neuron is denoted by j^*, so the output value of this neuron, y_{j^*}, is expressed as

$$y_{j^*} = \max_{1 \leqslant j \leqslant c} \{y_j\} \qquad (3.23)$$

where y_j is given by Equation (3.22).

Thus, the neuron j^* is the winner if

$$\mathbf{w}_{j^*}^T \mathbf{x} \geqslant \mathbf{w}_j^T \mathbf{x} \quad \text{for all } j \neq j^*$$

which can be written as

$$\|\mathbf{w}_{j^*} - \mathbf{x}\| \leqslant \|\mathbf{w}_j - \mathbf{x}\| \quad \text{for all } j \neq j^*$$

if $\|\mathbf{w}_j\| = 1$ for all $j = 1, \ldots, c$.

In this case, the winner is the neuron with the weight vector closest, in the sense of the Euclidean norm, to the input vector. More information about this kind of learning can be found in [165], [172], [584], as well as in other books on neural networks.

The competitive learning rule allows neurons to compete for the exclusive right to respond to a particular training input pattern. This method can be viewed as a sophisticated clustering technique, whose purpose is to divide a set of input patterns into a number of clusters such that patterns of the same cluster display a certain type of similarity [183]; see also e.g. [286]. In Sections 3.1.8 and 3.1.9 learning algorithms that use the WTA strategy and competitive learning are discussed.

In classical competitive learning, the weight vector of the winning neuron is the only one updated in a given unsupervised learning step. This is done by the following formula

$$\Delta \mathbf{w}_j = \eta \, (\mathbf{x} - \mathbf{w}_j) \qquad (3.24)$$

or, in the form of individual weight modification, by the expression

$$\Delta w_{ji} = \eta \, (x_i - w_{ji}) \qquad (3.25)$$

for $j = 1, \ldots, c$, where Δ denotes the difference between the new (updated) and the old (pre-modification) values of the weights (or weight vectors), η

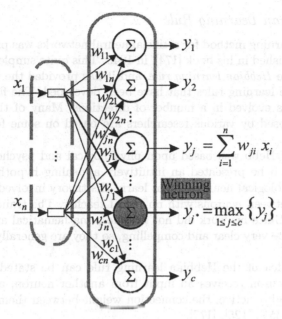

FIGURE 3.6. Illustration of the *winner takes all* strategy

is a small positive constant, which denotes the *learning rate*, and usually decreases during the learning process; see Sections 3.1.8 and 3.1.9, particularly: Equations (3.29) and (3.30).

In the WTA strategy, described above, only the winning neuron, j^*, is updated according formulas (3.24) or (3.24). The learning algorithm, presented in Section 3.1.8, modifies not only the weights of the winning neuron but also its neighbors' weight vectors.

Neural networks that employ competitive learning, in the simplest form, have a single layer of output neurons, each of which is fully connected to the input neurons. Moreover, the networks may include lateral connections among the output neurons [165], [172].

The idea of competitive learning was proposed in 1973, by von der Malsburg [510], who worked on self-organization with reference to orientation sensitive nerve cells in the striate cortex. A competitive learning network was also presented in [534]. Fukushima [138] introduced this idea of learning to the self-organizing multi-layer neural network known as the *cognitron*. Grossberg developed competitive learning to adaptive pattern classification networks [154], [155].

Competitive learning usually employs the Hebbian learning rule (see Section 3.1.7), in its extended form, and the WTA strategy.

3.1.7 Hebbian Learning Rule

The earliest learning method for artificial neural networks was proposed by Hebb and published in his book [174], in 1949. This quite simple algorithm is known as the *Hebbian learning rule*, and it has provided the inspiration for most of the learning rules that have been developed. The first version of this rule has evolved in a number of directions. Many of the learning methods proposed by various researchers are based on some form of the Hebbian rule.

The work of Hebb was based upon physiological and psychological research, in which he presented an intuitively appealing hypothesis about how a set of biological neurons might learn. His theory involved only local interactions between neurons with no global teacher. The training is thus unsupervised. Since his work did not include a mathematical analysis, his ideas seem to be very clear and compelling, so they are generally accepted; see e.g.[517].

The basic idea of the Hebbian learning rule can be stated simply as follows: If a neuron receives an input from another neuron, and if both neurons are highly active, the connection weight between them should be strengthened [355], [125], [172].

The Hebbian learning rule, in its simplest mathematical form, can be expressed as follows [487]

$$w_{jl}(t+1) = w_{jl}(t) + \eta \cdot y_j(t) \cdot x_l(t) \tag{3.26}$$

where w_{jl} is a connection weight between the l-th and j-th neurons, x_l denotes the output of the l-th neuron, entered into the input of the j-th neuron, y_j is the output of the j-th neuron, η is a positive constant that determines the *rate of learning*, and $t = 1, 2, \ldots$, is a time instant, indicating a learning step.

Two neurons considered with reference to this learning rule are illustrated in Fig. 3.7.

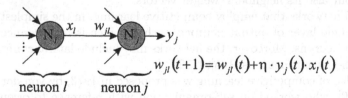

FIGURE 3.7. Two neurons peforming Hebbian learning

More information about the Hebbian learning rule is to be found in the literature on neural networks, e.g. those cited above, as well as many others.

It is worth emphasizing that in competitive learning, as described in Section 3.1.5, the output neurons compete among themselves in order to be the active (fired) one. Thus, only a single output neuron is active at any one time. In a neural network based on Hebbian learning several output neurons may be active simultaneously; see e.g. [172] for details.

The Hebbian rule is designed to train the network to function as a pattern associator. A stimulus pattern presented to the input of the network should produce an output pattern that is associated with the input pattern. Thus, the network ought to generate the output pattern that it has learned to associate with the input pattern. Alternatively, if a part of a pattern is presented to the network, it should generate a complete version of that pattern. This is basically the idea of *content-addresable memories* and *associative memories* [251].

Many modifications of the basic Hebbian learning rule have been carried out, for example, the methods known as Ojas' rule [368], as well as Yuille et al. rule [558], described in the literature on neural networks, e.g. [165], [379], [182].

3.1.8 Kohonen's Self-Organizing Neural Network

Self-organization is an unsupervised learning process whereby significant patterns or features in the input data are discovered. In the context of a neural network, this kind of learning is a process in which the weights of locally interacting neurons are adaptively modified in response to input excitations and in accordance with a learning rule until a final useful configuration develops. The local interaction of neurons means that the changes in the behavior of a neuron only directly affect the behavior of its immediate neighborhood. The configuration evolves via self-organization until it attains its final form.

The *self-organizing feature-mapping* (SOFM) algorithm, introduced by Kohonen [261] realizes the self-organization described above. The purpose of this method is to capture the topology and probability distribution of input data.

The self-organizing neural networks developed by Kohonen [263] are also called *topology-preserving maps*, since SOFM refers to topology-preserving competitive learning. The networks (self-organizing) can learn without being given the correct answer for an input pattern. They closely imitate the topology-preserving self-organizing mappings that exist in neurobiological systems. It is believed that biological topology-preserving maps are not entirely preprogrammed by genes and that some sort of unsupervised self-organizing learning phenomenon exists that tunes such maps during development. This feature is not implemented in other artificial neural networks.

Kohonen's self-organizing neural networks are suitable for data clustering and they can be used for unsupervised pattern recognition; see Section 6.3, in Chapter 6. The networks impose a neighborhood constraint on the output neurons, such that a particular topological property in the input data is reflected in the weights of output neurons.

The SOFM algorithm is supposed to convert patterns of arbitrary dimensionality into the responses of arbitrary one- or two-dimensional arrays of neurons. The basic SOFM network consists of two layers. The architecture of Kohonen's SOFM is illustrated in Fig. 3.8. The first layer is composed of input neurons and the second contains output neurons. The output layer can be one-dimensional, as Fig. 3.8 (a) presents, or two-dimensional, as Fig. 3.8 (b) portrays. The output neurons are extensively interconnected with many local connections.

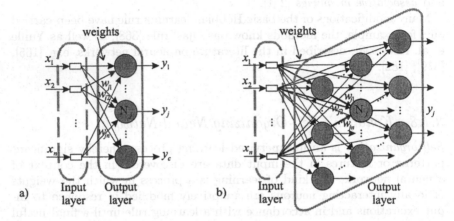

FIGURE 3.8. Kohonen's SOFM with a) one-dimensional, b) two-dimensional output layer

In Kohonen's SOFM algorithm, the output responses are ordered according to some characteristic feature of the input vectors. There are adjustable weights associated with connections between input and output neurons, as shown in Fig. 3.8. Every neuron thus has its own weights which are adaptive, in order to implement self-organization. Input vectors are presented sequentially in time without providing the desired output. The adaptive process of learning causes *clustering* (see Section 6.3) that samples the input space such that the point density function of the "cluster centers" tends to approximate the probability density function of the input vectors. In addition, the weights will be organized in such a way that topologically close neurons are sensitive to inputs that are physically similar. Thus, output neurons will be organized in a "natural" manner. In fact, the learning algorithm summarizes the history of the input data along with their topological relationships in the original pattern space.

The SOFM algorithm uses the unsupervised learning method to modify the weights to model the feature found in the training data. A topological map of the weight vectors is automatically created by a cyclic process of comparing input patterns to weight vectors for each neuron. The weight vector to which inputs are matched is optimized selectively to represent an average of the training data. As a result, all the training data are expressed by the weight vectors of the map which can be considered prototypes (cluster centers) of the input patterns.

The characteristics of topology-preserving mappings, with reference to this self-organizing algorithm, are observed in the context of neighborhood of the neurons. This means that the neurons located physically next to each other will respond to classes of input vectors that are likewise next to each other. The relationship among neurons can be easily visualized on two-dimensional maps, used in many applications. For details, see [263], and e.g. [304], [584], [85], [105], [165].

Kohonen's SOFM algorithm can be presented by the following steps:

- Initialize the weights w_{ji}, for $i = 1, ..., n$, and $j = 1, ..., c$, to small values, at random; n and c denote the number of neurons in the input and output layers, respectively. Set the initial radius of the neighborhood around neuron j as $N_j(0)$.

- Present the current (at time t) input data $x_1(t), ..., x_n(t)$, where $t = 1, 2, ...$, is a time instant, indicating a learning step.

- Calculate the distances, d_j, between the input vector and weight vectors

$$d_j(t) = \sum_{i=1}^{n} (x_i(t) - w_{ji}(t))^2 \qquad (3.27)$$

for $j = 1, ..., c$.

- Determine the output neuron j^* with the minimal distance, that is

$$d_{j^*}(t) = \min_{1 \leqslant j \leqslant c} \left\{ \sum_{i=1}^{n} (x_i(t) - w_{ji}(t))^2 \right\} \qquad (3.28)$$

- Update the weights for the *winning* output neuron j^* and all its neighbors in the neighborhood defined by $N_{j^*}(t)$. The new weights are modified according to the formula

$$w_{ji}(t+1) = w_{ji}(t) + \eta(t)(x_i(t) - w_{ji}(t)) \qquad (3.29)$$

where $\eta(t)$ is the learning rate; $0 < \eta(t) < 1$. Both $\eta(t)$ and $N_{j^*}(t)$ decrease as t increases. The neighborhood $N_{j^*}(t)$ can be a square, rectangular or hexagonal neighborhood; see e.g. [263], [584], [304].

- If the stopping criteria are not met, modify the neighborhood function, the learning rate, and return to the second step, otherwise stop.

This algorithm is similar to that of competitive learning networks. Not only are the winning neuron's weights updated, however, but also the weights of the neurons in the neighborhood around the winning neuron. As the algorithm states, the neighborhood size slowly decreases with each iteration. The function $N_{j*}(t)$ can be viewed as a square, rectangular or hexagonal neighborhood, and only the weights of neurons in this neighborhood are modified using formula (3.29). However, the neighborhood can be defined by the so-called *neighborhood function*. In this case, $N_{j*}(t)$ can play the role of a neighborhood function that may be defined in several ways; see e.g. [101], including the *rectangular neighborhood*. Treating $N_{j*}(t)$ as a neighborhood function, it is convenient to rewrite Equation (3.29) as follows

$$w_{ji}(t+1) = w_{ji}(t) + \eta(t) N_{j*}(t) (x_i(t) - w_{ji}(t))$$

taking the neighborhood function into account.

This form of the formula updates, in the same way, only the weights of neurons in the neighborhood defined by this function. The rectangular neighborhood function is expressed by

$$N_{j*}(t) = \begin{cases} 1 & \text{for} \quad d_{j*}(t) \leqslant \lambda(t) \\ 0 & \text{otherwise} \end{cases}$$

where $\lambda(t)$ determines the size of the winner neuron's neighborhood and decreases with iterations t. Both the neighborhood size as well as the learning rate, $\eta(t)$, decrease gradually with each iteration – in order to achieve a better convergence of the algorithm.

The distance denoted as d_j is a distance in the sense of a Euclidean norm – between the input vector composed of $x_1(t), \ldots, x_n(t)$ and the weight vector of the output neuron j, where $j = 1, \ldots, c$. Each distance, d_j, for $j = 1, \ldots, c$, can be treated as the output of neuron j. After the input data has been fed into the network, the weights are updated, according to Equation (3.29), and tend to partition the input data space, resulting in c clusters, corresponding to each output neuron. The weight vectors associated with the neurons j, for $j = 1, \ldots, c$, can be considered as "centers" of these clusters, i.e. the *prototypes* characterizing the clusters; see Sections 3.1.9 and 6.3.1. As we can see, the number of clusters, in this case, equals the number of output neurons, so it is obvious that this must be prespecified for the network.

Kohonen's learning method differs significantly from the Hebbian rule (see Section 3.1.7). The basic idea of Kohonen's network is to have an output layer of neurons which arrange their weight vectors such that they are distributed in $\mathbf{R}^n$ approximately proportional to the probability density function used to select the input vectors provided to train the network. Thus, the training data for this network is assumed to consist of a sequence of input vectors, drawn at random in accordance with a fixed probability density function [263], [177]. The graphic illustrations of the weight vector distribution during the ordering process, performed by Kohonen's network presented in the literature, e.g. [263], [304], [584], [85], [105], [165], on $\mathbf{R}^2$, usually refer to uniform distribution of input data vectors.

The graphical visualizations mentioned above portray how the SOFM algorithm adaptively transforms the input data in a topologically ordered fashion. The first figure usually refers to the initial, randomly chosen weight vectors, and shows the points concentrated around the center of the input space, i.e. the weights initialized randomly near a certain point (in the center). The next figures illustrate how the weight vectors spread out to fill almost all the space, in accordance to the uniform distribution of the input vectors. It can be observed that there are two phases to the formation of the map: an ordering phase and a convergence phase. Initial formation of the correct topological ordering of the weight vectors takes place during the first (ordering) phase, resulting in this task being roughly accomplished. Then, fine-tuning of the map is performed during the convergence phase, when the map converges asymptotically to a solution that approximates to the probability density function according to which the input vectors have been chosen. During this phase, values of the neighborhood size and the learning rate are very small – to keep the convergence slow. For good results, the convergence phase may involve many more iterations than the ordering phase (see [165] for the details). The density of the weight vectors in the weight space then follows the uniform probability distribution of the input vectors.

The architecture of Kohonen's SOFM network often consists of a two-dimensional structure, in the form of an array of linear neurons, where each neuron receives the same input vector, in $\mathbf{R}^n$; see Fig. 3.8 (b). Each neuron in the array is characterized by an n-dimensional weight vector. The weight vector of the neuron j, for $j = 1, ..., c$, may be viewed as a position vector that defines a "virtual position" for neuron j in $\mathbf{R}^n$. This interpretation allows the changes of the weight vectors (such as that portrayed in the above mentioned figures) to be illustrated as movements of the neurons associated with the weight vectors. It is important to emphasize that, in fact, no physical movements of the neurons take place during the self-organizing learning process. However, this may be confusing, since, for better visualization, the illustrations that show the changes of the weights display the lines connecting the weight vectors of the neurons that are topologically closest neighbors.

It have been explained that Kohonen's SOFM algorithm realizes unsupervised clustering of the input data; see also, e.g. [203]. Improved classification performance can be obtained by using this algorithm with a supervised learning technique, such as *learning vector quantization* (LVQ), described in Section 3.1.9. The SOFM learning method may be viewed as the first of two stages of a classification algorithm which employs the LVQ to perform the second stage. This approach is presented, for instance, in [172]. Vector quantization is one of many applications of Kohonen's SOFM algorithm. Others refer, for example, to a phonetic typewriter [264], equalization problems [266], [171], texture segmentation [369], control of robot arms [315]; see also [172]. In practical tasks, many input patterns are presented to the network, one at a time. These networks are therefore suitable for processing a large amount of data. Moreover, the input vectors are often high dimensional.

3.1.9 Learning Vector Quantization

Quantization is usually viewed as the process of transforming an analog or continuous valued variable into a discrete variable. *Vector quantization* (VQ) *networks* learn to quantize and encode input patterns from the environment. The *vector quantization theory* refers to the theoretical basis of the idea of vector quantization. The motivation behind this theory is dimensionality reduction or data compression [153], [145]. The main aim of vector quantization is to store a large set of data vectors (input vectors) by finding a smaller set of *prototypes*, so as to provide a "good" approximation of the original data (input) space.

One common application of competitive learning (Section 3.1.5) is adaptive vector quantization for data compression, e.g. image or speech data. In image processing or speech recognition, large quantities of data must be stored, processed, and possibly transmitted over communication channels. The vector quantization approach is very helpful in such situations when a large amount of data is to be reduced, for transmission or storage purposes. This technique allows the input space to be divided into a number of distinct regions, with a *template* (*prototype*) defined for each of them. The problem is to categorize a given set of data into the templates, so instead of using the data (vectors) itself, the corresponding templates, which represent encoded versions of the data vectors, may be employed. The template is treated as a "reconstruction vector", and also is called a *codevector* (or *prototype*); see Section 6.3.1. If a new input vector is presented, the region in which this vector lies is first determined, and then – the encoded version of the "reconstruction vector" corresponding to this region is obtained as a result of vector quantization. The set of all possible codevectors (prototypes) is usually called a *codebook*, and the prototypes – codebook vectors. In [263], the terms *reference vector* and *reference set*, corresponding to *prototype* and *codebook*, respectively, are used.

Learning vector quantization (LVQ), proposed by Kohonen [262] in 1986, and later improved [265], is a pattern classification method, which is a supervised learning technique. Three versions of this algorithm are described in [265]: LVQ1, LVQ2, LVQ3. Improvements have been introduced to better conform to classifiers based on the Bayesian approach; see e.g. in [116]. The differences between these LVQ methods are also presented, e.g. in [243], and a comparison with other algorithms in [42]. General information about vector quantization and learning vector quantization can be found, for example, in [172], [379], [229], [101], [285].

The architecture of an LVQ neural network is essentially the same as that of a Kohonen's SOFM, but with no topological structure assumed for the output neurons. In addition, each output neuron is associated with a class that it represents. Thus, the network looks like that portrayed in Fig. 3.8 (a), except that each of the output neurons is assigned to a given class. A very simple example is depicted in Fig. 3.9, assuming that input vector is three-dimensional, that is $n = 3$, and the input space is divided into five clusters, $c = 5$, so there are five output neurons, associated with two classes. Neurons 1, 2, 3 represent clusters that belong to class 1. The clusters of neurons 4, 5 are in class 2.

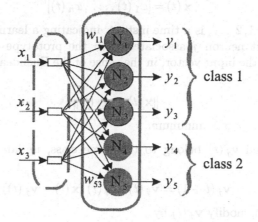

FIGURE 3.9. A simple example of LVQ network

It was stated in Section 3.1.8 that the weight vectors obtained after the learning process, by Kohonen's SOFM network, can be viewed as cluster centers (prototypes). The clusters are associated with the output neurons corresponding to these weights. It has also been mentioned that the convergence phase of this learning algorithm, i.e. the fine-tuning process, usually takes many iterations in order to obtain good results. To improve the network's classification performance, the LVQ algorithm has been proposed to realize two-stage learning. In the first stage, the unsupervised SOFM method is employed, and then, in the second stage, the supervised LVQ algorithm is applied to correct the values of the prototypes. The second stage uses information about the known classes for each item of training input data. In fact, the LVQ is a method that modifies the prototype values according to the classification results. This is done based on initial values of cluster prototypes, for example, produced by the SOFM algorithm (or generated in other ways), and a learning sequence containing input vectors and the corresponding classes. If an input data vector is misclassified, then

the prototype value of the winning output neuron is updated in the form of
"punishment" for this false classification. Otherwise, the updating formula
"rewards" the winning neuron. The LVQ algorithm can be presented in the
following steps.

- Initialize the cluster prototypes, using for instance, Kohonen's SOFM
  method, resulting in the initial values $v_1(0), \ldots, v_c(0)$.

- Label each prototype vector (cluster), assigning each of them a proper
  class.

- Present the current (at time t) input data vector, $x(t)$, selected at
  random

$$x(t) = [x_1(t), \ldots, x_n(t)]^t$$

where $t = 1, 2, \ldots$, is a time instant, indicating a learning step. Find
the output neuron j associated with the prototype vector that is
closest to the input vector, in the sense of the Euclidean norm, i.e. so
that

$$\|x(t) - v_j(t)\|$$

for $j = 1, \ldots, c$ is a minimum.

- If $x(t)$ and $v_j(t)$ belong to the same class, update $v_j(t)$ by the
  formula

$$v_j(t+1) = v_j(t) + \eta(t)(x(t) - v_j(t)) \tag{3.30}$$

Otherwise, modify $v_j(t)$ by

$$v_j(t+1) = v_j(t) - \eta(t)(x(t) - v_j(t)) \tag{3.31}$$

The learning rate $\eta(t)$ is a positive small constant and it decreases
with each iteration, t.

- If the stopping criteria (e.g. the desired number of iterations) are not
  met, change the value of the learning rate appropriately, and return to
  the third step, otherwise stop. The algorithm can also be terminated
  if no misclassifications occur.

The learning rate $\eta(t)$ is initially chosen as a small number and it is
reduced linearly to zero after a prespecified number of iterations. The updating formulas (3.30) and (3.31) move the prototype vectors towards the
input vectors that belong to the same class and away from the input vectors
from other classes.

The algorithm presented is the basic version of the LVQ families, and
applies to the LVQ1. The improved versions, LVQ2 and LVQ3 attempt to
use the training data more efficiently by updating not only the weights of
the winning neurons but also the weights of their neighbors. For details,
see e.g. [243], [407].

3.1.10   Other Types of Neural Networks

Neural networks are usually trained using either supervised or unsupervised learning methods (see Section 3.1.5). The perceptron, as well as the RBF network (portrayed in Sections 3.1.2 and 3.1.4, respectively) are examples of networks that employ supervised learning. For both of these, the idea of the back-propagation algorithm can be applied. The LVQ network presented in Section 3.1.9 also uses a supervised algorithm. Kohonen's SOFM network, however, considered in Section 3.1.8, is an example of the networks that apply unsupervised learning methods. As mentioned in Section 3.1.7, there are various forms of the Hebbian learning rule. Different neural networks apply this in its supervised or unsupervised version (see e.g. [379]).

There are many other neural networks known in the literature, apart from those networks mentioned above and presented in the previous sections. They implement supervised or unsupervised learning methods, or both, in a hybrid approach. Some of them will be described briefly in this section.

Hopfield networks, introduced and developed in [192], [193], [194], [196], can employ supervised or unsupervised learning methods [379]. These networks may be viewed as nonlinear *associative memories* (also called *content-addressable memories*) [172], [584], [125]. This means that they can store a set of pattern associations, i.e. input-output vector pairs, and recall patterns that are similar to the input patterns (see also Section 3.1.7). It is worth emphasizing that the networks not only learn the specific pattern pairs that were used for training. They are also able to recall the desired response patterns in situations where the input patterns entered into the networks are similar, but not identical, to the training input patterns. The architecture of an associative memory neural network may be feed-forward or recurrent (iterative). In feed-forward networks, information flows from the input to the output neurons, while in recurrent networks, there are connections between the neurons that form closed (feedback) loops. Thus, in this case, the output signals can also be propagated to the input neurons. The Hopfield network is a single-layer feedback (recurrent) neural network. Different versions of this network, introduced in [192], [193], [194], [196], are described e.g. in [125], as well as the *Bidirectional Associative Memory* (BAM), developed by Kosko [271], [272]. Both kinds of networks are closely related. The interested reader can find more information about the Hopfield networks and BAMs in, [105], [177], [243], [584]. The Hopfield network, presented in [195], has been applied to solve the well-known *traveling salesman problem* (TSP), which is an NP-complete, optimization task.

The so-called ART (*Adaptive Resonance Theory*) networks, i.e. the ART1, ART2, and ART3, are known as Carpenter/Grossberg's networks [155], [69], [70], [71], [156], [72]. These networks perform unsupervised clustering and prototype generation, similarly to the networks that employ a single Kohonen's layer with competitive learning (see Sections 3.1.5 and 3.1.8). A novel feature of the ART1 network is the controlled discovery of clusters, so the user can control the degree of similarity of patterns placed on the same cluster. Moreover, this network can deal with new clusters without affecting the storage or recall capabilities for clusters already learned. Thus, these networks imitate the ability of human memory to learn many new things without forgetting material learned in the past. The ART1 network has been designed for clustering binary vectors, ART2 accepts continuous-valued vectors. They are described in many books on neural networks, e.g. [125], [134], [165], [243], [286], [379], [584].

The neural network called the *cognitron*, introduced by Fukushima [138], and the new version, called the *neocognitron* [140], also employ unsupervised learning. The more recent neocognitron [139] is a hierarchical feed-forward network that can use either supervised or unsupervised learning methods. These networks are based on biological visual neural systems. They have been applied to handwritten character recognition.

The network introduced by Hecht-Nielsen [175], [176], which is called the *counterpropagation network*, applies both unsupervised and supervised learning methods, as a hybrid approach. This network looks like a two-layer perceptron (with an input layer, one hidden layer, and an output layer); see Section 3.1.2. It is trained in two stages. Firstly, a competitive learning and the WTA strategy (see Section 3.1.6) are employed, so unsupervised learning takes place. During this stage of learning, the input vectors are clustered, similarly to Kohonen's network with a one-dimensional output layer (see Section 3.1.8). The intermediate layer is thus called the *clustering layer*. During the second stage of learning, the weights associated with connections between the clustering layer and the output layer are updated to produce the desired response. This is realized by supervised learning. The counterpropagation network can be applied in pattern classification, data compression, function approximation, statistical analysis. More information about this network can be found, for example, in [125], [243], [584].

Other types of neural networks are presented in the literature, for instance, *probabilistic neural networks*, introduced by Specht [476], [477]. They use probability density functions and incorporate Bayesian decision theory; see e.g. [379].

Different neural network paradigms and their applications are to be found in [471].

3.2   Fuzzy Neural Networks

The name *fuzzy neural networks* suggests that it refers to neural networks that are *fuzzy*. This means that some kind of fuzziness has been introduced to standard neural networks, resulting in the networks with fuzzy signals, and fuzzy weights. This name applies, therefore, to networks obtained by the direct fuzzification of signals and weights, or networks composed of fuzzy neurons [427]. Multi-layer feed-forward neural networks, fuzzified in this way, have been studied in [57], [60], [61], [169], [170], [56], as well as in [215], [205], [216], [207], [206], [208]. Other types of neuro-fuzzy networks, for example networks created by employing fuzzy set operators (T-norms and S-norms) to standard neural networks, may be called *hybrid neural networks* [56]. The connectionist networks that represent fuzzy logic systems are called *fuzzy inference neural networks* rather than *fuzzy neural networks*, because they are, in fact, not fuzzy. These kind of networks will be presented in Section 3.3. However, different connectionist neuro-fuzzy systems are called *fuzzy neural networks* in the literature [159], [384], [551], [581].

Several types of *fuzzy neurons* have been introduced with the aid of logic operations, as fuzzy set connectives [382], [385], [386], [387]. The AND and OR neurons realize "pure" logic operations on the membership values. The standard implementation of the fuzzy set connectives involves triangular norms that mean that the AND and OR operators are realized by some T-norms and S-norms, respectively. As a straightforward extension of these two neurons, the OR/AND neuron has been constructed by putting several AND and OR neurons into a single two-layer structure [185]. This fuzzy neuron is treated as a single computational entity, but it can also be seen as a small fuzzy neural network proposed by the authors. The AND, OR, as well as OR/AND neurons are called logic-based neurons. A nonlinear processing element, which realizes the sigmoidal function, for example, can be added to the logic-based neuron.

It is worth mentioning that, in fact, the first ever neuron, historically introduced by McCulloch and Pitts [317], performed logical operations, i.e. *inclusive OR* and *AND* [327], [9]. In [317] the authors describe a logical calculus of neural networks.

In [56] the *hybrid neural network* combines signals and weights using the T-norm or S-norm operator and then inputs the result into a transfer function. Thus, the neurons perform similarly to the AND and OR fuzzy neurons proposed in [382], with the nonlinear element.

Another kind of fuzzy neuron, called the *OWA-neuron*, has been proposed by Yager [542]. The OWA-neuron is based on the *Ordered Weighted Averaging (OWA)* operator introduced by Yager in [543]; see also [548]. The OWA aggregation operators are closely related to linguistic quantifiers. The OWA-neurons have the same inputs as classical neurons. However, instead of using an activation function, they are described by an OWA weighting vector, which determines the output or firing level of the OWA-neuron [544], [545].

Fuzzy neurons and *fuzzy neural networks* were first introduced by Lee and Lee [292], [293], [294], in the early 1970s. Their fuzzy neurons were understood as a fuzzy generalization of the McCulloch-Pitts' neuron model. The fuzzy neural networks were developed by incorporating fuzzy sets into neural networks. However, very little research was done on the subject at that time. Later, the classical perceptron [409] was considered with the addition of membership functions, and called the *fuzzy perceptron* [248]. Then, Yamakawa's fuzzy neuron was proposed [552], [550], [551], [553]. The term *fuzzy perceptron* with reference to the multi-layer perceptron (see Section 3.1.2) is used in [249], [372], [330], [333]. Thus, after the very little activity in this field during 1980s, more papers on fuzzy neural networks have appeared since 1990; examples of these are cited above.

A *fuzzy neural network* with fuzzy signals and fuzzy weights is presented in the form of classical multi-layer neural network (see Fig. 3.3), where signals and weights are fuzzy numbers, which are usually triangular fuzzy sets. The neurons realize the same operations in both classical neural networks and fuzzy neural networks. They multiply signals by corresponding weights and add up the results. Transfer functions then change the results of this linear operation to neuron outputs. The transfer functions are most often sigmoidal functions (see Section 3.1). There are basically two ways of computing the output signals in a fuzzy neural network. One of them uses the *extension principle* (Section 2.1.1), another one α-*cuts* (Definition 12 in Section 2.1.1) and interval arithmetic [56]. Fuzzy neural networks can be trained by use of fuzzified versions of the back-propagation algorithm. In [57], [58], [60], [61], [170] direct fuzzification of the back-propagation method, called the *fuzzified delta rule*, was applied. Another algorithm for training fuzzy neural networks, based on the standard back-propagation method, was developed in [204], [217], [206]. A two-stage training algorithm was proposed in [64], [279], [405]. These methods are also described in [56].

The following definition of a *fuzzy neural network* is formulated in [343]:

Definition 32 *A fuzzy neural network is a structure* $FNN(U, \mathbf{W}, \mathbf{X}, \mathbf{Y}, L)$ *with the specifications.*

- *U is a non-empty set of fuzzy neurons and auxiliary units.*
- *The structure and parameters of the fuzzy neural network are described by the weight matrix $\mathbf{W}$ given by Cartesian product $U \times U \to D_W$, where D_W is the domain of weihgts.*
- *The vector of fuzzy inputs $\mathbf{X} \in D_X$ describes the input for the fuzzy neural network; D_X is the domain of the input vector.*
- *The vector of fuzzy outputs $\mathbf{Y} \in D_Y$ describes the output for the fuzzy neural network; D_Y is the domain of the output vector.*
- *The learning algorithm L describes the mechanism for learning and adaptation to the new information; usually by changing the weight matrix $\mathbf{W}$.*

It should be noted that, according to this definition, the term *fuzzy neural network* is frequently applied in the literature without a rationale or sufficient specifications. It is suggested in [343] to use the name *fuzzy network* for the connectionist architecture based on fuzzy logic or fuzzy arithmetic operations but not having the real neuron-like processing units. Two groups of fuzzy neural networks have been distinguished: *fuzzy arithmetic neural networks* and *fuzzy logic neural networks*. The former operate on fuzzy numbers using fuzzy arithmetic, while the latter operate on fuzzy sets of linguistic terms using fuzzy logic. It is also explained in [343] that most fuzzy neural networks introduced so far have employed fuzzy logic operations to handle fuzzy sets. Applying the term *fuzzy neural network* to various types of networks incorporating fuzziness can thus be compared to the commonly use of the term *fuzzy logic* for all techniques based on the theory of fuzzy sets, sometimes called "fuzzy logic in the wide sense".

3.3   Fuzzy Inference Neural Networks

Let us consider the fuzzy logic system described in Section 2.3.1, with the singleton fuzzifier, defined by formula (2.97), and the discrete form of the defuzzifier, given by Equation (2.107). The inference of the fuzzy system, performed by the single rule (2.94), for $k = 1, \ldots, N$, is expressed by formula (2.122). From Equations (2.107), (2.110), (2.115), and (2.122), we obtain the following description of the fuzzy system

$$\overline{y} = \frac{\sum_{k=1}^{N} \overline{y}^k \lambda_k}{\sum_{k=1}^{N} \lambda_k} \tag{3.32}$$

where

$$\lambda_k = \begin{cases} \displaystyle\mathop{\mathbf{S}}_{j=1}^{N} \mu_{A^j \to B^j}\left(\overline{\mathbf{x}}, \overline{y}^k\right) & \text{for the Mamdani approach} \\ \displaystyle\mathop{\mathbf{T}}_{j=1}^{N} \mu_{A^j \to B^j}\left(\overline{\mathbf{x}}, \overline{y}^k\right) & \text{for the logical approach} \end{cases} \tag{3.33}$$

Equation (4.2) represents the general mathematical description of the fuzzy system based on the Mamdani approach.

Formula (2.122) expresses the equality $\mu_{A^j \to B^j}(\overline{\mathbf{x}}, y) = \mu_{\overline{B}^j}(y)$. Hence, it is easy to represent the fuzzy system described by Equations (3.32) and (3.33) in the form of the multi-layer network illustrated in Fig. 3.10. The first layer contains elements which realize the membership functions of fuzzy sets $A^j = A_1^j \times \cdots \times A_n^j$, for $j = 1, \ldots, N$. These elements are denoted by $A^1, A^2, \ldots, A^n$, where n is the number of inputs. This layer is called the *antecedent layer*, since it refers to the antecedent part of the IF-THEN rules (2.94) or (2.108). The second layer consists of the elements which calculate the values of the membership functions of fuzzy sets $\overline{B}^j$, for $j = 1, \ldots, N$, inferred by the inference process (see Sections 2.3.3 and 2.3.4), in the points $\overline{\mathbf{x}}$ and $\overline{y}^k$, for $k = 1, \ldots, N$. These elements correspond to fuzzy relations that represent the fuzzy IF-THEN rules. They are denoted in Fig. 3.10 by $R^j\left(\overline{x},\overline{y}^k\right)$. This layer is called the *inference layer*. The outputs of this layer are membership values $\mu_{\overline{B}^j}\left(\overline{y}^k\right)$. The third layer is composed of the elements which realize the *S*-norm or *T*-norm operator, according to formula (3.33). This layer performs the aggregation operation (see Section 2.3.2), and is therefore called the *aggregation layer*. The last layer contains only three elements: two adders and one element which carry out the division operation. This layer, called the *defuzzification layer*, performs the defuzzification (2.107). This layer can be presented in the form of two layers: the adder layer, which is the classical neuron layer and the division layer (see Sections 4 and 5).

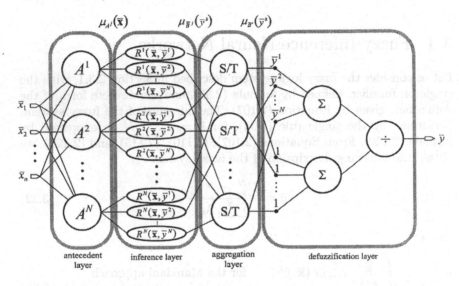

FIGURE 3.10. General form of fuzzy inference neural network

Modern neuro-fuzzy systems are very often represented in the form of multi-layer feed-forward connectionist networks. Some of them can be treated as a special case of the architecture portrayed in Fig. 3.10. Neuro-fuzzy systems are popularly viewed as fuzzy systems trained by a learning algorithm that usually comes from neural network theory [347]. The idea of the back-propagation algorithm (described in Section 3.1.3) is frequently applied in order to train neuro-fuzzy systems. However, it should be noted that the gradient methods developed in order to train the systems of this kind (Section 6.1), as a matter of fact, can be traced directly to the steepest descent optimization method [98], not to neural network learning. Therefore, what actually makes these systems neuro-fuzzy is their representation in the form of connectionist, multi-layer, architectures, similar to that of neural networks. These architectures allow analogous learning procedures to be incorporated. The importance of the architectures from the learning point of view is explained in Section 6.1.3, where special software for architecture-based learning is described. Of course, neuro-fuzzy systems are also created by including other methods of learning neural networks than the back-propagation algorithm. The reinforcement learning [25], which is explained briefly in Section 3.1.5, is one example.

Having the connectionist architectures of neuro-fuzzy systems, we can visualize the data flow through the systems. It is thus very convenient to analyze and compare different types of these systems. Besides, if a fuzzy system is represented in the form of a connectionist network, it is easier to adopt some (learning) tools developed and used for neural networks. Similarly to the reinforcement learning mentioned above, we can apply, for instance, competitive learning strategies (Section 3.1.6), in order to train neuro-fuzzy systems.

4

Neuro-Fuzzy Architectures
Based on the Mamdani Approach

The fuzzy inference neural networks (see Section 3.3) that realize the inference based on the Mamdani approach are the subject of this chapter. Different, multi-layer, architectures of the neuro-fuzzy systems are portrayed. The systems with various fuzzifiers (singleton, non-singleton), defuzzifiers, and inference operations, are considered. All these systems can be trained, when applied to solve practical problems, similarly to neural networks. Learning methods of neuro-fuzzy systems are presented in Chapter 6, including the architecture-based learning, proposed in Section 6.1.3. Interested readers may also be referred to [420], [434].

4.1 Basic Architectures

The fuzzy systems described in Section 2.3.3 and depicted in Lemmas 1 and 2 can be represented in the form of connectionist multi-layer architectures, similar to the neural networks [513]. The fuzzy logic systems given by Equations (2.126) and (2.127) can be easily portrayed as the networks illustrated in Figs. 4.1 and 4.2, respectively.

The first layer contains elements which realize the membership functions $\mu_{A_i^k}(\overline{x}_i)$, for $i = 1, \ldots, n$, and $k = 1, \ldots, N$. The Gaussian membership functions, defined by Equation (2.131), are marked in the figures. However, triangular or other-shaped functions can be used. The crisp values $\overline{x}_1, \ldots, \overline{x}_n$ constitute the input vector $\overline{\mathbf{x}} = [\overline{x}_1, \ldots, \overline{x}_n]^T$. The outputs of the first layer in both figures are membership values of the antecedent fuzzy

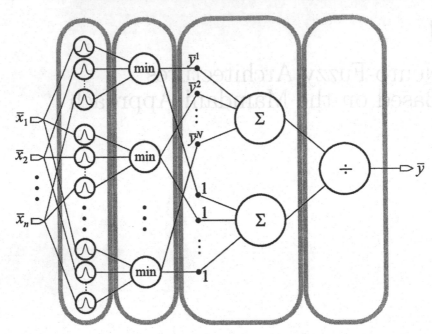

FIGURE 4.1. Basic neuro-fuzzy architecture of the *Mamdani system*

sets $A_1^k, \ldots, A_n^k$, for $k = 1, \ldots, N$, in the crisp points $\overline{x}_i$, for $i = 1, \ldots, n$, that is $\mu_{A_i^k}(\overline{x}_i)$. The number of these elements is equal to $n \cdot N$, where n is the number of inputs and N is the number of fuzzy IF-THEN rules (2.94).

The second layer, in both architectures, contains elements which realize the Cartesian product of the membership values $\mu_{A_i^k}(\overline{x}_i)$, for $i = 1, \ldots, n$. There are N elements in this layer. Each of them corresponds to one rule $R^{(k)}$, expressed by Equation (2.94), for $k = 1, \ldots, N$. These elements in the architecture presented in Fig. 4.1 perform the *min* operation, while in the architecture shown in Fig. 4.2 they realize the *product* operation. Therefore, as explained in Section 2.3.3, the fuzzy logic systems portrayed in Figs. 4.1 and 4.2 are called the *Mamdani* and *Larsen systems*, respectively.

The basic neuro-fuzzy architectures illustrated in Figs. 4.1 and 4.2 refer to Fig. 2.20. The first layer, the same in both figures, corresponds to Fig. 2.20 (a), which shows the membership functions in the antecedent part of the rules. The second layer realizes the Cartesian product of the antecedent fuzzy sets. This layer in Fig. 4.1 conducts the Cartesian product defined by the *min* operator and corresponds to Fig. 2.20 (b). The second layer in Fig. 4.2 realizes the Cartesian product defined by the *product* operator and refers to Fig. 2.20 (c).

The last two layers in each figure are defuzzification layers. They perform the defuzzification by the *center-average* method (see Section 2.3.1), based

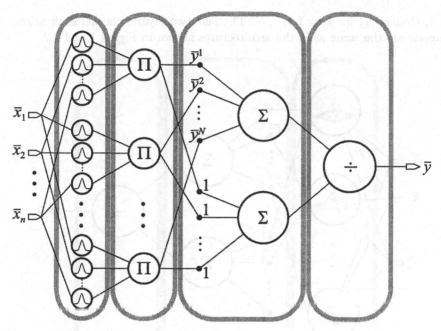

FIGURE 4.2. Basic neuro-fuzzy architecture of the *Larsen system*

on the fuzzy sets $\overline{B}^k$, $k = 1, \ldots, N$, inferred by FITA *max-min* or *max-product* inference, respectively (see Section 2.3.3, Figs. 2.21 and 2.22).

It is easy to notice in Figs. 2.21 and 2.22 that the *antecedent matching degrees* $\tau_k = \mu_{\overline{B}^k}(\overline{y}^k)$. On the other hand τ_k is given by Equation (2.130). Thus, τ_k, for $k = 1, \ldots, N$, are outputs of the second layer and also inputs of the defuzzification layers.

The last two layers realize the defuzzification defined by Equation (2.105), where $\overline{y}^k$ is the peak point (*center*) of the membership function $\mu_{\overline{B}^k}$. The values of $\overline{y}^k$, for $k = 1, \ldots, N$, are visible in the first defuzzification layer. They play the role of *weights* of *neurons* in neural networks. There are two elements which perform addition, realizing the model of the classical neuron. The *weights* to the other adder equal one. The element of the last layer conducts division operation, dividing the numerator by the denominator of the expression (2.105), which is the same as Equation (2.129). The crisp value $\overline{y}$, obtained from these equations, is the output of the last layer.

The first two layers of the architectures, illustrated in Figs. 4.1 and 4.2, correspond to the conjunction in the rule premises (antecedents). Therefore, these architectures can be viewed as examples of the three-layer architecture depicted in Fig. 4.3. In this case, the elements of the first layer realize the conjunction represented by the Cartesian product of the antecedent fuzzy sets. The outputs of the first layer in this figure are the same as the outputs of the second layer of the architectures portrayed in Figs. 4.1 and

4.2, that is τ_k, for $k = 1, \ldots, N$. The last two layers, the defuzzification layers, are the same as in the architectures shown in Figs. 4.1 and 4.2.

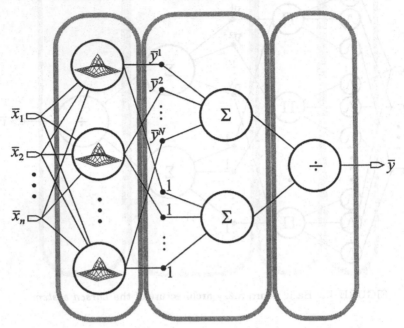

FIGURE 4.3. Basic architecture of the Mamdani approach fuzzy systems

The neuro-fuzzy architectures, depicted in Figs. 4.1, 4.2, as well as in Fig. 4.3, are *basic* architectures of the neuro-fuzzy systems, also called *fuzzy inference neural networks*. These architectures are similar to the neural networks and they incorporate fuzzy inference (see Section 3.3).

Let us assume that the membership functions realized by the elements of the first layer of the architecture illustrated in Fig. 4.2 are Gaussian membership functions, given by Equation (2.131), with the same *width* values, which means that $\sigma_i^k = \sigma^k$ for $i = 1, \ldots, n$. Thus, the elements of the first layer of the architecture shown in Fig. 4.3 perform the following functions (see Example 1 in Section 2.1.2)

$$\mu_{A^k}(\overline{\mathbf{x}}) = \exp\left[-\frac{\left\|\overline{\mathbf{x}} - \overline{\mathbf{x}}^k\right\|}{\sigma^k}\right]^2 \tag{4.1}$$

where $A^k = A_1^k \times \cdots \times A_n^k$, vector $\overline{\mathbf{x}} = [\overline{x}_1, \ldots, \overline{x}_n]^T$ is the input vector, $\overline{\mathbf{x}}^k = [\overline{x}_1^k, \ldots, \overline{x}_n^k]^T$ is a vector of the *centers* of the membership functions $\mu_{A_i^k}(\overline{x}_i)$, and $\|\cdot\|$ is the Euclidean norm, so $\left\|\overline{\mathbf{x}} - \overline{\mathbf{x}}^k\right\|^2 = (\overline{\mathbf{x}} - \overline{\mathbf{x}}^k)^T (\overline{\mathbf{x}} - \overline{\mathbf{x}}^k)$.

The neuro-fuzzy architecture depicted in Fig. 4.3, with the elements of the first layer realizing the functions given by Equation (4.1), represents a normalized version of the RBF neural network [341]; see Section 3.1.4. In this case the function (4.1) is the radial basis function.

Functional equivalence between RBF networks and fuzzy inference systems is shown in [228]. As mentioned in Section 3.1.4, RBF neural networks are universal approximators. It has also been proven that certain types of fuzzy systems are universal approximators [274], [512], [77]. The latter reference item refers to special kinds of fuzzy controllers. Moreover, fuzzy systems as universal approximators are studied, e.g. in [78], [270], [5].

4.2 General Form of the Architectures

Let us consider the fuzzy logic system described in Section 2.3.1, with the singleton fuzzifier, defined by formula (2.97), and the discrete form of the defuzzifier, given by Equation (2.107). The inference of the fuzzy system, performed by the single rule (2.94), for $k = 1, \ldots, N$, is expressed by formula (2.122). From Equations (2.107), (2.110), and (2.122), we obtain the following description of the fuzzy system

$$\overline{y} = \frac{\sum_{k=1}^{N} \overline{y}^k \underset{j=1}{\overset{N}{S}} \mu_{A^j \to B^j}\left(\overline{x}, \overline{y}^k\right)}{\sum_{k=1}^{N} \underset{j=1}{\overset{N}{S}} \mu_{A^j \to B^j}\left(\overline{x}, \overline{y}^k\right)} \tag{4.2}$$

Equation (4.2) represents the general mathematical description of the fuzzy system based on Mamdani approach. It is a special case of formula (3.32).

The fuzzy system described by Equation (4.2) corresponds to the neuro-fuzzy architecture illustrated in Fig. 3.10, where the elements of the *inference layer* realize the membership function

$$\mu_{\overline{B}^j}(y) = \begin{cases} \min\left\{\mu_{A^j}(\overline{x}), \mu_{B^j}(y)\right\} & \text{for the Mamdani rule} \\ \mu_{A^j}(\overline{x})\ \mu_{B^j}(y) & \text{for the Larsen rule} \end{cases} \tag{4.3}$$

and the elements of the *aggregation layer* perform the S-norm operator.

The Mamdani rule in Equation (4.3) means the *min* operation as the fuzzy relation (2.120), while the Larsen rule signifies the *product* operation as the fuzzy relation $A^j \to B^j$, for $j = 1, \ldots, N$. This network represents a general form of the neuro-fuzzy architecture of the fuzzy system based on Mamdani's approach.

Note that the S-norm in Equation (4.2) can be expressed as follows

$$\underset{j=1}{\overset{N}{S}} \mu_{A^j \to B^j}\left(\overline{x}, \overline{y}^k\right) = S\left(\mu_{A^k \to B^k}\left(\overline{x}, \overline{y}^k\right), \underset{\substack{j=1 \\ j \neq k}}{\overset{N}{S}} \mu_{A^j \to B^j}\left(\overline{x}, \overline{y}^k\right)\right) \tag{4.4}$$

We usually assume that the fuzzy sets B^k, for $k = 1, \ldots, N$, are *normal* fuzzy sets (see Definition 6). In this case the *centers* of the membership functions of these fuzzy sets fulfil the following condition

$$\mu_{B^k}\left(\overline{y}^k\right) = 1 \tag{4.5}$$

as a result of Equation (2.106).

From formulas (2.122), (4.3), and (4.5) Equation (4.4) becomes

$$\overset{N}{\underset{j=1}{S}}\,\mu_{A^j \to B^j}\left(\overline{x}, \overline{y}^k\right) = S\left(\mu_{A^k}\left(\overline{x}\right), \underset{\underset{j \neq k}{j=1}}{\overset{N}{S}}\,\mu_{A^j \to B^j}\left(\overline{x}, \overline{y}^k\right)\right) \tag{4.6}$$

If the following condition is satisfied

$$\mu_{B^j}\left(\overline{y}^k\right) = 0 \qquad \forall\; j \neq k \tag{4.7}$$

then from Equations (4.6), (2.122), (4.3), (4.7), and from the first *boundary condition* of the S-norm (see Definition 18) we will conclude that

$$\overset{N}{\underset{j=1}{S}}\,\mu_{A^j \to B^j}\left(\overline{x}, \overline{y}^k\right) = \mu_{A^k}\left(\overline{x}\right) \tag{4.8}$$

Note that the same conclusion, given by Equation (4.8), can be deduced if

$$\mu_{B^j}\left(\overline{y}^k\right) \approx 0 \qquad \forall\; j \neq k \tag{4.9}$$

Figure 4.4 illustrates an example of *non-overlapping consequent fuzzy sets* (NOCFS). If the membership functions of the consequent fuzzy sets B^k, for $k = 1, \ldots, N$, are adjacent (as the figure shows, for $k = 4$) or disjunctive, then assumption (4.9) is fulfilled for Gaussian membership functions and assumption (4.7) is satisfied for triangular membership functions. The centers $\overline{y}^k$ of membership functions of the fuzzy sets B^k, for $k = 1, \ldots, 4$, are marked in the figure. The singleton consequent fuzzy sets are a special case of NOCFS. They satisfy condition (4.7).

If assumption (4.7) or (4.9) is fulfilled, then the fuzzy system which refers to NOCFS is described by the following formula

$$\overline{y} = \frac{\sum_{k=1}^{N} \overline{y}^k\,\mu_{A^k}\left(\overline{x}\right)}{\sum_{k=1}^{N} \mu_{A^k}\left(\overline{x}\right)} \tag{4.10}$$

obtained from Equations (4.2) and (4.8).

If the *min* operation is chosen as the Cartesian product $A_1^k \times \cdots \times A_n^k$, that is $\mu_{A^k}\left(\mathbf{x}\right) = \min\left(\mu_{A_1^k}\left(x_1\right), \ldots, \mu_{A_n^k}\left(x_n\right)\right)$, then formula (4.10) becomes Equation (2.126) and the architecture of the system described by

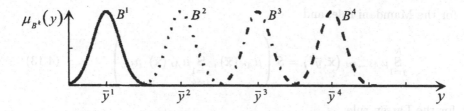

FIGURE 4.4. Example of non-overlapping consequent fuzzy sets

this formula is illustrated in Fig. 4.1. Similarly, if the Cartesian product $A_1^k \times \cdots \times A_n^k$ is realized by the *product* operation, that is $\mu_{A^k}(\mathbf{x}) = \mu_{A_1^k}(x_1) \cdots \mu_{A_n^k}(x_n)$, then formula (4.10) becomes Equation (2.127) and the architecture of the system represented by this formula is portrayed in Fig. 4.2. The architecture depicted in Fig. 4.3 corresponds directly to the system description (4.10).

Figure 4.5 presents the *overlapping consequent fuzzy sets* (OCFS); the example for Gaussian membership functions and $k = 4$. A similar illustration can be shown for triangular or other-shaped membership functions of the fuzzy sets B^k in the consequent part of the IF-THEN rules, for $k = 1, \ldots, N$. The centers $\bar{y}^k$ of membership functions of the fuzzy sets B^k, for $k = 1, \ldots, 4$, are marked in the figure. The OCFS usually fulfil neither condition (4.7) nor (4.9). They constitute a more general case of the consequent fuzzy sets, so the NOCFS systems can be treated as special cases of the OCFS systems.

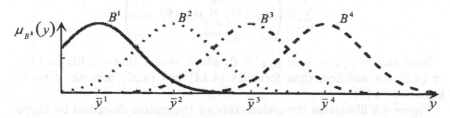

FIGURE 4.5. Example of overlapping consequent fuzzy sets

Let us denote

$$p_{j,k} = \mu_{B^j}\left(\bar{y}^k\right) \tag{4.11}$$

From Equations (4.6), (2.122), (4.3), and (4.11) we conclude that

$$\mathop{S}_{j=1}^{N} \mu_{A^j \to B^j}\left(\bar{\mathbf{x}}, \bar{y}^k\right) = S\left(\mu_{A^k}(\bar{\mathbf{x}}), \mathop{S}_{\substack{j=1 \\ j \neq k}}^{N} \min\left(\mu_{A^j}(\bar{\mathbf{x}}), p_{j,k}\right)\right) \tag{4.12}$$

for the Mamdani rule, and

$$\overset{N}{\underset{j=1}{S}} \mu_{A^j \to B^j}\left(\overline{x}, \overline{y}^k\right) = S\left(\mu_{A^k}(\overline{x}), \underset{\substack{j=1 \\ j \neq k}}{\overset{N}{S}} \mu_{A^j}(\overline{x})\, p_{j,k}\right) \qquad (4.13)$$

for the Larsen rule.

From formulas (4.2) and (4.12) we obtain the following mathematical description of the OCFS system based on the Mamdani rule

$$\overline{y} = \frac{\displaystyle\sum_{k=1}^{N} \overline{y}^k\, S\left(\mu_{A^k}(\overline{x}), \underset{\substack{j=1 \\ j \neq k}}{\overset{N}{S}} \mu_{A^j}(\overline{x}) \wedge p_{j,k}\right)}{\displaystyle\sum_{k=1}^{N} S\left(\mu_{A^k}(\overline{x}), \underset{\substack{j=1 \\ j \neq k}}{\overset{N}{S}} \mu_{A^j}(\overline{x}) \wedge p_{j,k}\right)} \qquad (4.14)$$

Analogously, from formulas (4.2) and (4.13) we have a description of the OCFS system based on the Larsen rule

$$\overline{y} = \frac{\displaystyle\sum_{k=1}^{N} \overline{y}^k\, S\left(\mu_{A^k}(\overline{x}), \underset{\substack{j=1 \\ j \neq k}}{\overset{N}{S}} \mu_{A^j}(\overline{x})\, p_{j,k}\right)}{\displaystyle\sum_{k=1}^{N} S\left(\mu_{A^k}(\overline{x}), \underset{\substack{j=1 \\ j \neq k}}{\overset{N}{S}} \mu_{A^j}(\overline{x})\, p_{j,k}\right)} \qquad (4.15)$$

Note that if $p_{j,k} = 0$ or $p_{j,k} \approx 0$, which means that conditions (4.7) or (4.9) are satisfied, then formulas (4.14) and (4.15) take the form of Equation (4.10).

Figure 4.6 illustrates the architecture of the system described by Equation (4.14) and Fig. 4.7 shows the architecture of the system represented by formula (4.15).

It was concluded in Section 2.3.3, looking at Fig. 2.23, that the CA defuzzification, defined by Equation (2.105), gives the same result as the special case of the COA defuzzification, expressed by formula (2.107). It is obvious that both defuzzification methods determine the same crisp output if the membership functions of the consequent fuzzy sets $\overline{B}^k$, for $k = 1, \dots, N$, are non-overlapping. It is worth noticing that these membership functions in Fig. 2.23 are in fact overlapping. However, the following condition is fulfilled

$$\mu_{B^k}\left(\overline{y}^k\right) \gg \mu_{B^k}\left(\overline{y}^j\right) \qquad (4.16)$$

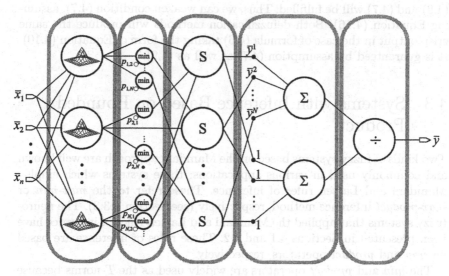

FIGURE 4.6. Architecture of OCFS system based on the Mamdani rule

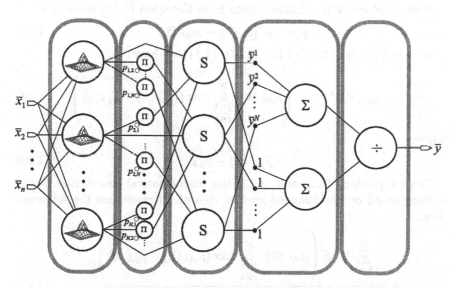

FIGURE 4.7. Architecture of OCFS system based on the Larsen rule

for $k, j = 1, \ldots, N$. If assumption (4.16) is satisfied, then also conditions (4.9) and (4.7) will be fulfilled. Thus, we can weaken condition (4.7), assuming Equation (4.16). Both defuzzification methods will produce the same crisp output in the case of formula (4.6) taking the form of Equation (4.10). It is guaranteed by assumption (4.7) as well as (4.9).

4.3 Systems with Inference Based on Bounded Product

Two kinds of fuzzy systems based on the Mamdani approach are well known and commonly used in various applications: these systems which employ Mamdani and Larsen rules of inference. These refer to the *max-min* or *max-product* inference method, respectively (see Section 2.3.3). The neuro-fuzzy systems that applied the Mamdani and Larsen rules of inference have been presented in Sections 4.1 and 4.2. These rules of inference are based on *min* and *product* operators, respectively.

The *min* and *product* operators are widely used as the T-norms because of their mathematical forms, which are easy to calculate. However, other T-norm operators can be employed, for example the *bounded product* (see Table 2.1). The inference rule is expressed by this T-norm as follows

$$\mu_{A^k \to B^k}(\mathbf{x}, y) = \max(\mu_{A^k}(\mathbf{x}) + \mu_{B^k}(y) - 1, 0) \qquad (4.17)$$

If assumption (4.5) is fulfilled, then from Equation (4.17) we obtain

$$\mu_{A^k \to B^k}(\overline{\mathbf{x}}, \overline{y}^k) = \mu_{A^k}(\overline{\mathbf{x}}) \qquad (4.18)$$

and from formulas (4.4), (4.18), (4.17), (4.11) we have

$$\overset{N}{\underset{j=1}{S}} \mu_{A^j \to B^j}(\overline{\mathbf{x}}, \overline{y}^k) = S\left(\mu_{A^k}(\overline{\mathbf{x}}), \underset{\substack{j=1 \\ j \neq k}}{\overset{N}{S}} \max(\mu_{A^j}(\overline{\mathbf{x}}) - \widetilde{p}_{j,k}, 0)\right) \qquad (4.19)$$

where

$$\widetilde{p}_{j,k} = 1 - p_{j,k} \qquad (4.20)$$

From Equations (4.2) and (4.19) the mathematical description of the system based on the *bounded product* rule of inference has the following form

$$\overline{y} = \frac{\displaystyle\sum_{k=1}^{N} \overline{y}^k \, S\left(\mu_{A^k}(\overline{\mathbf{x}}), \underset{\substack{j=1 \\ j \neq k}}{\overset{N}{S}} \max(\mu_{A^j}(\overline{\mathbf{x}}) - \widetilde{p}_{j,k}, 0)\right)}{\displaystyle\sum_{k=1}^{N} S\left(\mu_{A^k}(\overline{\mathbf{x}}), \underset{\substack{j=1 \\ j \neq k}}{\overset{N}{S}} \max(\mu_{A^j}(\overline{\mathbf{x}}) - \widetilde{p}_{j,k}, 0)\right)} \qquad (4.21)$$

If condition (4.7) or (4.9) is satisfied, it is easy to conclude, that Equation (4.21) takes the form of formula (4.10). Thus, in this case, a fuzzy system based on the *bounded product* rule of inference is described by the same mathematical formula as the systems based on the Mamdani (*min*) or Larsen (*product*) rule of inference. The multi-layer architecture of this system is illustrated in Fig. 4.3. If the *min* operation is chosen as the Cartesian product to realize the membership values $\mu_{A^k}(\overline{\mathbf{x}})$, for $k = 1, \ldots, N$, in Equation (4.10), then the neuro-fuzzy architecture has the form presented in Fig. 4.1. If the *product* operation is chosen as the Cartesian product, then the architecture of the system is as depicted in Fig. 4.2.

The architecture of the system described by Equation (4.21) is presented in Fig. 4.8.

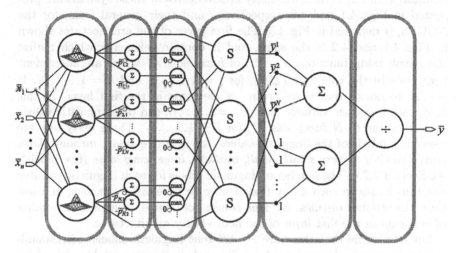

FIGURE 4.8. Architecture of OCFS system based on the *bounded product* rule

It is very simple to portray the inference process, based on the *bounded product* rule, in a similar way to that shown in Fig. 2.23, in Section 2.3.3. The membership functions of the fuzzy sets $\overline{B}^k$, inferred by use of the Mamdani rule, in Fig. 2.23 are "clipped" versions of the membership functions of the consequent fuzzy sets B^k. The membership functions of fuzzy sets $\overline{B}^k$, inferred by use of the Larsen rule, are "scaled" forms of the membership functions of the consequent fuzzy sets B^k, for $k = 1, \ldots, N$. In the case of the *bounded product* inference rule, the membership functions of the inferred fuzzy sets $\overline{B}^k$ are similar in shape to the "scaled" membership functions. In fact, however, they are shifted down, so the maximal values of the membership functions $\overline{B}^k$ are equal to the *antecedent matching degrees*

τ_k, and cut from the bottom to obtain membership values greater or equal to zero. This is illustrated in [437].

Other T-norm operators can also be proposed to perform inference of the Mamdani approach type. However, as we have seen on the example of the *bounded product* rule, in the case of NOCFS different T-norm operators lead to the same neuro-fuzzy architectures. In the case of OCFS the architectures for other T-norm operators can be more complicated.

4.4   Simplified Architectures

Now let us consider the *Mamdani* and *Larsen* systems (see Section 2.3.3, Lemmas 1 and 2). The neuro-fuzzy architectures of these systems are presented in Figs. 4.1 and 4.2, respectively, and their general form, for the NOCFS, is depicted in Fig. 4.3. The first layer of the architectures shown in Figs. 4.1 and 4.2 is the same, and it contains elements which realize the membership functions $\mu_{A_i^k}(\overline{x}_i)$ of fuzzy sets A_i^k which are antecedent fuzzy sets in the rule base (2.94), for $i = 1, \ldots, n$, and $k = 1, \ldots, N$. It is easy to notice that there are $n \cdot N$ elements in the first layer. In this case, each linguistic variable, x_i, for $i = 1, \ldots, n$, can take linguistic values corresponding to N fuzzy sets A_i^k, for $k = 1, \ldots, N$. These fuzzy sets are viewed as labels of the linguistic values, for example *small, medium, large* (three labels), or *very small, small, medium, large, very large* (five labels); see Section 2.2.4. The number of linguistic labels for each linguistic variable can thus be set in such a way that it may be different for each x_i and less than the number of rules, N. This results, of course, in a smaller number of elements in the first layer of the neuro-fuzzy architectures.

Let us assume that there are N_i different linguistic labels, corresponding to fuzzy sets denoted as A_{i,h_i}, for each linguistic variable, x_i, where $i = 1, \ldots, n$, and $h_i \in \{1, \ldots, N_i\}$, and $N_i \leqslant N$. In this case, the first layer of the neuro-fuzzy architectures contains elements performing the membership functions $\mu_{A_{i,h_i}}(\overline{x}_i)$, and the number of these elements is

$$\sum_{i=1}^{n} N_i \leqslant n \cdot N$$

The rule base with fuzzy sets A_{i,h_i}, in the antecedent part of the rules, has the following form

$R^{(k)}$: **IF** x_1 is A_{1,h_1} **AND** x_2 is A_{2,h_2} **AND** ... **AND** x_n is A_{n,h_n}

   THEN y is B^k (4.22)

where each rule number, k, is associated with a sequence $h_1 h_2 \cdots h_n$, in which $h_1 \in \{1, \ldots, N_1\}$, $h_2 \in \{1, \ldots, N_2\}$, ..., $h_n \in \{1, \ldots, N_n\}$; and $k = 1, \ldots, N$.

It is obvious that the same fuzzy sets A_{i,h_i} can be included to antecedent parts of many rules, but the values of the sequence $h_1 h_2 \cdots h_n$ must be different in each rule, which mean different combinations of the fuzzy sets.

Figure 4.9 illustrates the simplified neuro-fuzzy architecture that corresponds to the rule base (4.22). The first layer is composed of the elements which perform the membership functions $\mu_{A_{i,h_i}} (\overline{x}_i)$ of fuzzy sets A_{i,h_i} given input values $\overline{x}_i$, for $i = 1, \dots, n$. Since a fuzzy set is completely determined by its membership function (Section 2), the notation of fuzzy sets A_{i,h_i} is used in the figure instead of $\mu_{A_{i,h_i}}$, understanding that the elements realize the membership functions. The second layer consists of the elements that perform the Cartesian product operator, which is the minimum or product (see Definition 25). The number of these elements is equal to the number of rules, N.

It is easy to notice that if $N_1 = N_2 = \cdots = N_n = N$, then the rule base (4.22) takes the form (2.94) and the architecture shown in Fig. 4.9 becomes the same as the basic architectures presented in Figs. 4.1 and 4.2. In this case, the first layer of each architecture contains the elements that perform membership functions A_i^k, for $i = 1, \dots, n$, and $k = 1, \dots, N$. Thus, $A_1^k = A_{1,h_1}, A_2^k = A_{2,h_2}, \dots, A_n^k = A_{n,h_n}$, tor $k = 1, \dots, N$.

If the assumption $A_i^1 \neq A_i^2 \neq \cdots \neq A_i^N$, for $i = 1, \dots, n$, is not satisfied, the basic architecture can be reduced to the simplified one, because instead of using several elements, in the first layer, realizing the same membership function, only one can be applied and connected to several elements in the second layer. In the basic architecture, each element in the first layer is connected with only one element in the second layer.

In the simplified architecture depicted in Fig. 4.9 an element of the first layer can be connected to more than one element of the second layer. The connections correspond to the IF-THEN rules (4.22). The maximal number of rules that can be created in this way, denoted as $N_{\max}$, is

$$N_{\max} = \prod_{i=1}^{n} N_i \tag{4.23}$$

In situations when $N = N_{\max}$, the following expression [420], [366] can be used to determine the rule number, k, based on the sequence $h_1 h_2 \cdots h_n$

$$k = \sum_{i=1}^{n} \left[(h_i - 1) \prod_{l=0}^{i-1} N_l \right] + 1 \tag{4.24}$$

where $N_0 = 1$.

Let us notice that, in this case, from formula (4.24), if $h_1 = h_2 = \cdots = h_n = 1$, we obtain $k = 1$, and if $h_1 = h_2 = \cdots = h_n = N_{\max}$, then $k = N_{\max}$. It is worth emphasizing that if we presented the simplified architecture with the maximal number of rules, given by Equation (4.23), in the form of the basic architectures, the first layer would contain $n \cdot N_{\max}$ elements, which is much more than $N_1 + N_2 + \cdots + N_n$.

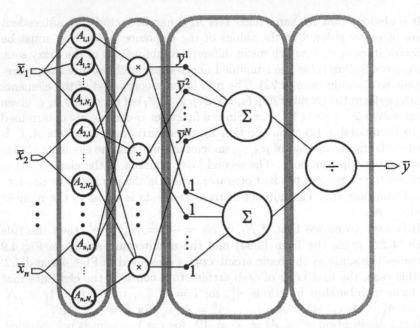

FIGURE 4.9. A simpified architecture of neuro-fuzzy systems

However, the rule base of a neuro-fuzzy system does not usually include
the maximal number of rules. Initially, the architecture for $N_{\max}$ rules can
be created, but later a pruning procedure may be applied in order to reduce
the rule base, so

$$N \leqslant \prod_{i=1}^{n} N_i \qquad (4.25)$$

Equation (4.24) may be applied in order to assign a number to each rule
during the pruning procedure. Moreover, this is helpful for a mathematical
description of neuro-fuzzy systems represented by the simplified architectures. In particular, it is useful for determining the formulas which constitute learning algorithms for these systems. These kind of learning procedures, similar to the back-propagation method, are depicted in [420]. However, this kind of learning algorithm can be realized based on the system's
architecture, as mentioned in Section 3.3, so it is not always necessary to
employ these mathematical formulas.

The mathematical description of the system with the rule base (4.22) is
given by the following equations

$$\bar{y} = \frac{\sum_{k=1}^{N} \bar{y}^k \prod_{i=1}^{n} \mu_{A_{i,h_i}}(\bar{x}_i)}{\sum_{k=1}^{N} \prod_{i=1}^{n} \mu_{A_{i,h_i}}(\bar{x}_i)} \qquad (4.26)$$

or

$$\bar{y} = \frac{\sum_{k=1}^{N} \bar{y}^k \min\left\{\mu_{A_{1,h_1}}(\bar{x}_1), \ldots, \mu_{A_{n,h_n}}(\bar{x}_n)\right\}}{\sum_{k=1}^{N} \min\left\{\mu_{A_{1,h_1}}(\bar{x}_1), \ldots, \mu_{A_{n,h_n}}(\bar{x}_n)\right\}} \tag{4.27}$$

for the product or minimum as the Cartesian product operator, respectively; where k is associated with the sequence $h_1 h_2 \cdots h_n$, and can be expressed by formula (4.24).

It is worth mentioning that Equation (4.24) serves as an example of the methods that allow numbering of the rules by assigning them to sequences $h_1 h_2 \cdots h_n$. It can, of course, be done in a different way.

Each of the neuro-fuzzy architectures presented in this book can also be considered in a simplified version, since this is a special case of the basic architecture, where some of the first-layer elements realize the same membership functions.

4.5 Architectures Based on Other Defuzzification Methods

The neuro-fuzzy architectures described in this chapter are based on the *center average* defuzzifier. The general form of the multi-layer connectionist architectures, shown in Fig. 3.10, in Section 3.3, has been determined using the discrete form of the *center-of-area* defuzzification method, also called the *center-of-gravity*. These methods, among others, are described in Section 2.3.1. The *center of sums* defuzzification applied to a specific kind of system is the subject of Section 4.5.1. In Section 4.5.2 a neural network is used as a defuzzifier.

4.5.1 COS-Based Architectures

The neuro-fuzzy systems presented in Figs. 4.1 and 4.2, and depicted, respectively, in Lemmas 1 and 2 in Section 2.3.3, were obtained using the *center average* defuzzification method (see Section 2.3.1). Applying the *center of sums* defuzzification (COS), defined by Equation (2.103), instead of the *center average* method, we can determine the following description of the system [420], [427]

$$\bar{y} = \frac{\sum_{k=1}^{N} \bar{y}^k \sigma^k \prod_{i=1}^{n} \mu_{A_i^k}(\bar{x}_i)}{\sum_{k=1}^{N} \sigma^k \prod_{i=1}^{n} \mu_{A_i^k}(\bar{x}_i)} \tag{4.28}$$

assuming that the rule base (2.94) is used, and Gaussian membership functions of fuzzy sets B^k, for $k = 1, \ldots, N$, given by

$$\mu_{B^k}(y) = \exp\left[-\left(\frac{y - \overline{y}^k}{\sigma^k}\right)^2\right] \tag{4.29}$$

are employed; $\overline{y}^k$ and σ^k denote *center* and *width* parameters, respectively, of these membership functions.

System description (4.28) can easily be determined by substituting expression (2.122) into Equation (2.103), which means that the singleton fuzzifier is applied. Then the Larsen (product) operation should be chosen as fuzzy relation $A^k \rightarrow B^k$, and the product operation as the Cartesian product $A^k = A_1^k \times \cdots \times A_n^k$, so

$$\mu_{A^k \rightarrow B^k}(\overline{\mathbf{x}}, y) = \mu_{B^k}(y) \prod_{i=1}^{n} \mu_{A_i^k}(\overline{x}_i) \tag{4.30}$$

The functions (5.16) fulfil the following equation

$$\int_{-\infty}^{\infty} \mu_{B^k}(y)\, dy = \sigma^k \sqrt{\pi} \tag{4.31}$$

and

$$\int_{-\infty}^{\infty} y \mu_{B^k}(y)\, dy = \overline{y}^k\, \sigma^k \sqrt{\pi} \tag{4.32}$$

Thus, from formulas (2.103), (2.122), 4.30, and (4.31), (4.32), we obtain the system description expressed by Equation (4.28).

Analogously to the lemmas 1 and 2, presented in Section 2.3.3, we can now formulate the following lemma:

Lemma 4 *The fuzzy logic systems with rule base (2.94), singleton fuzzifier (2.97), COS defuzzifier (2.103), product operation as fuzzy relation $A^k \rightarrow B^k$, product operation as Cartesian products $A_1^k \times \cdots \times A_n^k$, and Gaussian membership functions of the consequent fuzzy sets B^k, for $k = 1, \ldots, N$, given by formula (5.16), are described by Equation (4.28).*

The neuro-fuzzy architecture of the system referred to in lemma 4 is illustrated in Fig. 4.10. It is easy to notice the difference between this system and that depicted in lemma 2, with the neuro-fuzzy architecture shown in Fig. 4.2. The system based on the COS defuzzification method takes into account the *width* parameters of the consequent Gaussian membership functions, while its counterpart based on the *center average* defuzzification includes only the *center* parameters.

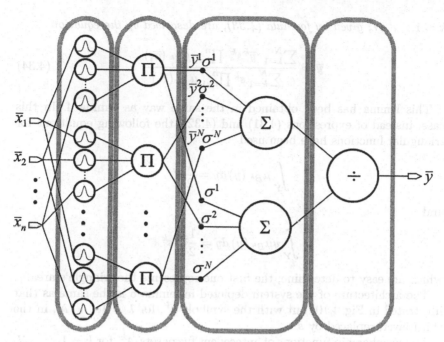

FIGURE 4.10. A neuro-fuzzy architecture based on the COS defuzzification method

If the consequent fuzzy sets B^k, for $k = 1, \ldots, N$, are singletons, the neuro-fuzzy architecture portrayed in Fig. 4.2 is, of course, sufficient. However, for non-singleton consequent fuzzy sets, the architecture presented in Fig. 4.10 contains more information about the system.

Similar system can be considered if the membership functions of fuzzy sets B^k, for $k = 1, \ldots, N$, are triangular functions defined by

$$\mu_{B^k}(y) = \begin{cases} 1 - 2\left|y - \overline{y}^k\right|/s^k & \text{if} \quad \left|y - \overline{y}^k\right| \leqslant s^k/2 \\ 0 & \text{otherwise} \end{cases} \quad (4.33)$$

where $\overline{y}^k$ and s^k denote the *center* and *width* parameters, respectively, of the triangular membership functions; see Fig. 2.1. The *center* is the one-point *core* of the triangular function (Definition 4) and the *width* is determined by the *support* (Definition 2) of this membership function.

Lemma 5 *Fuzzy logic systems with rule base (2.94), singleton fuzzifier (2.97), COS defuzzifier (2.103), product operation as fuzzy relation $A^k \rightarrow B^k$, product operation as Cartesian products $A_1^k \times \cdots \times A_n^k$, and triangular membership functions of the consequent fuzzy sets B^k, for*

$k = 1, \ldots, N$, given by formula (4.33), are described by the equation

$$\bar{y} = \frac{\sum_{k=1}^{N} \bar{y}^k s^k \prod_{i=1}^{n} \mu_{A_i^k} (\bar{x}_i)}{\sum_{k=1}^{N} s^k \prod_{i=1}^{n} \mu_{A_i^k} (\bar{x}_i)} \tag{4.34}$$

This lemma has been obtained in the same way as lemma 4. In this case, instead of expressions (4.31) and (4.32), the following equations for triangular functions have been used

$$\int_Y \mu_{B^k} (y) \, dy = \frac{1}{2} s^k$$

and

$$\int_Y y \mu_{B^k} (y) \, dy = \frac{1}{2} \bar{y}^k s^k$$

which are easy to determine; the first one represents the triangle's area.

The architecture of the system depicted in lemma 5 is the same as that illustrated in Fig. 4.10, but with the symbols σ^k, for $k = 1, \ldots, N$, in the third layer, replaced by s^k.

The membership functions of antecedent fuzzy sets A_i^k, for $k = 1, \ldots, N$, can be chosen as Gaussian, triangular, or other shaped functions.

Gradient learning formulas for tuning *center* and *width* parameters of the systems with Gaussian and triangular (antecedent and consequent) membership functions are presented in [420]; see also [427].

4.5.2 Neural Networks as Defuzzifiers

The defuzzification task in fuzzy systems, which transforms fuzzy outputs into crisp values, can be treated as a mapping from a high-dimensional space to a lower-dimensional space. Neural networks have the ability to learn this mapping if some good training samples are provided. This approach, using neural networks as defuzzifiers, is applied e.g. in [475], [474], [290], [291], [420], [422]. In these papers, multi-layer feed-forward neural networks (MLPs) are employed to perform defuzzification tasks. This approach utilizes the fact that single-hidden-layer MLPs are universal approximators (see Section 3.1.2), so they can approximate any continuous function to any degree of accuracy. Some interesting properties of defuzzification neural networks are presented in [474]. Other papers, cited above, include learning methods (usually based on back-propagation, as described in Section 3.1.3), as well as results of application experiments.

Neural networks can be employed as defuzzifiers in different kinds of neuro-fuzzy architectures, by replacing the last layers which realize the defuzzification task. Figure 4.11 illustrates the architecture that corresponds to the neuro-fuzzy systems portrayed in Figs. 4.1 and 4.2, as well as in

Fig. 4.10, in which the neural network plays the role of the defuzzifier. Analogously, we can replace these two layers by a neural network in the simplified architecture shown in Fig. 4.9, and in others.

Let us notice that Figs. 4.1 and 4.2 refer to the *center average* defuzzification method, while the architecture depicted in Fig. 4.10 incorporates the *center of sums* defuzzifier. Other neuro-fuzzy architectures considered in this book have been determined based on the discrete form of the *center-of-area* method used for defuzzification. Neural networks can therefore replace various defuzzification formulas.

The performance of the neural network defuzzifiers depends on the training samples that constitute the learning sequence. The weights of the neural network are tuned during a learning procedure, rather than the *center* (and *width*) parameters of the consequent fuzzy sets. By tuning the neural network weights we do not confine the information about shapes of the consequent membership functions only to these parameters. On the other hand, the weights, in contrast to the *center* and *width* parameters, have no physical interpretation.

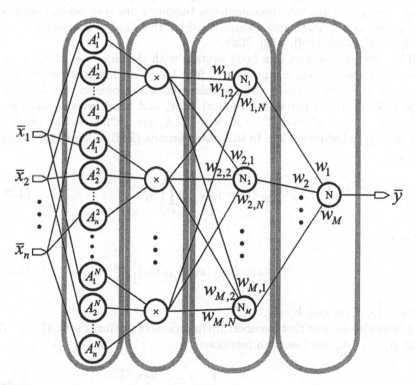

FIGURE 4.11. A neuro-fuzzy architecture with a neural network as a defuzzifier

As mentioned in Section 3.1.4, RBF networks are also universal approximators and they are capable of accurately mimicking specified MLP neural networks (and vice versa). Therefore, it is possible to apply an RBF network as a defuzzifier, instead of an MLP. This idea is presented in [425].

4.6 Architectures of Systems with Non-Singleton Fuzzifier

The most commonly used fuzzifier in fuzzy and neuro-fuzzy systems is the singleton fuzzifier, also applied in all the neuro-fuzzy architectures considered in this book. The singleton fuzzifier (2.97) is very convenient from the computational point of view, since in this case Equation (2.96), known as the *sup-star composition*, is expressed by the very simple formula (2.122). However, this kind of fuzzifier may not always be applicable, for example in the situations when input data (or training data) are corrupted by noise and there is a need to account for uncertainty in the input values. An example of the non-singleton fuzzifier is given by Equation (2.98). Fuzzy or neuro-fuzzy systems with non-singleton fuzzifiers are very seldom studied in the literature. The papers which consider this kind of fuzzifier are e.g. [342], [386], [420], [424], [432], [436].

The inference process of a fuzzy system with the rule base (2.94) is expressed by the sup-star composition (2.96). Let us assume that the product operator is chosen as the T-norm in this equation. Moreover, the fuzzy relation $A^k \to B^k$ is Larsen's (product) type, and the Cartesian products $A^k = A_1^k \times \cdots \times A_n^k$ and $A^k = A_1' \times \cdots \times A_n'$ are defined by the product (according to Definition 25). In this case, formula (2.96) takes the following form

$$\mu_{\overline{B}^k}(y) = \mu_{B^k}(y) \prod_{i=1}^{n} \gamma_i^k \qquad (4.35)$$

where

$$\gamma_i^k = \sup_{x_i} \left[\mu_{A_i'}(x_i) \, \mu_{A_i^k}(x_i) \right] \qquad (4.36)$$

for $i = 1, \ldots, n$, and $k = 1, \ldots, N$.

Let us also assume that membership functions of the fuzzy sets $A_1^k, \ldots, A_n^k$ and $A_1', \ldots, A_n'$ are Gaussian functions

$$\mu_{A_i^k}(x_i) = \exp\left[-\left(\frac{x_i - \overline{x}_i^k}{\sigma_i^k} \right)^2 \right] \qquad (4.37)$$

and

$$\mu_{A_i'}(x_i) = \exp\left[-\left(\frac{x_i - \widehat{x}_i}{\sigma_i}\right)^2\right] \tag{4.38}$$

respectively.

By maximizing the function $\mu_{A_i'}(x_i)\,\mu_{A_i^k}(x_i)$, in formula (4.36), using Equations (4.37) and (4.38), we find that the point $\widetilde{x}_i^k$, which corresponds to the maximal value of this function, is expressed as follows

$$\widetilde{x}_i^k = \frac{(\sigma_i)^2\,\overline{x}_i^k + (\sigma_i^k)^2\,\widehat{x}_i}{(\sigma_i)^2 + (\sigma_i^k)^2} \tag{4.39}$$

Substituting $\widetilde{x}_i^k$, given by Equation (4.39), into $\mu_{A_i'}(x_i)\,\mu_{A_i^k}(x_i)$ we can easily obtain γ_i^k, defined by Equation (4.36), in the form

$$\gamma_i^k = \exp\left[-\left(\frac{\widehat{x}_i - \overline{x}_i^k}{\sigma_i^{l_0}}\right)^2\right] \tag{1.40}$$

where

$$\bar{\sigma}_i^k = \sqrt{(\sigma_i)^2 + (\sigma_i^k)^2} \tag{4.41}$$

Now we can substitute γ_i^k, expressed by Equation (4.40), into formula (4.35) and then determine a description of a fuzzy system based on a specific defuzzification method, for example the *center average* (2.105) or the *center of sums* (2.103). Hence, a system with the *center average* defuzzifier is described as

$$\overline{y} = \frac{\sum_{k=1}^{N} \overline{y}^k\,\tau_k}{\sum_{k=1}^{N} \tau_k} \tag{4.42}$$

and a system with the *center of sums* defuzzifier by

$$\overline{y} = \frac{\sum_{k=1}^{N} \overline{y}^k\,\sigma^k\,\tau_k}{\sum_{k=1}^{N} \sigma^k\,\tau_k} \tag{4.43}$$

where

$$\tau_k = \prod_{i=1}^{n} \exp\left[-\left(\frac{\widehat{x}_i - \overline{x}_i^k}{\bar{\sigma}_i^k}\right)^2\right] \tag{4.44}$$

Equation (4.43) has been determined in the same way as the system description (4.28) in Section 4.5.1. Formula (4.42) has the same form as the description of the system depicted in lemma 2, in Section 2.3.3. Thus, the neuro-fuzzy architectures of the systems with the non-singleton fuzzifier is fundamentally the same but there is a difference in the first layer. It is easy to notice that in the non-singleton case, elements of the first layers in both architectures perform Gaussian functions with different *center* and *width* parameters, according to formula (4.44). The architecture that corresponds to Equation (4.42) is presented in Fig. 4.2, while the architecture of the system described by Equation (4.43) is illustrated in Fig. 4.10, where the Gaussian functions realized by the first layer's elements are expressed by formula (4.40). Note that this means that input values are centers, $\widehat{x}_i$, of the Gaussian membership functions $\mu_{A'_i}(x_i)$, for $i = 1, \dots, n$. Of course, we can assume that $\widehat{x}_i = \overline{x}_i$, where $\overline{x}_i$, for $i = 1, \dots, n$, are crisp input values. Moreover, we can also assume that the *width* parameters of the membership functions $\mu_{A'_i}(x_i)$ are the same for each $i = 1, \dots, n$, so $\sigma_i = \sigma$. In this case, the *degree of rule activation*, τ_k, is expressed as

$$\tau_k = \prod_{i=1}^{n} \exp\left[-\left(\frac{\overline{x}_i - \overline{x}_i^k}{\bar{\sigma}_i^k}\right)^2\right] \qquad (4.45)$$

where

$$\bar{\sigma}_i^k = \sqrt{\sigma^2 + \left(\sigma_i^k\right)^2} \qquad (4.46)$$

so the only difference between the architectures for the singleton and non-singleton cases is in the *width* parameters of the Gaussian functions performed by the first layers' elements. These parameters are σ_i^k for the singleton architectures and $\bar{\sigma}_i^k$ given by Equation (4.46) in the non-singleton case.

Gradient learning algorithms for tuning parameters of the antecedent and consequent membership functions are similar to their singleton counterparts. These formulas are presented in [420], [424].

5

Neuro-Fuzzy Architectures
Based on the Logical Approach

The fuzzy inference neural networks (see Section 3.3) that realize the inference based on the logical approach are the subject of this chapter. Firstly, in Section 5.1, the mathematical descriptions of the neuro-fuzzy systems employing different fuzzy implications are determined. Then, the connectionist, multi-layer, architectures, which correspond to the implication-based systems, are presented. These architectures are proposed in [366]. The neuro-fuzzy systems of this kind are considered in [367], [430], [433], and also in the papers that refer to a specific implication, e.g. [429]. In Section 5.4, the performance analysis of the implication-based systems is illustrated. The results of computer simulations with regard to examples of function approximation, control, and classification problems, are portrayed in Section 5.5. In order to train the systems, gradient, genetic, or hybrid algorithms can be applied. The learning methods are described in Chapter 6. In particular, the architecture-based learning, outlined in Section 6.1.3, is recommended.

5.1 Mathematical Descriptions of Implication-Based Systems

Let us consider the fuzzy logic system presented in Section 2.3.1, with the singleton fuzzifier defined by formula (2.97), and the discrete form of the defuzzifier given by Equation (2.107). The inference of the fuzzy system, performed by the single rule (2.94), for $j = 1, \ldots, N$, is expressed

by formula (2.122). From Equations (2.107), (2.115), and (2.122), we obtain
the following description of the fuzzy system

$$\overline{y} = \frac{\sum_{k=1}^{N} \overline{y}^k \ \underset{j=1}{\overset{N}{\mathbf{T}}} \mu_{A^j \to B^j} \left(\overline{\mathbf{x}}, \overline{y}^k \right)}{\sum_{k=1}^{N} \underset{j=1}{\overset{N}{\mathbf{T}}} \mu_{A^j \to B^j} \left(\overline{\mathbf{x}}, \overline{y}^k \right)} \tag{5.1}$$

Equation (5.1) represents the general mathematical description of the
fuzzy system based on the logical approach. This is a special case of formula (3.32).

The T-norm in Equation (5.1) can be written as follows

$$\underset{j=1}{\overset{N}{\mathbf{T}}} \mu_{A^j \to B^j} \left(\overline{\mathbf{x}}, \overline{y}^k \right) = T \left(\mu_{A^k \to B^k} \left(\overline{\mathbf{x}}, \overline{y}^k \right), \underset{\substack{j=1 \\ j \neq k}}{\overset{N}{\mathbf{T}}} \mu_{A^j \to B^j} \left(\overline{\mathbf{x}}, \overline{y}^k \right) \right) \tag{5.2}$$

The logical implications applied to fuzzy inference are depicted in Section 2.3.4. The Kleene-Dienes, Łukasiewicz, Zadeh, Reichenbach, Goguen,
Gödel, Dubois-Prade implications are defined by Equations (2.132), (2.135),
(2.137), (2.138), (2.145), (2.146), (2.147), respectively. These implications
are listed in Table 2.2; see Section 2.2.2. In addition, the following implications are presented in Section 2.3.4: the stochastic, Fodor, Willmott, as well
as Sharp, and Yager fuzzy implications, given by formulas (2.139), (2.141),
(2.142), (2.144), (2.143), respectively.

It is easy to show that if assumption (4.5) is fulfilled, then

$$\mu_{A^k \to B^k} \left(\overline{\mathbf{x}}, \overline{y}^k \right) = 1 \tag{5.3}$$

for the Kleene-Dienes, Łukasiewicz, Reichenbach, Goguen, Gödel, Dubois-
Prade, stochastic, Fodor, Sharp, Yager implications, and

$$\mu_{A^k \to B^k} \left(\overline{\mathbf{x}}, \overline{y}^k \right) = \max \left(1 - \mu_{A^k} \left(\overline{\mathbf{x}} \right), \mu_{A^k} \left(\overline{\mathbf{x}} \right) \right) \tag{5.4}$$

for the Zadeh and Willmott implications.

From Equations (5.1), (5.2), (5.3), and the second *boundary condition* of
the T-norm (see Definition 17), we have the expression

$$\overline{y} = \frac{\sum_{k=1}^{N} \overline{y}^k \ \underset{\substack{j=1 \\ j \neq k}}{\overset{N}{\mathbf{T}}} \mu_{A^j \to B^j} \left(\overline{\mathbf{x}}, \overline{y}^k \right)}{\sum_{k=1}^{N} \underset{\substack{j=1 \\ j \neq k}}{\overset{N}{\mathbf{T}}} \mu_{A^j \to B^j} \left(\overline{\mathbf{x}}, \overline{y}^k \right)} \tag{5.5}$$

for the Kleene-Dienes, Łukasiewicz, Reichenbach, Goguen, Gödel, Dubois-
Prade, stochastic, Fodor, Sharp, Yager implications, and from formula (5.4),

the equation

$$\overline{y} = \frac{\sum\limits_{k=1}^{N} \overline{y}^k \; T\left(\max\left(1 - \mu_{A^k}\left(\overline{\mathbf{x}}\right), \mu_{A^k}\left(\overline{\mathbf{x}}\right)\right), \mathop{T}\limits_{\substack{j=1 \\ j \neq k}}^{N} \mu_{A^j \to B^j}\left(\overline{\mathbf{x}}, \overline{y}^k\right)\right)}{\sum\limits_{k=1}^{N} T\left(\max\left(1 - \mu_{A^k}\left(\overline{\mathbf{x}}\right), \mu_{A^k}\left(\overline{\mathbf{x}}\right)\right), \mathop{T}\limits_{\substack{j=1 \\ j \neq k}}^{N} \mu_{A^j \to B^j}\left(\overline{\mathbf{x}}, \overline{y}^k\right)\right)} \tag{5.6}$$

for the Zadeh and Willmott implications.

Thus, in the more general case of OCFS systems, with denotation (4.11), from Equations (5.5), and the corresponding formulas which define the fuzzy implications, we obtain the following mathematical descriptions of the implication-based fuzzy systems

$$\overline{y} = \frac{\sum\limits_{k=1}^{N} \overline{y}^k \mathop{T}\limits_{\substack{j=1 \\ j \neq k}}^{N} \max\left(1 - \mu_{A^k}\left(\overline{\mathbf{x}}\right), p_{j,k}\right)}{\sum\limits_{k=1}^{N} \mathop{T}\limits_{\substack{j=1 \\ j \neq k}}^{N} \max\left(1 - \mu_{A^k}\left(\overline{\mathbf{x}}\right), p_{j,k}\right)} \tag{5.7}$$

for the Kleene-Dienes fuzzy implication, given by Equation (2.132), and

$$\overline{y} = \frac{\sum\limits_{k=1}^{N} \overline{y}^k \mathop{T}\limits_{\substack{j=1 \\ j \neq k}}^{N} \min\left(1, 1 - \mu_{A^k}\left(\overline{\mathbf{x}}\right) + p_{j,k}\right)}{\sum\limits_{k=1}^{N} \mathop{T}\limits_{\substack{j=1 \\ j \neq k}}^{N} \min\left(1, 1 - \mu_{A^k}\left(\overline{\mathbf{x}}\right) + p_{j,k}\right)} \tag{5.8}$$

for the Łukasiewicz fuzzy implication, given by Equation (2.135), and

$$\overline{y} = \frac{\sum\limits_{k=1}^{N} \overline{y}^k \mathop{T}\limits_{\substack{j=1 \\ j \neq k}}^{N} \left(1 - \mu_{A^k}\left(\overline{\mathbf{x}}\right) + \mu_{A^k}\left(\overline{\mathbf{x}}\right) p_{j,k}\right)}{\sum\limits_{k=1}^{N} \mathop{T}\limits_{\substack{j=1 \\ j \neq k}}^{N} \left(1 - \mu_{A^k}\left(\overline{\mathbf{x}}\right) + \mu_{A^k}\left(\overline{\mathbf{x}}\right) p_{j,k}\right)} \tag{5.9}$$

for the Reichenbach fuzzy implication, given by Equation (2.138), and

$$\overline{y} = \frac{\sum\limits_{k=1}^{N} \overline{y}^k \mathop{T}\limits_{\substack{j=1 \\ j \neq k}}^{N} \min\left\{1, 1 - \mu_{A^k}\left(\overline{\mathbf{x}}\right) + \mu_{A^k}\left(\overline{\mathbf{x}}\right) p_{j,k}\right\}}{\sum\limits_{k=1}^{N} \mathop{T}\limits_{\substack{j=1 \\ j \neq k}}^{N} \min\left\{1, 1 - \mu_{A^k}\left(\overline{\mathbf{x}}\right) + \mu_{A^k}\left(\overline{\mathbf{x}}\right) p_{j,k}\right\}} \tag{5.10}$$

for the stochastic fuzzy implication, given by Equation (2.139), as well as

$$\overline{y} = \frac{\sum\limits_{k=1}^{N} \overline{y}^k \mathop{\mathbf{T}}\limits_{\substack{j=1 \\ j \neq k}}^{N} (p_{j,k})^{\mu_{A^k}(\overline{\mathbf{x}})}}{\sum\limits_{k=1}^{N} \mathop{\mathbf{T}}\limits_{\substack{j=1 \\ j \neq k}}^{N} (p_{j,k})^{\mu_{A^k}(\overline{\mathbf{x}})}} \tag{5.11}$$

for the Yager fuzzy implication, given by Equation (2.143).

In the same way, we obtain the following formula

$$\overline{y} = \frac{\sum\limits_{k=1}^{N} \overline{y}^k \mathop{\mathbf{T}}\limits_{\substack{j=1 \\ j \neq k}}^{N} \min\left(1, \frac{p_{j,k}}{\mu_{A^k}(\overline{\mathbf{x}})}\right)}{\sum\limits_{k=1}^{N} \mathop{\mathbf{T}}\limits_{\substack{j=1 \\ j \neq k}}^{N} \min\left(1, \frac{p_{j,k}}{\mu_{A^k}(\overline{\mathbf{x}})}\right)} \tag{5.12}$$

for the Goguen fuzzy implication, defined by Equation (2.145); note that if $\mu_{A^k}(\overline{\mathbf{x}}) = 0$, then $\min\left(1, \frac{p_{j,k}}{\mu_{A^k}(\overline{\mathbf{x}})}\right) = 1$.

Let us define the function

$$\rho(a, b) = \begin{cases} 1 & \text{if} \quad a \leqslant b \\ 0 & \text{if} \quad a > b \end{cases} \tag{5.13}$$

It is easy to show that Equation (2.146), in the form

$$\mu_{A^k \to B^k}(\overline{\mathbf{x}}, \overline{y}^k) = \begin{cases} 1 & \text{if} \quad \mu_{A^k}(\overline{\mathbf{x}}) \leqslant \mu_{B^k}(\overline{y}^k) \\ \mu_{B^k}(\overline{y}^k) & \text{otherwise} \end{cases} \tag{5.14}$$

can be replaced by the following formula

$$\mu_{A^j \to B^j}(\overline{\mathbf{x}}, \overline{y}^k) = \min\left(1, \mu_{B^j}(\overline{y}^k) + \rho\left(\mu_{A^j}(\overline{\mathbf{x}}), \mu_{B^j}(\overline{y}^k)\right)\right) \tag{5.15}$$

where ρ is given by Equation (5.13). Thus, from formulas (5.5), (5.15), and (4.11), we obtain the mathematical description of the OCFS system based on the Gödel fuzzy implication, in the form

$$\overline{y} = \frac{\sum\limits_{k=1}^{N} \overline{y}^k \mathop{\mathbf{T}}\limits_{\substack{j=1 \\ j \neq k}}^{N} \min\left(1, p_{j,k} + \rho\left(\mu_{A^j}(\overline{\mathbf{x}}), p_{j,k}\right)\right)}{\sum\limits_{k=1}^{N} \mathop{\mathbf{T}}\limits_{\substack{j=1 \\ j \neq k}}^{N} \min\left(1, p_{j,k} + \rho\left(\mu_{A^j}(\overline{\mathbf{x}}), p_{j,k}\right)\right)} \tag{5.16}$$

In the similar way, we can present the formula which defines Fodor implication, given by Equation (2.141), as follows

$$\mu_{A^j \to B^j}(\overline{\mathbf{x}}, \overline{y}^k) = \min(1, \max\left(1 - \mu_{A^j}(\overline{\mathbf{x}}), \mu_{B^j}(\overline{y}^k)\right)$$
$$+ \rho\left(\mu_{A^j}(\overline{\mathbf{x}}), \mu_{B^j}(\overline{y}^k)\right)) \tag{5.17}$$

where ρ is given by Equation (5.13). Thus, from formulas (5.5), (5.17), and (4.11), we determine the following description of the OCFS system based on the Fodor fuzzy implication

$$\bar{y} = \frac{\sum\limits_{k=1}^{N} \bar{y}^k \mathop{\mathbf{T}}\limits_{\substack{j=1 \\ j \neq k}}^{N} \min\left(1, \max\left(1 - \mu_{A^j}\left(\bar{\mathbf{x}}\right), p_{j,k}\right) + \rho\left(\mu_{A^j}\left(\bar{\mathbf{x}}\right), p_{j,k}\right)\right)}{\sum\limits_{k=1}^{N} \mathop{\mathbf{T}}\limits_{\substack{j=1 \\ j \neq k}}^{N} \min\left(1, \max\left(1 - \mu_{A^j}\left(\bar{\mathbf{x}}\right), p_{j,k}\right) + \rho\left(\mu_{A^j}\left(\bar{\mathbf{x}}\right), p_{j,k}\right)\right)} \tag{5.18}$$

Note that formula (2.144) which defines Sharp fuzzy implication, can be expressed directly by function (5.13), so the mathematical description of the OCFS system based on this implication, determined from formulas (5.5), (2.144), (5.13), and (4.11), has the form

$$\bar{y} = \frac{\sum\limits_{k=1}^{N} \bar{y}^k \mathop{\mathbf{T}}\limits_{\substack{j=1 \\ j \neq k}}^{N} \rho\left(\mu_{A^j}\left(\bar{\mathbf{x}}\right), p_{j,k}\right)}{\sum\limits_{k=1}^{N} \mathop{\mathbf{T}}\limits_{\substack{j=1 \\ j \neq k}}^{N} \rho\left(\mu_{A^j}\left(\bar{\mathbf{x}}\right), p_{j,k}\right)} \tag{5.19}$$

It is also easy to show [431] that Equation (2.147), which represents the Dubois-Prade implication, can be expressed by

$$\mu_{A^j \to B^j}\left(\bar{\mathbf{x}}, \bar{y}^k\right) = \min(1, 1 - \mu_{A^j}\left(\bar{\mathbf{x}}\right) + \mu_{B^j}\left(\bar{y}^k\right)$$
$$+ \tilde{\delta}\left(\left(1 - \mu_{A^j}\left(\bar{\mathbf{x}}\right)\right)\mu_{B^j}\left(\bar{y}^k\right)\right)) \tag{5.20}$$

where

$$\tilde{\delta}(a) = \begin{cases} 0 & \text{if} \quad a = 0 \\ 1 & \text{otherwise} \end{cases} \tag{5.21}$$

From formulas (5.5), (5.20), and (4.11), the description of the system based on this implication is given as follows

$$\bar{y} = \frac{\sum\limits_{k=1}^{N} \bar{y}^k \mathop{\mathbf{T}}\limits_{\substack{j=1 \\ j \neq k}}^{N} \min\left(1, 1 - \mu_{A^j}\left(\bar{\mathbf{x}}\right) + p_{j,k} + \tilde{\delta}\left(\left(1 - \mu_{A^j}\left(\bar{\mathbf{x}}\right)\right)p_{j,k}\right)\right)}{\sum\limits_{k=1}^{N} \mathop{\mathbf{T}}\limits_{\substack{j=1 \\ j \neq k}}^{N} \min\left(1, 1 - \mu_{A^j}\left(\bar{\mathbf{x}}\right) + p_{j,k} + \tilde{\delta}\left(\left(1 - \mu_{A^j}\left(\bar{\mathbf{x}}\right)\right)p_{j,k}\right)\right)} \tag{5.22}$$

From formulas (5.6), (4.11), and (2.137), we conclude that the OCFS system based on Zadeh implication is described by Equation (3.32), where

$$\lambda_k = T\left(\left(1 - \mu_{A^k}\left(\bar{\mathbf{x}}\right)\right) \vee \mu_{A^k}\left(\bar{\mathbf{x}}\right), \mathop{\mathbf{T}}\limits_{\substack{j=1 \\ j \neq k}}^{N} \left(\left(1 - \mu_{A^j}\left(\bar{\mathbf{x}}\right)\right) \vee \left(\mu_{A^j}\left(\bar{\mathbf{x}}\right) \wedge p_{j,k}\right)\right)\right)$$

$$\tag{5.23}$$

In the same way, from formulas (5.6), (4.11), and (2.142), we obtain the mathematical description of the OCFS system based on the Willmott implication expressed by Equation (3.32), where

$$\lambda_k = T((1 - \mu_{A^k}(\overline{\mathbf{x}})) \vee \mu_{A^k}(\overline{\mathbf{x}}), \underset{\substack{j=1 \\ j \neq k}}{\overset{N}{\mathbf{T}}} ((1 - \mu_{A^j}(\overline{\mathbf{x}})) \vee p_{j,k})$$

$$\wedge (\mu_{A^k}(\overline{\mathbf{x}}) \vee \widetilde{p}_{j,k} \vee ((1 - \mu_{A^k}(\overline{\mathbf{x}})) \wedge p_{j,k})) \tag{5.24}$$

and $\widetilde{p}_{j,k}$ is given by Equation (4.20).

In the case of NOCFS, we assume that condition (4.7) is fulfilled. Thus, substituting $p_{j,k} = 0$ into formulas (5.7), (5.8), (5.9), (5.10), (5.11), (5.12), (5.16), (5.18), (5.19), (5.22), (5.23), and (5.24), we determine the descriptions of the NOCFS systems. In this way, we obtain the same expressions for systems based on the Kleene-Dienes, Łukasiewicz, Reichenbach, stochastic, Dubois-Prade, and Fodor implications. The following equation describes the systems based on these fuzzy implications

$$\overline{y} = \frac{\sum_{k=1}^{N} \overline{y}^k \underset{\substack{j=1 \\ j \neq k}}{\overset{N}{\mathbf{T}}} (1 - \mu_{A^j}(\overline{\mathbf{x}}))}{\sum_{k=1}^{N} \underset{\substack{j=1 \\ j \neq k}}{\overset{N}{\mathbf{T}}} (1 - \mu_{A^j}(\overline{\mathbf{x}}))} \tag{5.25}$$

The NOCFS systems based on the Goguen, Gödel, Sharp, and Yager implications, are represented by the formula

$$\overline{y} = \frac{\sum_{k=1}^{N} \overline{y}^k \underset{\substack{j=1 \\ j \neq k}}{\overset{N}{\mathbf{T}}} \delta(\mu_{A^j}(\overline{\mathbf{x}}))}{\sum_{k=1}^{N} \underset{\substack{j=1 \\ j \neq k}}{\overset{N}{\mathbf{T}}} \delta(\mu_{A^j}(\overline{\mathbf{x}}))} \tag{5.26}$$

where

$$\delta(a) = \begin{cases} 1 & \text{if } a = 0 \\ 0 & \text{if } a > 0 \end{cases} \tag{5.27}$$

It is easy to notice that functions ς and δ, defined by Equations (5.21) and (5.27), respectively, satisfy the following relation

$$\widetilde{\delta} = 1 - \delta \tag{5.28}$$

The NOCFS systems based on Zadeh or Willmott fuzzy implication are described by the following expression

$$
\bar{y} = \frac{\sum\limits_{k=1}^{N} \bar{y}^k \, T\left(\max\left(1 - \mu_{A^k}\left(\bar{\mathbf{x}}\right), \mu_{A^k}\left(\bar{\mathbf{x}}\right)\right), \underset{\substack{j=1 \\ j\neq k}}{\overset{N}{\mathbf{T}}}\left(1 - \mu_{A^j}\left(\bar{\mathbf{x}}\right)\right) \right)}{\sum\limits_{k=1}^{N} T\left(\max\left(1 - \mu_{A^k}\left(\bar{\mathbf{x}}\right), \mu_{A^k}\left(\bar{\mathbf{x}}\right)\right), \underset{\substack{j=1 \\ j\neq k}}{\overset{N}{\mathbf{T}}}\left(1 - \mu_{A^j}\left(\bar{\mathbf{x}}\right)\right) \right)}
\tag{5.29}
$$

It should be noted that the NOCFS systems are represented by Equations (5.25), (5.26), (5.29) if condition (4.7). Unlike in the case of the Mamdani approach (see Section 4.2), where this assumption can be weakened, i.e. replaced by formula (4.9) or (4.16), this is not generally possible for systems based on logical approach. Although assumption (4.9) leads to the same description of a system which employs the Kleene-Dienes implication, it will be different, in this case, for example, for the Łukasiewicz fuzzy implication.

The connectionist, multi-layer architectures of the NOCFS and OCFS systems will be depicted in the next sections. The mathematical formulas which describe the systems will be used to build the architectures.

5.2 NOCFS Architectures

The NOCFS fuzzy systems fulfil assumption (4.7). Examples of non-overlapping consequent fuzzy sets are shown in Fig. 4.4. Three mathematical formulas which describe the NOCFS implication-based systems were determined in Section 5.1. Formula (5.25) represents fuzzy systems based on the Kleene-Dienes, Łukasiewicz, Reichenbach, stochastic, Dubois-Prade, and Fodor implications. Fuzzy systems based on the Goguen, Gödel, Sharp, and Yager implications were described by Equation (5.26). The mathematical description of the systems based on the Zadeh or Willmott fuzzy implication was expressed by formula (5.29). Each of these three equations is a special case of formula (3.32), where

$$
\lambda_k = \underset{j=1}{\overset{N}{\mathbf{T}}}\mu_{A^j \to B^j}\left(\bar{\mathbf{x}}, \bar{y}^k\right) = \begin{cases} \underset{\substack{j=1 \\ j\neq k}}{\overset{N}{\mathbf{T}}}\left(1 - \mu_{A^j}\left(\bar{\mathbf{x}}\right)\right) & \text{for the Kleene-Dienes} \\ & \text{group} \\ \underset{\substack{j=1 \\ j\neq k}}{\overset{N}{\mathbf{T}}}\delta\left(\mu_{A^j}\left(\bar{\mathbf{x}}\right)\right) & \text{for the Goguen group} \end{cases}
\tag{5.30}
$$

and

$$\lambda_k = T \left((1 - \mu_{A^k} (\overline{\mathbf{x}})) \vee \mu_{A^k} (\overline{\mathbf{x}}), \underset{\substack{j=1 \\ j \neq k}}{\overset{N}{T}} (1 - \mu_{A^j} (\overline{\mathbf{x}})) \right) \quad \text{for the Zadeh group}$$

$$(5.31)$$

where δ is given by Equation (5.27).

Thus, these systems can generally be represented in the form of a connectionist, multi-layer network, similar to that illustrated in Fig. 3.10, in Section 3.3, as well as to the architectures depicted in Section 4.2. The neuro-fuzzy architectures which correspond to formulas (5.25), (5.26), and (5.29) are shown in Figs. 5.1, 5.2, 5.3, respectively. We will refer to the systems based on the Kleene-Dienes, Goguen, and Zadeh group of implications, respectively. The first group consists of those systems which employ the Kleene-Dienes, Łukasiewicz, Reichenbach, stochastic, Dubois-Prade, and Fodor implications, as well as others which are described by Equation (5.25). The Goguen group of implications refers to the group of Goguen, Gödel, Sharp, Yager, as well as other implications that lead to the same mathematical description of the fuzzy systems expressed by formula (5.26). The latter group corresponds to the systems described by Equation (5.29), i.e. the systems based on the Zadeh and Willmott implications, as well as others with the same mathematical description. Hence, in the case of NOCFS, the implications used in neuro-fuzzy systems can be classified from the point of view of the mathematical formulas which describe the systems. Each of these groups of systems is represented by a different neuro-fuzzy architecture, portrayed in Figs. 5.1, 5.2, 5.3, respectively.

We should note that the mathematical descriptions of the NOCFS systems based on the Kleene-Dienes and Zadeh group of implications, given by Equations (5.25), and (5.29), respectively, are actually very similar. However, they are different from the description of the systems based on the Goguen group of implications, expressed by formula (5.26). It is easy to see that the architectures of the systems based on the Kleene-Dienes and Zadeh group of implications, illustrated in Figs. 5.1 and 5.3, respectively, are very similar. The latter only differs from the former with regard to the third layer, composed of elements performing the *max* operation. This layer is included in the architecture of the systems based on the Zadeh group of implications, while it does not occur in the architecture of the neuro-fuzzy systems based on the Kleene-Dienes group of implications. Thus, it seems that the performance of the systems based on the Zadeh and Kleene-Dienes group of implications may be similar but can be different from the performance of the systems based on the Goguen group of implications. This will be illustrated in Section 5.4.

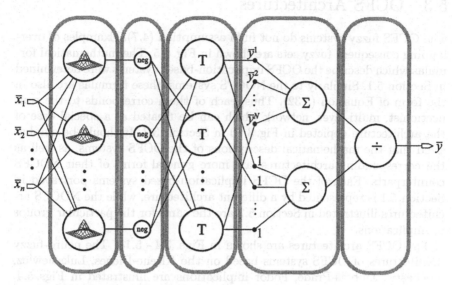

FIGURE 5.1. Neuro-fuzzy architecture of the NOCFS system based on the Kleene-Dienes group of implications

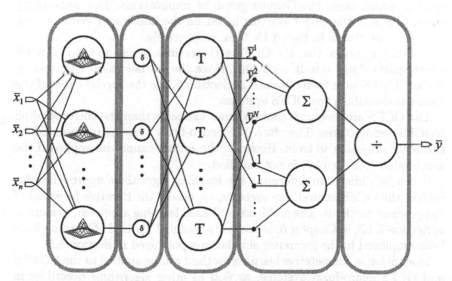

FIGURE 5.2. Neuro-fuzzy architecture of the NOCFS system based on the Goguen group of implications

5.3   OCFS Architectures

The OCFS fuzzy systems do not fulfil assumption (4.7). Examples of overlapping consequent fuzzy sets are shown in Fig. 4.5. The mathematical formulas which describe the OCFS implication-based systems were determined in Section 5.1. Similarly to the NOCFS systems, these formulas are also in the form of Equation (3.32). Thus, each of them corresponds to the connectionist, multi-layer, network which can be treated as a special case of the architecture depicted in Fig. 3.10 in Section 3.3. It should be emphasized that the mathematical descriptions of the OCFS systems, as well as the corresponding architectures, are more general forms of their NOCFS counterparts. Each of the OCFS implication-based systems portrayed in Section 5.1 is represented by a different architecture, while the NOCFS architectures illustrated in Section 5.2 are the same for the particular groups of implications.

The OCFS architectures are shown in Figs. 5.4 - 5.14. The neuro-fuzzy architectures of OCFS systems based on the Kleene-Dienes, Łukasiewicz, stochastic, Dubois-Prade, Fodor implications are illustrated in Figs. 5.4, 5.5, 5.6, 5.7, 5.8, respectively. They belong to the group of neuro-fuzzy systems which employ the Kleene-Dienes group of implications (see Section 5.2). The neuro-fuzzy architectures of the OCFS systems based on the Goguen, Gödel, Sharp, and Yager implications are portrayed in Figs. 5.9, 5.10, 5.11, 5.12, respectively. These constitute the group of neuro-fuzzy systems which apply the Goguen group of implications. The neuro-fuzzy architectures of the OCFS systems based on the Zadeh and Willmott implications are shown in Figs. 5.13, 5.14, respectively.

It is easy to notice that the OCFS architectures reduce to their NOCFS counterparts if $p_{j,k} = 0$. It is obvious, since the mathematical descriptions of the NOCFS have been obtained in Section 5.1 as the special cases of the formulas describing the OCFS systems.

The OCFS architectures contain more elements than the corresponding NOCFS architectures. Therefore, the neuro-fuzzy systems represented by the latter are easier to train. However, the former cannot be applied if the assumption (4.7) or (4.9) is not satisfied.

It can be difficult to determine the learning algorithms appropriate for each of the OCFS neuro-fuzzy systems, especially the iterative formulas of the gradient methods. The architecture-based learning approach, presented in Section 6.1.3, in Chapter 6, is thus very useful. This kind of learning have been employed in the computer simulations portrayed in Section 5.5.

In addition, a competetive learning method can be applied to the NOCFS and OCFS neuro-fuzzy systems, as well as other algorithms described in Chapter 6, especially a hybrid approach.

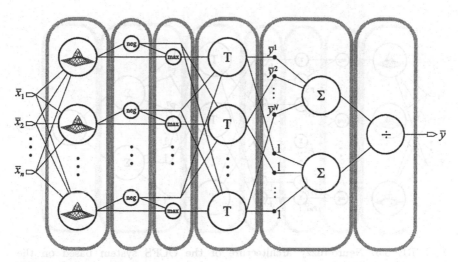

FIGURE 5.3. Neuro-fuzzy architecture of the NOCFS system based on the Zadeh group of implications

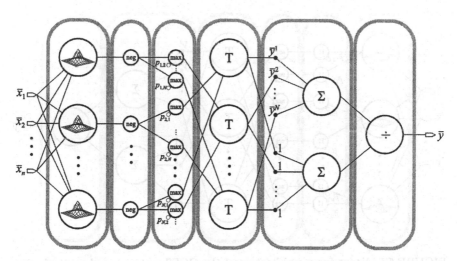

FIGURE 5.4. Neuro-fuzzy architecture of the OCFS system based on the Kleene-Dienes implication

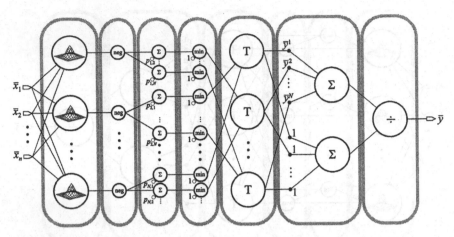

FIGURE 5.5. Neuro-fuzzy architecture of the OCFS system based on the Łukasiewicz implication

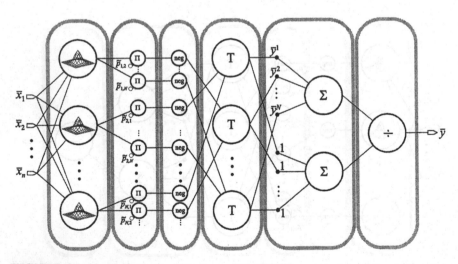

FIGURE 5.6. Neuro-fuzzy architecture of the OCFS system based on stochastic implication

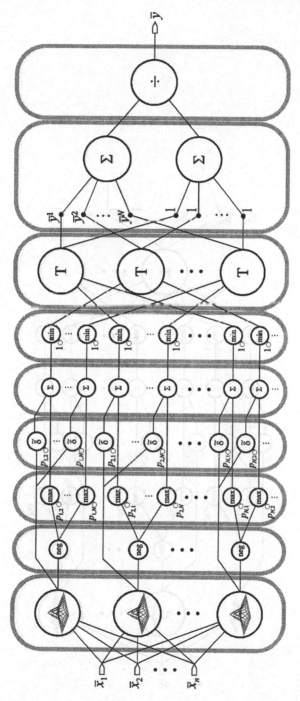

FIGURE 5.7. Neuro-fuzzy architecture of the OCFS system based on the Dubois-Prade implication

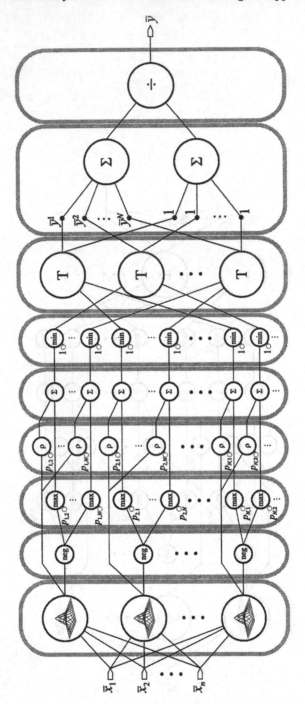

FIGURE 5.8. Neuro-fuzzy architecture of the OCFS system based on the Fodor implication

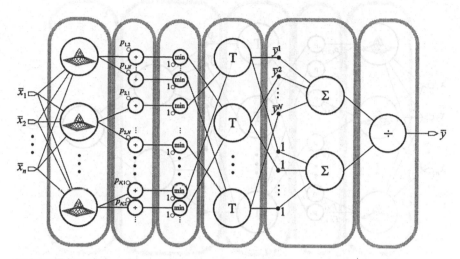

FIGURE 5.9. Neuro-fuzzy architecture of the OCFS system based on the Goguen implication

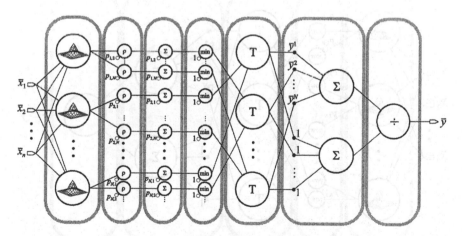

FIGURE 5.10. Neuro-fuzzy architecture of the OCFS system based on the Gödel implication

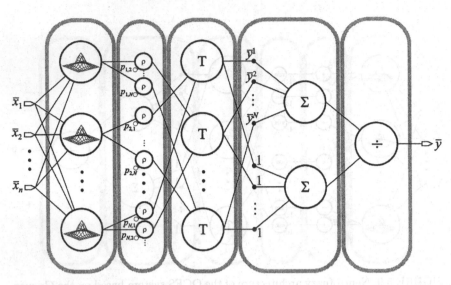

FIGURE 5.11. Neuro-fuzzy architecture of the OCFS system based on the Sharp implication

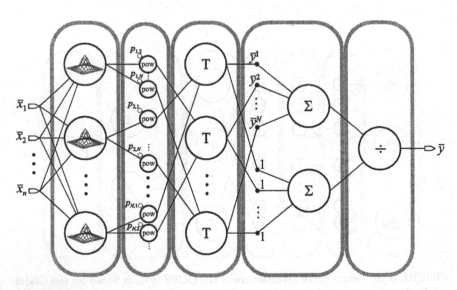

FIGURE 5.12. Neuro-fuzzy architecture of the OCFS system based on the Yager implication

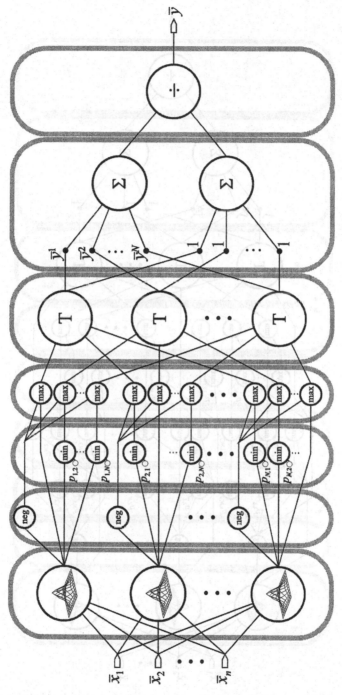

FIGURE 5.13. Neuro-fuzzy architecture of the OCFS system based on the Zadeh implication

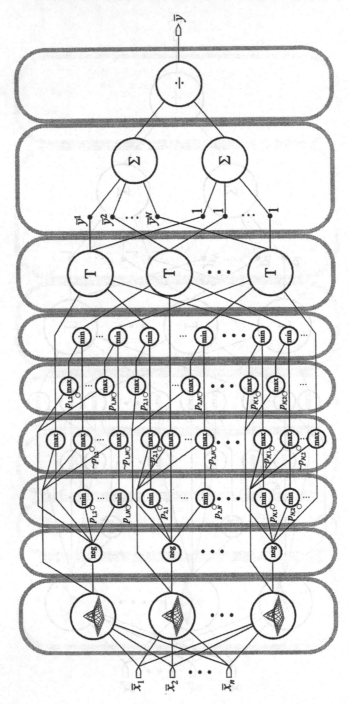

FIGURE 5.14. Neuro-fuzzy architecture of the OCFS system based on the Will-mott implication

5.4   Performance Analysis

In order to analyze the performance of the neuro-fuzzy systems presented in this chapter as well as in Sections 4.1, 4.2, 4.3, let us consider a system with the following rule base

$$R^{(k)} : \textbf{IF } x \text{ is } A^k \textbf{ THEN } y \text{ is } B^k \tag{5.32}$$

where $x \in X \subset \mathbf{R}$, and $y \in Y \subset \mathbf{R}$, are linguistic variables corresponding to the input and output of the system, and $k = 1, ..., N$. Assume that $N = 4$. Formula (5.32) is a special case of the rule base (2.94) and (2.108). This means that we have a single-input, single-output (SISO) system, with 4 rules in the rule base. The crisp input and crisp output are denoted by $\bar{x}$ and $\bar{y}$, respectively.

Each neuro-fuzzy architecture of the systems under consideration therefore contains 4 elements in the first layer. These elements realize the membership functions $\mu_{A^k}(x)$ of the fuzzy sets A^k, for $k = 1, ..., 4$. Gaussian or triangular functions are usually chosen; see Fig. 2.1. The first layer is called the *antecedent layer* in Fig. 3.10. The *aggregation layer* also contains 4 elements which realize the S-norm or T-norm operator, depending whether the Mamdani or logical approach, respectively, is used (Chapter 4 or 5).

In order to compare the performance of these systems, we analyze the outputs of the *aggregation layer*, $\mu_{B'}(\bar{y}^k)$, of each neuro-fuzzy architecture and outputs of the systems, $\bar{y}$, as a function of the input $\bar{x}$, for the same inputs and the same membership functions $\mu_{A^k}(x)$ and $\mu_{B^k}(y)$; $k = 1, ..., 4$.

Figures 5.15 and 5.16 show the Gaussian antecedent fuzzy sets and Gaussian consequent fuzzy sets (the OCFS case), respectively, i.e. the membership functions $\mu_{A^k}(x)$ and $\mu_{B^k}(y)$, for $k = 1, ..., 4$, used to illustrate the system performance. Different types of lines (solid, dotted, dotted-dashed, and dashed) correspond to the four individual rules in the rule base (5.32). The case of the NOCFS need not be portrayed, since only the centers of membership functions $\mu_{B^k}(y)$, for $k = 1, ..., 4$, are important, and there are the same as in Fig. 5.16.

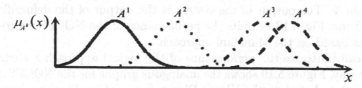

FIGURE 5.15. Gaussian antecedent fuzzy sets

Instead of the Gaussian antecedent fuzzy sets presented in Fig. 5.15, we can employ triangular functions, in the form shown in Fig. 5.17. Note that all the values of the Gaussian membership functions are greater than zero, while the triangular membership functions can take values equal to zero.

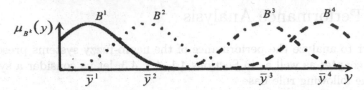

FIGURE 5.16. Gaussian consequent fuzzy sets (OCFS)

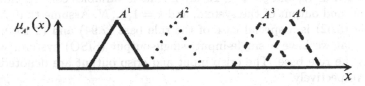

FIGURE 5.17. Triangular antecedent fuzzy sets

Outputs of the *antecedent layer* in the neuro-fuzzy architectures, expressed as functions of inputs $\bar{x}$, are in the form depicted in Figs. 5.15 and 5.17, respectively, where x is replaced by $\bar{x}$. In this way, four functions, $\mu_{A^k}(\bar{x})$, for $k = 1, ..., 4$, corresponding to the output of each element of the antecedent layer, are portrayed in one figure (with the same coordinate axis). Analogously, outputs of the aggregation layer as functions of inputs $\bar{x}$, can be illustrated, using the same types of lines, i.e. solid, dotted, dotted-dashed, and dashed, which are associated with $k = 1, 2, 3, 4$, respectively.

Comparing the general architecture shown in Fig. 3.10 with the NOCFS Mamdani approach system presented in Fig. 4.3, we see that the outputs of the aggregation layer in the latter architecture are the same as the outputs of the antecedent layer. Thus the membership values $\mu_{B'}(\bar{y}^k)$, as functions of $\bar{x}$, have the same form as $\mu_{A^k}(\bar{x})$; see also Equation (4.8). The graphs of these functions, for the Gaussian antecedent fuzzy sets depicted in Fig. 5.15, are shown in Fig. 5.18, which also portrays the output $\bar{y}$ as a function of the input $\bar{x}$. The output of the system is the output of the defuzzification layer. Thus, Fig. 5.18 exhibits the performance of the NOCFS neuro-fuzzy systems based on the Mamdani approach.

We can illustrate the performance of the logical approach systems in a similar way. Figure 5.19 shows the analogous graphs for the NOCFS neuro-fuzzy system based on the Kleene-Dienes group of implications, presented in Fig. 5.1. In this case, the membership values $\mu_{B'}(\bar{y}^k)$, as a function of $\bar{x}$, do not depend on the values of $\mu_{A^k}(\bar{x})$ but on $\mu_{A^j}(\bar{x})$ for $j \neq k$; see Equation (5.30). It is interesting to note that the values of $\bar{x}$ with small antecedent matching degrees (small values of the rule activation degrees), for all rules, i.e. for $k = 1, ..., 4$, imply output values $\bar{y}$ close to the arithmetical average of the centers of the consequent membership functions, $\bar{y}^k$.

The explanation to Equation (5.33) concerning the next neuro-fuzzy system described in this section, also refers to this conclusion.

The graphs that portray the performance of NOCFS systems based on the Zadeh group of implications, depicted in Fig. 5.3, are shown in Fig. 5.20. In this case, the values of $\mu_{B'}\left(\overline{y}^k\right)$, as a function of $\overline{x}$, depend on the values of each $\mu_{A^k}(\overline{x})$ for $k = 1, ..., 4$; see Equation (5.31). Thus, these systems behave similarly to the NOCFS neuro-fuzzy system based on the Kleene-Dienes group of implications. However, the additional influence of those values of $\mu_{A^k}(\overline{x})$ which are taken into account in the Mamdani approach systems, is observed. Normal antecedent fuzzy sets (see Definition 6) are used in Fig. 5.15, so we can easily notice that for the points of $\overline{x}$ which satisfy $\mu_{A^k}(\overline{x}) < 0.5$, the functions $\mu_{B'}\left(\overline{y}^k\right)$, for $k = 1, ..., 4$, in Fig. 5.20 take the same values. From Equation (2.107), which represents the defuzzification method incorporated into the neuro-fuzzy architectures (the defuzzification layer in Fig. 3.10), we conclude that the output values, $\overline{y}$, corresponding to these input points, $\overline{x}$, is equal to the arithmetic average of $\overline{y}^k$, for $k = 1, ..., 4$, that is

$$\overline{y} = \frac{1}{N} \sum_{i=1}^{N} \overline{y}^k \qquad (5.33)$$

for $N = 4$. This constant value of the output $\overline{y}$ is clearly visible for some intervals of the input values $\overline{x}$, at the beginning, two middle parts, and at the end of the graph depicted in Fig. 5.20. For the same values of $\overline{x}$, the output values $\overline{y}$ of the previous system (based on the Kleene-Dienes group of implications) are close to the arithmetical average of $\overline{y}^k$, expressed by Equation (5.33). The values of $\overline{y}$ that correspond to the input values $\overline{x}$ with the highest rule activation degrees are the same for both neuro-fuzzy systems (those based on the Kleene-Dienes as well as the Zadeh group of implications). Note that these input values also give the same output values for the NOCFS system based on the Mamdani approach (Fig. 5.18).

In order to illustrate the performance of the NOCFS neuro-fuzzy system based on the Goguen group of implications, presented in Fig. 5.2, the triangular antecedent fuzzy sets portrayed in Fig. 5.17 have been used instead of the Gaussian ones. This system is described by Equation (5.26). As in the case of systems based on the Kleene-Dienes group of implications, the values of $\mu_{B'}\left(\overline{y}^k\right)$, as a function of $\overline{x}$, do not depend on $\mu_{A^k}(\overline{x})$ but only on $\mu_{A^j}(\overline{x})$ for $j \neq k$; see Equation (5.30). However, the values may be 0 or 1, according to Equation (5.27). Let us notice that in the case of Gaussian antecedent fuzzy sets, the denominator in formula (5.26) always equals zero, so the system can not work. For the triangular antecedent fuzzy sets, the graphs that show the performance of the NOCFS systems based on the Goguen group of implications, are depicted in Fig. 5.21. Comparing the graphs of $\overline{y}$ in Figs. 5.20 and 5.21, we see that the same values of $\overline{x}$ that imply the output values $\overline{y}$ equal to the arithmetical average of $\overline{y}^k$,

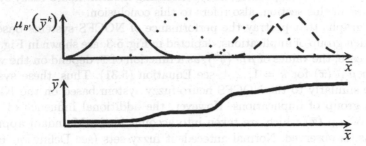

FIGURE 5.18. Performance of the NOCFS Mamdani approach neuro-fuzzy system; with Gaussian membership functions

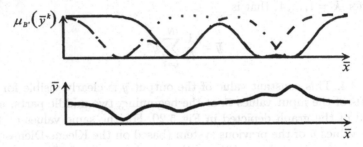

FIGURE 5.19. Performance of the NOCFS neuro-fuzzy system based on the Kleene-Dienes group of implications; with Gaussian membership functions

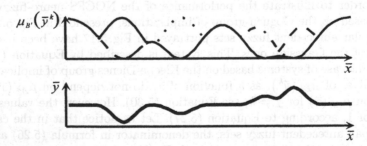

FIGURE 5.20. Performance of the NOCFS neuro-fuzzy system based on the Zadeh group of implications; with Gaussian membership functions

expressed by Equation (5.33), give the same values of $\bar{y}$ for both neuro-fuzzy systems, based on the Zadeh and the Goguen group of implications. Moreover, the system based on the Goguen group of implications produces the same values of the output $\bar{y}$ as all the previously considered systems, for the input values $\bar{x}$ with the highest rule activation degrees.

Triangular antecedent fuzzy sets can be used for all the kinds of systems under consideration. Similar illustrations of the performance of the NOCFS Mamdani approach system, as well as the systems based on the Kleene-Dienes and Zadeh group of implications, can be found in [433].

The performance of the OCFS neuro-fuzzy systems may be portrayed in the same way. Using the Gaussian consequent fuzzy sets shown in Fig. 5.16, we obtain the graphs that do not differ much either from their NOCFS counterparts, or from each other within the groups of implications. To explain this situation, we can observe that values of the $p_{j,k}$ defined by Equation (4.11) are rather small. The higher these values are, the greater are the differences between the graphs, i.e. the performance of the particular neuro-fuzzy systems differ more significantly.

For the OCFS depicted in Fig. 5.16, graphs illustrating how the Mamdani approach systems perform are presented in Figs. 5.22 and 5.23, respectively, for systems based on the Mamdani and Larsen rules of inference, with the architectures shown in Figs. 4.6 and 4.7. These systems are described by Equations (4.14) and (4.15). In this case, the output values $\bar{y}$ depend also on $p_{j,k}$, so the influence of the shapes of the consequent fuzzy sets is visible on the graphs.

The performance of the OCFS neuro-fuzzy systems based on the logical approach, for the Gaussian consequent fuzzy sets, shown in Fig. 5.16, are portrayed by the following graphs. For the Kleene-Dienes group of implications, Figs. 5.24 and 5.25 illustrate the performance of the systems based on the Kleene-Dienes and Łukasiewicz implications, respectively (Figs. 5.4 and 5.5); described by Equations (5.7) and (5.8). Similar graphs represent the behavior of other systems from this implication group. In particular, those that exhibit the performance of the neuro-fuzzy systems based on the Fodor and stochastic implications look almost the same as the graphs depicted in Figs. 5.24 and 5.25, respectively. The mathematical descriptions of these systems are expressed by formulas (5.18) and (5.10). Their architectures are shown in Figs. 5.8 and 5.6.

For the Zadeh group of implications, Fig. 5.26 portrays the graphs illustrating the performance of the OCFS system based on the Zadeh implication. The neuro-fuzzy architecture of this system is depicted in Fig. 5.13 and the mathematical description is given by formulas (3.32), (5.23). A very similar graph has been obtained for the neuro-fuzzy system based on Willmott implication, presented in Fig. 5.14 and described by Equations (3.32), (5.24). The shapes of the functions $\mu_{B'}\left(\bar{y}^k\right)$ are the same as those shown in Fig. 5.26 but the graphs of these functions are slightly separated from each other. The functions of $\bar{y}$ are almost identical for both systems.

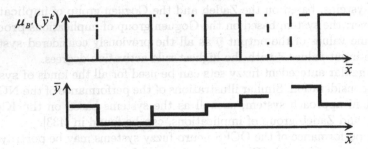

FIGURE 5.21. Performance of the NOCFS neuro-fuzzy system based on the Goguen group of implications; with triangular membership functions

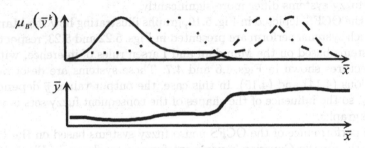

FIGURE 5.22. Performance of the OCFS neuro-fuzzy system based on the Mamdani rule of inference; with Gaussian membership functions

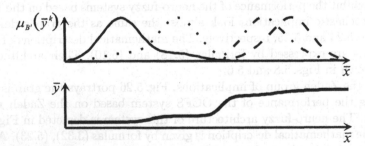

FIGURE 5.23. Performance of the OCFS neuro-fuzzy system based on the Larsen rule of inference; with Gaussian membership functions

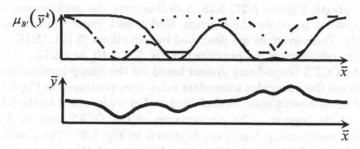

FIGURE 5.24. Performance of the OCFS neuro-fuzzy system based on the
Kleene-Dienes implication; with Gaussian membership functions

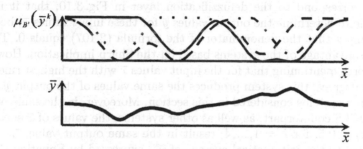

FIGURE 5.25. Performance of the OCFS neuro-fuzzy system based on the
Łukasiewicz implication; with Gaussian membership functions

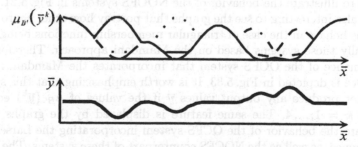

FIGURE 5.26. Performance of the OCFS neuro-fuzzy system based on the Zadeh
implication; with Gaussian membership functions

Now let us consider the OCFS systems related to the Goguen group of implications. Figures 5.27, 5.28, 5.29 illustrate the performance of the OCFS systems based on the Goguen, Gödel, and Yager implications, respectively. These systems are described by Equations (5.12), (5.16), (5.11) and their architectures are presented in Fig. 5.9, 5.10, and 5.12.

For the OCFS neuro-fuzzy system based on the Sharp implication, it is better to use the triangular antecedent fuzzy sets, portrayed in Fig. 5.17, instead of the Gaussian ones, as explained earlier with regard to the NOCFS version of this system. The performance of the OCFS system, for the triangular membership functions, is shown in Fig. 5.30. The mathematical description of this system is given by Equation (5.19), so it is clear that the values of $\mu_{B'}\left(\overline{y}^k\right)$, as a function of $\overline{x}$, are 0 or 1; as also in the NOCFS versions (with the performance illustrated in Fig. 5.21). The neuro-fuzzy architecture of the OCFS system is depicted in Fig. 5.11. As we see in Figs. 5.21 and 5.30, there are some points of $\overline{x}$ where the values of $\mu_{B'}\left(\overline{y}^k\right)$ equal 0, for each $k = 1, ..., 4$. It is easy to conclude from Equation (2.107), which correspond to the defuzzification layer in Fig. 3.10, that it is not possible to determine the output values $\overline{y}$ for these input values $\overline{x}$, because they imply that the denominator of the formula (2.107) equals 0. This is one disadvantage of the systems based on the Sharp implication. However, it is worth mentioning that for the input values $\overline{x}$ with the highest rule activation degrees, this system produces the same values of the output $\overline{y}$ as all the other systems considered in this section. Moreover, in the same way as its NOCFS counterpart, as well as other systems, the values of $\overline{x}$ such that $\mu_{A^k}\left(\overline{x}\right) < 0.5$, for $k = 1, ..., 4$, result in the same output values $\overline{y}$, which are equal to the arithmetical average of $\overline{y}^k$, expressed by Equation (5.33).

In order to compare the performance of the neuro-fuzzy systems related to the Goguen group of implications, in both cases, i.e. the NOCFS and OCFS, graphs for systems based on the Goguen and Gödel implications are presented in Figs. 5.31 and 5.32, respectively. The triangular antecedent fuzzy sets are used, since triangular membership functions have been employed to illustrate the behavior of the NOCFS systems in Fig. 5.21.

It is also interesting to see the graphs that portray how other neuro-fuzzy systems behave in the case of triangular membership functions being used, especially those systems based on the Mamdani approach. Therefore the performance of the OCFS system that incorporates the Mamdani rule of inference is depicted in Fig. 5.33. It is worth emphasizing that this system does not produce any output values $\overline{y}$ if the values of $\mu_{B'}\left(\overline{y}^k\right)$ equal 0 for all $k = 1, ..., 4$. The same feature is displayed by the graphs which illustrate the behavior of the OCFS system incorporating the Larsen rule of inference, as well as the NOCFS counterpart of these systems. The graph of $\mu_{B'}\left(\overline{y}^k\right)$, as a function of $\overline{x}$, in the case of the NOCFS system, with the triangular membership functions, exactly reflects the shape of these functions (Fig. 5.17); just as in the system with Gaussian antecedent fuzzy sets (see Fig. 5.18).

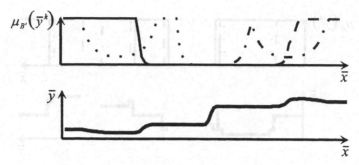

FIGURE 5.27. Performance of the OCFS neuro-fuzzy system based on the Goguen implication; with Gaussian membership functions

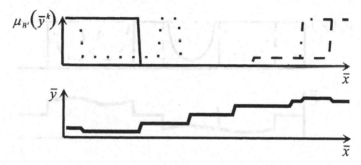

FIGURE 5.28. Performance of the OCFS neuro-fuzzy system based on the Gödel implication; with Gaussian membership functions

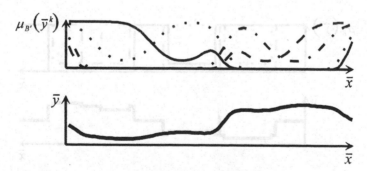

FIGURE 5.29. Performance of the OCFS neuro-fuzzy system based on the Yager implication; with Gaussian membership functions

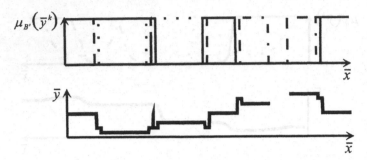

FIGURE 5.30. Performance of the OCFS neuro-fuzzy system based on the Sharp implication; with triangular membership functions

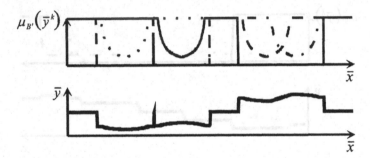

FIGURE 5.31. Performance of the OCFS neuro-fuzzy system based on the Goguen implication; with triangular membership functions

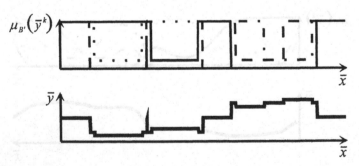

FIGURE 5.32. Performance of the OCFS neuro-fuzzy system based on the Gödel implication; with triangular membership functions

Figures 5.34 and 5.35 exhibit graphs that illustrate the performance of the NOCFS systems based on the Kleene-Dienes group of implications and the OCFS system based on the Lukasiewicz implication, respectively. The latter system is an example of the logical approach systems that belong to the Kleene-Dienes group of implications. The analogical graphs that correspond to other neuro-fuzzy systems included in this group look the same. For instance, the behavior of the OCFS system based on the Kleene-Dienes as well as Fodor implications are portrayed by almost the same graphs as depicted in Fig. 5.34. All the graphs related to the logical approach systems show that those input values $\bar{x}$ which do not imply any output values for the systems based on the Mamdani approach produce the average output values in the systems based on the logical approach.

It is worth mentioning that similar graphs to that depicted in Figs. 5.22 and 5.23 illustrate the performance of the OCFS system based on the bounded product rule of inference (see Section 4.3). The architecture of this system is presented in Fig. 4.8 and the mathematical description is expressed by Equation (4.21). Of course, the graphs are not the same. There are some differences between these graphs and those shown in Figs. 5.22 and 5.23 but, in general, they are much alike, especially the graphs that portray the output values $\bar{y}$ of the systems. It should be emphasized that each of these systems is based on the Mamdani approach.

In this section, the SISO system has been considered with 4 rules for the sake of simplicity, in order to clearly illustrate the performance of different implication-based neuro-fuzzy systems. The perceived features of the systems presented can be generalized for their MISO counterparts, with more rules in the form (2.94) or (2.108). The very important conclusion, obtained from the graphs of the performance, is that all the systems give the same results for the input values with the highest rule activation degrees. The difference between the systems based on the Mamdani and logical approaches may also be observed using the graphs of their behavior. For example, the former systems (Mamdani approach) require complete partitioning of the input space by the antecedent fuzzy sets. They cannot work properly in situations when the activation degree of every rule is equal to zero. The latter systems (logical approach) in this case determine the average output value.

In the next section applications of the neuro-fuzzy systems, based on both the Mamdani and logical approaches, are described. They illustrate the practical performance of the different systems, showing that all of them can be helpful. Their behavior depends on the number of fuzzy IF-THEN rules. The systems must be trained for specific problems, using learning algorithms.

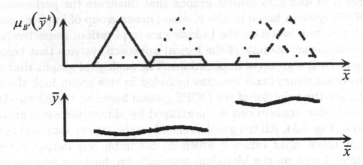

FIGURE 5.33. Performance of the OCFS neuro-fuzzy system based on the Mamdani rule of inference; with triangular membership functions

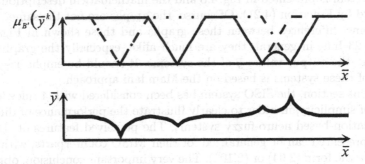

FIGURE 5.34. Performance of the NOCFS neuro-fuzzy system based on the Kleene-Dienes group of implications; with triangular membership functions

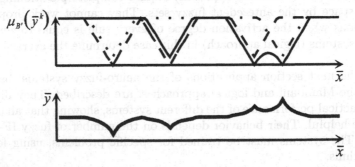

FIGURE 5.35. Performance of the OCFS neuro-fuzzy system based on the Łukasiewicz implication; with triangular membership functions

5.5 Computer Simulations

The neuro-fuzzy systems presented in this book can be employed to solve various tasks. An appropriate neuro-fuzzy architecture with a learning method (usually, a hybrid approach; see Section 6) constitute a system for practical applications. In order to illustrate how different neuro-fuzzy systems perform solving some typical problems, they have been applied to the following tasks: function approximation, control examples, classification problems. The FLiNN program [395], briefly described in Section 6.1.3, has been used to train the systems. The results are portrayed in this section.

5.5.1 Function Approximation

Function approximation is typical of the problems that can be solved by neural networks. In [92] the behavior of different implication-based fuzzy logic systems is tested on the task of linear function approximation ($y = x$). Therefore, this example has also been used to portray the performance of the neuro-fuzzy systems. The simple linear function $y = x$ and the nonlinear function $y = x_1^2 + x_2^2$ have been chosen to be approximated by the systems. Figures 5.36 and 5.37 show the results of approximation of these two functions, respectively. These illustrations refer to most of the neuro-fuzzy system architectures described in Chapter 4 and Sections 5.2, 5.3 of this chapter. A perfect approximation has been obtained for the systems based on the Mamdani approach. Almost all implication-based systems, except the Sharp and Goguen implications, give very good results that are similar to the perfect one or to those portrayed in Figs. 5.36 and 5.37. Of course, the approximation results depend on the number of fuzzy IF-THEN rules incorporated into the systems. It is obvious that the function $y = x_1^2 + x_2^2$ requires more rules than the linear function. It has been observed that the OCFS systems give better results than their NOCFS counterparts [431].

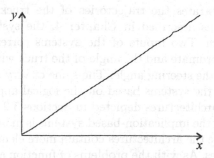

FIGURE 5.36. Approximation of the linear function

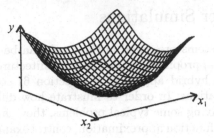

FIGURE 5.37. Approximation of the square function

5.5.2 Control Examples

Control tasks are typical of the problems that are solved by fuzzy systems called fuzzy controllers. The truck backer-upper control problem and the inverted pendulum are very popular examples of control tasks. These examples are most often used in the literature to test performance of fuzzy systems as well as neural networks; see e.g. [359], [166], [360], [268], [273], [513], [200], [470]. Therefore, they have also been chosen to illustrate how the neuro-fuzzy systems, considered in this book, solve control problems.

The truck backer-upper task refers to a truck and its loading zone. The aim is to get the truck to arrive at the loading dock (a small rectangle in the upper side of the loading zone). The truck moves backwards by a fixed unit distance at every stage. The truck position is exactly determined by three state variables: two coordinates that specify the position in the plane (loading zone), and the angle of the truck with the vertical. The control variable is the steering angle, produced while backing the truck up to the loading dock from any initial position and any angle in the loading zone. For the sake of simplicity, we assume that enough clearance exists between the truck and the loading dock, so we can ignore the vertical position coordinate.

Figure 5.38 illustrates the trajectories of the truck controlled by the neuro-fuzzy systems described in Chapter 4, the systems based on the Mamdani approach. Two inputs of the systems correspond to the horizontal position coordinate and the angle of the truck with the vertical. The output variable is the steering angle. The same or very similar results have been obtained for the systems based on the logical approach presented in this chapter (the architectures depicted in Sections 5.2, 5.3). However, the process of training the implication-based systems is more difficult and takes more time, because the architectures contain more elements, especially the OCFS architectures. As with the problems of function approximation (Section 5.5.1), the systems based on the Sharp and Goguen implications are not well suited to solving control tasks. However, it is possible to get the result shown in Fig. 5.38 by use of the Sharp implication-based system

[430]. The truck backer-upper control example has also been used to test a neuro-fuzzy system with a non-singleton fuzzifier (Section 4.6) in [424].

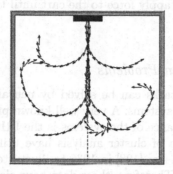

FIGURE 5.38. Illustration of the truck backer-upper control problem

The inverted pendulum problem, applied in testing neuro-fuzzy systems' performance, gives similar conclusions to that of the truck backer-upper control problem. Figure 5.39 is an illustration of the inverted pendulum stabilization by neuro-fuzzy systems with two inputs corresponding to the angle and the angular velocity. More details about this control example and similar results obtained by testing a system with a neural network as a defuzzifier (Section 4.5.2) and hybrid learning are presented in [422].

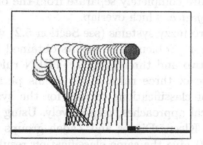

FIGURE 5.39. Illustration of the inverted pendulum control problem

The inverted pendulum example is a classical control task with two state variables and one control variable. The first state variable is the *angle* of the pendulum shaft (pole) with respect to the vertical. The pole is balanced on the moving cart and is free to rotate on the vertical plane of the cart. The vertical position of the pole corresponds to the zero value of the angle. Positive values of the angle are to the right of the vertical, negative values are to the left. Thus the angle ranges from -90 to 90. The second state variable is the *angular velocity* of the pole, i.e. the instantaneous rate of change of angle values, usually measured, in practice, as the difference between successive angle values. The control variable is the motor (cart) velocity, which can be positive if the pendulum falls to the left, negative if it falls to the right, and zero if the pendulum successfully balances on the vertical. The goal is to apply force to the cart until the pole is balanced in a vertical position.

5.5.3   Classification Problems

Various classification tasks can be solved by neural-networks, fuzzy systems, and neuro-fuzzy systems. A very well known problem, which is often chosen to test performance of the systems is the IRIS classification. Many researchers in the area of cluster analysis have utilized Anderson's IRIS data, firstly used by Fisher [128] in 1936 to illustrate the concept of linear discriminant analysis. Therefore, these data have also been applied to test the systems described in Chapter 4 and Sections 5.2, 5.3. Moreover, other classification tasks have been solved by these systems, including medical diagnosis problems. The so-called *semi-ring classification* problem is presented in this section, and results of some medical applications are outlined.

The IRIS data set is composed of 150 data items, containing flower measurements from three species of iris: *Setosa*, *Versicolor*, and *Virginica*. The data include information about four features of the iris flowers: *sepal length*, *sepal width*, *petal length*, *petal width*. In this data set, there are 50 data items corresponding to each of the iris species. It is worth mentioning that the data of *Setosa* are completely separate from the other two classes, i.e. *Versicolor*, and *Virginica*, which overlap.

The NOCFS neuro-fuzzy systems (see Section 5.2) were applied to solve the IRIS classification problem. The results obtained by the systems constructed based on two and three fuzzy IF-THEN rules are shown in Table 5.1. In the case of three rules, the systems perform similarly, with 97.33% and 98% of classifications correct for the systems based on the Mamdani and logical approaches, respectively. Using only two rules, systems based on the Kleene-Dienes and Zadeh groups of implications (see Section 5.1 and 5.2) give the same classification results as systems based on the Mamdani approach that incorporate three rules. For the Goguen group of implications, the neuro-fuzzy systems perform much worse: in the case of two rules, almost the same as the systems with the Mamdani approach type of inference. These results are also presented in [430].

TABLE 5.1. Results of IRIS classification

NOCFS neuro-fuzzy systems	2 rules	3 rules
The Mamdani approach systems	66.67%	97.33%
The Kleene-Dienes group of implications	97.33%	98.00%
The Goguen group of implications	67.33%	98.00%
The Zadeh group of implications	97.33%	98.00%

Another task is related to the semi-ring regions located within the area of a square, as shown in Fig. 5.40 (a). This problem is referred to as the *semi-ring classification*. Each point in the square area belongs to one of three classes. Two of them are the semi-rings and the third class is composed of the points not included in the semi-rings. The points which belong to the first and second classes are associated with numbers 1 and -1, respectively. The points located in the area beyond the regions of the semi-rings (the third class) are assigned to number 0. In order to perform the classification, a learning sequence of 1089 points, evenly placed on the square area, with properly associated numbers 1, -1, or 0, has been created.

Different neuro-fuzzy systems, based on the Mamdani and logical approaches, were applied to solve the semi-ring classification task. The two coordinate values of the points in the square area were fed to the inputs of the systems. The output represented the class corresponding to a classified point. The architectures of the systems incorporated ten fuzzy IF-THEN rules in the form (2.108), where $n = 2$, and $N = 10$. Five of these rules referred to the first class, and the other five to the second class. Figure 5.40 (b) portrays 10 points that are the centers of the membership functions of the fuzzy sets in the antecedent parts of the rules. The centers of the membership functions of the fuzzy sets in the consequent parts of the rules equaled 1 or -1, respectively, depending on the class. We should remember that there are no rules concerning the third class.

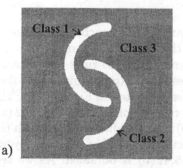 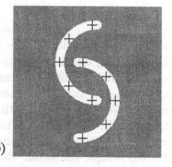

FIGURE 5.40. Illustration of the semi-ring classification: a) class arrangement, b) location of the centers of antecedent membership functions

After the learning process, with Gaussian membership functions, the systems were tested on a sequence of 4225 points, evenly placed on the square area. The results are presented in [430]. The general conclusion is that logical implication-based systems can solve the semi-ring classification task using the rules depicted in Fig. 5.40 (b), which is not sufficient for the systems based on Mamdani approach. The latter systems need additional rules related to the third class, i.e. rules with centers of antecedent membership functions located in the area beyond the semi-rings. This is shown in [428], using the basic Larsen system (Fig. 4.2) and the NOCFS system based on the Kleene-Dienes implication (Fig. 5.1). The NOCFS Larsen system as well as the Mamdani system (Fig. 4.1), i.e. the NOCFS systems based on the Mamdani approach (Fig. 4.3), cannot perform the classification without the additional rules and give the result illustrated in Fig. 5.41 (a). The NOCFS systems based on the Kleene-Dienes implication (and Łukasiewicz, Reichenbach, Fodor implications), with the same rules, classify points in the square area as shown in Fig. 5.41 (b).

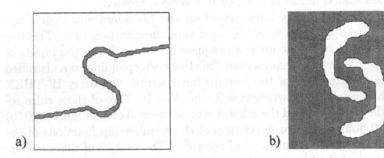

FIGURE 5.41. Classification results: a) for NOCFS systems based on the Mamdani approach, b) for NOCFS systems based on the Kleene-Dienes group of implications

The NOCFS systems based on the Mamdani approach, as mentioned earlier, need additional rules concerning the third class in order to solve the semi-ring classification task. If the systems use 10 rules with 6 rules corresponding to the semi-rings and 4 rules related to the third class, they perform better than in the case of the rules presented in Fig. 5.40 (b). The result of the classification with the 6 plus 4 rules is portrayed in Fig. 5.42 (a). Applying the rules depicted in Fig. 5.40 (b) plus 4 additional rules with the centers of the antecedent membership functions located in the area beyond the semi-rings, the result shown in Fig. 5.42 (b) is obtained. As we see, this result is similar to that illustrated in Fig. 5.41 (b), which refers to the NOCFS systems based on the Kleene-Dienes group of implications.

The classification results of neuro-fuzzy systems based on both the Mamdani and logical approaches are much better than those presented in Figs. 5.41 (b) and 5.42 (b) if the number of rules is increased. In this case, results of the semi-ring classification by both kinds of the systems bear much more resemblance to the class arrangement illustrated in Fig. 5.40. However, it is worth emphasizing that systems based on logical implications can solve classification problems in situations where systems based on the Mamdani approach do not.

Another conclusion that can be drawn from the comparison of the semi-ring classification performed by different neuro-fuzzy systems [430] is the

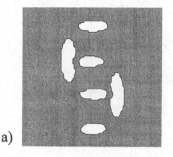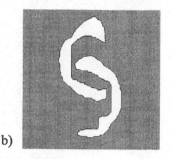

a)   b)

FIGURE 5.42. Results of the classification by NOCFS system based on the Mamdani approach: with 6+4=10 rules, b) with 10+4=14 rules

following: in many cases, the OCFS systems give better results than their
NOCFS counterparts.

One of the medical diagnosis problems refers to tumors in the mucous
membrane of the uterus. The data of 65 women (52 sick and 13 healthy)
were collected and analyzed. Each woman's record contains 9 attributes,
namely: period of time after menopause, body mass index, luteinizing hormone, follicle-stimulating hormone, prolactin, estrone, estriadol, aromatase,
estrogenic receptor. A final attribute, which is a diagnosis of the tumor, is
also included in each of the records. The diagnosis is expressed as values
of 0 or 1, for healthy or sick women, respectively. The data were received
from a hospital in Czestochowa, Poland [420].

Various neuro-fuzzy systems can be created in order to solve the medical
diagnosis problem. They can incorporate different numbers of rules. However, two rules in the form (2.108) are sufficient to obtain a result with
100% (or almost 100%) correct answers concerning the diagnosis. The systems have 9 inputs corresponding to the attributes and one output that
refers to the diagnosis. All the kinds of systems presented in Chapter 4 and
Sections 5.2, 5.3 of this chapter, after a proper learning process, in most
cases give the same very good final result. For details, see [420], [367], [429].

Other medical diagnosis tasks that can be solved by neuro-fuzzy systems
are described in Section 6.5.3, in Chapter 6. For example, the percentage
of correct system responses concerning the diagnosis of the breast cancer
problem ranges from 97.87% to 98.72%, depending on the kind of systems
employed.

It has been shown that neuro-fuzzy systems based on logical implication can solve various classification problems, such as IRIS, the semi-ring
task, and medical diagnosis, with better results than systems based on
the Mamdani approach, especially in situations where the number of fuzzy
IF-THEN rules is not great, which means that it is not sufficient for the
latter systems but good enough for the former ones.

6
Hybrid Learning Methods

In Chapters 4 and 5 the connectionist, multi-layer architectures of fuzzy systems, called *fuzzy inference neural networks*, were presented. These architectures are similar to neural networks (see Section 3.1), so learning algorithms can be proposed to tune the parameters of the networks, analogously to tuning *weights* in neural networks. The parameters of the neuro-fuzzy architectures define the shape of membership functions of the fuzzy sets in the IF-THEN rules. Tuning these parameters thus optimizes the form of the rules. Moreover, the number of rules in the rule base of the fuzzy systems can be determined using a learning method. The number of elements in the first layers of the neuro-fuzzy architectures depends on the number of the rules, so this kind of algorithms determines the architectures. Hybrid learning, which is the subject of this chapter, consists of a combination of different learning methods, such as gradient, genetic, and clustering algorithms. These methods are first described, and then the hybrid algorithms for rule generation and parameter tuning are presented, including the algorithms proposed in [479], [438], [439], [440], [480], [481].

6.1 Gradient Learning Algorithms

The most popular method of neural network learning is the *back-propagation* algorithm (see Section 3.1.3). It allows *weights* of neural networks to be tuned to the optimal values. The idea for the back-propagation learning comes from the steepest descent optimization algorithm [98], which is a gradient method. This idea has also been employed in order to adjust parameters of fuzzy (neuro-fuzzy) systems. These parameters are usually *centers* and *widths* of membership functions of fuzzy sets in the IF-THEN rules. The methods of tuning the parameters are iterative formulas, similar to the back-propagation algorithm, but applied to neuro-fuzzy systems in the form of a connectionist, multi-layer, architecture. Therefore, it is often stated that this kind of fuzzy system learning has been derived from neural networks. However, the formulas of learning fuzzy and neuro-fuzzy systems can be obtained directly from the steepest descent optimization method.

6.1.1   Learning of Fuzzy Systems

Fuzzy systems applied as fuzzy controllers can be designed as adaptive control systems [14]. These kind of systems possess an adaptation mechanism which allows them to alter their parameters in order to achieve better performance. Fuzzy controllers are knowledge-based systems. The knowledge base consists of a data base and a rule base. Both the data base and the rule base contain fuzzy sets (membership functions) representing the meaning of the linguistic values of the process state and control output variables. Adaptive fuzzy controllers that modify the rules are called *self-organizing* controllers. They can either modify an existing set of rules or they can start with no rules at all and then "learn" their control strategy. In the former case, the systems are similar to *self-tuning* controllers, which only adjust parameters of the membership functions, so they alter the shapes of the fuzzy sets defining the meaning of linguistic values. Recent work has been focused on the use of mathematical optimization techniques to tune the fuzzy controllers.

The membership functions employed in the rule base can be tuned by the gradient descent method. This method relies on having a set of training data against which the system (controller) is tuned. If a reliable set of controller input-output data is available, it is possible to tune the membership functions, using a numerical optimization procedure. A basic example of this is given in [363], where the gradient descent method is applied to tune simple (triangular) membership functions (see also [111]). For details on the steepest descent algorithm, see e.g. [446].

The rule base of the control system considered in this example is in the form (2.94), where $x_1, \dots, x_n$ are the controller inputs (process-state variables), and y is the control output variable, $A_1^k, \dots, A_n^k$ are the linguistic values of the rule antecedent, and B^k is the linguistic value of the rule consequent, k is the rule number, $k = 1, \dots, N$. The membership functions of A_i^k, for $i = 1, \dots, n$, are triangular functions (simple symmetrical triangles) with *centers* $\overline{x}_i^k$ and *support* s_i^k. The triangular membership functions are shown in Fig. 2.1, as well as in Fig. 6.1 in the next section. The *centers* are the peak points, i.e. points in the universe of discourse (real numbers **R**) with the maximal values of the membership functions (equal

1), that is the *core* (Definition 4). The *support* (Definition 2) represents the *width* parameter of the triangular membership function. The following formula expresses this membership function:

$$\mu_{A_i^k}(x_i) = \begin{cases} 1 - \frac{2|x_i - \overline{x}_i^k|}{s_i^k} & \text{for} \quad |x_i - \overline{x}_i^k| \leqslant \frac{s_i^k}{2} \\ 0 & \text{otherwise} \end{cases} \tag{6.1}$$

The control-output membership functions of B^k, for $k = 1, \ldots, N$, in the example presented in [363] and [111], are *fuzzy singletons* (see Definition 3), $\overline{y}^k$, defined on the real number universe of discourse. The system under consideration is the multi-input, single-output (MISO) system. Remember that the fuzzy systems described in Section 2.3.3 employ the *non-singleton*, i.e. Gaussian, triangular (or other types) output membership functions, where $\overline{y}^k$ denote the *centers* of the membership functions. The *singletons* B^k are characterized by the membership function, $\mu_{B^k}(y)$, which is equal to 1 for $y = \overline{y}^k$, and 0 for $y \neq \overline{y}^k$.

The *max-product* composition (Section 2.3.3) and the *center-of-area* defuzzification method (Section 2.3.1) have been used in this example of fuzzy control systems. Thus, the crisp output, inferred from the rule base, is given by Equations (2.129), (2.130), and (6.1), where $\overline{y}^k$, for $k = 1, \ldots, N$, denote the *singleton* values. It is obvious that the same formulas would describe the system if the *center average* defuzzification method, given by Equation (2.105), was applied instead of the COA method.

If a set of operating data that represents the desirable control-output, denoted by y^*, is available for various values of the process-state, $x_1^*, \ldots, x_n^*$, then the fuzzy controller can be optimized by minimizing one of the criteria on the error between the controller output, expressed by Equations (2.129), (2.130), (6.1), and the desired output given by the reference data. By substitution of formulas (6.1) and (2.130) into (2.129), we have an expression for the crisp control-output, $\overline{y}$, in terms of the membership function parameters $\overline{x}_i^k$, s_i^k, and $\overline{y}^k$, for $i = 1, \ldots, n$, and $k = 1, \ldots, N$. These are the parameters to be tuned by the optimization procedure.

The following objective function E, was minimized in [363]

$$E = \frac{1}{2}(\overline{y} - y^*)^2 \tag{6.2}$$

where y^* is the desired real-valued control output as given by the reference data, and $\overline{y}$ is the controller output for a particular process-state (input).

The steepest descent optimization algorithm is applied in [363] in order to minimize criterion (6.2). This algorithm is an iterative method that seeks to decrease the value of the objective function with each iteration. It relies on the fact that the objective function decreases most rapidly from any point in the direction of the negative gradient vector of its parameters at that point. If we have, for instance, the objective function $E(\Omega)$, where

$\Omega = [\omega_1, \ldots \omega_r]^T$ is the vector of the parameters, then the gradient vector is in the form

$$\left[-\frac{\partial E}{\partial \omega_1}, \ldots, -\frac{\partial E}{\partial \omega_r} \right]$$

If $\omega_j(t)$ is the value of the j-th parameter, $j = 1, \ldots, r$, at iteration t, the steepest descent algorithm seeks to decrease the value of the objective function by modifying this parameter via the following recursion

$$\omega_j(t+1) = \omega_j(t) - \eta \frac{\partial E(\Omega)}{\partial \omega_j(t)} \qquad (6.3)$$

where η is a constant which controls how much the parameters are altered at each iteration. It can be difficult to choose a suitable value for the stepsize constant (see e.g. [446] for details). As the iterations proceed, the objective function converges to a local minimum.

In the case of the fuzzy system under consideration, the parameters to be modified according to formula (6.3) are parameters of the triangular membership functions, $\overline{x}_i^k$, s_i^k, as well as the output singleton values $\overline{y}^k$, for $i = 1, \ldots, n$, and $k = 1, \ldots, N$. Thus, the parameter vector Ω is

$$[\omega_1, \ldots \omega_r]^T = \left[\overline{x}_1^1, \ldots, \overline{x}_n^N, s_1^1, \ldots, s_n^N, \overline{y}^1, \ldots, \overline{y}^N \right]^T$$

where $r = 2nN + N$.

Substituting Equations (2.130) and (2.129) into (6.2) gives the objective function E, in terms of the membership functions defined by formula (6.1), that is

$$E = \frac{1}{2} \left(\frac{\sum_{k=1}^{N} \overline{y}^k \prod_{i=1}^{n} \mu_{A_i^k}(x_i^*)}{\sum_{k=1}^{N} \prod_{i=1}^{n} \mu_{A_i^k}(x_i^*)} - y^* \right)^2 \qquad (6.4)$$

It should be noted that the value of E, determined from Equation (6.4), depends on the values of the input-output data x_i^* and y^*.

The steepest descent algorithm, applied to the parameters $\overline{x}_i^k$, s_i^k, $\overline{y}^k$, for $i = 1, \ldots, n$, and $k = 1, \ldots, N$, uses the iterative formulas

$$\overline{x}_i^k(t+1) = \overline{x}_i^k(t) - \eta_1 \frac{\partial E}{\partial \overline{x}_i^k} \qquad (6.5)$$

$$s_i^k(t+1) = s_i^k(t) - \eta_2 \frac{\partial E}{\partial s_i^k} \qquad (6.6)$$

$$\overline{y}^k(t+1) = \overline{y}^k(t) - \eta_3 \frac{\partial E}{\partial \overline{y}^k} \qquad (6.7)$$

where η_1, η_2, η_3 are constants. Taking the partial derivatives of E, using Equation (6.1), the following recursions have been obtained from (6.5), (6.6), (6.7); see [363], [111]

$$\overline{x}_i^k (t+1) = \overline{x}_i^k (t) - \eta_1 \frac{\tau_k \left(\overline{y} - y^*\right) \left(\overline{y}^k (t) - \overline{y}\right)}{\sum_{j=1}^{N} \tau_j} \frac{2sgn \left(x_i^* - \overline{x}_i^k\right)}{s_i^k (t) \, \mu_{A_i^k} (x_i^*)} \tag{6.8}$$

$$s_i^k (t+1) = s_i^k (t) - \eta_2 \frac{\tau_k \left(\overline{y} - y^*\right) \left(\overline{y}^k (t) - \overline{y}\right)}{\sum_{j=1}^{N} \tau_j} \frac{\left(1 - \mu_{A_i^k} (x_i^*)\right)}{s_i^k (t) \, \mu_{A_i^k} (x_i^*)} \tag{6.9}$$

$$\overline{y}^k (t+1) = \overline{y}^k (t) - \eta_3 \frac{\tau_k}{\sum_{j=1}^{N} \tau_j} \left(\overline{y} - y^*\right) \tag{6.10}$$

where τ_k is given by Equation (2.130), replacing $\overline{x}_i$ by x_i^*, and $\mu_{A_i^k} (x_i^*)$ is defined by formula (6.1).

Once a set of reliable controller input-output data $\{x_1^*, \dots, x_n^*, y^*\}$ has been collected, the optimization procedure according to recursions (6.8), (6.9), (6.10) can be performed, assuming initial values of the parameters $\overline{x}_i^k$, s_i^k, $\overline{y}^k$, for $t = 0$. The membership functions $\mu_{A_i^k} (x_i)$ are initially defined such that the input domains are divided equally, by a suitable choice of the *centers* $\overline{x}_i^k$, and the sets overlap, by a suitable choice of their *supports* s_i^k. The output *singleton* values $\overline{y}^k$ are chosen to give a suitable range of controller outputs covering, for example, a large decrease, small decrease, no change, small increase, and a large increase.

The optimization procedure is conducted as follows:

- The IF-THEN rules are fired on the input data $\{x_1^*, \dots, x_n^*\}$ to obtain the antecedent values, τ_k, for $k = 1, \dots, N$, and the crisp (real-valued) control-output, $\overline{y}$, using Equation (2.129).

- Parameters $\overline{y}^k$ are updated according to recursion (6.10).

- Rule firing is repeated applying the new values of $\overline{y}^k$.

- Parameters $\overline{x}_i^k$ and s_i^k are updated by recursions (6.8) and (6.9), using the new values of $\overline{y}^k$, τ_k, and $\overline{y}$.

- The inference error is calculated according to Equation (6.2).

- If the change-of-error, obtained from Equation (6.2), is suitably small, the optimization is complete; otherwise it is repeated from the beginning (first step).

This procedure will modify the actual values, $\bar{y}^k$, used for the controller outputs, and will change the *centers* $\bar{x}_i^k$ and *width* parameters s_i^k of the antecedent fuzzy sets A_i^k, for $i = 1, \ldots, n$. In this way the fuzzy IF-THEN rules will be adjusted in order to achieve the best performance of the controller (the minimal value for the inference error).

The optimization procedure has been employed in several simulated systems, including the problem of a mobile robot avoiding a moving obstacle, with some success; see [363] and [111].

The gradient descent method described above is essentially for use offline. However, adaptive controller architectures have also been developed for on-line tuning by this method, for example [148]; but in this system only the rule consequent membership functions can be tuned via Equation (6.10). Other adaptive controllers, which modify their membership functions on-line, have been proposed, applying methods other than the gradient descent optimization; see e.g. [19].

The iterative formulas (6.8), (6.9), (6.10) constitute the learning algorithm of the fuzzy systems under consideration. These systems are Mamdani approach systems, MISO, with a singleton fuzzifier, triangular antecedent membership functions, singleton consequent membership functions, the *max-min* inference method, and the COA defuzzifier (see Section 2.3). Similar learning algorithms can be determined for the antecedent membership functions which are different from the triangular ones.

We should note that the gradient learning algorithm, given by recursions (6.8), (6.9), (6.10), refers to the system described by Equation (2.129). The same mathematical description has been obtained for systems with non-singleton consequent fuzzy sets and the CA defuzzification method (see Section 2.3.3). Thus the learning algorithm presented in this section can also be suitable for systems with triangular antecedents as well as consequent fuzzy membership functions. In this case, the consequent membership functions could also be Gaussian or other-shaped functions, since only the *centers* of this functions are significant.

It is worth emphasizing that the possibility of applying the gradient learning algorithm to fuzzy systems does not mean that these systems have the same learning ability as neural networks. As mentioned before, the gradient algorithm is usually employed off-line. In this way the fuzzy IF-THEN rules are extracted, so a suitable rule base (with the optimized rules) is created, to solve the problem (for example, a control problem). Thus, this "learning" algorithm is in fact a method of generating fuzzy IF-THEN rules from input-output data, and in this sense it can be viewed in a similar way as, for instance, the table-lookup scheme of rule generating [513]. Although, the latter method is also called a "learning" or "training" method, because it uses *learning* (*training*) input-output data, the key idea of this method is to generate fuzzy rules from the input-output pairs, collect the rules into a rule base, and construct a fuzzy logic system. This system thus works, using the prepared rule base, in order to solve a certain problem.

Unlike neural networks, which modify their weights during performance, the constructed fuzzy system does not change the generated rule base when it is solving the problem.

6.1.2   Learning of Neuro-Fuzzy Systems

In Section 6.1.1 the gradient learning algorithm of the Mamdani approach fuzzy systems, with triangular membership functions, was presented. It was mentioned that a similar algorithm can be determined for the membership functions of other shapes. However, it might be very difficult to obtain iterative formulas for tuning the parameters of the membership functions, if these functions are not differentiable. From this point of view, the Gaussian membership functions are very convenient, even more so than the triangular ones.

In [513] the gradient algorithm, similar to that described in Section 6.1.1, was determined for the fuzzy logic systems, MISO, using the Mamdani approach, with a singleton fuzzifier, CA defuzzifier, and Gaussian membership functions. Lemmas 1 and 2, included in Section 2.3.3, were formulated for these systems. In general, the steepest descent optimization method can be employed to tune the parameters of the membership functions to the fuzzy systems described by Equations (2.126) or (2.127). Triangular or Gaussian membership functions (as well as others) can be used. The parameters, which can be modified during the learning algorithm, are indicated in Figs. 6.1 and 6.2. The triangular function parameters, *centers* $\bar{x}_i^k$ and *widths* s_i^k, tuned by the algorithm presented in Section 6.1.1, are shown in Fig. 6.1. The analogical parameters, also called *centers* and *widths*, denoted $\bar{x}_i^k$ and σ_i^k, respectively, for the Gaussian membership function, are illustrated in Fig. 6.2.

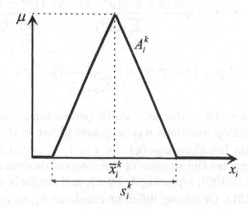

FIGURE 6.1. *Center* and *width* parameters of triangular membership function

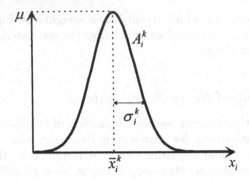

FIGURE 6.2. *Center* and *width* parameters of Gaussian membership function

It is easier to determine the gradient learning algorithm for the system described by Equation (2.127) with Gaussian membership functions. This system is referred to in Lemma 2, and uses the *product* operation, while the system depicted in Lemma 1 employs the *min* operation. Unfortunately, the *min* is not a differentiable function, but it is possible to determine the learning algorithm in this case; see e.g. [420]. Now, let us consider a system with the *product* operation and Gaussian membership functions. In the same way as in Section 6.1.1, by applying the steepest descent optimization method to minimize the objective function (6.2), the following recursions have been obtained in [513]; see also [300], [301], [434]

$$\overline{x}_i^k(t+1) = \overline{x}_i^k(t) - \eta \frac{\tau_k(\overline{y} - y^*)(\overline{y}^k(t) - \overline{y})}{\sum_{j=1}^{N} \tau_j} \frac{2(x_i^* - \overline{x}_i^k)}{(\sigma_i^k(t))^2} \tag{6.11}$$

$$\sigma_i^k(t+1) = \sigma_i^k(t) - \eta \frac{\tau_k(\overline{y} - y^*)(\overline{y}^k(t) - \overline{y})}{\sum_{j=1}^{N} \tau_j} \frac{2(x_i^* - \overline{x}_i^k)^2}{(\sigma_i^k(t))^3} \tag{6.12}$$

$$\overline{y}^k(t+1) = \overline{y}^k(t) - \eta \frac{\tau_k}{\sum_{j=1}^{N} \tau_j}(\overline{y} - y^*) \tag{6.13}$$

where $\overline{x}_i^k$, σ_i^k are the *center* and *width* parameters, respectively of the Gaussian membership functions $\mu_{A_i^k}(x_i)$, and $\overline{y}^k$ are *centers* of the consequent membership functions $\mu_{B^k}(y)$, for $i = 1, \dots, n$, and $k = 1, \dots, N$, the constant η denotes the stepsize of the steepest descent algorithm, τ_k is given by formula (2.130), replacing $\overline{x}_i$ by x_i^*, and similarly $\mu_{A_i^k}(x_i)$ defined by Equation (2.131). Of course, different constants η_1, η_2, η_3 can be used in these recursions instead of η.

The *momentum* terms $\beta(\overline{x}_i^k(t) - \overline{x}_i^k(t-1))$, $\beta(\sigma_i^k(t) - \sigma_i^k(t-1))$, and $\beta(\overline{y}^k(t) - \overline{y}^k(t-1))$, where $t = 0, 1, , 2, \dots$, and β is a constant, called the *momentum coefficient* (see Section 3.1), can be added to Equations (6.11), (6.12), and (6.13), respectively, in order to speed up the convergence [424], [423]. Different values of the β coefficients can be used in each recursion, as can different values of the learning coefficient, η.

The iterative expressions (6.11), (6.12), (6.13) constitute the algorithm for tuning the parameters $\overline{x}_i^k$, σ_i^k, $\overline{y}^k$, for $i = 1, \ldots, n$, and $k = 1, \ldots, N$, of the Gaussian membership functions, in the same way as the analogical equations determined in Section 6.1.1 for tuning the parameters of the triangular membership functions. Thus, this algorithm can be performed in the same way and viewed as a method of generating fuzzy IF-THEN rules from input-output data. From this point of view, it can be treated as a method of "learning" fuzzy systems off-line.

However, the algorithm realized by Equations (6.11), (6.12), (6.13), as well as the similar method of learning presented in Section 6.1.1, can be viewed as an error back-propagation procedure with reference to the neuro-fuzzy connectionist network [513], [300], [301], [434]. The fuzzy logic systems considered in this and the previous section are described by Equation (2.129). It was shown in Section 4.1 that these fuzzy systems can be represented in the form of connectionist multi-layer architectures, similar to the feed-forward multi-layer neural networks. These architectures, illustrated in Figs. 4.1 and 4.2, can be trained in the same way as neural networks, by use of a back-propagation method based on the steepest descent optimization algorithm.

Applying the idea of error back-propagation to the connectionist neuro-fuzzy architecture, the recursions (6.11), (6.12), (6.13) are obtained in [513]; see also [300], [301], [434]. This learning algorithm refers to the architecture depicted in Fig. 4.2, with the *product* operator and Gaussian membership functions. For the same architecture, but with triangular membership functions, we can apply the recursions (6.8), (6.9), (6.10) as the learning algorithm.

If we represent the fuzzy systems in the form of connectionist multi-layer networks, we can realize the learning procedures in the same way as the back-propagation algorithm in neural networks. These algorithms can be performed on-line, and the fuzzy systems viewed as connectionist networks possess learning ability in the same sense as the neural networks.

Moreover, if the fuzzy systems are represented in the form of the connectionist multi-layer architectures, they can be trained by incorporating the idea of back-propagation, using software such as the FLiNN program [395], which does not require the mathematical equations (6.11), (6.12), (6.13) or (6.8), (6.9), (6.10). The FLiNN program realizes the error back-propagation for any connectionist architecture built by use of the basic components which can serve as the elements of particular layers. This program allows any multi-layer network to be constructed from these elements, and can perform back-propagation learning based on the architecture, rather than on the mathematical recursions. This feature of the program is very important and advantageous, because it is much easier to build the connectionist architecture of a fuzzy system than determine the iterative equations of a learning algorithm. The latter is especially difficult when nondifferentiable functions appear in the system description. It is also very easy to replace, for example, *product* operator elements by *min* elements, or Gaussian function elements by triangular function elements in the architectures constructed employing the FLiNN program. These changes, without a program like FLiNN, are not so easy to realize by use of the mathematical formulas. Therefore, instead of determine the learning algorithms in the form of mathematical recursions, for different fuzzy systems, for instance with the inference based on the logical implications, we can represent the systems as connectionist neuro-fuzzy architectures and apply software for learning the networks.

6.1.3   FLiNN - Architecture Based Learning

The FLiNN program [395] realizes the back-propagation method of learning neural networks or neuro-fuzzy systems based on their architectures. This approach was introduced in [394], [396]. FLiNN stands for *Fuzzy Logic and Neural Networks*. This program is a *universal network trainer* that can tune the parameters (weights) of any neural network or neuro-fuzzy architecture. The most important advantage of architecture-based learning is the fact that it does not need the mathematical formulas of the gradient learning algorithms. The traditional approach requires iterative formulas of learning for each kind of neuro-fuzzy architectures (see e.g. [420]). It is worth emphasizing that in many cases it is very difficult to determine these formulas, especially when the architecture contains elements performing non-differentiable functions. Software that incorporates architecture-based learning is thus a very useful tool for training neuro-fuzzy systems.

The special *Feedforward Network Description Language* (FNDL) is proposed in [394], [396] to realize architecture-based learning in the FLiNN program, and a library of the basic elements has been created. These elements perform such operations like addition, multiplication, division, minimum, maximum, exponent, as well as the Gaussian and triangular functions. For details, see [396], [395]. The sigmoidal function, and others, can also be employed by use of these elements. For a feed-forward network (neural network or neuro-fuzzy architecture), which consists of a limited number of elements organized in layers, the FLiNN program can construct the architecture and tune its parameters according to the back-propagation method. Networks (architectures) are described in the FNDL language, which allows to specify the elements and connections between them. In case of any modification of a network, the FLiNN program automatically updates its learning algorithm, without knowing the mathematical formulas that describe the gradient learning method for different network architectures. This can be done in the manner presented in [394], [396]. The main idea of this method reflects the way of error back-propagation within a network and the fact that every element "knows" how to propagate the error signal from its output to the outputs of the elements in the preceding layer. Thus the knowledge expressed by the learning (mathematical) formulas is incorporated into the corresponding network architectures.

The FLiNN software is a tool for creating, training, and testing various neural network and neuro-fuzzy architectures. It also contains several very useful options, like extracting fuzzy rules from training data, creation and visualization of 3D control surfaces, visualization of training errors, and many others. The program of this kind is especially helpful when applied to the implication-based neuro-fuzzy systems presented in Chapter 5, as well as to the systems described in Chapter 4.

6.2   Genetic Algorithms

The gradient learning algorithms presented in Section 6.1 suffer from one main drawback, namely that they perform local optimization. This means that they seek optimal solutions, which depend on the starting points, i.e. the initial values of the tuned parameters. If the starting point is close to a local optimum, the gradient method will find this optimum as the solution, while it should search for the global optimum.

Some research has been carried out in order to choose a proper starting point for the gradient method such as the back-propagation. Several random initialization schemes are compared in [498], using a very large number of computer experiments. Other ideas concerning the initialization of the gradient algorithm, not based on random initial values, have also been proposed, as well as alternative global optimization algorithms. The methods very often applied to eliminate the drawback of the gradient algorithms are genetic algorithms, and clustering algorithms, described in this section and the next one, respectively.

6.2.1   Basic Genetic Algorithm

Genetic algorithms (GAs) are search methods based on natural selection and genetics. They were invented to mimic some of the processes observed in natural evolution. This kind of algorithm was proposed and developed by Holland [188], [189] as an efficient search mechanism in artificially adaptive systems. GAs have mainly been applied in optimization problems. The idea incorporated in these algorithms imitates the phenomenon of survival of the fittest individual in a population. The individuals are represented by *chromosomes*, in the form of strings of *genes*. The mechanics of a simple (basic) genetic algorithm (GA) are actually very simple, mostly copying the strings and swapping parts of them. In this way, a new population of chromosomes is created, employing the following basic operations: *selection*, *crossover*, and *mutation*. The chromosomes in each population are evaluated according to an appropriately defined *fitness function*. In optimization tasks, this evaluation function is usually chosen as the optimized function, also called the *objective function*. Potential solutions of the problem under consideration are coded into the chromosomes and the best one, with regard to the fitness value, obtained from this algorithm is treated as the optimal (or near optimal) solution. GAs are described in detail, e.g. in [150], [103], [325], [132].

The basic GA is illustrated by the flowchart shown in Fig. 6.3. The first step of the algorithm is initialization of a population of chromosomes. In the simple GA the chromosomes are binary strings of potential solutions, and the population is created randomly. Then, each chromosome in this population is evaluated by means of the fitness function. The best chromosome can be chosen from this population. Usually, however, the algorithm does not stop at this point. The next step is the selection operation. Different methods of selection can be employed. In the basic GA, this operation is realized using the *roulette wheel* method, which will be presented later in this section. The selection is applied in order to choose the chromosomes that will participate in the process of creating a new population, by use of the crossover and mutation operators. In this way, the initial (previous) population improves, replacing some chromosomes by better ones, with reference to their fitness values. The chromosomes that constitute the population obtained after the crossover and mutation operations (the new generation of chromosomes) are evaluated according to the fitness function, and the process is repeated until the stop criterium is attained. The idea is that the new population will contain better chromosomes than the old one, and the best chromosome in the final population, produced by the algorithm, is treated as the solution to the problem.

Now, let us explain how the potential solutions of a problem under consideration are coded into the chromosomes, and how the selection, as well as the main genetic operators (i.e. crossover and mutation), work.

To use the simple GA we must first code values of the variables of our problem in the form of binary strings, called chromosomes. The method of this coding depends on the problem under consideration. For example, if the variables take values from a domain $D = [d_B, d_E] \subset \mathbf{R}$, where d_B, and d_E refer to the beginning and end of this real-valued interval D, respectively, then the real-values of the variables can be coded with certain required precision. Let us assume that we wish to achieve a precision of b decimal places. In this case, the domain D should be cut into $(d_E - d_B) \cdot 10^b$ equal size ranges. Let us denote the smallest integer by s so that

$$(d_E - d_B) \cdot 10^b \leqslant 2^s - 1$$

Then the representation of values of the variables in the form of binary strings of length s clearly satisfies the precision requirement. The following

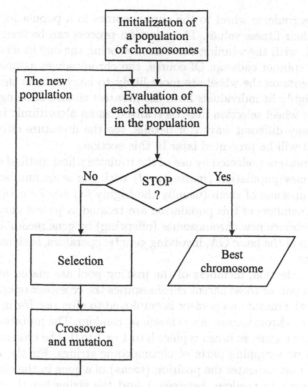

FIGURE 6.3. Flowchart of basic GA

formula interprets this way of coding the value of a variable $x \in D$ into the binary string (chromosome composed of s genes)

$$x = d_B + y \cdot \frac{d_E - d_B}{2^s - 1}$$

where y expresses the decimal value of this binary string (of length s). This coding method can be applied in optimization problems of a function with many variables (see [325]). In the special, very simple case, where the variables take only integer values from the domain D, the coding procedure is much easier. For example, using 4-bit strings and the well-known notation of a binary integer, we can code the integer numbers from $[0, 15]$ as follows

0000 0001 0010 0011 0100 0101 0110 0111
1000 1001 1010 1011 1100 1101 1110 1111

In the same way, we can represent the integer numbers from $[0, 31]$, employing 5-bit strings, and so on.

The selection applied in the basic GA is referred to as the roulette wheel method, because it can be viewed as allocating pie-shaped slices (segments, sectors) on a roulette wheel to the chromosomes in a population, proportionally to their fitness values. The selection process can be seen as a spin of the wheel, with the winning chromosome being the one in whose sector the roulette spinner ends up. Of course, the chromosomes associated with bigger segments on the wheel are more likely to be chosen as the winners. Thus, the highly fit individuals have the greatest chance of being selected. The roulette wheel selection may be realized as an algorithmic implementation in many different ways (for details, see the literature cited above). One of them will be presented later in this section.

The chromosomes selected by use of the roulette wheel method constitute a tentative new population (*mating pool*) with the same number of chromosomes, but some of them (usually the highly fit) can be copied several times. The members of this population are treated as parent chromosomes which can produce new chromosomes (offspring) by gene recombination, in the next step of the basic GA, involving genetic operators, such as crossover and mutation.

After the selection, members of the mating pool are mated at random, and for each pair of these parent chromosomes the crossover operator is applied. Then the mutation operator is employed to alter one (or more) genes in some of the chromosomes, also chosen at random. The mutation changes the value of one gene, so it can replace 0 to 1 or 1 to 0. The crossover recombines genes by swapping parts of chromosome strings. Firstly, an integer number, L, that indicates the position (*locus*) of a gene in the chromosome string is chosen at random, between 1 and the string length (number of genes in the chromosome) minus 1. Then, two new chromosomes are created by swapping all the genes located after the position L. To illustrate these operations, let us assume that the following chromosomes (composed of 8 genes) have been selected as parents to produce two offspring, by use of the crossover operator, with the locus $L = 3$

Parent 1: **01110101**	*Offspring 1:* **01101010**
Parent 2: **11001010**	*Offspring 2:* **11010101**

and the offspring 1 has been chosen for the mutation operation on the position 5, so the offspring after this mutation is

01100010

The offspring chromosomes, after the mutation, are introduced into the new population, which constitutes a new generation of chromosomes, characterized by a higher average fitness value. It is worth mentioning that the mutation takes place with very low probability, so the main genetic operator in the basic GA is the crossover. However, the mutation is necessary because it introduces more diversity to the populations of chromosomes. Otherwise, premature convergence could occur. This means that we can obtain a population in which all the chromosomes are the same, but they do not represent the optimal solution. The mutation prevents such a situation arising.

To explain the above operations more precisely, let c_i, for $i = 1, \ldots, K$, denotes chromosomes in a population of size K, so the number of chromosomes in this population equals K. The chromosomes are composed of genes. Assuming that the number of genes in the chromosomes equals m, the chromosomes in the population can be presented as follows

$$c_1 = \{a_{1,1} \quad a_{1,2} \quad \cdots \quad a_{1,m}\}$$
$$c_2 = \{a_{2,1} \quad a_{2,2} \quad \cdots \quad a_{2,m}\}$$
$$\cdots$$
$$c_K = \{a_{K,1} \quad a_{K,2} \quad \cdots \quad a_{K,m}\}$$

where $a_{i,j}$, for $i = 1, \ldots, K$, and $j = 1, \ldots, m$, denote values of genes (called *alleles*), which in the basic GA can be 0 or 1. Let F be a fitness function that evaluates the chromosomes. Thus, the total fitness of the population is

$$F_{pop} = \sum_{i=1}^{K} F(c_i)$$

and F_{pop}/K is the average fitness value of the population.

The following formula expresses the probability of chromosome c_i being selected by the roulette wheel method

$$p(c_i) = \frac{F(c_i)}{F_{pop}}$$

The roulette wheel selection can be formalized in the following way: Generate a number, r, at random from the interval $[0, 1]$. Calculate a cumulative probability, q_i, for each chromosome c_i; $i = 1, \ldots, K$, as

$$q_i = \sum_{l=1}^{i} p(c_l)$$

If $r < q_1$ then select the first chromosome, c_1, otherwise choose the i-th, that is c_i, for $2 \leqslant i \leqslant K$, such that $q_{i-1} < r \leqslant q_i$. As mentioned earlier, some chromosomes might be selected more than once.

Let us assume that the recombination operator (crossover) is applied to chromosomes c_1 and c_2. In fact the selection of the parent chromosomes takes place according to a *probability of crossover*, p_c, which is one of the parameters of GAs. This probability gives the information about the number of chromosomes expected to undergo the crossover operation. For each chromosome in the population (mating pool) a number, r, from the interval $[0, 1]$, is generated at random. If $r < p_c$ then the chromosome associated with this number is chosen for the crossover operation. The selected chromosomes are mated randomly. Then, for each pair of coupled parent chromosomes an integer number is generated at random from the interval $[1, m-1]$. This number indicates the locus, L, of the crossing point. The crossover operation applied to the chromosomes c_1 and c_2, with the crossing point L, is illustrated as follows. The parent chromosomes

$$c_1 = \{a_{1,1} \quad a_{1,2} \quad \cdots \quad a_{1,L} \quad a_{1,L+1} \quad \cdots \quad a_{1,m}\}$$
$$c_2 = \{a_{2,1} \quad a_{2,2} \quad \cdots \quad a_{2,L} \quad a_{2,L+1} \quad \cdots \quad a_{2,m}\}$$

are replaced by the following pair of their offspring

$$c_1' = \{a_{1,1} \quad a_{1,2} \quad \cdots \quad a_{1,L} \quad a_{2,L+1} \quad \cdots \quad a_{2,m}\}$$
$$c_2' = \{a_{2,1} \quad a_{2,2} \quad \cdots \quad a_{2,L} \quad a_{1,L+1} \quad \cdots \quad a_{1,m}\}$$

In the above illustration of the crossover operation, it was assumed that the locus of genes corresponds to the order of their location in the chromosome. This is true in the basic GA, it may, however, be different in some evolutionary algorithms. The crossover operation in the simple GA is referred to as *one-point crossover*, because only one crossing point is chosen to perform the crossover.

The mutation operator, as already shown in this section, changes the value of a selected gene, from 0 to 1 or vise versa. The mutation is performed according to a *probability of mutation*, p_m, which is another parameter of GAs. It gives information about the expected number of mutated genes. For each chromosome in the current (i.e. post-crossover) population, and for each gene within the chromosome, a number, r, from the interval $[0, 1]$, is generated at random. If $r < p_m$ then the selected gene is mutated. As mentioned before, values of the probability of mutation, for problems solving by GAs, are usually very small, much less than the values of the probability of crossover.

It is worth mentioning that the evaluation of each chromosomes by use of the fitness function, F, actually takes place on decoded versions of the chromosomes, i.e. on the corresponding values of the variables represented by the chromosomes. These values are referred to as *phenotypes*, while their chromosomal representations - as *genotypes*. This vocabulary, as well as other words used in GAs, is borrowed from natural genetics.

The algorithm (basic GA) is usually terminated after some number of generations, if no further improvement is observed. However, it can be stopped after a fixed number of iterations, depending on speed or other criteria.

As we can see, GAs differ from classical optimization and search techniques. Firstly, they perform searches from a population of potential solutions, not from a single point (in the search space). Therefore, they can find the optimal solution more easily, without getting trapped in a local optimum. Secondly, they operate on coded versions of the potential solutions, not directly on the points of the search space. Thirdly, they do not use derivatives, only the objective (fitness) function. Fourthly, they employ probabilistic rather than deterministic transition rules.

The theoretical foundations of GAs are based on a binary string representation of solutions, and on the notion of a schema, i.e. a template that allows similarities to be sought among chromosomes and helps to explain how a GA works. Interested readers are referred to e.g. [189], [150], [325]. A theorem has been formulated, called the Schema Theorem, which says that a schema occurring in chromosomes with above-average evaluations (by the fitness function) will tend to appear more frequently in the next generation, and a schema that occurs in chromosomes with below-average evaluations will tend to appear less frequently (ignoring the effect of crossover and mutation). This feature of GAs has been described by Holland as one of *intristic parallelism*, in that the algorithm is manipulating a large number of schema in parallel. A hypothesis called the Building Block Hypothesis has also been formulated. It says that a GA seeks near optimal performance through the juxtaposition of a special kind of schema (building blocks).

6.2.2   Evolutionary Algorithms

The simple GA, presented in Section 6.2.1, that is the GA in its basic form, uses binary chromosomes, roulette wheel selection, and one-point crossover. A great deal of research has been devoted to investigating many different variations of the basic genetic operators, encoding schemes, and so on. New versions of GAs have thus been introduced. Various modifications of the simple GA have led to algorithms that differ greatly from the basic one. Other similar methods based on the process of natural evolution have also been proposed independently. Examples include *evolution strategies*, developed in Germany by Schwefel [456], [457], and *evolutionary programming* in USA, by Fogel [130], [131], both during the 1960s; see also [132], as well as [325]. Another is *genetic programming*, introduced by Koza in 1990 to find the most appropriate computer program to solve a particular problem [276], [277]. Information about other evolution-based algorithms can be found e.g. in [325], [150]. All of them are referred to as *evolutionary algorithms* rather than genetic algorithms.

Let us now present some modifications of the classical (basic) GA, intended to improve its performance. Firstly, instead of the binary chromosomes that are applied in the basic GA, real-valued genes can be used in chromosomes. This way the chromosomes are not as long as their binary counterparts. Different alternative methods concerning the selection process have been investigated; see e.g. [150]. One of the most frequently employed, apart from the roulette wheel method, is *tournament selection*; it will be described later in this section. Some of the modifications concern the crossover and mutation. Other genetic operators have also been proposed.

In order to keep the best fit chromosomes in new populations, the so-called *elitist strategy* [106] and *steady-state GA* [525], [488] have been proposed; see also [103]. The elitist strategy preserves the best chromosome of each generation by copying it into the next generation. In some implementations of GAs, if no increasingly fit individual (chromosome) has been discovered between generations, the elitist strategy simply carries forward the most fit chromosome from the previous generation into the next. However, in some optimization problems, this strategy can sometimes lead to premature convergence.

In the steady-state GA, the number of new chromosomes (offspring) to be created in order to replace the same number of parent chromosomes can be chosen as a parameter. In the basic GA, the number of these chromosomes equals the *population size* (i.e. the number of chromosomes in the population, denoted by K), which is the main parameter of GAs. Many practitioners, using the steady-state GA, replace just one or two chromosomes at a time. Further modifications have been suggested, for example, the steady-state GA without duplicates. In this algorithm the chromosomes created (offspring) that are duplicates of ones in the current population are discarded rather than inserted. Therefore every chromosome (in the population) will be different. For details, see e.g. [103].

Another modification of the simple GA, proposed in [11], is a GA with a *Varying Population Size*. This algorithm does not employ any variation of the selection mechanism but rather introduces the concept of "age" of a chromosome, which is equivalent to the number of generations the chromosome stays "alive". Thus the age of the chromosome supersedes the concept of selection, and it influences the size of the population at every stage of the algorithm, since it depends on the fitness of the chromosome. The idea of this approach came from natural environments, where the aging process is well-known. This evolutionary algorithm is also presented in [325].

Many other different improvements have been introduced to the basic GA. The interested reader can find information in the literature on GAs; see e.g. [150], [103], [325]. In this section only tournament selection, and some genetic operators such as crossover and mutation, will be described.

Different selection methods are examined in [51]. One of them is tournament selection; see also e.g. [49]. This method selects a number, κ, of chromosomes from the population, and then chooses the best one to enter the next generation. This process is repeated K times, where K is the population size. It is clear that large values of κ increase the selective pressure of this procedure. A typical value, accepted by many applications, is $\kappa = 2$. Thus, after drawing a pair of successive chromosomes, the one with the higher fitness value is declared the winner and inserted into the new population, and another pair is drawn. This process continues until the population is full (K times). Many experiments have demonstrated the superiority of the tournament selection over the roulette wheel method. The reader interested in other selection methods may also be referred to [150], [325].

Although one-point crossover was inspired by biological processes, its algorithmic counterpart, employed in the simple GA, has some drawbacks; see [103]. Therefore, two-point crossover, as well as other crossover operators, with many crossing points, has been proposed.

Two-point crossover, as its name indicates, realizes a crossover operation with two crossing points. Let L_1 and L_2 denote these two crossing points. In this case, the two-point crossover can be illustrated as follows. The parent chromosomes, in the form

$$\mathbf{c}_1 = \{a_{1,1} \ a_{1,2} \ \cdots \ a_{1,L_1} \ a_{1,L_1+1} \ \cdots \ a_{1,L_2} \ a_{1,L_2+1} \cdots \ a_{1,m}\}$$
$$\mathbf{c}_2 = \{a_{2,1} \ a_{2,2} \ \cdots \ a_{2,L_1} \ a_{2,L_1+1} \ \cdots \ a_{2,L_2} \ a_{2,L_2+1} \cdots \ a_{2,m}\}$$

are replaced by the following pair of their offspring

$$\mathbf{c}'_1 = \{a_{1,1} \ a_{1,2} \ \cdots \ a_{1,L_1} \ a_{2,L_1+1} \ \cdots \ a_{2,L_2} \ a_{1,L_2+1} \cdots \ a_{1,m}\}$$
$$\mathbf{c}'_2 = \{a_{2,1} \ a_{2,2} \ \cdots \ a_{2,L_1} \ a_{1,L_1+1} \ \cdots \ a_{1,L_2} \ a_{2,L_2+1} \cdots \ a_{2,m}\}$$

Thus, the offspring chromosomes take the first and the last part of the genes (set apart by the crossing points) from one parent and the middle part from another parent. Analogously, the crossover operation can be realized with more than two crossing points, called *multi-point crossover*; see e.g. [103].

Another kind of crossover operation is described in [488] and called *uniform crossover*. Two parents are selected for the crossover and two offspring chromosomes are produced; just as in the one-point and multi-point crossover. However, the process of gene swapping between the parent chromosomes proceeds in a different manner. For each gene position (locus) on the two offspring, it is decided randomly which parent contributes its gene value (allel) to which offspring. For each locus on the parent chromosomes, a special template (generated randomly) indicates which parent will deliver its value in that position to the first offspring. The second offspring receives the allel in this locus from the other parent. The template is a pattern composed of 0 and 1 values, generated at random. The length of this template is equal to the number of genes in the chromosomes. The values 1 or 0, in particular positions in this template mean that the alleles associated with that loci come from the first or the second parent, respectively. Assuming that $m = 12$ and the following template has been generated randomly

$$[0 \ 1 \ 0 \ 1 \ 1 \ 0 \ 1 \ 1 \ 1 \ 0 \ 1 \ 1]$$

and the parent chromosomes are in the form

$$\mathbf{c}_1 = \{a_{1,1} \ a_{1,2} \ a_{1,3} \ a_{1,4} \ a_{1,5} \ a_{1,6} \ a_{1,7} \ a_{1,8} \ a_{1,9} \ a_{1,10} \ a_{1,11} \ a_{1,12}\}$$
$$\mathbf{c}_2 = \{a_{2,1} \ a_{2,2} \ a_{2,3} \ a_{2,4} \ a_{2,5} \ a_{2,6} \ a_{2,7} \ a_{2,8} \ a_{2,9} \ a_{2,10} \ a_{2,11} \ a_{2,12}\}$$

their pair of offspring, produced by uniform crossover, according the above template, are represented as

$$c_1' = \{a_{2,1}\ a_{1,2}\ a_{2,3}\ a_{1,4}\ a_{1,5}\ a_{2,6}\ a_{1,7}\ a_{1,8}\ a_{1,9}\ a_{2,10}\ a_{1,11}\ a_{1,12}\}$$
$$c_2' = \{a_{1,1}\ a_{2,2}\ a_{1,3}\ a_{2,4}\ a_{2,5}\ a_{1,6}\ a_{2,7}\ a_{2,8}\ a_{2,9}\ a_{1,10}\ a_{2,11}\ a_{2,12}\}$$

An example of uniform crossover is also depicted in [103].

The mutation operator in the basic GA is related to the binary representation of chromosomes, and changes the alleles equalling 0 to 1 and vice versa. It is obvious that this operator must be modified if real coding is employed. In this case, the alleles are real-valued numbers, so the mutation operator that changes the value of one single gene should be defined in a different way. For example, mutation can change the real value of a gene by adding a small randomly generated real value to it.

Other types of crossover and mutation operators have been proposed for specific problems to be solved by GAs. For instance, combinatorical tasks, where chromosomes represent potential solutions in the form of permutations of genes, require different crossover and mutation operators from those used in classical GAs. The genetic operators, called *position-based crossover* and *position-based mutation*, investigated in [370], as well as the operators called *order-based crossover* and *order-based mutation*, studied in [489], are suitable for such tasks (e.g. the Traveling Salesman Problem or Scheduling Problem). The *edge recombination crossover*, described in detail in [528], has also been created to be applied to these problems.

It is worth mentioning that, as well as the crossover and mutation operators, the *inversion* operator has also been introduced, by Holland [189]. This operator inverts the order of genes between two randomly chosen positions (loci) in a chromosome. In spite of the fact that the idea of using this operator was inspired by a biological process, it is rarely employed in GAs. However, such an operator can be helpful when applied to combinatorical tasks, for example to solve the Traveling Salesman Problem by a GA; see e.g. [325].

Although the GAs with various modifications of the classical genetic operators, selection strategies, and so on, are referred to as evolutionary algorithms rather than genetic algorithms, the latter name is often used in the literature in this broader sense, and not only with reference to the basic GA.

A great number of different implementations of the evolutionary (genetic) algorithms have been produced in the form of computer software. They usually realize many options, including various modifications of the basic GA. For example, the FlexTool (GA) employs binary representations of individuals, but in order to reduce the length of the chromosomes, it can also apply a special kind of coding, called *logarithmic coding*; see [587], as well as [434]. Besides, the program allows the selection method to be chosen, for example the roulette wheel or tournament selection. The

Evolver [588] is software that can solve different optimization problems, including combinatorical tasks. It uses real-valued chromosomes and realizes the steady-state GA. There are many different evolutionary algorithms implemented for special applications. As an example, let us point out the Genetic Training Option (GTO), which cooperates with the Brain Maker [589], i.e. the software applied in order to train neural networks. The genetic operators (crossover and mutation) in GTO are specially designed for this kind of application, which is neural network optimization using combinations of the BrainMaker and GTO; see [590].

6.3   Clustering Algorithms

This section addresses *clustering*, also known as *unsupervised learning* or *self-organization* (see Section 3.1.8). By clustering, we usually mean the partitioning of a collection of objects (data) into subsets, called *clusters*, that contain elements with common properties which distinguish them from the members of the other clusters. *Cluster analysis* is thus essentially the classification of a given data set into a certain number of clusters where the elements within each cluster should be as similar as possible and dissimilar from those of other clusters. This implies the existence of a measure of distance or similarity between the elements to be classified. *Clustering algorithms* are mathematical tools for detecting similarities between members of a collection of objects. Most cluster analysis methods require a measure of similarity to be defined for every pairwise combination of the entities to be clustered. Clustering algorithms produce partitions of a given data set, resulting in a number of clusters.

6.3.1   Cluster Analysis

The aim of cluster analysis is to partition a given set of data or objects into clusters (subsets, groups, classes). As mentioned earlier, this partition should have the two following properties: the data that belong to the same cluster should be as similar as possible, and the data that belong to different clusters should be as different as possible. The former feature is referred to as *homogeneity*, and the latter one as *heterogeneity*. Thus, the clusters should be formed as *homogeneous* subsets. The concept of "similarity" has to be specified according to the data. In different tasks of cluster analysis, the data may come from the area of medical diagnosis in the form of a database about patients, they may describe states of an industrial production plant, they may be available as images, etc. In most cases, where the data are represented as real-valued vectors, the Euclidean distance between data can be used as a measure of their similarity. Generally, the data may be qualitative, quantitative, or both. They may be numerical, pictorial, textual, linguistic, etc., as well as any combinations thereof.

Cluster analysis has played an important role in solving many problems, especially in *pattern recognition*, where classification of objects is a field of intensive research and practical applications. The term "pattern recognition" may be defined in different ways. A survey of the definitions is provided in [509]. Quite simply, we can say that pattern recognition is a *search for structure in data* [33]. One of the survey papers (published in the 1960s), which describes the role of cluster analysis in pattern recognition is [344], but there are many other papers (also very good survey papers), textbooks, and monographs on this subject, e.g. [500]. In [116], for example, Bayesian classifiers, which are most often employed in pattern recognition, are described, and there are also valuable references to the related literature. The books [8], [502], [164] refer explicitly, in their titles, to cluster analysis or clustering algorithms.

Cluster analysis is a field of *data analysis*; see e.g. [33], [197]. There is a difference between *clustering* and *classification*. Let $\mathbf{X} = \{\mathbf{x}_1, \mathbf{x}_2, \ldots, \mathbf{x}_q\}$ be a data set of q items $\mathbf{x}_j$, where $j = 1, \ldots, q$. *Clustering* in $\mathbf{X}$ has classically meant the identification of an integer c, such as $2 \leqslant c < q$, and a partitioning of $\mathbf{X}$ by c mutually exclusive, collectively exhaustive subsets of $\mathbf{X}$, i.e. the homogeneous clusters. The cluster *structure* in $\mathbf{X}$ may reveal associations between each data item $\mathbf{x}_j$. By the structure we mean the manner in which the information carried by the data is organized. Let $\mathbf{S}$ denote a data space from which $\mathbf{X}$ has been drawn, that is $\mathbf{X} \subset \mathbf{S}$. A *classifier* for $\mathbf{S}$ is a device or means whereby $\mathbf{S}$ itself is partitioned into c "decision regions". Explicit representation of these regions, as well as the role played by a sample data set $\mathbf{X}$ from data space $\mathbf{S}$ in classifier design, depends on the data, the search method performed in order to find the structure, and on the structure itself. The sample data set $\mathbf{X}$ is often used to "train" the classifier, that is to delineate the decision regions in $\mathbf{S}$. In *classification*, we search for structure in an entire data space $\mathbf{S}$. It is possible, though not necessary, to conduct this search by first clustering in a sample data set $\mathbf{X}$. For details, see [33].

The concept of pattern classification may be viewed as a partition of feature space or a mapping from feature space to decision space. In classical cluster analysis, clustering algorithms produce *hard partition* of a given data set, resulting in well separated clusters.

According to [33], hard partition can be defined in the following way, using a *matrix* representation. Let $\mathbf{V}_{cq}$ denote the vector space of $c \times q$ real matrices over $\mathbf{R}$, that is a real line. A matrix $\mathbf{U} = [u_{ij}]$; $i = 1, \ldots, c$; $j = 1, \ldots, q$, where $\mathbf{U} \in \mathbf{V}_{cq}$, represents a hard c-partition of $\mathbf{X}$ if and only if its elements satisfy three conditions

$$u_{ij} \in \{0, 1\} \quad \text{for } i = 1, \ldots, c; j = 1, \ldots, q \qquad (6.14)$$

$$\sum_{i=1}^{c} u_{ij} = 1 \quad \text{for } j = 1, \dots, q \tag{6.15}$$

$$0 < \sum_{j=1}^{q} u_{ij} < q \quad \text{for } i = 1, \dots, c \tag{6.16}$$

Row i of matrix $\mathbf{U}$, say $\mathbf{U}_{(i)} = (u_{i1}, \dots, u_{iq})$, exhibits values of the characteristic function of the ith partitioning subset of $\mathbf{X}$, where

$$u_{ij} = u_i(\mathbf{x}_j) \tag{6.17}$$

is 1 if $\mathbf{x}_j$ belongs to the ith subset of $\mathbf{X}$, and 0 if it does not belong to this subset (cluster).

Equation (6.14) expresses the characteristic function (6.17), which can take only values 0 or 1, so the partitioning subsets are classical (crisp) sets. Equation (6.15) means that each data item $\mathbf{x}_j$ is in exactly one of the c subsets. Equation (6.16) ensures that no subset is empty, and no subset is all of $\mathbf{X}$; in other words, $2 \leqslant c < q$ Thus, the hard c-partition of $\mathbf{X}$ is represented by the matrix $\mathbf{U}$, which contains exact information about this partition. The rows of this matrix correspond to the clusters, and the columns to the data items. The elements of the rows, taking values of 1, indicate the data items that belong to the corresponding clusters. It is easy to notice that each row can consist of at least one value equal to 1, but not all of them. Otherwise, this cluster is empty or contains all the data items; so the condition (6.16) must be fulfilled. Analogously, more than one value equal to 1, in a column, would suggest that the corresponding data item belongs to more than one cluster, which is not true in the hard partition. Therefore, condition (6.15) must be satisfied.

The set of admissible solutions for the conventional (hard) cluster analysis problem with respect to $\mathbf{X}$, defined above, is denoted by M_c and expressed as follows

$$M_c = \left\{ \mathbf{U} \in \mathbf{V}_{cq} \mid u_{ij} \in \{0,1\} \;\; \forall i,j; \sum_{i=1}^{c} u_{ij} = 1 \;\; \forall j; 0 < \sum_{j=1}^{q} u_{ij} < q \;\; \forall i \right\} \tag{6.18}$$

Different solutions of the hard partition problem, represented by Equation (6.18), in the form of the matrix $\mathbf{U}$, can be obtained using clustering algorithms. An inherent difficulty in cluster analysis is the fact that various algorithms can suggest radically different substructures in the same data set. The most important requirement for solving a clustering problem is a suitable measure of "clusters" – what *clustering criterion* should be used? The choice of the clustering criterion can be rather problematic. No clustering criterion or measure of similarity will be universally applicable. Selection of a particular criterion is at least partially subjective, and always open to question; see [33] for details. The clustering criteria, in general, refer to the mathematical properties of the data, such as distance, angle, curvature, symmetry, connectivity, intensity, etc. Similarity measures are thus building blocks for clustering criteria. However, in the simplest models, a measure of similarity can serve as a clustering criterion.

The classical objective functional is perhaps the most intensively studied clustering criterion which generates hard clusters in $\mathbf{X}$. Let J_W denote the functional, defined as

$$J_W(\mathbf{U}, \mathbf{v}) = \sum_{j=1}^{q} \sum_{i=1}^{c} u_{ij} (d_{ij})^2 \qquad (6.19)$$

where

$$d_{ij} = d(\mathbf{x}_j, \mathbf{v}_i) = \|\mathbf{x}_j - \mathbf{v}_i\| = \left[\sum_{k=1}^{p} (x_{jk} - v_{ik})^2 \right]^{\frac{1}{2}} \qquad (6.20)$$

is a similarity measure, expressed by the Euclidean norm metric, and vector

$$\mathbf{v} = (\mathbf{v}_1, \ldots, \mathbf{v}_c) \in \mathbf{R}^{cp}, \quad \mathbf{v}_i \in \mathbf{R}^p \ \forall i \qquad (6.21)$$

is a set of c prototypical "cluster centers", $\mathbf{v}_i$, for $i = 1, \ldots, c$, is the cluster center of the hard cluster represented by $u_i \in \mathbf{U}$. The "cluster centers" are treated as *prototypes* that characterize the clusters. They can be calculated according to the formula

$$\mathbf{v}_i = \frac{\sum_{j=1}^{q} u_{ij} \mathbf{x}_j}{\sum_{j=1}^{q} u_{ij}} \qquad (6.22)$$

so the name *mean vectors* is used for these prototypes. There are many synonyms for the word "prototype": centroid, vector quantizer (VQ), signature, template, codevector, paradigm, exemplar, etc., but in the context of clustering it is usually referred as the cluster center of a crisp cluster [42].

One of the most popular algorithms for approximating the minima of the functional J_W, defined by Equation (6.19), is iterative optimization, performed by the algorithm, called the *hard c-means* or basic *ISODATA* method [116]; see also [33]. It can be presented in the following steps

- Fix the number of clusters, c, such as $2 \leqslant c < q$, and initialize the first matrix $\mathbf{U}^{(0)} \in M_c$. The matrices $\mathbf{U}^{(l)}$, for $l = 1, 2, \ldots$, will be determined in the next steps. Besides, set the stopping condition, ε_L.

- Calculate the c mean vectors $\left\{ \mathbf{v}_i^{(l)} \right\}$ using Equation (6.22).

- Update $\mathbf{U}^{(l)}$, obtaining new memberships, for $i = 1, \ldots, c$, and $j = 1, \ldots, q$, as

$$u_{ij}^{(l+1)} = \begin{cases} 1 & \text{for } d_{ij}^{(l)} = \min_{1 \leqslant k \leqslant c} \left\{ d_{kj}^{(l)} \right\} \\ 0 & \text{otherwise} \end{cases} \qquad (6.23)$$

- Compare $\mathbf{U}^{(l)}$ to $\mathbf{U}^{(l+1)}$ in a convenient matrix norm. If

$$\left\| \mathbf{U}^{(l+1)} - \mathbf{U}^{(l)} \right\| \leqslant \varepsilon_L \qquad (6.24)$$

then stop, otherwise set $l = l + 1$ and return to the second step.

This algorithm is quite reasonable from an intuitive standpoint. We should guess the number c of the hard clusters, find their "centers" (prototypes), reallocate cluster memberships to minimize squared errors between the data and current prototypes, and stop when looping ceases to lower the value of J_W.

A simple example of using the 2-*means* algorithm is illustrated in [33].

6.3.2 Fuzzy Clustering

In 1969 Ruspini [414] suggested employing fuzzy sets, introduced by Zadeh [559] in 1965, in cluster analysis. He proposed a fuzzy partition to represent the clusters in a data set. This idea has also been described in his other papers; e.g. [415], [416], [417], [418]. In 1973 Dunn [119] defined the first fuzzy generalization of the well-known ISODATA clustering algorithm [17]. It was called *fuzzy ISODATA*. Since 1973, this algorithm has been studied and improved by Bezdek, e.g. [28], [29], [30], [37], [31], [39], [45], [32], [47], [33], also Bezdek and Dunn [38], as well as Dunn [121], [120], [122], and known as *fuzzy c-means*. As Zadeh wrote, in the foreword to the book [33], "... the work of Dunn and Bezdek on the *fuzzy ISODATA* (or *fuzzy c-means*) algorithms became a landmark in the theory of cluster analysis, that the relevance of the theory of fuzzy sets to cluster analysis and pattern recognition became clearly established. Since then, the theory of fuzzy clustering has developed rapidly and fruitfully ... ". It is worth mentioning that in 1966 a paper about fuzzy sets and pattern classification, with Zadeh as a co-author, was published [23]. Many publications concerning fuzzy clustering by Bezdek as well as others, appeared later; see e.g. [40], [43], [44].

Analogously to the definition of hard partition, by Equation (6.18), *fuzzy c-partition* is expressed as follows [33]

$$M_{fc} = \left\{ \mathbf{U} \in \mathbf{V}_{cq} \mid u_{ij} \in [0,1] \ \forall i, j; \sum_{i=1}^{c} u_{ij} = 1 \ \forall j; 0 < \sum_{j=1}^{q} u_{ij} < q \ \forall i \right\}$$

$$(6.25)$$

where $\mathbf{X} = \{\mathbf{x}_1, \mathbf{x}_2, \dots, \mathbf{x}_q\}$ is a data set, $\mathbf{V}_{cq}$ is a set of real $c \times q$ matrices, c is an integer, such that $2 \leqslant c < q$, and $\mathbf{U}$ is the matrix that represents the fuzzy partition. Note that the difference between Equations (6.18) and (6.25) is that, in the former, elements of $\mathbf{U}$ take only values of 0 and 1, but in the latter they take real values from the interval $[0, 1]$. Thus, in the latter case, the function (6.17) denotes a membership function of a fuzzy subset, instead of the characteristic function (of a crisp subset) used in the hard partition. The fuzzy partition produces fuzzy subsets as clusters. In spite of the fact that, in this case, elements of matrix $\mathbf{U}$ take values of the membership functions, it is obvious that conditions (6.15) and (6.16) remain the same. Equation (6.15) means that the sum of each column is 1, so the total membership of each data item $\mathbf{x}_j$ in $\mathbf{X}$ is still 1. Since Equation (6.16) is satisfied, it is possible for each $\mathbf{x}_j$, $j = 1, \dots, q$, to have an otherwise arbitrary distribution of membership among the c fuzzy subsets $\{u_i\}$ partitioning $\mathbf{X}$. There may, of course, be one or more columns of $\mathbf{U}$ which assign all of the membership of some $\mathbf{x}_j$ to a single u_i; indeed M_c is clearly a finite subset of M_{fc}. More details, as well as examples, can be found in [33].

The fuzzy c-partition defined by Equation (6.25) can be realized by the *fuzzy c-means* clustering algorithm, which is a generalization of the *hard c-means* (or basic ISODATA method), described in Section 6.3.1. This algorithm is based on the generalized version of the functional expressed by Equation (6.19), and can be presented as follows, according to [28], [33]:

- Fix the number of clusters, c, such that $2 \leqslant c < q$, choose any inner product metric for $\mathbf{R}^p$, and fix m, such that $1 \leqslant m < \infty$. Initialize the first matrix $\mathbf{U}^{(0)} \in M_{fc}$. The matrices $\mathbf{U}^{(l)}$, for $l = 1, 2, \dots$, will be determined in the next steps. In addition, set the stopping condition, ε_L.

- Calculate the c fuzzy cluster centers $\left\{ \mathbf{v}_i^{(l)} \right\}$ using the formula

$$\mathbf{v}_i = \frac{\sum_{j=1}^{q} (u_{ij})^m \mathbf{x}_j}{\sum_{j=1}^{q} (u_{ij})^m} \tag{6.26}$$

for $i = 1, \dots, c$.

- Update $\mathbf{U}^{(l)}$, obtaining new memberships, for $i = 1, \dots, c$, and $j = 1, \dots, q$, applying the following equation

$$u_{ij} = \left[\sum_{k=1}^{c} \left(\frac{d_{ij}}{d_{kj}} \right)^{\frac{2}{m-1}} \right]^{-1} \tag{6.27}$$

where $d_{ij} = \| \mathbf{x}_j - \mathbf{v}_i \|$, and if the norm $\| \cdot \|$ is the Euclidean norm metric, then d_{ij} is the similarity measure (6.20) between the data item vector $\mathbf{x}_j$ and the cluster center value obtained in the preceding step.

- Compare $\mathbf{U}^{(l)}$ to $\mathbf{U}^{(l+1)}$ in a convenient matrix norm. If Equation (6.24) is fulfilled, then stop, otherwise set $l = l + 1$ and return to the second step.

The *fuzzy c-means* clustering algorithm, presented above, reduces to the *hard c-means* method, described in Section 6.3.1, in the nonsingular case when $m = 1$ and the norm on $\mathbf{R}^p$ is the Euclidean norm. The parameter m, introduced to the fuzzy version of the *c-means* method, expresses a degree of "fuzziness". As $m \to 1$, *fuzzy c-means* converges to *hard c-means*. Conversely, the larger m is, the "fuzzier" are the membership assignments; see [33], for the details.

A simple example of using the *fuzzy 2-means* algorithm is also illustrated in [33], as well as much more information about both versions of the *c-means* algorithm. Moreover, other variants of these methods have been considered. Some of them realize slightly different types of partition of a given data set, for example the so-called *possibilistic c-partition*, as well as *degenerate c-partitions*, considered in [33].

As mentioned earlier, clustering algorithms are usually viewed as learning methods (*unsupervised, self-organizing learning*). They can be compared with the learning algorithms of clustering neural networks (see Section 3.1.8). One way of combining the Kohonen's learning method with the fuzzy *c*-means clustering algorithm is presented in [46]. Kohonen's self-organizing algorithm has been extended to a fuzzy version, which can produce both hard and fuzzy partitioning; see [332].

Clustering algorithms are called *unsupervised learning*, because they use *unlabeled* data vectors, which means that the learning input vectors are not associated with the classes to which they belong. These algorithms can solve a clustering problem, that is the identification of an "optimal" partition of the input data set, by grouping together unlabeled object data vectors that share some well-defined (mathematical) similarity, without being presented with examples of *labeled* data vectors, i.e. assigned to the proper classes. Another term, more recently used for this kind of clustering method, is *self-organizing learning*.

It is worth noticing that the number of clusters is usually assumed to be known for a clustering algorithm, otherwise this value becomes part of the clustering problem.

6.4   Hybrid Learning

This section is devoted to hybrid learning methods, which are combinations of the algorithms described in Sections 6.1, 6.2, and 6.3, i.e. gradient, genetic, and clustering algorithms, respectively. Firstly, in Section 6.4.1, the different types of hybridizations presented in the literature are mentioned. Then, applications of the hybrid learning methods to tuning weights of neural networks or parameters of neuro-fuzzy systems, and to rule generating, are considered in Section 6.4.2 and 6.4.3, respectively. It should be emphasized that, in general, hybrid learning approach to neuro-fuzzy systems can be viewed as a two-stage learning process, with a rule generation method at the first stage and a parameter tuning algorithm at the second stage. Both the former and the latter can be performed by use of hybrid methods as well.

6.4.1   Combinations of Gradient Methods, GAs, and Clustering Algorithms

There has been a great deal of research into combining neural networks, fuzzy systems, and genetic (evolutionary) algorithms in various schemes of their hybridizations. The integration of these techniques allows to create intelligent knowledge-based systems with learning abilities that take advantage from the merits of each implemented method.

The idea of using genetic algorithms (Section 6.2) in order to perform a neural network learning is presented e.g. in [526], [151], [338]. The backpropagation algorithm (Section 3.1.3), which is a gradient method, is applied in combination with GAs to train neural networks in [339], [21], [22], and others. In [64], this kind of hybrid learning is employed for fuzzy neural networks (Section 3.2). A bibliography on applications GAs to neural networks, fuzzy systems, neuro-fuzzy systems, and fuzzy neural networks is available on the Internet [90], Section: *Fuzzy Neural Networks*, and in [91].

Different supportive and collaborative combinations of GAs and neural networks are described in [453], as well as in [452]. The latter paper also includes fuzzy systems. Examples of a synergy of GAs (or evolutionary algorithms) and neural networks are depicted in [468], [521]. In this section, GAs are very often understood in the broader sense, i.e. as evolutionary techniques; see Section 6.2.2.

GAs are also powerful tools for structure (architecture) optimization of neural networks; e.g. [326], [257], [527]. The problem of architecture optimization, using GAs, is in fact, a problem of evolutionary learning, and the GAs, as mentioned earlier, are rather evolutionary algorithms. The learning of the architectures is part of a general evolutionary learning scheme, presented in [555], which includes the learning of weights, and architectures, as well as the learning rules of neural networks, by evolutionary algorithms. In [218] GAs are applied in order to optimize the architectures of fuzzy neural networks.

GAs (or evolutionary algorithms) for optimization of both weights and neural network architectures are presented in [163], [278], as well as in many other papers. With reference to neuro-fuzzy systems, GAs have been used for optimizing the parameters of membership functions and for generating fuzzy rules; see e.g. [191]. This problem can also be solved by hybrid learning methods, described in Sections 6.4.2 and 6.4.3.

Similarly to neural network learning by GAs, in order to find optimal weight values, fuzzy systems are trained to adjust parameters of membership functions, e.g. in [241], [242], [486], [180], [20]. A bibliography on this subject is also available on the Internet [90], Section: *Fuzzy Logic Controllers (Design, Learning, Tuning, Applications)*. Hybrid methods that combine GAs with gradient learning algorithms can be employed; see Section 6.4.2. In addition, GAs are often used in order to generate fuzzy IF-THEN rules of a fuzzy (neuro-fuzzy) system. Some details are presented in Section 6.4.3.

Neuro-fuzzy-genetic combinations are considered in the literature and applied to hybrid learning; e.g. [303], [2], [420], [582], [223]. Moreover, these methods can also be combined with clustering algorithms.

In [41], GAs are employed to optimize fuzzy clustering criteria (Section 6.3.2), and to perform a global search of the space of possible data partitions given a choice of the number of clusters (or classes) in the data, for determining the number of clusters. Other papers concerning similar applications of GAs to fuzzy clustering are e.g. [160], [557], which refer to *genetic* (or *evolutionary*) *fuzzy clustering*, and [478] which applies a GA for clustering and classification. Integration of neural networks with GAs and clustering is considered in [454]. A hybrid algorithm that is a combination of a GA and the k-nearest neighbor method of classification is presented in [250]. A bibliography concerning GA-based approaches to fuzzy clustering is available on the Internet [90], Section: *Fuzzy Clustering*.

There are many examples of successful practical applications of different hybrid learning methods described in the literature, e.g. for use in controlling intelligent systems in robotics and mechatronics [136].

With regard to hybrid learning methods, it is worth mentioning that such combinations as *fuzzy genetic algorithms* are also considered in the literature, e.g. [26], [297], [181], [390]. These are genetic algorithms that use fuzzy logic based techniques or fuzzy tools to improve their behavior. In these algorithms, some components may be designed with fuzzy logic tools. Examples are fuzzy operators and fuzzy connectives for designing genetic operators with different properties, fuzzy logic systems for controlling the GA parameters according to certain performance measures, fuzzy stop criteria, and others [91]. Fuzzy genetic algorithms understood, in a narrow sense, as genetic algorithms which breed fuzzy logic controllers as agent programs, are considered in [146]. A bibliography concerning fuzzy genetic algorithms is available on the Internet [90], Sections: *Fuzzy Genetic Algorithms* and *Fuzzy Optimization*. Apart from those papers cited above, it includes e.g. [62], [449].

6.4.2   Hybrid Algorithms for Parameter Tuning

In was written in Section 3.1.5 that the learning process in artificial neural networks can be viewed as an optimization task, that is, a "search" in a multidimensional parameter (weight) space for a solution which gradually optimizes a prespecified objective (criterion) function. It implies that GAs, which are optimization algorithms, can be applied in order to train neural networks. They are even more suitable for this task than the back-propagation method, because they search for a global (near global) optimum, and do not usually stop at a local optimum. Similarly, neuro-fuzzy systems can be trained by GAs. However, as stated in Section 6.4.1, the method suggested is a combination of both algorithms. First a GA is employed to get a result pretty close to the global optimum, and then back-propagation to tune the weights or parameters of the neuro-fuzzy system to the globally optimal solution. Figure 6.4 illustrates this kind of hybrid approach.

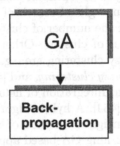

FIGURE 6.4. Hybrid learning: GA plus back-propagation

Apart from the main disadvantage of the back-propagation algorithm, that is its tendency to get trapped at local optima, the speed of convergence also justifies the hybrid approach. The comparison study is presented in [256], [556]. The conclusion is the following: GAs converge very quickly to an approximate solution during the early stage and go slow at the end of the algorithm run. It is thus reasonable to employ a GA at the first stage to obtain quickly an initial value for the back-propagation method, which then modifies this value very fast to get the global optimal solution.

As mentioned in Section 6.4.1, membership functions of antecedent and consequent fuzzy sets (in fuzzy IF-THEN rules) are adjusted by GAs in [241], [242], [486], [180], [20]. Some other papers concerning this subject are cited in Section 6.4.3. The bibliography available on the Internet [90], Section: *Fuzzy Logic Controllers (Design, Learning, Tuning, Applications)*, includes more reference items on tuning membership functions of a fuzzy rule base by means of genetic (evolutionary) algorithms.

The gradient algorithms employed in order to adjust parameters of membership functions (see Section 6.1) are alternative methods of learning fuzzy (or neuro-fuzzy) systems. These algorithms are based on the steepest descent optimization technique, which is also incorporated into the back-propagation method applied to train neural networks. Since the idea of this kind of learning is the same for both fuzzy (neuro-fuzzy) systems and neural networks, each of these gradient algorithms suffer from the same drawbacks. The main disadvantage is the tendency to get trapped at local optima. Therefore, the hybrid learning method that combines a GA with the gradient algorithm used for a fuzzy (neuro-fuzzy) system, in the same way as presented in Fig. 6.4, is recommended. Instead of the back-propagation method, which tune weights of a neural network, the gradient algorithm is employed, using the initial values of the parameters obtained from the GA which is applied at the first stage. Thus the values of the parameters of membership functions (usually the *centers* and *widths*), determined by the GA, are sufficiently close to the global optimum solution, which is then quickly found by the gradient method of parameter tuning. This approach is presented e.g. in [420] for Gaussian and triangular membership functions.

6.4.3 Rule Generation

Fuzzy IF-THEN rules, in fuzzy and neuro-fuzzy systems, are usually derived from human experts. However, several approaches have recently been proposed for generating these rules automatically, from numerical data, without domain experts. The method developed by Wang and Mendel [515], [514] is frequently employed. A collection of fuzzy IF-THEN rules is generated from input-output pairs. The input and output domain spaces are divided into subspaces (regions). A membership function is associated with each region, so the membership values of given numerical data in different regions are determined. Since each data pair generates one rule, the degrees that are calculated based on the membership values are assigned to each rule in order to evaluate the rules. Then, the rule with the maximum degree is accepted from a group of conflicting rules. For details, see also [513]. This method allows to incorporate into a table-lookup representation of a fuzzy rule base both the rules generated from numerical data as well as linguistic rules provided by a human expert. It is assumed that the linguistic rules have degrees assigned by the expert, depending on the importance of the rules. This method of generating fuzzy IF-THEN rules from numerical input-output data is implemented in the FLiNN software (Section 6.1.3).

One example of various rule generation algorithms is presented in [12], for a single output fuzzy model. In this method, an input space is iteratively fuzzy partitioned by the ratio of 1/2 in the subregions where the value of the output inference error takes the maximum. This algorithm has been extended to the multiple output fuzzy model in [245], where three methods, called the *equal fixed grid method*, $1/2^n$ *fixed grid method*, and *free grid method* are compared.

Other approaches to rule generation are proposed in the literature, mainly, with regard to control and classification rules. Most of them are briefly described in [329], which is a survey paper on this subject. The problem of fuzzy rule extraction from numerical data, for function approximation, is presented e.g. in [1]. Generating fuzzy rules for system identification and system modeling are studied in [412] and [516], respectively. The latter refers to extracting important fuzzy rules from a given rule base to construct a "parsimonious" fuzzy model with a high generalization ability. A hybrid algorithm is considered. The rule extracting is done by a GA, and the Kalman filter is used in order to estimate parameters of the model.

In [210] a rule generation method from numerical data, based on fuzzy partition of a two-dimensional pattern space by a simple grid, is proposed for classification problems. The fuzzy classification simultaneously employs all the fuzzy rules generated for several fuzzy partitions of different sizes. In this approach, the number of fuzzy rules is enormous, especially for high-dimensional pattern spaces. In order to reduce the number of rules, a GA-based method is applied in [211], [212]. GAs are also employed to generate fuzzy classification rules in [214], [213]. In these cases, compact fuzzy classification systems are automatically constructed from numerical data by selecting a small number of significant fuzzy rules using genetic algorithms. Since significant rules are selected and unnecessary rules are removed, this method can be viewed as a knowledge acquisition tool for classification problems.

As mentioned in Section 6.4.1, GAs have been widely used for generating fuzzy IF-THEN rules, as well as for tuning membership functions of antecedent and consequent fuzzy sets (see Section 6.4.2). For example, in [499], [126], [280], GAs are employed for generating fuzzy IF-THEN rules. Both fuzzy rule generation and tuning membership functions are realized by GAs in [254], [450], [191], [373], [419]. The number of fuzzy IF-THEN rules is also obtained by GAs in [364], [306], [296], [218]. Hierarchical structures of fuzzy IF-THEN rules are determined by GAs in [466]. In these GA-based approaches, a collection of fuzzy IF-THEN rules is coded as individual rules. In [209], for instance, where fuzzy IF-THEN rules are generated by a GA for pattern classification problems, a collection of these rules is represented by a single chromosome. Another example of coding the whole rule base in a single chromosome is presented e.g. in [465].

As we can see, two main approaches are distinguished in the literature on rule generation by GAs. The first one involves coding each single rule in the form of one chromosome, and in the second approach a collection of rules is coded as one chromosome. The former approach refers to the so-called Michigan method [190], and the latter one to the so-called Pittsburgh method [473]; named after the universities in which they were invented. These two approaches as applied to fuzzy classifiers are described e.g. in [76].

In the Michigan approach, chromosomes represent individual rules, and the collection of rules (rule base) corresponds to the entire population of the chromosomes. In the Pittsburgh approach, each chromosome encodes a whole rule base. The crossover operation used in this method serves to provide a new combination of rules and mutation creates new rules. Other approaches have also been proposed based on the Michigan and Pittsburgh methods, for example, the *iterative rule learning approach*, [91]. In this method, as in the Michigan one, each chromosome in the population represents a single rule. However, unlike in the Michigan approach, only the best chromosome is accepted (considered as the solution), the remaining chromosomes in the population being discarded. The fitness of each chromosome is computed individually, without taking into account cooperation with other chromosomes. This substantially reduces the search space, because in each sequence of iterations only one rule is searched for. For details, see [91], as well as [89]. It is worth mentioning that the latter paper refers explicitly to the GA as a hybrid learning algorithm.

Apart from the papers on generating fuzzy rules by means of GAs, mentioned above, there are many others in the literature, e.g. [179], [354], [537], [97], [108]. A bibliography on this subject is also available on the Internet [90], Sections: *Fuzzy Logic Controllers (Design, Learning, Tuning, Applications)*, as well as *Fuzzy Classifier Systems*, and *Fuzzy Classification – Concept Learning*.

Neural networks can be employed in order to determine fuzzy rules from training data. In this case, clustering neural networks are usually applied, for example the SOFM depicted in Section 3.1.8. Instead of neural networks, fuzzy clustering algorithms (Section 6.3.2) may by used. This approach, with Kohonen's SOFM proposed for generating linguistic rules, is presented in [389]; see also [347]. It is similar to the way of creating fuzzy IF-THEN rules by means of *Fuzzy Associative Memory* (FAM), introduced by Kosko [273]; and described in [347]. In this method, fuzzy rules are interpreted as associations between antecedents and consequents. Thus, neural associative memories (Section 3.1.10) can be applied to store fuzzy rules. Neural networks, along with other methods of knowledge acquisition, can help by inducing the rules from examples.

Generally, a FAM system consists of a bank of different FAM associations [273]. It should be noted that the table-lookup representation of a fuzzy rule base in the Wang and Mendel's method of rule generation, in fact, realizes a FAM bank based on both the generated rules and linguistic rules of human experts.

In [74], [75] knowledge in the form of fuzzy IF-THEN rules is derived from a supervised learning neural network called *fuzzy ARTMAP* [73]. This neural network performs incremental supervised learning of recognition categories (pattern classes) and multi-dimensional maps for both binary and analog input patterns. When applied to a classification task, the fuzzy ARTMAP network formulates recognition categories of input patterns, and associates each category with its respective prediction. The knowledge that the network discovers during learning is equivalent to IF-THEN rules which link fuzzy sets in their antecedent and consequent parts. At any point during the incremental learning, the network architecture can be translated into a collection of fuzzy IF-THEN rules. However, the number of these rules is usually too big, so a prunning method is applied in order to reduce the rule-base, corresponding to the network architecture, by removing excessive recognition categories and weights. Thus the compact rule-base, which maintains the predictive accuracy of the full network, is extracted.

The idea of using ARTMAP networks for rule generation, and employing the fuzzy ARTMAP in order to solve classification tasks, is developed by other researchers; see e.g. [495], [269], [469]. The rules associated with the network provide a readability of the classification results. A modified fuzzy ARTMAP for pattern recognition is proposed in [67]. An ART-based neural architecture for extracting membership functions from training data is used in [15] for fuzzy controllers in robotics. More examples can be found.

Different methods of rule extraction from neural networks are briefly described in [329]. The connectionist networks presented in [144] and [448] are used for rule generation with regard to medical applications. The latter is a multi-layer neural network for the headache detection. However, the number of rules extracted for a relatively simple problem is exceedingly large. A reasonably compact collection of rules with high predictive accuracy is obtained in [462]. Linguistic rules are also generated in [585], using a neuro-fuzzy framework. Logical rules are extracted from neural networks in [114]. A recurrent neural network for rule extraction is presented in [80]. A survey on extracting rules from trained artificial neural networks is also done in [10]. Many papers on rule generating from neural networks are cited in [10] and [329]. The method developed in [135], as well as others, are mentioned in [329]. Some of them employ genetic algorithms, e.g. [308], [137].

6.5 Hybrid Learning Algorithms for Neuro-Fuzzy Systems

This section is devoted to neuro-fuzzy systems trained by hybrid learning methods. At first, the neuro-fuzzy systems well-known from the literature are briefly described (Section 6.5.1). Then, two hybrid learning algorithms proposed for rule generating and parameter tuning are depicted (Section 6.5.2), as well as results of their application to medical diagnosis problems (Section 6.5.3).

6.5.1 Examples of Hybrid Learning Neuro-Fuzzy Systems

Different examples of neuro-fuzzy systems are presented e.g. in [347]. Among others, three neuro-fuzzy systems that use hybrid learning for rule generating and parameter tuning have been described. The first system is called NEFCON, which stands for *NEuro-Fuzzy CONtroller*. This is a system for control applications. The next one is NEFCLASS, which stands for *NEuro-Fuzzy CLASSifier*, and was designed for classification problems, or more precisely, for pattern recognition. The third system, called NEFPROX, which stands for *NEuro-Fuzzy function apPROXimation*, can be applied to function approximation.

These systems are based on the *generic fuzzy perceptron* [347], [345], which is a kind of fuzzy neural networks (see Section 3.2). The generic fuzzy perceptron has the architecture of a classical MLP, described in Section 3.1.2, but the weights are modelled as fuzzy sets. The idea behind using the fuzzy perceptron is to provide a framework for learning algorithms to be interpreted as a system of linguistic rules, and to be able to use prior knowledge in the form of fuzzy IF-THEN rules. Interpretation of the perceptron architecture is possible in the form of linguistic rules, because the fuzzy weights can be associated with linguistic terms.

Each of these systems can learn a rule-base and then tune the parameters of the membership functions. A fuzzy perceptron, like a classical MLP, is used for function approximation. Thus, the rule-base can be obtained as an approximation of an (unknown) function. The linguistic rules which perform this approximation, and define the system, are determined from a sequence of examples by learning. The fuzzy perceptron is composed of an input layer, one hidden layer, and an output layer. In contrast to classical MLPs, the connections are weighted with fuzzy sets instead of real numbers. Some connections always have the same weight, which means that there are *shared weights*, to make sure that for each linguistic value there can be only one representation as a particular fuzzy set. The connections between input neurons and hidden neurons are labeled with linguistic terms corresponding to the antecedent fuzzy sets. Connections that come from the same input neurons and have identical labels always carry the same fuzzy weight. These connections are called linked connections and their weight is called shared weight. The output layer is different in each neuro-fuzzy system.

In the NEFCON system [346], [349], [348], for neuro-fuzzy control applications, the input variables are state variables of a technical system which has to be controlled. The output variable is the control action applied to this system. The neurons of the hidden layer represent fuzzy rules in the form (2.94). This system has only one output neuron.

In the NEFCLASS system [350], [352], [351], for classification, the rule-base approximates a function that represents a classification problem and maps an input pattern to proper class. This system does not use membership functions in the rule's consequents.

The NEFPROX system [347], for function approximation, has output connections similar to that of the NEFCON, with shared weights, but more than one output neuron can be included in this system.

Architectures of these systems and hybrid learning algorithms are presented in [347].

The learning process for the NEFCON system consists of two stages: learning fuzzy rules and learning fuzzy sets. The first stage involves structure (architecture) learning, the second is parameter learning. The knowledge base (rule base) of the system is implicitly given by the network architecture. As a matter of fact, there are several different learning methods for this system. The rule base can be given, or else obtained by learning. Then, the parameters are adjusted to modify the membership functions.

Similarly, in the NEFCLASS system, after the rule base is created, the learning procedure tunes the membership functions of the antecedents of the rules. There are also different methods of rule generation and a simple heuristic procedure for the modification of fuzzy sets. In this case the learning algorithm is simpler.

In the NEFPROX system, some rules can be known and the remaining rules may be found by learning. However, the whole rule base can be generated by the rule learning algorithm, which selects fuzzy rules based on a predefined partitioning of the input space, the same as in the NEFCLASS system. This partitioning is given by initial fuzzy sets. As in NEFCON and NEFCLASS, the learning procedure for fuzzy sets is a simple heuristic. For details, see [347].

The rule learning methods for these systems may be incremental or decremental. The latter approach means that the algorithm starts with all the rules that can be created and then eliminates some rules. In the former, incremental learning, the number of rules can be increased by adding rule after rule; starting with an initial fuzzy partition for each variable. Decremental rule learning can be used if there are only a few input variables with not too many fuzzy sets.

There are also other examples of neuro-fuzzy systems presented in the literature, but many of them do not employ any algorithms for rule generating, so the rule base must be known in advance. They can only adjust the parameters of the antecedent and consequent fuzzy sets. One system of this kind is ANFIS (Adaptive-Network-based Fuzzy Inference System). This system implements the Takagi-Sugeno type of rules [494], which have a functional form (linear combination of input variables) of the consequent part; see Section 2.3.1. The architecture is five-layer feed-forward, where the first two layers are the same as in the basic architecture presented in Fig. 4.2. The next layers correspond to the consequent part of the rules. This system was introduced by Jang [225], [226], [227]. This is one of the first hybrid neuro-fuzzy systems for function approximation. For details see also e.g. [347]. Different methods have been proposed for tuning parameters, including hybrid learning.

6.5.2 Description of Two Hybrid Learning Algorithms for Rule Generation

The neuro-fuzzy systems called NEFCON, NEFCLASS, and NEFPROX, described briefly in Section 6.5.1, can generate fuzzy IF-THEN rules using incremental or decremental rule learning. In addition, these systems are based on a fuzzy neural network (fuzzy perceptron). In this section, examples of hybrid learning algorithms, which may be used for the neuro-fuzzy systems presented in this book, are outlined. This kind of algorithm determines fuzzy rules when the number of rules is not known. Then, after the rule base is created, a supervised method for adjusting parameters can be employed.

A clustering algorithm can be applied to rule generating but the number of clusters, which corresponds to the number of rules, usually needs to be fixed. Classical clustering methods are thus combined with some heuristic techniques in order to generate the correct number of rules. The algorithms proposed in [479], [440], [438], [439] are examples of this kind of method. They incorporate some ideas that come from LVQ and *fuzzy c-means* algorithms (see Sections 3.1.9, and 6.3.2, respectively), as well as heuristic methods. One of these algorithms can be presented as follows.

Let $\mathbf{Z} = [\mathbf{z}_1, \ldots , \mathbf{z}_q]^T \in \mathbf{R}^{qn}$ be a given data set.

- Fix D, B, and α_1.

- Set the initial number of clusters $c = 1$, and $i = 1$, $k = 1$.

- Create cluster $\mathbf{W}_i$ with data vector $\mathbf{z}_k \in \mathbf{W}_i$ and the cluster center $\mathbf{v}_i = \mathbf{z}_k$.

- For $k = 2, \ldots , q$, check the Euclidean distance between data vector $\mathbf{z}_k$ and the center $\mathbf{v}_i$ of cluster $\mathbf{W}_i$, according to the following condition

$$\|\mathbf{z}_k - \mathbf{v}_i\| \leqslant D \tag{6.28}$$

- If inequality (6.28) is satisfied, check the distance between data vector $\mathbf{z}_k$ and each cluster different from $\mathbf{W}_i$, if any exist, according to the condition

$$d\left(\mathbf{z}_k, \mathbf{W}_j\right) > B \tag{6.29}$$

for $j \neq i$, where $j = 1, \ldots , c$, and $\mathbf{W} = \{\mathbf{W}_1, \ldots , \mathbf{W}_c\}$ is a set of clusters. The distance, d, between data vector $\mathbf{z}_k$ and cluster $\mathbf{W}_j$ is defined as the minimum of the Euclidean distances between vector $\mathbf{z}_k$ and each element belonging to cluster $\mathbf{W}_j$.

- If inequality (6.29) is fulfilled, assign data vector $\mathbf{z}_k$ to cluster $\mathbf{W}_i$ and update the cluster center $\mathbf{v}_i$ using the formula

$$\mathbf{v}_i := \mathbf{v}_i + \alpha_i \left(\mathbf{z}_k - \mathbf{v}_i\right) \tag{6.30}$$

where $\alpha_i \in [0, 1]$ is the learning rate, which decreases with each iteration of the algorithm, depending on the number of elements in the cluster.

- For $k = 1, \ldots, q$, and $z_k \notin W_i$, do:

For $i = 1, \ldots, c$, check the distance between data vector z_k and cluster W_i, according to the condition

$$d(z_k, W_i) > B \tag{6.31}$$

If inequality (6.31) is satisfied, check the distance between data vector z_k and each cluster created which differs from W_i, using Equation (6.29). If this condition is fulfilled, assign vector z_k to cluster W_i and update the cluster center v_i by formula (6.30). Otherwise, change the value of the constant B as follows

$$B = \min_{1 \leqslant j \leqslant c} d(z_k, W_j) \tag{6.32}$$

and return to the second step of this algorithm.

If inequality (6.31) is not fulfilled, increase the number of clusters, c, increase index i, and return the third step of the algorithm in order to create a new cluster with the initial center vector z_k.

As a result of this algorithm, we obtain the number of clusters, c, and the clusters $W_1, \ldots, W_c$, with the values of their centers: $v_1, \ldots, v_c$.

Note that Equation (6.30) is the same as the updating formula (3.30) in the LVQ algorithm described in Section 3.1.9.

Another algorithm, presented in [479], incorporates a similar idea for creating new clusters and updating their centers, but without using constant B. This method creates clusters, starting with a very small value of D. Thus, the number of clusters obtained in the first iteration of this algorithm is very large, almost the same as the amount of data. Then, in the proceeding iterations the data vectors are replaced by the cluster centers and the value of D increases, resulting in lower number of new clusters. For the data set $Z = [z_1, \ldots, z_q]^T \in \mathbf{R}^{qn}$, this algorithm can be presented in the following steps:

- Fix D, τ, and α_1.

- Set $c = 1$, and $i = 1$, $k = 1$.

- Create cluster W_i with data vector $z_k \in W_i$ and the cluster center $v_i = z_k$.

- For $k = 2, \ldots, q$, check the Euclidean distance between data vector z_k and the center v_i of cluster W_i, according to condition (6.28).

- If inequality (6.28) is satisfied, include data vector $\mathbf{z}_k$ into cluster $\mathbf{W}_i$ and update the cluster center $\mathbf{v}_i$ using formula (6.30), where, in a similar way to the previous algorithm, the learning rate, $\alpha_i \epsilon [0, 1]$, decreases with each iteration.

- For $k = 2, \ldots, q$, and $i = 1, \ldots, c$, if $\mathbf{z}_k \notin \mathbf{W}_i$, create new clusters by returning to the third step with $c := c + 1$.

- If the stopping criteria (for example, a desired number of clusters) are not met, increase the value of D as follows

$$D := D + \tau$$

and replace the data set $\mathbf{Z}$ by the prototypes (cluster centers) $\mathbf{v}_i$, for $i = 1, \ldots, c$; then return to the first step. Hence, the cluster centers play the role of data vectors. Otherwise, stop.

The algorithm can be terminated using different stopping criteria. It is possible to apply a desired number of clusters if this is known. In practice, a neuro-fuzzy system is usually constructed based on the fuzzy IF-THEN rules that correspond to the clusters obtained, and the performance of this system is tested. In this way, we can decrease the number of rules (clusters) in subsequent iterations of the algorithm until the system works properly.

Different heuristic techniques, as well as various modifications of the methods proposed, may be introduced to produce clusters when their number is not fixed and must be find by the algorithm.

The fuzzy rules generated from the methods described above are expressed in the form (2.94), where membership functions of the fuzzy sets can be Gaussian or other shaped functions with centers that are components of the vector centers $\mathbf{v}_1, \ldots, \mathbf{v}_c$ obtained from the presented algorithm. The width parameter vector, σ_i, for $i = 1, \ldots, c$, can be determined using the following formula

$$\sigma_{ij} = \left(\frac{\sum_{k=1}^{n} u_{ik} \left(z_{kj} - v_{ij}\right)^2}{\sum_{k=1}^{n} u_{ik}} \right)^{\frac{1}{2}} \tag{6.33}$$

where σ_{ij} and v_{ij} are components of the vectors σ_i and $\mathbf{v}_i$, respectively, for $i = 1, \ldots, c$; the components of matrix $\mathbf{U}$, denoted as u_{ik}, are calculated according to Equation (6.27), which means that vectors $\mathbf{v}_1, \ldots, \mathbf{v}_c$ are treated as the centers of fuzzy clusters. Thus, the idea of *fuzzy c-partition* (Section 6.3.2) is incorporated. A formula similar to Equation (6.33) is used in [81].

The architecture of the neuro-fuzzy system corresponding to this rule base can be the same as that presented, for example, in Fig. 4.2, where elements of the first layer realize the antecedent membership functions and the third-layer parameters are center values of the consequent membership functions, with the centers and width parameters obtained from the algorithms described above. The number of rules, which is equal to the number of clusters, $N = c$, determines the number of elements in the second layer of the architecture.

The parameters of the membership functions can be tuned by a gradient method, similarly to that depicted in Section 6.1.2; see formulas (6.11), (6.12), (6.13).

The algorithms of rule generating presented in this section can be applied to the multi-segment architecture proposed in [479], and also considered in [480]. Each segment of this architecture is a neuro-fuzzy system that is responsible for recognizing only one class when the system is solving a classification task. In this case, the latter of the two clustering methods described above is especially suitable. It is worth mentioning that the data should be scaled before use in this algorithm.

6.5.3   Medical Diagnosis Applications

The algorithms described in Section 6.5.2 have been used to generate fuzzy IF-THEN rules in order to solve various medical diagnosis problems. One of these is the case of heart disease. Data from the Cleveland Clinic Foundation are available on the Internet [324]. The published experiments with the Cleveland database mostly concentrate on simply attempting to determining presence or absence of the disease. They use 14 attributes which represent features such as age, sex, chest pain type, resting blood pressure, serum cholestorol, fasting blood sugar, resting electrocardiographic results, maximum heart rate achieved, exercise induced angina, etc. The final attribute is the diagnosis of heart disease, expressed as values 0 or 1. This is the predicted attribute, which depends on the values of the 13 previous attributes. The data that have been used constitute 297 vectors with different values of the 14 attributes. In order to solve the diagnosis problem, the neuro-fuzzy system represented by the architecture shown in Fig. 4.2 has been employed, with the number of elements in the second layer determined by the algorithm described in Section 6.5.2; i.e. 26 rules. The number of inputs is equal to the number of attributes, that is 14. In order to tune the parameters of the membership functions, the data set was split into 257 items of training data and 40 vectors of testing data. The gradient learning method presented in Section 6.1.2 was applied. The result was very good, with only one mistake [440].

Another medical diagnosis problem that can be solved by the algorithms described in Section 6.5.2 is breast cancer. The data available on the Internet [324] come from the University of Wisconsin Hospitals. The database contains information concerning 10 attributes, such as clump thickness, uniformity of cell size, uniformity of cell shape, marginal adhesion, single epithelial cell size, bare nuclei, bland chromatin, normal nucleoli, mitoses. The final attribute concerns the diagnosis of breast cancer, with two distinguished values for benign and malignant cases of the disease. The data set contained 487 different data vectors, each composed of 10 components, corresponding to the attributes. This data set was divided into 387 learning vectors and 100 testing vectors. The same architecture was employed, with 36 elements in the second layer, determined by the number of rules generated, and 9 inputs. The same gradient algorithm was applied to tune the parameters of the membership functions. In this case, for the testing sequence of 100 vectors, there were 4 mistakes, so the result is also good, similar to or even better than the results obtained by other methods [324], [536].

In order to solve problems in which there are more than two different classes to be distinguished, for example the case of heart disease with several kinds of diagnosis, the multi-segment architecture is recommended. This consists of the neuro-fuzzy systems which are called segments. When applied to classification tasks, the number of segments is equal to the number of discerned classes. Each segment is trained to recognize a particular class, so it should decide whether an input data vector belongs to this class or not. There are two possible ways of realising a multi-segment system of this kind; these are described in [479], [480], and in [481], [441], respectively.

In the former, the first segment receives all the input data vectors entered into the multi-segment system. If the data vector is identified as a member of the class associated with this segment, the output value of the segment differs from zero and indicates the class, otherwise the output value equals zero. If the input data is discarded as not belonging to the first class (assigned to the first segment), it is fed into the input of the second segment, which is responsible for recognizing the second class. If this segment does not accept this data vector as a member of its class, the data is entered into the third segment, and so on. In this way, the second segment does not receive the input data identified with the class associated with the first segment. Similarly, the data vectors accepted as members of the second class do not need to be transmitted to the input of the third and subsequent segments. The output value of the multi-segment system, for a given input data vector, is equal to the output of the segment which has identified this input vector as belonging to its class.

In the latter system, all the input data vectors are entered into every segment in parallel. The output value of the segment which accepts the input vector as a member of its class differs from zero, while the output values of the remaining segments equal zero. The output values of the system are equal to the non-zero output values of the segments which have accepted the corresponding input vectors as members of their classes. A multi-segment system of this type is illustrated in Fig. 6.5. As with the first way, it is composed of M segments and an output unit which transmits the output value of the appropriate segment to the output of the system. This value represents the class associated with the input data vector. It should be noted that the parallel multi-segment system performs classification faster than the former system.

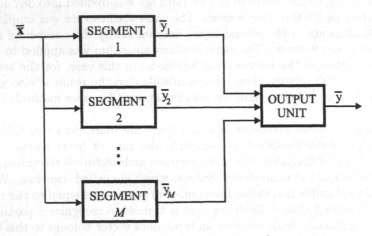

FIGURE 6.5. The multi-segment neuro-fuzzy system

The number of segments in the multi-segment architectures can equal the number of classes minus one, because the last segment is not necessary since the previous ones should identify all the input data vectors that do not belong to the class associated with the last segment. Thus it is obvious that the class which is not assigned to any segment contains those input data vectors which have not been accepted by the segments of the architecture as members of their classes. Of course, the architecture can include this (additional) segment, in order to make sure that the extant segments perform classification correctly. In this case, the output values of the multi-segment system always differ from zero, if not this means that the input data does not belong to any classes represented by the segments.

Each segment of the multi-segment architectures presented in the above cited literature is a classical neuro-fuzzy system with the modifications proposed in [479]. An additional layer has been added (before the defuzzification layers) to the architecture shown in Fig. 4.2. This layer contains elements that realize sigmoidal functions with parameters corresponding to degrees of rule activation. Moreover, the so-called *zero rule* (with the value of the consequent fuzzy set equal to zero) is taken into account, so the additional parameter representing the degree of activation of this rule is entered into the second adder of the defuzzification layer. Of course, other architectures can be proposed as segments of multi-segment systems.

As mentioned earlier, each segment is trained to recognize those data items that belong to its class and identify other data vectors as not belonging to its class. The rule bases of the segments differ from each other in numbers of rules and parameter values which are obtained as a result of a learning process. Thus it is obvious that the architectures of the neuro-fuzzy segments, which reflect the collections of rules, are different. Hybrid learning, composed of a rule generating algorithm and a parameter tuning method, can be employed. In the medical applications, described above, the algorithms presented in Section 6.5.2, especially the second one, determined the rules. Then the gradient algorithms, depicted in Section 6.1.2, were used to adjust the *center* and *width* parameters of the Gaussian membership functions. If the center parameters are properly chosen during the rule generating process, only the width parameters need be tuned by the gradient algorithm.

One advantage of applying neuro-fuzzy systems in the form of multisegment architectures is clear even in the case of only two classes. It is much easier to train a system that incorporates a smaller number of rules in its rule base. It is obvious that each segment needs less rules than the classical neuro-fuzzy system constructed to identify all classes. Moreover, the multisegment system is suitable for realizing an intelligent system that can learn from mistakes [441], by modifying the architecture of a particular segment based on the mistake observed. This system improves its performance, so the longer it works the less mistakes occur, and eventually it should produce only correct answers. The systems of this kind can be especially helpful as medical expert systems, with the possibility of many different decisions concerning a diagnosis.

7
Intelligent Systems

The neuro-fuzzy architectures and hybrid learning procedures, described in the previous chapters, can be employed to create so-called *intelligent computational systems*. A general schema of these kind of systems is presented in this chapter. Intelligent systems usually refer to the field of *Artificial Intelligence* (AI) or *Computational Intelligence* (CI). The difference between these branches of Computer Science is explained in Section 7.1. Then, expert systems are outlined (Section 7.2). Intelligent computational systems (Section 7.3) can be viewed as a special type of expert systems. Finally, in Section 7.4, perception-based systems are considered as intelligent systems in AI.

7.1 Artificial and Computational Intelligence

AI deals with methods, and systems for solving problems that normally require human intelligence [18], [79], [535], [147]. The main goal of AI is to construct computer based systems that solve tasks which are routinely performed by human beings.

There are many definitions of AI. The following explanation can be found in Webster's dictionary: " AI is the branch of computer science that studies how smart a machine can be, which involves the capability of a device to perform functions normally associated with human intelligence, such as reasoning, learning, and self improvement"; see [591], and also [36]. The ability to reason, which is a very important aspect of human intelligence, is called the commonsense knowledge by AI researchers [147], [316]; see also [546].

AI was started in 1950s, after the publication of Turing's famous article [504], which described the *Turing test*, and another influential paper by Shannon [464] on the possibility of computer chess. However, the name *artificial intelligence* was not used until the *Dartmouth Conference* in 1956 at Dartmouth College in Hanover, New Hampshire. This was probably the first time that the term *artificial intelligence* was proposed, in spite of the fact that it seemed rather contentious [79]. Earlier, the works of Turing and Shannon referred to *computer intelligence*. The *Turing test* was proposed to put forward the idea that computers could be programmed so as to exhibit intelligent behavior. In fact, a computer chess program seems to confirm this idea.

As mentioned earlier, many definitions of AI have been suggested since this term was introduced. A very short one, presented in [79], states: "AI is the study of mental faculties through the use of computational models", and explains that this definition may be viewed as the use of computers to study the mental faculties of people, such as vision or natural language. It should be noted that on this understanding of AI, the word *computational*, which is related to *computers*, was emphasized.

Computational Intelligence was a new term suggested as a title for conferences that comprised neural networks, fuzzy systems, genetic algorithms, as well as other similar subjects [586]. There is also a journal entitled *Computational Intelligence* (Blackwell). In the preface to the book [586], which contains contributions to the *1994 IEEE World Congress on Computational Intelligence*, it is stated that originally the congress had "intelligent systems" instead of "computational intelligence" in its title. However, recognizing that *intelligent systems* had a specific meaning in the AI community, so the contents of the congress was not consistent with this meaning, the title was changed. In the first paper presented in [586] the difference between CI and AI is explained by Bezdek [36]. He introduced this new term, and had earlier discussed the relationship between neural networks, pattern recognition and intelligence in [35]. The article published by Marks [314] also concerns *computational* and *artificial intelligence*. Later, publications on CI, by other authors, appeared, e.g. [133], [387]. Now, many conferences and books have the term *computational intelligence* in their titles.

The term *computational* in [36] refers to *mathematics + computers*, which is similar to the definition of AI presented above. However, it is obvious that both CI and AI use computers, the "computational" in the sense of CI means that the *computational systems* depend on numerical data, while intelligent systems in AI apply a symbolic form of the data, and incorporate knowledge in a way that the systems in CI do not. Bezdek's definition of CI is as follows: "A system is *computationally intelligent* when if deals only with numerical (low-level) data, has a pattern recognition component, and does not use knowledge in the AI sense; and additionally, when it (begins to) exhibit (i) computational adaptivity; (ii) computational fault tolerance; (iii) speed approaching human-like turnaround, and (iv) error rates that approximate human performance". According to Bezdek, an *artificially intelligent* system is a CI system whose added value comes from incorporating knowledge in a non-numerical way.

The definition of CI presented in [314] focuses on the contributing technologies: "...neural networks, genetic algorithms, fuzzy systems, evolutionary programming, and artificial life are the building blocks of CI."

The following definition of CI is given in [133]: "... These technologies of neural, fuzzy and evolutionary systems were brought together under the rubric of Computational Intelligence, ... to generally describe methods of computation that can be used to adapt solutions of new problems and do not rely on explicit human knowledge."

When the concept of CI arose the methods mentioned above, as well as their combinations, were proposed as a way of creating "intelligent systems" that were, of course, different from the systems which had been constructing in AI. In particular, the connectionist (neural) expert systems significantly differ from classical expert systems (see Section 7.2). The idea of using the term *computational* comes from an earlier paper written by Bezdek [34], where he compared pattern recognition, neural networks, and artificial intelligence, based on three levels: *numeric*, *symbolic*, and *organic*. The *symbolic* level is associated with the term "artificial", that is non-biological (man-made). The *organic* level refers to "biological", and the *numeric* level corresponds to "computational". The same approach is presented in [35]. Thus the term *computational* is most closely related to connectionist networks, which process numerical data and do not possess a knowledge base in the form of IF-THEN rules. Fuzzy systems are different since they use linguistic fuzzy rules and accept symbolic (linguistic) values. However, fuzzy systems with a fuzzifier and a defuzzifier, as well as neuro-fuzzy systems, employ numerical (crisp) input and output values, but they have a collection of rules as their knowledge base. Of course, they are different from the systems developed in AI.

Recently we have observed the tendency to create more hybrid systems that combine neural networks, fuzzy systems, genetic algorithms, as well as classical expert systems together; This is mentioned in Section 7.2.2. Thus the new trend leads to the building of intelligent systems in the sense of AI, employing methods used in CI.

It should be added that the methods applied in CI to create intelligent systems, for example, neural networks, fuzzy systems, genetic algorithms belong to the area called *Soft Computing* [573], [549], [443], [232]. In contrast to *hard computing*, the *soft computing* methods deal with uncertainty, impreciseness, and vagueness. The probability theory and chaotic theory are also assigned to this field.

7.2   Expert Systems

Expert systems [221], [518] are the main branch of applications of AI. *Knowledge engineering*, which is the research area concerned with the basic technology for construction of expert systems, can be called *practical artificial intelligence* since it is a field of research oriented towards applications of AI, and expert systems are concrete products in this area [497]. In addition to classical expert systems, the soft computing methods, i.e. neural networks, fuzzy systems, as well as genetic algorithms, have been recently employed to perform various tasks of expert systems or to support these systems.

7.2.1   Classical Expert Systems

Expert systems are often called *rule-based systems* or *knowledge-based systems*; see e.g. [79], [355], [54], [282]. Typically an expert system consists of an inference engine and a knowledge base. Figure 7.1 shows the basic structure of an expert system. The *explanation facility* block in this structure represents the tools, developed in most expert systems, that allow the inference process performed by the system to be explained. This means that users can understand questions being asked, as well as inferred conclusions. The *interface* serves to communicate with users and *knowledge engineers* whose job is *knowledge acquisition*. Knowledge engineers gather knowledge from human experts and deliver it to the system. As we see, the main part of the system is the block that contains the knowledge base to store the knowledge and the inference engine for using it to infer conclusions (answers) to the questions and data provided by users.

One of the best known expert systems, produced in 1970s, is the medical diagnostic system called MYCIN [467]. This is a computer program designed to diagnose and then prescribe treatment for an infectious disease, in particular, a bacterial infection of the blood. The system should decide what bacterium is causing the disease (or what are the most likely possibilities), and then – based upon this decision – determine what antibiotic to give the patient to kill the bacterium.

Many different medical diagnosis expert systems have been proposed in addition to the MYCIN program. An example is CADUCEUS, a system created in order to diagnose diseases of internal organs, like heart, lungs, and liver; see [401], [399], [400]. Moreover, a large number of expert systems for other applications have been constructed. One of them is PROSPECTOR, a well-known program, designed to predict the location of ore deposits [118], [115]. These two examples represent the first group of expert systems introduced in 1970s. Since then, a great number of others have been proposed.

The MYCIN expert system has been put to use for medical diagnosis and treatment, but in its development it has been tied to a system called TEIRESIAS (see [104]), and furthermore, in 1980, the expert system called EMYCIN was built. This system can be widely employed and is not restricted to medical diagnosis applications.

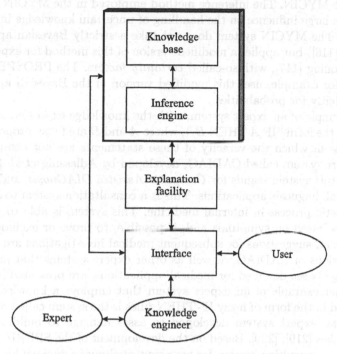

FIGURE 7.1. Basic structure of an expert system

Most expert systems available for use are "shells". They consist of the software programs required, but do not contain any knowledge bases. Thus users can introduce the knowledge appropriate for the problems to be solved by the systems. The big advantage of these shells is that they can be employed in various applications, without the necessity of creating a software system specific for each problem. Since this kind of systems puts the knowledge of experts or the experience of specialists into the memory of a computer and uses it, such a system is called an expert system.

The knowledge in knowledge-based systems (expert systems) is usually expressed in the form of IF-THEN statements; more precisely: IF *premise* THEN *conclusion*.

The EMYCIN expert system was constructed as a shell. Therefore, the possibility of its application goes beyond medical diagnosis problems. If the knowledge of an expert in any field can be expressed in the form of the IF-THEN statements, the system may be used. The EMYCIN stands for *Empty* MYCIN, which means the expert system shell for the MYCIN.

7.2.2   Fuzzy and Neural Expert Systems

The role of fuzzy sets is well understood, and evidence of its use is wide-spread, including in expert systems, for example in medical diagnostic systems, like MYCIN. The inference method employed in the MYCIN system has had a large influence on the handling of uncertain knowledge in expert systems. The MYCIN system does not take a strictly Bayesian approach (see e.g. [116]) but applies a modified version of this method for expert system reasoning [117], with so-called *certainty factors*. The PROSPECTOR system, for example, uses this modified version of the Bayesian approach but explicitly for probabilities.

An example of an expert system, with the knowledge expressed as statements in the form "IF A THEN B ", where A and B are fuzzy propositions, and those in which the veracity of these statements are not complete, is the expert system called CADIAG, developed by Adlassnig *et al.* [3]. The name of this system stands for *Computer Assisted DIAGnosis*, and relates to medical diagnosis applications. This is a consultation system to support a diagnostic process in internal medicine. This system is able to propose diagnoses based on symptoms and, if possible, to prove or exclude them. If necessary, suggestions for subsequent medical investigations are offered. New versions of CADIAG, as well as other expert systems that use fuzzy knowledge bases designed for medical applications, are presented in [4].

Another example of an expert system that employs a knowledge base expressed in the form of fuzzy IF-THEN rules is the system called SPERIL. This is an expert system developed to asses damage to buildings after earthquakes [219], [220]. Based on the development of the SPERIL system, a practical consulting system for assessing earthquake damage for non-life insurance companies in Japan has been constructed. Information about these systems can be found in [497]. The inference process in the SPERIL expert system is based on Dempster-Shafer theory [107], [463], for handling uncertainty for which Bayesian probability was inappropriate. It is worth mentioning that the Dempster-Shafer's idea of *upper* and *lower* probability includes Bayesian probability as a special case (see e.g. [497]). In order to use a knowledge base expressed by fuzzy sets, the Dempster-Shafer theory has been extended to fuzzy sets without losing its essence.

Expert systems with the inference based on the Dempster-Shafer theory can also be developed for medical diagnosis applications; see e.g. [482], [483]. These systems deal with knowledge accompanied by uncertainty and fuzziness.

As explained in Section 7.2.1, an expert system is a computer-based system that emulates the reasoning process of a human expert within a specific domain of knowledge. In *fuzzy expert systems*, the knowledge is usually represented by a collection of fuzzy IF-THEN rules; see e.g. [236], [161], [455]. A fuzzy inference system based on IF-THEN rules is practically an expert system if the rules are developed via expert knowledge [27]. It is worth noticing that fuzzy expert systems are software oriented, while fuzzy controllers are often built as hardware applications.

Different methods for handling uncertainty and vagueness in expert systems are presented in [282]. Approximate reasoning in expert systems is discussed e.g. in [571], [158].

Genetic algorithms (see Section 6.2) can be employed to create the knowledge base in fuzzy expert systems, as well as for knowledge filtering [391], [580]. A bibliography on combinations of GAs and fuzzy expert systems is available on the Internet [90], Section: *Fuzzy Expert Systems*. Neural networks are also applied to expert and fuzzy expert systems, see e.g. [391].

Neural networks can be used as an alternative to conventional rule-based expert systems [584]. Neural networks can solve various classification problems, particularly in diagnosis, pattern recognition, etc. In contrast to classical expert systems, they acquire knowledge without extracting IF-THEN rules from human experts being based on training data. After the learning process, neural networks have the potential to perform like expert systems. The learning ability of neural networks might ease the knowledge acquisition bottleneck that impedes the development of classical expert systems.

Connectionist expert systems have been considered mainly for medical diagnosis [144], [199], [448], as well as for fault diagnosis of an automobile engine, for instance; see [313], and also [584]. The medical diagnosis systems are neural networks, in which the input layer neurons take the information about selected symptoms of a patient's diseases, expressed by numerical values. The number of diseases that the system can recognize equals the number of output layer neurons. Special care needs to be taken in order to choose the number of hidden layer neurons. The connectionist expert system for the fault diagnosis task is a single-hidden layer neural network trained by the back-propagation algorithm. This neural network-based expert system can identify 26 different faults such as a shorted plug, an open plug, a broken fuel injector, etc. The training sequence consists of 16 sets of data for each failure, each of the sets representing a single engine cycle. A total of 16×26 data vectors with 52 components in each vector has been employed for training, and the problem of defective engine diagnosis has been successfully solved; see [313] or [584], for more details. Several examples of existing neural networks for medical diagnosis and fault diagnosis are presented in [312].

A drawback of neural networks is the lack of explanation facilities, typical for expert systems. Thus a neural network expert system is usually unable to inform users about the reasons for the decisions made by the system. However, there are some ideas to solve this problem, for instance, genetic algorithms can be used to design the explanation facilities [124], [123].

Fuzzy systems and neural networks are both soft computing approaches to modelling expert behavior [573]; see also [347]. The purpose is to imitate the actions of an expert who solves complex tasks. This means that we do not need to use a mathematical model of the problem that we want to solve but we examine how the expert deals successfully to obtain the solution. A learning process of neural networks or neuro-fuzzy systems can be part of knowledge acquisition. The learning method used is usually supervised, because it looks for examples provided by a teacher (expert), mostly in the form of a training data sequence. Thus the learning process is performed based on trial and error guided by an error signal that tells how well the system works. Fuzzy systems employ fuzzy IF-THEN rules that can be gathered from examples of this kind. Thus, in this way, the knowledge base expressed in linguistic rules is acquired. In this sense, fuzzy systems, neural networks, and neuro-fuzzy systems are suitable tools for modelling expert behavior. It is worth emphasizing that classical expert systems, which try to model the knowledge or the behavior of human experts, usually by means of logical representations based on symbolic structures, encounter trouble in dealing with uncertainty and vagueness [110]. As mentioned earlier, traditional expert systems employ probability theory, in particular the Bayesian approach, for handling of uncertain knowledge. It should be explained that on this understanding of modelling expert behavior, the intention is not to model an expert exactly, but to create a system that produces results which are similar to the decisions made by a real expert. More information about expert systems of this kind can be found in [347].

In addition to the role of neural networks as an alternative to the conventional rule-based systems, they can be combined with classical expert systems to create more powerful hybrid systems [319], [320], [321]. Such integrated systems have proven to be useful for developing real-world applications, including diagnostic systems, as well as control systems, also in robotics. This kind of integrated systems may be considered as intelligent agents in multi-agent systems (see e.g. [522]). In the literature, cited above, various configurations of expert system - neural network couplings are presented, and practical examples of the neuro-expert systems employed in industry are described.

A neural expert system with a fuzzy input is depicted in [168]. This means that fuzzy neural networks (see Section 3.2) play the role of fuzzy expert systems. It has been shown [170] that neural networks with fuzzy signals and fuzzy weights are ideal for modeling fuzzy expert systems with fuzzy IF-THEN rules. The fuzzy neural networks, after successful learning, operate as fuzzy expert systems [55], [65]. This kind of fuzzy expert systems are also described in [56]. In the earlier papers, a computational equivalence of fuzzy expert systems and classical neural networks is shown [63]. Similar equivalence concerns hybrid neural networks, which are in fact, fuzzy inference neural networks [59]. Thus neural networks, fuzzy neural networks, fuzzy inference neural networks, and fuzzy systems, can be viewed as alternatives for classical expert systems. Besides, all of them can be combined together to create more powerful intelligent systems.

A study of neuro-fuzzy expert systems may be found in [331]. These systems incorporate fuzzy reasoning into connectionist expert systems. In [333] the fuzzy MLP, proposed in [372], and mentioned in Section 3.2, has been applied to design such connectionist (neural) systems. The presented system can handle uncertainty and/or impreciseness in the input data, inferring, for a classification problem, output class membership values. The system is able to justify its decision, to the user, in the form of IF-THEN rules. It is worth emphasizing that, in this case, the rules are not explicitly included in the knowledge base but are generated from the learned connection weights, if the system is asked by the user for explanations.

7.3   Intelligent Computational Systems

In Section 7.1, the difference between AI and CI has been explained. According to Bezdek [36], the "intelligent systems" created by means of neural networks, fuzzy systems and genetic algorithms (as well as other *soft computing* methods) should be treated as *computationally intelligent systems*. This means that the systems of this kind are intelligent in the sense of Computational Intelligence rather than Artificial Intelligence. The name *intelligent computational systems* [420] is also suitable. It emphasizes that these systems are realized as computer programs that can solve various (computational) problems and possess some attributes of intelligence, for example knowledge acquisition, inference, learning ability. However, the term *computational* may be viewed in a broader sense. In that, it does not necessarily refer to computations of numbers (numerical data) but also to symbolic (linguistic) information with regard to computing with words (CW); see Section 2.2.6. If the system applies a symbolic form of data, and incorporates knowledge, it can be treated as an intelligent system, not only in CI but also in AI.

Intelligent computational systems should be constructed based on the soft computing methods such as fuzzy systems, neural networks, and genetic algorithms. The systems of this kind ought to be able to solve various problems, including classification and control tasks. A concept of an intelligent computational system is presented in Fig. 7.2. As we see, the main part is a fuzzy system with a fuzzifier and a defuzzifier. This means that input and output values are crisp (numerical) data. Neural networks (NNs) may be employed in different ways. First of all, they can be incorporated in a neuro-fuzzy architecture. Moreover, a neural network can play the role of a defuzzifier (Section 4.5.2). It is also possible to use a neural network to approximate the functions performed by elements of the first layer of the neuro-fuzzy architecture. This layer refers to a fuzzifier, in particular if the non-singleton fuzzification method is employed (Section 4.6). Besides, a learning algorithm is very often based on a neural network, especially if a clustering network is used in order to generate fuzzy rules. If a neural network is applied as a defuzzifier, the back-propagation algorithm adjusts weights of the network to tune membership functions of antecedent and consequent fuzzy sets. The gradient learning algorithms, employed in order to optimize values of the weights or parameters of membership functions, can be supported by a genetic algorithm (GA). In addition, GAs may be used as a method of rule generation; see Section 6.4.3.

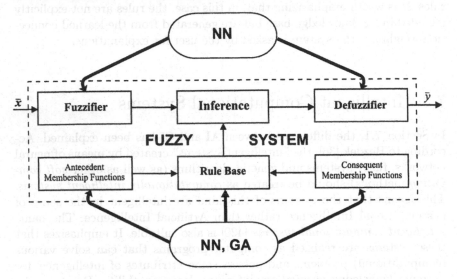

FIGURE 7.2. Basic schema of an intelligent computational system

As mentioned in Chapter 1, neuro-fuzzy architectures plus hybrid learning constitute intelligent systems. In particular, the neuro-fuzzy architectures presented in this book, with a learning algorithm can be viewed as intelligent computational systems. Figure 7.3 portrays the way of realizing the systems of this kind, according to the conception illustrated in Fig. 7.2. A fuzzy system combined with a neural network creates a form of a neuro-fuzzy architecture. The learning ability of the neuro-fuzzy system is performed by means of a hybrid method, which is a neural network training with support by a GA. The neuro-fuzzy system with the learning ability can be treated as an intelligent computational system. In general, the hybrid learning should include a rule generation algorithm and a method of parameter tuning; see Sections 6.4.3 and 6.4.2.

Different neuro-fuzzy architectures have been presented in this book. Each of them can be trained by various learning methods, usually hybrid ones. Thus many kinds of intelligent computational systems may be created. They can solve specific problems after a proper learning process. Some examples of their applications have been described in Sections 5.5 and 6.5.3.

It should be noted that the same neuro-fuzzy architectures with the same learning methods can be employed to solve various kinds of problems, for instance, control and classification tasks; see also [435]. Since control and classification problems differ from each other, they usually require different neuro-fuzzy architectures applied in order to solve these problems. These architectures are constructed based on the fuzzy IF-THEN rules, which differ in the consequent part, depending on the task under consideration. The NEFCON and NEFCLASS systems described in Section 6.5.1 are examples of these.

Intelligent computational systems should be able to solve different kinds of problems. Possessing such an ability, they resemble *general problem solvers*, understood as systems (computer programs) designed not for specific tasks but as tools for various applications. These kind of systems are important from the viewpoint of Artificial Intelligence; however, they are usually difficult to implement. The *intelligent computational systems* presented in this book may be viewed as examples of their successful implementations. The systems of this kind can play the role of expert systems as well as intelligent controllers (see e.g. [377]) and can be realized in a software or hardware form, similarly to neural networks.

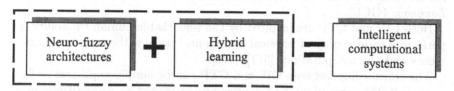

FIGURE 7.3. Architectures plus learning as intelligent systems

The concept of intelligent computational systems, presented in this section, is based on a synergy of fuzzy systems, neural networks, and genetic (evolutionary) algorithms. Neuro-fuzzy-genetic combinations are considered e.g. in [303], [2], [582], [223]. Different forms of integration of fuzzy systems with neural networks, including GAs, are described in [493]. Other papers on the subject of creating intelligent systems as a fusion of these methods, can be found in the literature, e.g. [86]. As mentioned in Section 7.1, neural networks, fuzzy systems, and genetic algorithms are *soft computing* methods. They should be viewed as complementary rather than competitive tools for constructing systems in CI or AI. It should be noted that each of these methods has some advantages as well as drawbacks; for details, see e.g. [303]. Incorporating several methods in one intelligent system allows to utilize their merits and reduce (or avoid) disadvantages, resulting in better performance of the system.

7.4 Perception-Based Intelligent Systems

According to the definition adapted from [447] and cited in [172], the aim of artificial intelligence is to develop paradigms or algorithms that allow machines to perform tasks that involve *cognition* when performed by humans. In this statement the term *cognition* is purposely used rather than *intelligence*. Thus the tasks tackled by artificial intelligence include *perception* and *language* as well as problem solving, *conscious* as well as *subconscious* processes [322]. There are many definitions of artificial intelligence. However, it seems to be obvious that perception as well as language plays an important role in intelligent systems created within artificial or computational intelligence (Section 7.1). Thus a theory that incorporates both perception and language, and can be applied to intelligent systems, is considered in this section.

The *computational theory of perceptions* (CTP), introduced by Zadeh [577], [578], is based on the methodology of *computing with words* (CW), presented in Section 2.2.6, in Chapter 2. In CTP, words play the role of labels of perceptions. The assumption is that perceptions are described in a natural or synthetic language. Humans employ mostly words in computing and reasoning. Thus, in CTP, perceptions are expressed as propositions in a natural language, and then translated into so-called *Generalized Constraint Language* (GCL).

Both CW and CTP are inspired by the remarkable human capability to perform a wide variety of physical and mental tasks without any measurements and any computations [577], [578].

The relationship between CW and CTP can be simply explained as follows. In CTP perceptions and queries are expressed as propositions in a natural language. Then, the propositions and queries are processed by CW-based methods to yield answers to queries.

The two core issues concerning CW have been mentioned in Section 2.2.6, i.e. the issue of representation of fuzzy constraints and the issue of fuzzy constraint propagation. Both of them will be considered with reference to CTP.

In CTP, reasoning with perceptions is a process of arriving at an answer, a, to a specific question, q, given a collection of perceptions as propositions expressed in a natural language. This process of reasoning is viewed as the constraint propagation from premises to a conclusion, which plays the role of an answer to a question. The following very simple example illustrates this process. Let us assume that the premises are the perceptions

$$p_1 : \quad Thomas \text{ is } young$$

$$p_2 : \quad John \text{ is } a \text{ few years older than Thomas}$$

and the question is

$$q: \quad How \ old \ is \ John?$$

Explicitation of p_1 and p_2 leads to the constraints

$$p_1 \to Age\,(Thomas) \ is \ young$$

$$p_2 \to (Age\,(John)\,.Age\,(Thomas)) \ is \ few.years.older$$

The answer, a, to the question, q, obtained by constraint propagation, is

$$a\,(q): \quad young + few$$

In this expression, *young* and *few* play the role of fuzzy numbers and their sum can be computed through the use of fuzzy arithmetic [247]. The presented example of reasoning with perceptions comes from [578].

The first step of the reasoning in CTP concerns a description of the given perceptions as propositions expressed in a natural language, resulting in the initial data set. The second step involves translation of the propositions in the initial data set into the generalized constraint language (GCL), to obtain the antecedent constraints (fuzzy constraints in premises) in explicit canonical forms. The third step pertains to translation of the question into GCL; the result is an explicit form of the question, i.e. the canonical form. The fourth step is an augmentation of antecedent constraints, resulting in the augmented data set, which consist of constraints induced by the initial data set and the external knowledge base (also formulated as propositions). Application of the rules governing generalized constraint propagation to constraints in the augmented data set leads to consequent constraints in the terminal data set, which refers to the constraints in conclusion. The fifth step, which is the last one, involves retranslation of the consequent constraints into the answer, a, to the question, q. This process of reasoning with perceptions is illustrated in Fig. 7.4.

A general schema that shows the relationship between CW and CTP is depicted in Fig. 7.5. Perceptions in the initial perception set are converted into propositions which describe them. The obtained set of the propositions, represented in a natural language, constitutes the initial data set, which is processed by CW-based methods. As a result, the terminal data set, which contains the consequent constraints (see Fig. 7.4), is inferred. Then, the terminal data set is retranslated into the answer, a, to the question, q.

Comparing Fig. 7.5 with Fig. 7.4, we see the CW-based methods realize the following tasks. Propositions in the initial data set are converted into their canonical forms, expressed in the generalized constraint language (GCL) which defines the meaning of these propositions. The collection of the canonical forms constitutes the initial constraint set (antecedent constraints). Then, the initial constraint set is augmented with canonical forms

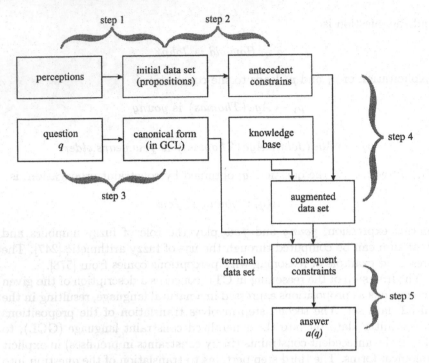

FIGURE 7.4. Basic schema of reasoning with perceptions

of those propositions in the external knowledge base which are needed to derive the answer, a, to the question, q. By successive application of the rules of generalized constraint propagation, the generalized constraints which are resident in the resulting augmented initial constraint set are transformed into a terminal constraint set, which is the canonical form of the question, q.

In CTP, reasoning is viewed as a form of computation. As was pointed out already, computation with perceptions is based on propagation of generalized constraints from premises (antecedent propositions) to conclusions (consequent propositions). The representation of the meaning of propositions is drawn from a natural language as a constraint on a variable. A variety of constraints of different types can be used. This is what underlines the concept of a generalized constraint, introduced in [572].

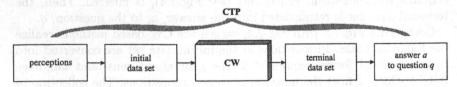

FIGURE 7.5. Illustration of the relationship between CW and CTP

A generalized constraint is represented as

$$X \; \text{isr} \; R$$

where **isr** (pronounced "ezar") is a variable copula which defines the way in which R constrains X. Let us explain more specifically: the role of R in relation to X is defined by the value of the discrete variable, r, which can take the following values, interpreted as listed below

e	equal; abbreviated to $=$
d	disjunctive (possibilistic); abbreviated to blank
v	veristic
p	probabilistic (probability distribution)
λ	probability value
rs	random set
rfs	random fuzzy set
fg	fuzzy graph
ps	rough set
	...

The list of values presented above can be extended to include other values. All of them represent different constraints. The first one is an equality constraint, which means that $r = e$, and **ise** is abbreviated to $=$. The second constraint is disjunctive (possibilistic); $r = d$ and **isd** is abbreviated to **is**, leading to the expression

$$X \; \text{is} \; R$$

in which R is a fuzzy relation which constrains X, and in this case R defines the possibility distribution of X, implying that

$$Poss\{X = u\} = \mu_R(u)$$

where μ_R is the membership function of R, and X takes values in a universe of discourse, $U = \{u\}$.

The veristic constraint, $r = v$, refers to R as the verity (truth) distribution of X. The expression

$$X \; \text{isv} \; R$$

means that if the grade of membership of u in R is μ, then $X = u$ has truth value μ. For example, a canonical form of the proposition

Stephan is half Pole, quarter German and quarter Czech

may be written as

Ethnicity (*Stephan*) **isv** (0.5 | *Pole* + 0.25 | *German* + 0.25 | *Czech*) in which $0.5, 0.25, 0.25$ represent, respectively, the truth values of the propositions *Stephan is a Pole, Stephan is a German, Stephan is a Czech.*

In the probabilistic constraint, $r = p$, we assume that X is a random variable and R is its probability distribution. For example

$$X \text{ isp } N(m, \sigma)$$

where X is a real-valued random variable which is normally distributed with mean m and variance σ.

In the probability value constraint, $r = \lambda$, the formula

$$X \text{ is}\lambda \ R$$

signifies that what is constrained is the probability of a specified event, X **is** A. More precisely

$$X \text{ is}\lambda \ R \rightarrow Prob\{X \text{ is } A\} \text{ is } R$$

For instance, if $A = tall$ and $R = likely$, then X **is**λ *likely* means that $Prob\{X$ **is** $tall\}$ is *likely*.

The random set constraint, $r = rs$, is a composite constraint which is a combination of probabilistic and possibilistic (or veristic) constraints. The expression

$$X \text{ isrs } R$$

results from the probabilistic constraint

$$Y \text{ isp } P$$

and the joint possibilistic constraint on X and Y

$$(X, Y) \text{ is } Q$$

or the joint veristic constraint on X and Y

$$(X, Y) \text{ isv } Q$$

respectively; where R is a random set, that is, a set-valued random variable.

It is worth mentioning that the Dempster-Shafer theory of evidence [463] is, in essence, a theory of random set constraints.

The random fuzzy set constraint, $r = rfs$, refers to the case in which X is a fuzzy-set-valued random variable and R is its fuzzy-set-valued probability distribution.

The fuzzy graph constraint, $r = fg$, pertains to the situation where R defines a fuzzy graph and X is a function which is approximated by R. More specifically, in the expression

$$X \text{ isfg } R$$

if X is a function, $U \to Z$, defined by a collection of fuzzy IF-THEN rules, i.e. the following fuzzy rule set

IF u is A_1 **THEN** z is B_1

IF u is A_2 **THEN** z is B_2

...

IF u is A_n **THEN** z is B_n

where A_i and B_i , for $i = 1, \ldots , n$, are linguistic values of u and z, respectively, in U and Z, then R is the fuzzy graph

$$R = A_1 \times B_1 + A_2 \times B_2 + \cdots + A_n \times B_n$$

where $A_i \times B_i$ is the Cartesian product of A_i and B_i, and symbol $+$ represents disjunction or, more generally, an S-norm; see Section 2.2.5, in Chapter 2.

A fuzzy graph constraint may be represented as a possibilistic constraint on the function which is approximated. Thus

$$X \ \mathbf{isfg} \ R \ \to \ X \ \mathbf{is} \ \left(\sum_{i=1}^{n} A_i \times B_i \right)$$

For a more detailed explanation of the above conclusion, see [576].

The rough set constraint, $r = ps$, incorporates the concept of a rough set [380], [381]. Other examples of generalized constraints can be found in [574], [577], [579].

The constraint X **isr** R is referred to as a *canonical form* of a proposition expressed in a natural language. The canonical form places in evidence the variable, X, that is constrained, and the constraining relation R, as well as the way, r, in which R constrains X. It makes explicit the constraint that is usually implicit in the proposition. Equivalently, we can say that explicitation may be viewed as a translation of the proposition into the language of canonical forms (i.e. GCL). Explicitation may or may not be simple, depending on the complexity of the proposition. In general, explicitation can be carried out through the use of test-score semantics (see [570], [574]).

In CW, the starting point is a collection of propositions which play the role of premises. In many cases, the canonical forms of these propositions are constraints of the basic, possibilistic type. Both X and R are assumed to be expressed in words. For example, in *Thomas is young*, $X = Age\,(Thomas)$, and $R = young$.

It was mentioned, in Section 2.2.5, that the principal types of granules are: possibilistic, veristic and probabilistic. The concept of generalized constraints, presented here, provides a basis for this classification of fuzzy granules. To illustrate this idea, let us explain that a granule is viewed as a clump of points characterized by a generalized constraint. Thus a granule denoted by G is expressed as

$$G = \{X \mid X \ \text{ isr } \ R\}$$

In this context, the type of a granule is determined by the type of constraint which defines it. The possibilistic, veristic and probabilistic granules are defined, respectively, by possibilistic, veristic and probabilistic constraints. The following are examples

$$G = \{X \mid X \ \text{ is } \textit{big}\}$$

is a possibilistic granule. Analogously,

$$G = \{X \mid X \ \text{ isv } \textit{big}\}$$

is a veristic granule, and

$$G = \{X \mid X \ \text{ isp } N(m, \sigma)\}$$

is a probabilistic (Gaussian) granule [576].

It was said in Sections 2.2.5 and 2.2.6 that the concept of a granule plays a pivotal role in CW, since a word (for example, *big*) is treated as a label of a fuzzy granule. It was also emphasized that a key role in CW is played by fuzzy constraint propagation from premises to conclusions. It was also mentioned in this section that fuzzy constraint propagation is the latter of two core issues concerning CW; the former is the issue of representation of fuzzy constraints, already described.

Once the propositions in the initial data set are formulated in their canonical forms, the groundwork is laid for fuzzy constraint propagation. The rules governing constraint propagation are, in effect, the rules of inference in fuzzy logic. However, it is helpful to have additional rules that govern fuzzy constraint modification.

The simple example of reasoning with perceptions, presented in this section, employed the inference rules of fuzzy logic. Another, similar example which illustrates the use of these rules comes from [574]. The propositions are formulated as follows

$$p_1 : \quad \textit{most students are young}$$

$$p_2 : \quad \textit{most young students are single}$$

The question might be

$$q : \textit{How many students are single?}$$

The conclusion (answer) drawn from p_1 and p_2, using the inference rules of fuzzy logic, is

$$a\,(q) : most^2 \; students \; are \; single$$

where $most^2$ represents the square of the fuzzy number $most$ in fuzzy arithmetic (see also Section 2.2.3).

As mentioned before, the rules of constraint propagation, basically, coincide with the rules of inference in fuzzy logic. These rules are presented in [574], [577], [578], [579]. They are written in such a way that antecedent and consequent constraints are separated by a horizontal line. For instance, assuming that $X \in U$, $A \subset U$, $Y \in V$, $B \subset V$, the following two inference rules are examples of conjunctive rules for possibilistic constraints

$$\frac{\begin{array}{c} X \;\; is \;\; A \\ X \;\; is \;\; B \end{array}}{X \;\; is \;\; A \cap B} \qquad \frac{\begin{array}{c} X \;\; is \;\; A \\ X \;\; is \;\; B \end{array}}{(X,Y) \;\; is \;\; A \times B}$$

Similar, disjunctive rules have the form

$$\frac{\begin{array}{c} X \;\; is \;\; A \\ X \;\; is \;\; B \end{array}}{X \;\; is \;\; A \cup B} \qquad \frac{\begin{array}{c} X \;\; is \;\; A \\ X \;\; is \;\; B \end{array}}{(X,Y) \;\; is \;\; A \times V \cup B \times U}$$

The compositional rule is expressed as

$$\frac{\begin{array}{c} X \;\; is \;\; A \\ (X,Y) \;\; is \;\; B \end{array}}{Y \;\; is \;\; A \circ B}$$

where $A \circ B$ denotes the composition of A and B; see Section 2.2.1 and Definition 26. This is a basic rule of inference in fuzzy logic. In a simplified form, A is a value of a linguistic variable, e.g. X is big, and B is a fuzzy relation on (X, Y).

Other examples, as well as general forms of the rules for the generalized constraints, can be found in the literature cited above. Among them, there is a principal rule of inference in CTP, i.e. the *generalized extension principle*, which plays a pivotal role in fuzzy constraint propagation; see also the extension principle described in Section 2.1.1. For possibilistic constraints, this rule may be formulated as follows

$$\frac{f\,(X) \;\; is \;\; R}{g\,(X) \;\; is \;\; g\left(f^{-1}\,(R)\right)}$$

where $f\,(X)$ is R plays the role of an antecedent constraint, i.e. an explicitation of a given perception or perceptions, X is the constrained variable, f and g are given functions, R is a relation that constraints $f\,(X)$, and $f^{-1}(R)$ is the preimage of R. In effect, $f(X)$ **is** R is a generalized constraint that represents the information conveyed by antecedent perception(s), while $g(X)$ **is** $g(f^{-1}(R))$ defines the induced generalized constraint on a specified function of X. An illustration, including a simple example, concerning this rule is depicted in [578].

According to Zadeh [578]: "CTP may be viewed as a first step toward the development of a better understanding of ways in which the remarkable human ability to reason with perceptions may be mechanized. Eventually, the ability of a machinery for computing with perceptions may have a profound impact on theories in which human decision-making plays an important role. Furthermore, in moving countertraditionally from measurements to perceptions, we may be able to conceive and construct systems with higher degree of machine intelligence (MIQ – *Machine Intelligence Quotient*) than those we have today."

The computational theory of perceptions (CTP), described in this section, suggests a new direction in Artificial Intelligence (AI). However, CTP is complementary rather than competitive to other methodologies developed in AI [579]. It should be emphasized that CTP is not intended to replace traditional measurement-based methods. In effect, CTP provides an additional tool which complements rather than competes with standard methods.

As mentioned earlier, the importance of CTP derives from the fact that much of human decision-making and commonsense reasoning is, in reality, perception-based. Thus it seems to be obvious that systems described by a collection of linguistic IF-THEN rules, in which values of the variables are fuzzy granular perceptions, and the inference incorporates CTP, can be applied as perception-based intelligent systems in AI.

8

Summary

It should be noted that the "pure" fuzzy system, depicted in Fig. 2.19, is a special case of perception-based systems, considered in Section 7.4. Since this system, with a fuzzifier and a defuzzifier, can be represented in the connectionist form of a neuro-fuzzy system, it seems that perception-based systems, or at least some types of them, may also be combined with neural networks to create perception-based neuro-fuzzy systems. These systems might be trained using different hybrid learning methods. Having learning ability makes these systems even more "intelligent." It would be interesting to combine these systems with fuzzy neural networks (see Section 3.2), and include genetic (evolutionary) algorithms to support the learning process. Fuzzy neural networks that process granular information refer to *granular neural networks* [388]. Networks of this kind may be applied with reference to perception-based systems, since the latter also use information granulation.

Perception-based systems may be realized employing different forms of neuro-fuzzy combinations [493] with granular neural networks or as granular neuro-fuzzy architectures with hybrid learning. Perception-based model of a system would consist of a collection of linguistic IF-THEN rules of the generic form, for example [579]

IF X_t is A_t AND S_t is B_t **THEN** S_{t+1} is C_t AND Y_t is D_t

for $t = 1, 2, \ldots$, where $X_1, X_2, \ldots$ are inputs, $Y_1, Y_2, \ldots$ outputs, and $S_1, S_2, \ldots$ states of the system, defined by the state transition function, f, as follows

$$S_{t+1} = f(S_t, X_t)$$

and the output function, g, as

$$Y_t = g(S_t, X_t)$$

In perception-based system modeling, the inputs, outputs, and states are assumed to be perceptions, as are the state transition function, f, and the output function, g. Thus in the collection of IF-THEN rules, A_t, B_t, C_t, D_t, for $t = 1, 2, \ldots$, are fuzzy granular perception of the values X_t, S_t, S_{t+1}, Y_t, respectively.

The example presented above shows that perception-based systems can be expressed in the form of IF-THEN rules with variables that take values which are fuzzy granules. This model is similar to the description of a fuzzy system in the form of IF-THEN rules in which the values of linguistic variables are fuzzy sets. As a matter of fact, the latter can be treated as a special case of a perception-based system. It should be noted that the fuzzy sets that are values of the linguistic variables in classical IF-THEN rules are also fuzzy granules. Thus many results obtained for classical fuzzy sets can be extended to perception-based systems. In this context, it seems that the Mamdani and logical approach to fuzzy inference (Section 2.3.2) should be considered with reference to perception-based systems. In particular, the logical approach might be useful since those fuzzy systems based on logical implications are more suitable for expert systems than for control systems. It is worth mentioning that among the inference rules of constraint propagation (see Section 7.4) there is the following [577], generalized modus ponens rule

$$\frac{X \text{ is } A}{\text{IF } X \text{ is } B \text{ THEN } Y \text{ is } C}{X \text{ is } A \circ \left(\widetilde{B} \oplus C\right)}$$

where the bounded sum $\widetilde{B} \oplus C$ represents Łukasiewicz's definition of implication (see Section 2.2.2).

It was explained in Section 7.3 that neuro-fuzzy architectures plus hybrid learning constitute intelligent computational systems that are intelligent systems in the sense of computational intelligence (see Section 7.1). The neuro-fuzzy systems which are perception-based systems, with a learning algorithm, may be fully treated as intelligent systems in the AI sense, because they process symbolic (not only numerical) information is in the form of fuzzy granules.

Since fuzzy sets were introduced by Zadeh [559] in 1965, researchers have found numerous ways to utilize this theory to generalize existing techniques and to develop new algorithms. In this way fuzzy neural networks, fuzzy clustering methods, fuzzy genetic algorithms, fuzzy expert systems, etc. have appeared. Together with the theoretical research, we have witnessed many important applications of fuzzy and neuro-fuzzy systems, based on fuzzy sets and fuzzy logic. It seems natural that fuzziness can be incorporated everywhere since the world is fuzzy. Now, in the new millennium, we will probably observe a new progressive trend in the area of AI, with reference to the conception of perception-based systems initiated by Prof. L. A. Zadeh.

A recent idea of incorporating fuzziness in existing methods, suggested for the new millennium [507], pertains to type 2 fuzzy sets, defined by Zadeh [565], [567]; see Section 2. Fuzzy sets of this kind have been investigated by other authors, e.g. [334], and applied [540], [511], [230], in particular to fuzzy systems [506], [238], [240], [239], [298], [299], [445]. It is stated in [323] that type 2 fuzzy sets, and type 2 fuzzy logic [238] are more suitable for CW, described in Sections 2.2.6 and 7.4, than type 1 fuzzy sets and fuzzy logic. Thus type 2 fuzzy sets have already been introduced to fuzzy and neuro-fuzzy systems, as well as to learning methods, e.g. to clustering [233]. The implication-based neuro-fuzzy systems presented in this book may also be considered using type 2 fuzzy sets, i.e. with fuzzy membership functions.

Fuzzy and neuro-fuzzy systems have been widely applied as fuzzy (neuro-fuzzy) controllers but also as fuzzy (neuro-fuzzy) classifiers. It is stated in [275] that fuzzy systems can be treated as probabilistic systems. In [228] a functional equivalence between fuzzy systems and RBF networks is presented; also see Section 4.1. Fuzzy systems can also be represented, under certain conditions, in the form of the standard neural network [421], [426]. It has been shown that RBF networks are asymptotically Bayes-optimal classifiers by proving their equivalence to the kernel type of nonparametric statistical classifiers [48], [95], [283]. Thus we can conclude that fuzzy systems are also asymptotically Bayes-optimal classifiers [284]. Moreover, neural networks can be considered as probabilistic neural networks (see [477] as well as e.g. [379] Chapter 13, and [337], [444]). As we see, the direction to combine different methods, i.e. fuzzy system, neural networks, Bayesian classifiers, and others, in one intelligent system seems to be reasonable and should be a subject of further research to incorporate architectures and learning algorithms into the systems created in the area of artificial (computational) intelligence.

The intelligent systems considered in this book can also be applied to multi-agent systems (see e.g. [252], [522]), in which different intelligent systems cooperate with each other as intelligent agents. The emerging opportunity of just such an application of hybrid expert systems, mentioned in Section 7.2.2, has been noted in [321], where also other soft computing techniques, i.e. fuzzy logic and genetic algorithms, are suggested to complement the hybrid systems.

List of Figures

List of Tables

References

[1] Abe S. and Lan M.S. (1995): *Fuzzy rules extraction directly from numerical data for function approximation*, IEEE Transactions on Systems, Man, and Cybernetics, Vol. 25, pp. 119-129.

[2] Adeli H. and S.-L. Hung (1995): *Machine Learning. Neural Networks, Genetic Algorithms, and Fuzzy Systems*, John Wiley & Sons, New York.

[3] Adlassnig K.-P., Kolarz G., and Scheithauer W. (1985): *Present state of the medical expert system CADIAG-2*, Method of Information in Medicine, Vol. 24, No. 1, pp. 13-20.

[4] Adlassnig K.-P. (1998): *Medical Expert and Knowledge-Based Systems*, Annual Report 1998, Department of Medical Computer Sciences, University of Vienna, Austria.

[5] Alimi A.M., Hassine R., and Selmi M. (2000): *Beta fuzzy logic systems: approximation properties in the SISO case*, International Journal of Applied Mathematics and Computer Science, Vol. 10, No. 4, pp. 857-875.

[6] Alsina C. (1985): *On a family of connectives for fuzzy sets*, Fuzzy Sets and Systems, Vol. 16, pp. 231-235.

[7] Alsina C., Trillas E., and Valverde L. (1981): *On some logical connectives for fuzzy set theory*, Journal of Mathematical Analysis and Applications, Vol. 93, pp. 15-26.

242   References

[8] Anderberg M.R. (1973): *Cluster Analysis for Applications*, Academic Press, New York.

[9] Anderson J.A. (1995): *An Introduction to Neural Networks*, The MIT Press, London.

[10] Andrew R., Diederich J., and Tickle A.B. (1995): *A survey and critique of techniques for extracting rules from trained artificial neural networks*, Knowledge-Based Systems, Vol. 8, pp. 373-389.

[11] Arabas J., Michalewicz Z., and Mulawka J. (1994): *GAVaPS - a genetic algorithm with varying population size*, In: Michalewicz Z., Kitano H., Schaffer D., Schwefel H.-P., and Fogel D. (Eds.), Proceedings of the IEEE Conference on Evolutionary Computation, Orlando, FL, USA

[12] Araki S., Nomura H., and Hayashi I. (1991): *A self-generating method of fuzzy inference rules*, Proceedings of the International Fuzzy Engineering Symposium (IFES'91), Yokohama, Japan, pp. 1047-1058.

[13] Assilian S. (1974): *Artificial Intelligence Techniques in the Control of Real Dynamic Systems*, Ph.D. Thesis, Queen Mary College, University of London, London, UK.

[14] Åström K.J., Wittenmark B. (1989): *Adaptive Control*, Addison-Wesley.

[15] Attolico G., Itta A., Cicirelli G., and D'Orazio T. (1999): *ART-based automatic generation of membership functions for fuzzy controllers in robotics*, In: Reusch B. (Ed.), Computational Intelligence. Theory and Applications, Proceedings of the International Conference: 6th Fuzzy Days, Dortmund, Germany, Lecture Notes in Computer Science, Vol. 1625, pp. 259-271.

[16] Babuška R. (1998): *Fuzzy Modeling for Control*, Kluwer Academic Publishers, Boston, Dordrecht, London.

[17] Ball G.H. and Hall D.J. (1967): *ISODATA, an iterative method of multivariate analysis and pattern classification*, Behavioral Science, Vol. 12, pp. 153-155.

[18] Barr A. and Feigenbaum E.A. (1981): *The Handbook of Artificial Intelligence*, Vols. I, II, Morgan-Kaufmann, Los Altos, CA.

[19] Bartolini G., Casalino G., Davoli F., Mastretta M., Minciardi R., and Morten E. (1982): *Development of performance adaptive fuzzy controllers with application to continuous casting plants*, In: Trappl R. (Ed.), Cybernetics and Systems Research, North Holland, Amsterdam, pp. 721-728.

[20] Bastian A. (1996): *A genetic algorithm for tuning membership functions*, Proceedings of the 4th European Congress on Intelligent Techniques and Soft Computing (EUFIT'96), Aachen, Germany, pp. 494-498.

[21] Belew R.K., McInerney J, and Schraudolph N. (1990): *Evolving networks: Using genetic algorithms with connectionist learning*, CSE Technical Report CS90-174, University of California at San Diego, La Jolla, CA, USA.

[22] Belew R.K., McInerney J, and Schraudolph N. (1992): *Evolving networks using the genetic algorithm with connectionist learning*, Artificial Life II, pp. 511-547.

[23] Bellman R., Kalaba R., and Zadeh L. (1966): *Abstraction and pattern classification*, Journal of Mathematical Analysis and Applications, Vol. 13, pp. 1-7.

[24] Berenji H.R. (1992): *Fuzzy logic controllers*, In: Yager R.R. and Zadeh L.A. (Eds.), An Introduction to Fuzzy Logic Applications and Intelligent Systems, Kluwer Academic Publishers, Boston.

[25] Berenji H.R. and Khedkar P. (1992): *Learning and tuning fuzzy logic controllers through reinforcements*, IEEE Transactions on Neural Networks, Vol. 3, pp. 724-740.

[26] Bergman A., Burgard W., and Hemker A. (1994): *Adjusting parameters of genetic algorithms by fuzzy control rules*, In: Becks K.H. and Gallix D.P. (Eds.), New Computer Techniques in Physics Research III, World Scientific, Singapore, pp. 235-240.

[27] Berkan R.C. and Trubatch S.L. (1997): *Fuzzy Systems Design Principles. Building Fuzzy IF-THEN Rule Bases*, IEEE Press, New York.

[28] Bezdek J.C. (1973): *Fuzzy Mathematics in Pattern Classification*, Ph.D. Thesis, Appl. Math., Cornell University, Ithaca, N.Y., USA.

[29] Bezdek J.C. (1974): *Cluster validity with fuzzy sets*, Journal of Cybernetics, Vol. 3, No. 3, pp. 58-72.

[30] Bezdek J.C. (1976): *A physical interpretation of fuzzy ISODATA*, IEEE Transactions on Systems, Man, and Cybernetics, Vol. SMC-6, pp. 387-390.

[31] Bezdek J.C. (1978): *Fuzzy partitions and relations; an axiomatic basis for clustering*, Fuzzy Sets and Systems, Vol. 1, pp. 111-127.

[32] Bezdek J.C. (1980): *A convergence theorem for the fuzzy ISODATA clustering algorithms*, IEEE Transactions on Pattern Analysis and Machine Intelligence, Vol. PAMI-2, No. 1, pp. 1-8.

[33] Bezdek J.C. (1981): *Pattern Recognition with Fuzzy Objective Function Algorithms*, Plenum Press, New York.

[34] Bezdek J.C. (1991): *Pattern recognition, neural networks, and artificial intelligence*, Applications of Artificial Intelligence, SPIE Volume 1468, pp. 924-935.

[35] Bezdek J.C. (1992): *On the relationship between neural networks, pattern recognition and intelligence*, International Journal of. Approximate. Reasoning, Vol. 6, No. 2, pp. 85-107.

[36] Bezdek J.C. (1994): *What is computational intelligence?*, In: Żurada J.M., Marks II R.J., and Robinson C.J. (Eds.), Computational Intelligence: Imitating Life, IEEE Press, New York, pp. 1-12.

[37] Bezdek J.C. and Castelaz P. (1977): *Prototype classification and feature selection with fuzzy sets*, IEEE Transactions on Systems, Man, and Cybernetics, Vol. SMC-7, No. 2, pp. 87-92.

[38] Bezdek J.C. and Dunn J.C. (1975): *Optimal fuzzy partitions: A heuristic for estimating the parameters in a mixture of normal distributions*, IEEE Transactions on Computers, Vol. C-24, pp. 835-838.

[39] Bezdek J.C. and Harris J.C. (1978): *Fuzzy partitions and relations: An axiomatic basis for clustering*, Fuzzy Sets and Syst., Vol. 1, No. 2, pp. 111-127.

[40] Bezdek J.C. and Hathaway R.J. (1988): *Recent convergence results for the fuzzy c-means clustering algorithms*, Journal of Classification, Vol. 5, No. 2, pp. 237-247.

[41] Bezdek J.C. and Hathaway R.J. (1994): *Optimization of fuzzy clustering criteria using genetic algorithms*, Proceedings of the First International Conference on Evolutionary Computation, Vol. 2, IEEE Press, Piscataway, pp. 589-594.

[42] Bezdek J.C., Keller J., Krisnapuram R., and Pal N.R. (1999): *Fuzzy Models and Algorithms for Pattern Recognition and Image Processing*, Kluwer Academic Publishers, Boston.

[43] Bezdek J.C. and Pal S.K. (1992): *Fuzzy Models for Pattern Recognition*, IEEE Press, Piscataway, N.J.

[44] Bezdek J.C. and Pal S.K. (1998): *Some new indexes of cluster validity*, IEEE Transactions on Systems, Man, and Cybernetics - Part B, Vol. SMC-28, No. 3, pp. 301-315.

[45] Bezdek J.C., Spillman B., and Spillman R. (1979): *Fuzzy relations spaces for group decision theory – An application*, Fuzzy Sets and Syst., Vol. 2, No. 1, pp. 5-14.

[46] Bezdek J.C., Tsao C.-K., and Pal S.K. (1992): *Fuzzy Kohonen clustering networks*, Proceedings of the 1st IEEE International Conference on Fuzzy Systems (FUZZ-IEEE'92), San Diego, CA, USA, pp. 1035-1043.

[47] Bezdek J.C., Windham M.P., and Ehrlich R. (1980): *Statistical parameters of cluster validity functionals*, International Journal of Computer and Information Sciences, Vol. 9, No. 4, pp. 324-326.

[48] Bishop C.M. (1995): *Neural networks for pattern recognition*, Clarendon Press, Oxford.

[49] Blickle T. and Thiele L. (1995): *A mathematical analysis of tournament selection*, In: Eshelman L.J. (Ed.), Proceedings of the Sixth International Conference on Genetics Algorithms, San Francisco, CA, Morgan Kaufmann Publishers.

[50] Bouchon-Meunier B. (Ed.) (1998): *Aggregation and Fusion of Imperfect Information*, Physica-Verlag, Heidelberg.

[51] Brindle A. (1981): *Genetic Algorithms for Function Optimization*, Ph.D. Thesis, University of Alberta, Edmonton.

[52] Broomhead D.S. and Lowe D. (1988): *Multivariable functional interpolation and adaptive networks*, Complex Systems, Vol. 2, pp. 321-355.

[53] Brown M. and Harris C. (1994): *Neurofuzzy Adaptive Modelling and Control*, Prentice Hall, New York.

[54] Buchanan B.G. and Shortliffe E.H. (Eds.) (1984): *Rule-Based Expert Systems*, Addison-Wesley.

[55] Buckley J.J. and Czogała E. (1991): *Linguistic approximate reasoning inference engine for expert systems (LARIEES)*, Proceedings of World Congress on Expert Systems, Orlando, FL, USA, Vol. 1, pp. 108-115.

[56] Buckley J.J. and Feuring T. (1999): *Fuzzy and Neural: Interactions and Applications*, Physica-Verlag, A Springer-Verlag Company, Heidelberg, New York.

[57] Buckley J.J. and Hayashi Y. (1992): *Fuzzy neural nets and applications*, Fuzzy Sets and Artificial Intelligence, Vol. 1, pp. 11-41.

[58] Buckley J.J. and Hayashi Y. (1993): *Direct fuzzification of neural networks*, Proceedings of the First Asian Fuzzy Systems Symposium, Singapore, pp. 560-567.

[59] Buckley J.J. and Hayashi Y. (1993): *Hybrid neural nets can be fuzzy controllers and fuzzy expert systems*, Fuzzy Sets and Systems, Vol. 60, pp. 135-142.

[60] Buckley J.J. and Hayashi Y. (1994): *Fuzzy neural nets: A survey*, Fuzzy Sets and Systems, Vol. 66, pp. 1-13.

[61] Buckley J.J. and Hayashi Y. (1994): *Fuzzy neural nets*, In: Zadeh L.A. and Yager R.R. (Eds.), Fuzzy Sets, Neural Networks and Soft Computing, Van Nostrand Reinhold, New York, pp. 233-249.

[62] Buckley J.J. and Hayashi Y. (1994): *Fuzzy genetic algorithm and applications*, Fuzzy Sets and Systems, Vol. 61, No. 2, pp. 129-136.

[63] Buckley J.J., Hayashi Y., and Czogała E. (1993): *On the equivalence of neural nets and fuzzy expert systems*, Fuzzy Sets and Systems, Vol. 53, pp. 129-134.

[64] Buckley J.J., Reilly K.D., and Penmetcha K.V. (1996): *Backpropagation and genetic algorithms for training fuzzy neural nets*, In: Herrera F. and Verdegay J.L. (Eds.), Genetic Algorithms and Soft Computing, Physica-Verlag, pp. 505-532.

[65] Buckley J.J., Siler W., and Tucker D. (1986): *Fuzzy expert system*, Fuzzy Sets and Systems, Vol. 20, pp. 1-16.

[66] Butnariu D. (1977): *L-fuzzy automata. Description of a neural model*, Proceedings of the International Congress on Cybernetics and Systems, Bucharest, Romania, Vol. 3, No. 2, pp. 119-124.

[67] Canuto A., Howells G., and Fairhurst M. (1999): *RePART: a modified fuzzy ARTMAP for pattern recognition*, In: Reusch B. (Ed.), Computational Intelligence. Theory and Applications, Proceedings of the International Conference: 6th Fuzzy Days, Dortmund, Germany, Lecture Notes in Computer Science, Vol. 1625, pp. 159-168.

[68] Cao Z. and Kandel A. (1989): *Applicability of some fuzzy implication operators*, Fuzzy Sets and Systems, Vol. 31, pp. 151-186.

[69] Carpenter G.A. and Grossberg S. (1986): *Neural dynamics of category learning and recognition: Attention, memory consolidation, and amnesia*, In: Davis J., Newburgh R., and Wegman E. (Eds.), Brain Structure, Learning, and Memory, AAAS Symposium Series, Westview Press, Boulder, CO, USA..

[70] Carpenter G.A. and Grossberg S. (1987): *A massively parallel architecture for a self-organizing neural pattern recognition machine*, Computer Vision, Graphics, and Image Processing, Vol. 37, pp. 54-115.

[71] Carpenter G.A. and Grossberg S. (1987): *ART2: Self-organization of stable category recognition codes for analog input patterns*, Applied Optics, Vol. 26, No. 23, pp. 4919-4930.

[72] Carpenter G.A. and Grossberg S. (1990): *ART3: Hierarchical search using chemical transmitters in self-organizing pattern recognition architectures*, Neural Networks, Vol. 3, No. 4, pp. 129-152.

[73] Carpenter G.A., Grossberg S., Markuzon N., Reynolds J.H., and Rosen D.B. (1992): *Fuzzy ARTMAP: a neural network architecture for incremental supervised learning of analog multidimensional maps*, IEEE Transactions on Neural Networks, Vol. 3, pp. 698-713.

[74] Carpenter G.A. and Tan A.-H. (1993): *Fuzzy ARTMAP, rule extraction and medical databases*, In: World Congress on Neural Networks, Portland, OR, USA, Vol. 1, Hillsdale, N.J., Lawrence Erlbaum Associates, pp. 501-506.

[75] Carpenter G.A. and Tan A.-H. (1995): *Rule extraction: From neural architecture to symbolic representation*, Connection Science, Vol. 7, No. 1, pp. 3-27.

[76] Carse B. and Fogarty T.C. (1994): *A fuzzy classifier system using the Pittsburgh approach*, In: Davidor Y., Schwefel H.-P., and Männer R. (Eds.), Parallel Problem Solving from Nature - PPSN III, Proceedings of the International Conference on Evolutionary Computation, Jerusalem Israel, Lecture Notes in Computer Science, Springer-Verlag, Berlin, pp. 260-269.

[77] Castro J.L. (1995): *Fuzzy logic controllers as universal approximators*, IEEE Transactions on Systems, Man, and Cybernetics, Vol. 25, No. 4, pp. 629-635 .

[78] Castro J.L. and Delgardo M. (1996): *Fuzzy systems with defuzzification are universal approximators*, IEEE Transactions on Systems, Man, and Cybernetics, Part B, Vol. 26, No. 1, pp. 149-152 .

[79] Charniak E. and McDermott (1987): *Introduction to Artificial Intelligence*, Addison-Wesley.

[80] Chen L.H., Chua H.C., and Tan P.B. (1998): *Grammatical inference using an adaptive recurrent neural network*, Neural Processing Letters, Vol. 8, pp. 211-219.

[81] Chen M.-S and Wang S.-W. (1996): *Fuzzy clustering for parameter identification of fuzzy membership functions*, Proccedings of the 4th International Conference on Soft Computing (IIZUKA'96), Iizuka, Japan, pp. 287-290.

[82] Chen S., Billings S.A., Cowan C.F.N., and Grant P.M. (1990): *Practical identification of NARMAX models using radial basis functions*, International Journal of Control, Vol. 52, No. 6, pp. 1327-1350.

[83] Chen S., Billings S.A., and Grant P.M. (1992): *Recursive hybrid algorithm for non-linear system identification using radial basis function networks*, International Journal of Control, Vol. 55, No. 5, pp. 1051-1070.

[84] Chen S. and Billings S.A. (1994): *Neural networks for nonlinear dynamic system modelling and identification*, In: Harris C.J. (Ed.), Advances in Intelligent Control, Taylor and Francis, London, Chapter 4.

[85] Chi Z., Yan H., and Pham T. (1996): *Fuzzy Algorithms: With Applications to Image Processing and Pattern Recognition*, World Scientific, Singapore.

[86] Cho S.B. (1996): *Towards an intelligent system based on fuzzy logic, neural networks and genetic algorithm*, In: Chiang W. and Lee J. (Eds.), Fuzzy Logic for the Applications to Complex Systems, World Scientific, Singapore, pp. 121-126.

[87] Chorayan O.G. (1982): *Identifying elements of the probabilistic neuronal ensembles from the standpoint of fuzzy sets theory*, Fuzzy Sets and Systems, Vol. 8, No. 2, pp. 141-147.

[88] Cichocki A. and Unbehauen R. (1993): *Neural Networks for Optimization and Signal Processing*, John Wiley & Sons.

[89] Cordòn O., and Herrera F. (1996): *A hybrid genetic algorithm-evolution strategy process for learning fuzzy logic controller knowledge bases*, In: Herrera F. and Verdegay J. (Eds.), Genetic Algorithms and Soft Computing, Physica Verlag, pp. 251-278.

[90] Cordòn O., Herrera F., and Lozano M. (1996): *A Classified Review on the Combination Fuzzy Logic-Genetic Algorithms Bibliography*, Technical Report DECSAI 95129, Department of Computer Science and Artificial Intelligence, University of Granada, Granada, Spain; also on the Internet: *Combination Fuzzy Logic-Genetic Algorithms Bibliography*, htttp://decsai.ugr.es/~herrera/fl-ga.html.

[91] Cordòn O., Herrera F., and Lozano M. (1997): *On the combination of fuzzy logic and evolutionary computation: A short review and bibliography*, In: Pedrycz W. (Ed.), Fuzzy Evolutionary Computation, Kluwer Academic Publishers, pp. 33-56.

[92] Cordòn O., Herrera F., and Peregrin A. (1997): *Applicability of the fuzzy operators in the design of fuzzy logic controllers*, Fuzzy Sets and Systems, Vol. 86, No. 1, pp. 15-41.

[93] Cordòn O., Herrera F., and Peregrin A. (1995): *T-norms vs. implication functions as implication operators in fuzzy control*, Proceedings

of the 6th International Fuzzy Systems Association World Congress (IFSA'95), Sao Paulo, Brazil, pp. 501-504.

[94] Cotter N.E. (1990): *The Stone-Weierstrass theorem and its application to neural networks*, IEEE Transactions on Neural Networks, Vol. 1, No. 4, pp. 290-295.

[95] Coultrip R.L. and Granger R.H. (1994): *Sparse random networks with LTP learning rules approximate Bayes classifiers via Parzen's method*, Neural Networks, Vol. 7, pp. 463-476.

[96] Cox E. (1994): *The Fuzzy Systems Handbook. A Practitioner's Guide to Building, Using, and Maintaining Fuzzy Systems*, Academic Press.

[97] Cupal J.J. and Wilamowski B.M. (1994): *Selection of fuzzy rules using a genetic algorithm*, Proceedings of the World Congress on Neural Networks (WCNN'94), Vol. 1, pp. 814-819.

[98] Curry H. (1944): *The method of steepest descent for non-linear minimization problems*, Quarterly of Applied Mathematics, Vol. 2, pp. 258-260.

[99] Cybenko G. (1989): *Approximation by superpositions of a sigmoidal function*, Mathematics of Control, Signals, and Systems, Vol. 2, pp. 303-314.

[100] Czogała E., Fodor J.C., and Leski J. (1997): *The Fodor fuzzy implication in approximate reasoning*, Systems Science, Vol. 23, No. 2, pp. 17-28.

[101] Czogała E. and Leski J. (2000): *Fuzzy and Neuro-Fuzzy Intelligent Systems*, Physica-Verlag, A Springer-Verlag Company, Heidelberg, New York.

[102] Czogała E. and Pedrycz W. (1985): *Elements and Methods of Fuzzy Set Theory*, PWN, Warsaw, Poland (in Polish).

[103] Davis L. (Ed.) (1991): *Handbook of Genetic Algorithms*, Van Nostrand Reinhold, New York.

[104] Davis R. (1982): *Knowledge-Based Systems in Artificial Intelligence*, McGraw-Hill, New York.

[105] Dayhoff J. (1990): *Neural Network Architectures. An Introduction*, Van Nostrand Reinhold, New York.

[106] De Jong K.A. (1975): *An Analysis of the Behavior of a Class of Genetic Adaptive Systems*, Ph.D. Thesis, University of Michigan.

250   References

[107] Dempster A.P. (1967): *Upper and lower probabilities induced by a multivalued mapping*, Annals of Mathematical Statistics, Vol. 37, pp. 325-339.

[108] Domanski P.D. and Arabas J. (1995): *On generating the fuzzy rule base by means of genetic algorithm*, Proceedings of the 3th European Congress on Intelligent Techniques and Soft Computing (EUFIT'95), Aachen, Germany, pp. 467-470.

[109] Dombi J. (1999): *DeMorgan class and negation*, Proceedings of EUROFUSE-SIC'99, Budapest, pp. 335-344.

[110] Dreyfus H.L. and Dreyfus S.E. (1986): *Mind over Machine*, Free Press, New York.

[111] Driankov D., Hellendoorn H., and Reinfrank M. (1993): *An Introduction to Fuzzy Control*, Springer-Verlag, Berlin, Heidelberg.

[112] Dubois D. and Prade H. (1980): *Fuzzy Sets and Systems: Theory and Applications*, Academic Press, London.

[113] Dubois D. and Prade H. (1991): *Fuzzy sets in approximate reasoning, Part I: Inference with possibility distribution*, Fuzzy Sets and Systems, Vol. 40, pp. 143-202.

[114] Duch W., Adamczak R., and Grabczewski K. (1998): *Extraction of logical rules from neural networks*, Neural Processing Letters, Vol. 7, pp. 211-219.

[115] Duda R.O., Gashing J.G., and Hart P.E. (1980): *Model design in the Prospector consultant system for mineral exploration*, In: Michie D. (Ed.), Expert Systems in the Microelectronic Age, Edinburgh University Press, Edinburgh, pp. 153-167.

[116] Duda R.O. and Hart P.E. (1973): *Pattern Classification and Sciene Analysis*, John Wiley & Sons, New York.

[117] Duda R.O., Hart P.E., and Nilsson N.J. (1976): *Subjective Bayesian Methods for Rule-Based Inference Systems*, Proceedings of the 1976 National Computer Conference (NCC), AFIPS Press.

[118] Duda R.O., Hart P.E., and Sutherland G.L. (1978): *Semantic network representations in rule-based inference systems*, In: Waterman D.A. and Hayes-Roth F. (Eds.), Pattern Directed Inference Systems, Academic Press, New York, pp. 203-221.

[119] Dunn J.C. (1973): *A fuzzy relative of the ISODATA process and its use in detecting compact well-separated clusters*, Journal of Cybernetics, Vol. 3, No. 3, pp. 32-57.

[120] Dunn J.C. (1974): *Some recent investigations of a new fuzzy partitioning algorithm and its application to pattern classification problems*, Journal of Cybernetics, Vol. 4., pp. 1-15.

[121] Dunn J.C. (1974): *Well separated clusters and optimal fuzzy partitions*, Journal of Cybernetics, Vol. 4., pp. 95-104.

[122] Dunn J.C. (1977): *Indices of partition fuzziness and the detection of clusters in large data set*, In: Gupta M.M., Saridis G.N., Gaines B.R. (Eds.), Fuzzy Automata and Decision Processes, North-Holland, Amsterdam, pp. 271-284.

[123] Eberhart R.C. (1992): *The role of genetic algorithms in neural network query-based learning and explanation facilities*, Proceedings of International Workshop on Combinations of Genetic Algorithms and Neural Networks (COGANN-92), pp. 169-183.

[124] Eberhart R.C. and Dobbins R.W. (1991): *Designing neural network explanation facilities using genetic algorithms*, Proceedings of the IEEE International Conference on Neural Networks, Singapore, pp. 1758-1763.

[125] Fausett L. (1994): *Fundamentals of Neural Networks. Architectures, Algorithms, and Applications*, Prentice-Hall, Inc., Englewood Cliffs, New Jersey.

[126] Feldman D.S. (1993): *Fuzzy network synthesis with genetic algorithms*, Proceedings of the 5th International Conference on Genetic Algorithms (ICGA), pp. 312-317.

[127] Filev D.P. and Yager R.R. (1995): *Simplified methods of reasoning in fuzzy models*, Proceedings of the IEEE International Conference on Fuzzy Systems, Yokohama, Japan, pp. 123-129.

[128] Fisher R.A. (1936): *The use of multiple measurements in taxonomic problems*, Ann. Eugenics, Vol. 7, pp. 179-188.

[129] Fodor J.C. (1991): *On fuzzy implication operators*, Fuzzy Sets and Systems, Vol. 42, pp. 293-300.

[130] Fogel L.J. (1962): *Autonomous Automata*, Industrial Research, Vol. 4, pp. 14-19.

[131] Fogel L.J., Owens A.J., and Walsh M.J. (1966): *Artificial Intelligence through Simulated Evolution*, John Wiley & Sons, New York.

[132] Fogel D.B. (1995): *Evolutionary Computation: Towards a New Philosophy of Machine Intelligence*, IEEE Press, New York.

252   References

[133] Fogel D.B. (1995): *Review of "Computational Intelligence: Imitating Life"*, IEEE Transactions on Neural Networks, Vol. 6, pp. 1562-1565.

[134] Freeman J.A. and Skapura D.M. (1991): *Neural Networks. Algorithms, Applications, and Programming Techniques*, Addison-Wesley.

[135] Fu L. (1994): *Rule generation from neural networks*, IEEE Transactions on Systems, Man, and Cybernetics, Vol. 24, No. 8, pp. 1114-1124.

[136] Fukuda T. and Shibata T. (1994): *Fuzzy-neuro-GA based intelligent robotics*, In: Zurada J.M., Marks II R.J., and Robinson C.J. (Eds.), Computational Intelligence: Imitating Life, IEEE Press, New York, pp. 352-363.

[137] Fukumi M. and Akamatsu N. (1999): *A new rule extraction method from neural networks*, Proceedings of the IEEE International Joint Conference on Neural Networks (IJCNN'99), Washington, DC, USA.

[138] Fukushima K. (1975): *Cognitron: A self-organizing multilayer neural network*, Biological Cybernetics, Vol. 20, pp. 121-136.

[139] Fukushima K. (1988): *Neocognitron: A hierarchical neural network model capable of visual pattern recognition*, Neural Networks, Vol. 1, No. 2., pp. 119-130.

[140] Fukushima K., Miyake S., and Ito T. (1983): *Neocognitron: A neural network model for a mechanism of visual pattern recognition*, IEEE Transactions on Systems, Man, and Cybernetics, Vol. 13, pp. 826-834.

[141] Fuller R. (2000): *Introduction to Neuro-Fuzzy Systems*, Advances in Soft Computing, Physica-Verlag, A Springer-Verlag Company, Heidelberg, New York.

[142] Funahashi K. (1989): *On the approximate realization of continuous mappings by neural networks*, Neural Networks, Vol. 2, pp. 183-192.

[143] Gaines B.R. (1976): *Foundations of fuzzy reasoning*, International Journal of Man-Machine Studies, Vol. 8, pp. 623-668.

[144] Gallant S.I. (1988): *Connectionist expert systems*, Communications of the ACM, Vol. 31, No. 2, pp. 152-169.

[145] Gersho A. and Gray R.M. (1992): *Vector Quantization and Signal Compression*, Kluwer Academic Publishers, Boston.

[146] Geyer-Schulz A. (1998): *Fuzzy genetic algorithms*, In: Nguyen H.T. and Sugeno M. (Eds.), Fuzzy Systems: Modeling and Control, Kluwer Academic Publishers, Boston, pp. 403-459.

[147] Ginsberg M.L. (1993): *Essentials of Artificial Intelligence*, Morgan Kaufmann, San Francisco.

[148] Glorennec P.Y. (1991): *Adaptive fuzzy control*, Proceedings of the 4th International Fuzzy Systems Association World Congress (IFSA'91), Brussels, Belgium, pp. 33-36.

[149] Goguen J.A. (1969): *The logic of inexact concepts*, Synthese, Vol. 19, pp. 325-373.

[150] Goldberg D.E. (1989): *Genetic Algorithms in Search, Optimization, and Machine Learning*, Addison-Wesley.

[151] Gonzalez-Seko J. (1992): *A genetic algorithm as the learning procedure for neural networks*, Proceedings of the International Joint Conference on Neural Networks, Baltimore, MD, pp. 835-840.

[152] Gorzałczany M. (1989): *An interval-valued fuzzy inference method – some basic properties*, Fuzzy Sets and Systems, Vol. 31, pp. 243-251.

[153] Gray R.M. (1984): *Vector quantization*, IEEE ASSP Magazine, Vol. 1, pp. 4-29.

[154] Grossberg S. (1972): *Neural expectation: Cerebellar and retinal analogs of cells fired by learnable or unlearned pattern classes*, Kybernetic, Vol. 10, pp. 49-57.

[155] Grossberg S. (1976): *Adaptive pattern classification and universal recording: Part I. Parallel development and coding of neural detectors. Part II. Feedback, expectation, olfaction, illusions*, Biological Cybernetics, Vol. 23, pp. 121-134, 187-202.

[156] Grossberg S. (1988): *Neural Networks and Natural Intelligence*, The MIT Press, Cambridge, MA.

[157] Gupta M.M. and Gorzałczany M.B. (1992): *Fuzzy neuro-comuputation technique and its application to modeling and control*, Proceedings of the 1st IEEE International Conference on Fuzzy Systems (FUZZ-IEEE'92), San Diego, CA, USA, pp. 1271-1274.

[158] Gupta M.M., Kandel A., and Bandler W. (Eds.) (1985): *Approximate Reasoning in Expert Systems*, North-Holland, New York.

[159] Gupta M.M. and Rao D. H. (1994): *On the principles of fuzzy neural networks*, Fuzzy Sets and Systems, Vol. 61, pp. 1-18.

[160] Hall L.O., Bezdek J.C., Boggavarpu S., and Bensaid A. (1994): *Genetic fuzzy clustering*, Proceedings of the North American Fuzzy Information Processing Society Biannual Conference (NAFIPS'94), San Antonio, TX, USA, pp. 411-415.

[161] Hall L.O. and Kandel A. (1986): *Designing Fuzzy Expert Systems*, Verlag TÜV Rheinland, Köln, Germany.

[162] Harris C.J., Moore C.G., and Brown M. (1993): *Intelligent Control. Aspects of Fuzzy Logic and Neural Nets*, World Scientific, Singapore.

[163] Harp S.A., Samad T., and Guha A. (1989): *Towards the genetic synthesis of neural networks*, In: Schaffer J.D. (Ed.), Proceedings of the Third International Conference on Genetic Algorithms and Their Applications, Morgan Kaufmann Publishers, San Mateo, CA, USA, pp. 360-369.

[164] Hartigan J. (1975): *Clustering Algorithms*, John Wiley & Sons, New York.

[165] Hassoun M.H. (1995): *Fundamentals of Artificial Neural Networks*, The MIT Press, Cambridge, MA.

[166] Hayashi I., Nomura H., and Wakami N. (1989): *Artificial neural network driven fuzzy control and its application to the learning of inverted pendulum system*, Proceedings of the 3rd International Fuzzy Systems Association World Congress (IFSA'89), Seatle, WA, USA, pp. 610-613.

[167] Hayashi I. and Takagi H. (1988): *Formulation of fuzzy reasoning by neural network*, Proceedings of the 4th IFSA Fuzzy System Symposium, Tokyo, Japan, pp. 55-60 (in Japanese).

[168] Hayashi Y. (1992): *A neural expert system using fuzzy teaching input*, Proceedings of the 1st IEEE International Conference on Fuzzy Systems (FUZZ-IEEE'92), San Diego, CA, USA, pp. 485-491.

[169] Hayashi Y., Buckley J.J., and Czogała E. (1992): *Direct fuzzification of neural network and fuzzified delta rule*, Proceedings of the 2nd International Conference on Fuzzy Logic & Neural Networks (IIZUKA'92), Iizuka, Japan, pp. 73-76.

[170] Hayashi Y., Buckley J.J., and Czogała E. (1993): *Fuzzy neural networks with fuzzy signals and weights*, International Journal of Intelligent Systems, Vol. 8, pp. 527-537.

[171] Haykin S. (1992): *Blind equalization formulated as a self-organized learning process*, Proceedings of the Twenty-Sixth Asilomar Conference on Signals, Systems, and Computers, Pacific Grove, CA, pp. 346-350.

[172] Haykin S. (1994): *Neural Networks. A Comprehensive Foundation*, Macmillan College Publishing Company, New York.

[173] He X. and Lapedes A. (1991): *Nonlinear Modeling and Prediction by Successive Approximation Using Radial Basis Functions*, Technical Report LA-UR-91-1375, Los Alamos National Laboratory, Los Alamos, NM.

[174] Hebb D.O. (1949): *The Organization of behaviour, A Neuropsychological Theory*, John Wiley & Sons, New York.

[175] Hecht-Nielsen R. (1987): *Counterpropagation networks*, Applied Optics, Vol. 26, No. 23, pp. 4979-4984.

[176] Hecht-Nielsen R. (1988): *Applications of counterpropagation networks*, Neural Networks, Vol. 1, pp. 131-139.

[177] Hecht-Nielsen R. (1990): *Neurocomputing*, Addison-Wesley.

[178] Hellendorn H. and Thomas C. (1993): *Defuzzification in fuzzy controllers*, Journal of Intelligent & Fuzzy Systems, Vol. 1, pp. 109-123.

[179] Herrera F., Lozano M., and Verdegay J.L. (1994): *Generating fuzzy rules from examples using genetic algorithms*, Proceedings of the 5th International Conference on Information Processing and Management of Uncertainty in Knowledge-Based Systems (IPMU'94), Paris, France, pp. 675-679.

[180] Herrera F., Lozano M., and Verdegay J.L. (1995): *Tuning fuzzy logic controllers by genetic algorithms*, International Journal of Approximate Reasoning, Vol. 12, pp. 299-315.

[181] Herrera F., Lozano M., and Verdegay J.L. (1996): *Dynamic and heuristic fuzzy connectives based crossover operators for controlling the diversity and convergence of real-coded genetic algorithms*, International Journal of Intelligent Systems, Vol. 11, No. 12, pp. 1013-1040.

[182] Hertz J., Krogh A., and Palmer R.G. (1991): *Introduction to the Theory of Neural Computation*, Addison-Wesley.

[183] Hinton G.E. (1987): *Connectionist learning procedure*, Technical Report CMU-CS-87-115, Carnegie Mellon University.

[184] Hirota K. (Ed.) (1993): *Industrial Applications of Fuzzy Technology*, Springer-Verlag, Tokyo, Berlin, Heidelberg, New York.

[185] Hirota K. and Pedrycz W. (1994): *OR/AND neuron in modeling fuzzy set connectives*, IEEE Transactions on Fuzzy Systems, Vol. 2, pp. 151-161.

[186] Hisdal E. (1981): *The IF THEN ELSE statement and interval-valued fuzzy sets of higher type*, International Journal of Man-Machine Studies, Vol. 15, pp. 385-455.

[187] Hoffmann N. (1994): *Simulating Neural Networks*, Verlag Vieweg, Wiesbaden.

[188] Holland J.H. (1969): *Adaptive plans optimal for payoff-only environments*, Proceedings of the Second Hawaii International Conference on System Sciences, pp. 917-920.

[189] Holland J.H. (1975): *Adaptation in Natural and Artificial Systems*, Ann Arbor: University of Michigan Press.

[190] Holland J.H. (1986): *Escaping brittleness: the possibilities of general-purpose learning algorithm applied to parallel rule-based systems*, Machine Learning, An Artificial Intelligence Approach, Vol. 2.

[191] Homaifar A. and McCornick E. (1995): *Simultaneous design of membership functions and rule sets for fuzzy controllers using genetic algorithms*, IEEE Transactions on Fuzzy Systems, Vol. 3, pp. 129-139.

[192] Hopfield J.J. (1982): *Neural networks and physical systems with emergent collective computational abilities*, Proceedings of the National Academy of Science of the USA, Vol. 79, pp. 2554-2558.

[193] Hopfield J.J. (1984): *Neurons with graded response have collective computational properties like those of two-state neurons*, Proceedings of the National Academy of Science of the USA, Vol. 81, pp. 3088-3092.

[194] Hopfield J.J. (1984): *Collective processing and neural states*, In: Nicollini C. (Ed.), Modeling and Analysis in Biomedicine, World Scientific, Singapore, pp. 370-389.

[195] Hopfield J.J. and Tank D.W. (1985): *Neural computation of decisions in optimization problems*, Biological Cybernetics, Vol. 52, pp. 141-152.

[196] Hopfield J.J. and Tank D.W. (1986): *Computing with neural circuits: A model*, Science, pp. 625-633.

[197] Höppner F., Klawonn F., Kruse R., and Runkler T. (1999): *Fuzzy Cluster Analysis. Methods for Classification, Data Analysis and Image Recognition*, John Wiley & Sons, LTD.

[198] Hornik K. and Stinchcombe M., and White H. (1989): *Multilayer feedforward networks are universal approximators*, Neural Networks, Vol. 2. pp. 359-366.

[199] Hripcsak G. (1988): *Problem-Solving Using Neural Networks*, SAIC Communication, San Diego, CA, USA.

[200] Huang S.J. and Hung C.C. (1996): *Genetic-evoved fuzzy systems for inverted pendulum controls*, In: Chiang W. and Lee J. (Eds.), Fuzzy Logic for the Applications to Complex Systems, World Scientific, Singapore, pp. 35-40.

[201] Huang W.Y., and Lippmann R.P. (1988): *Neural nets and traditional classifiers*, In: Anderson D.Z. (Ed.), Neural Information Processing Systems, Denver 1987, American Institute of Physics, New York, pp. 387-396.

[202] Hughes G.E. and Cresswell M.J. (1968): *An Introduction to Modal Logic*, Methuen, London.

[203] Huntsberger T.L. and Ajjimarangsee P. (1990): *Parallel self-organizing feature maps for unsupervised pattern recognition*, International Journal of General Systems, Vol. 16, No. 4, pp. 357-372.

[204] Ishibushi H., Fujioka R., and Tanaka H. (1993): *Neural networks that learn from fuzzy if-then rules*, IEEE Transactions on Fuzzy Systems, Vol. 1, pp. 85-97.

[205] Ishibushi H., Kwon K., and Tanaka H. (1993): *Learning of fuzzy neural networks from fuzzy inputs and fuzzy targets*, Proceedings of the 5th International Fuzzy Systems Association World Congress (IFSA'93), Seul, Korea, pp. 147-150.

[206] Ishibushi H., Kwon K., and Tanaka H. (1995): *A learning algorithm of fuzzy neural networks with triangular fuzzy weights*, Fuzzy Sets and Systems, Vol. 71, pp. 277-293.

[207] Ishibushi H., Morioka K., and Tanaka H. (1994): *A fuzzy neural network with trapezoidal fuzzy weights*, Proceedings of the 3rd IEEE International Conference on Fuzzy Systems (FUZZ-IEEE'94), Orlando, FL, USA, pp. 228-233.

[208] Ishibushi H., Morioka K., and Türksen I.B. (1995): *Learning by fuzzified neural networks*, International Journal of Approximate Reasoning, Vol. 13, pp. 327-358.

[209] Ishibushi H., Murata T., and Türksen I.B. (1997): *Single-objective and two-objective genetic algorithms for selecting linguistic rules for pattern classification problems*, Fuzzy Sets and Systems, Vol. 89, pp. 135-150.

[210] Ishibushi H., Nozaki K., and Tanaka H. (1992): *Distributed representation of fuzzy rules and its application to pattern classification*, Fuzzy Sets and Systems, Vol. 52, pp. 21-32.

[211] Ishibushi H., Nozaki K., and Yamamoto N. (1993): *Selecting fuzzy rules by genetic algorithm for classification problems*, Proceedings of the 2nd IEEE International Conference on Fuzzy Systems (FUZZ-IEEE'93), San Francisco, CA, USA, pp. 1119-1124.

[212] Ishibushi H., Nozaki K., Yamamoto N., and Tanaka H. (1993): *Genetic operations for rule selection in fuzzy classification systems*, Proceedings of the 5th International Fuzzy Systems Association World Congress (IFSA'93), Seoul, Korea, pp. 15-18.

[213] Ishibushi H., Nozaki K., Yamamoto N., and Tanaka H. (1994): *Construction of fuzzy classification systems with rectangular fuzzy rules using genetic algorithms*, Fuzzy Sets and Systems, Vol. 65, pp. 237-253.

[214] Ishibushi H., Nozaki K., Yamamoto N., and Tanaka H. (1995): *Selecting fuzzy If-Then rules for classification problems using genetic algorithms*, IEEE Transactions on Fuzzy Systems, Vol. 3, pp. 260-270.

[215] Ishibushi H., Okada H., and Tanaka H. (1992): *Learning of neural networks from fuzzy inputs and fuzzy targets*, Proceedings of the International Joint Conference on Neural Networks (IJCNN'92), Beijing, Vol. 3, pp. 447-452.

[216] Ishibushi H., Tanaka H., and Okada H. (1993): *Fuzzy neural networks with fuzzy weights and fuzzy biases*, Proceedings of the IEEE International Conference on Neural Networks (IEEE-ICNN'93), San Francisco, CA, USA, pp. 1650-1655.

[217] Ishibushi H., Tanaka H., and Okada H. (1994): *Interpolation of fuzzy if-then rules by neural networks*, International Journal of Approximate Reasoning, Vol. 10, pp. 3-27.

[218] Ishigami H., Fukuda T., Shibata T., and Arai F. (1995): *Structure optimization of fuzzy neural network by genetic algorithm*, Fuzzy Sets and Systems, Vol. 71, pp. 257-264.

[219] Ishizuka M., Fu K.S., and Yao J.T.P. (1982): *SPERIL: An expert system for damage assessment of existing structures*, Proceedings of the Sixth International Conference on Pattern Recognition, Munich, Germany.

[220] Ishizuka M., Fu K.S., and Yao J.T.P. (1983): *Rule-based damage assessment system for existing structures*, Solid Mechanics Archives, Vol. 8, pp. 99-118.

[221] Jackson P. (1990): *Introduction to Expert Systems*, Second Edition, John Wiley & Sons.

[200] Huang S.J. and Hung C.C. (1996): *Genetic-evoved fuzzy systems for inverted pendulum controls*, In: Chiang W. and Lee J. (Eds.), Fuzzy Logic for the Applications to Complex Systems, World Scientific, Singapore, pp. 35-40.

[201] Huang W.Y., and Lippmann R.P. (1988): *Neural nets and traditional classifiers*, In: Anderson D.Z. (Ed.), Neural Information Processing Systems, Denver 1987, American Institute of Physics, New York, pp. 387-396.

[202] Hughes G.E. and Cresswell M.J. (1968): *An Introduction to Modal Logic*, Methuen, London.

[203] Huntsberger T.L. and Ajjimarangsee P. (1990): *Parallel self-organizing feature maps for unsupervised pattern recognition*, International Journal of General Systems, Vol. 16, No. 4, pp. 357-372.

[204] Ishibushi H., Fujioka R., and Tanaka H. (1993): *Neural networks that learn from fuzzy if-then rules*, IEEE Transactions on Fuzzy Systems, Vol. 1, pp. 85-97.

[205] Ishibushi H., Kwon K., and Tanaka H. (1993): *Learning of fuzzy neural networks from fuzzy inputs and fuzzy targets*, Proceedings of the 5th International Fuzzy Systems Association World Congress (IFSA'93), Seul, Korea, pp. 147-150.

[206] Ishibushi H., Kwon K., and Tanaka H. (1995): *A learning algorithm of fuzzy neural networks with triangular fuzzy weights*, Fuzzy Sets and Systems, Vol. 71, pp. 277-293.

[207] Ishibushi H., Morioka K., and Tanaka H. (1994): *A fuzzy neural network with trapezoidal fuzzy weights*, Proceedings of the 3rd IEEE International Conference on Fuzzy Systems (FUZZ-IEEE'94), Orlando, FL, USA, pp. 228-233.

[208] Ishibushi H., Morioka K., and Türksen I.B. (1995): *Learning by fuzzified neural networks*, International Journal of Approximate Reasoning, Vol. 13, pp. 327-358.

[209] Ishibushi H., Murata T., and Türksen I.B. (1997): *Single-objective and two-objective genetic algorithms for selecting linguistic rules for pattern classification problems*, Fuzzy Sets and Systems, Vol. 89, pp. 135-150.

[210] Ishibushi H., Nozaki K., and Tanaka H. (1992): *Distributed representation of fuzzy rules and its application to pattern classification*, Fuzzy Sets and Systems, Vol. 52, pp. 21-32.

[234] Kacprzyk J. (1983): *Multistage Decision-Making Under Fuzziness: Theory and Applications*, ISR Series, Verlag TÜV Rheinland, Köln, Germany.

[235] Kacprzyk J. (1986): *Fuzzy Sets in System Analysis*, PWN, Warsaw, Poland (in Polish).

[236] Kandel A. (Ed.) (1991): *Fuzzy Expert Systems*, CRC Press, Boca Raton, FL.

[237] Karnik N.N. and Mendel J.M. (1998): *An Introduction to Type-2 Fuzzy Logic Systems*, University of Southern California Report. http://sipi.usc.edu/~mendel/report.

[238] Karnik N.N. and Mendel J.M. (1998): *Introduction to type 2 fuzzy logic systems*, Proceedings of the 7th IEEE International Conference on Fuzzy Systems (FUZZ-IEEE'98), Anchorage, AK, USA, pp. 915-920.

[239] Karnik N.N. and Mendel J.M. (1999): *Applications of type-2 fuzzy logic systems to forecasting of time-series*, Information Sciences, Vol. 120, pp. 89-111.

[240] Karnik N.N., Mendel J.M., and Liang Q. (1999): *Type-2 fuzzy logic systems*, IEEE Transactions on Fuzzy Systems, Vol. 7, No. 6, pp. 643-658.

[241] Karr C.L. (1991): *Design of an adaptive fuzzy logic controller using a genetic algorithm*, Proceedings of the 4th International Conference on Genetic Algorithms (ICGA), San Diego, CA, USA, pp. 450-457.

[242] Karr C.L. and Gentry E.J. (1993): *Fuzzy control of pH using genetic algorithms*, IEEE Transactions on Fuzzy Systems, Vol. 1, pp. 46-53.

[243] N.K. Kasabov (1996): *Fundations of Neural Networks, Fuzzy Systems, and Knowledge Engineering*, The MIT Press, Cambridge, MA.

[244] Kasabov N. and Kozma R. (Eds.) (1999): *Neuro-Fuzzy Techinques for Intelligent Information Systems*, Physica-Verlag, A Springer-Verlag Company, Heidelberg, New York.

[245] Katayama R, Kajitani Y., and Nishida Y. (1993): *A self generating and tuning method for fuzzy modeling using interior penalty method and its application to knowledge acquisition of fuzzy controller*, In: Kandel A. and Langholz G. (Eds.), Fuzzy Control Systems, CRC Press, Boca Raton, FL., pp. 198-224.

[246] Kaufmann A. (1975): *Theory of Fuzzy Subsets*, Academic Press, New York.

[247] Kaufmann A. and Gupta M.M. (1985): *Introduction to Fuzzy Arithmetic: Theory and Applications*, Van Nostrand Reinhold, New York.

[248] Keller J.M. and Hunt D. (1985): *Incorporating fuzzy membership functions into the perceptron algorithm*, IEEE Transactions on Pattern Analysis and Machine Intelligence, Vol. 7, pp. 693-699.

[249] Keller J.M. and Tahani H. (1992): *Backpropagation neural networks for fuzzy logic*, Information Sciences, Vol. 62, pp. 205-221.

[250] Kelly J.D. and Davis L. (1991): *Hybridizing the genetic algorithm and the k-nearest neighbors classification algorithm*, In: Belew R.K. and Booker L.B. (Eds.), Fourth International Conference on Genetic Algorithms, Morgan Kaufmann Publishers, San Mateo, CA, USA, pp. 377-383.

[251] Khanna T. (1990): *Foundations of Neural Networks*, Addison-Wesley.

[252] Khosla R. and Dillon T. (1997): *Engineering Intelligent Hybrid Multi-Agent Systems*, Kluwer Academic Publishers, Boston.

[253] Kickert W.J.M. (1978): *Fuzzy Theories on Decision Making*, Nijhoff, Leiden.

[254] Kinzel J., Klawonn F., and Kruse R. (1994): *Modification of genetic algorithms for designing and optimizing fuzzy controllers*, Proceedings of the IEEE International Conference on Evolutionary Computation (IEEE-ICEC'94), Orlando, FL, USA, pp. 28-33.

[255] Kiszka J., Kochańska M., and Śliwińska D. (1985): *The influence of some fuzzy implication operators on the accuracy of a fuzzy model, Part I and Part II*, Fuzzy Sets and Systems, Vol. 15, pp. 11-128, 223-240.

[256] Kitano H. (1990): *Empirical studies on the speed of convergence of neural network training using genetic algorithms*, Proceedings AAAI-90, pp. 789-795.

[257] Kitano H. (1990): *Designing neural networks using genetic algorithms with graph generation system*, Complex Systems, No. 4, pp. 461-476.

[258] Klement E.P., Mesiar R., and Pap E. (2000): *Triangular Norms*, Kluwer Academic Publishers, Dordrecht/Boston/London.

[259] Klir G.J. and Folger T.A. (1988): *Fuzzy Sets, Uncertainty, and Information*, Prentice Hall, Englewood Cliffs, New Jersey.

[260] Klir G.J. and Yuan B. (1995): *Fuzzy Sets and Fuzzy Logic: Theory and Applications*, Prentice Hall, Upper Saddle River, New Jersey.

[261] Kohonen T. (1982): *Self-organized formation of topologically correct feature maps*, Biological Cybernetics, Vol. 43, pp. 59-69.

[262] Kohonen T. (1986): *Learning vector quantization for pattern recognition*, Technical Report TKK-F-A601, Helsinki University of Technology, Finland.

[263] Kohonen T. (1984): *Self-organization and Associative Memory*, Springer-Verlag, Berlin.

[264] Kohonen T. (1988): *The "neural" phonetic typewriter*, Computer, Vol. 21, pp. 11-22.

[265] Kohonen T. (1990): *Improved versions of learning vector quantization*, Proceedings of the 4th International Joint Conference on Neural Networks, San Diego, CA, USA, pp. 545-550.

[266] Kohonen T., Kangas J., Laaksonen J., and Torkkola K. (1992): *LVQ-PAK: The learning vector quantization Program Package*, Helsinki University of Technology, Finland.

[267] Kolmogorov A (1957): *On the representations of continuous functions of many variables by superpositions of continuous functions of one variable and addition*, Dokladi Academii Nauk USSR, Vol. 114, pp. 953-956.

[268] Kong S.G. and Kosko B. (1990): *Comparison of fuzzy and neural truck backer-upper control systems*, Proceedings of the International Joint Conference on Neural Networks (IJCNN-90), Vol. 3, pp. 349-358.

[269] Kopco N., Sincak P., and Veregin H. (1999): *Extended methods for classification of remotely sensed images based on ARTMAP neural networks*, In: Reusch B. (Ed.), Computational Intelligence. Theory and Applications, Proceedings of the International Conference: 6th Fuzzy Days, Dortmund, Germany, Lecture Notes in Computer Science, Vol. 1625, pp. 206-219.

[270] Kosiński W. and Weigl M. (1998): *General mapping: approximation problems solving by neural and fuzzy inference networks*, Systems Analysis Modelling Simulation (SAMS), Vol. 30, No. 1, pp. 11-28.

[271] Kosko B. (1987): *Adaptive bidirectional associative memories*, Applied Optics, Vol. 26, No. 23, pp. 4947-4959.

[272] Kosko B. (1988): *Bidirectorial associative memories*, IEEE Transactions on Systems, Man, and Cybernetics, Vol. 18, No. 1, pp. 49-60.

[273] Kosko B. (1992): *Neural Networks and Fuzzy Systems. A Dynamical Systems Approach to Machine Intelligence*, Prentice Hall, Englewood Cliffs, New Jersey.

[274] Kosko B. (1994): *Fuzzy systems as universal approximators*, IEEE Transactions on Computers, Vol. 43, No. 11, pp. 1329-1332.

[275] Kosko B. (1995): *Combining fuzzy systems*, Proceedings of the 4th IEEE International Conference on Fuzzy Systems (FUZZ-IEEE'95), Yokohama, Japan, pp. 1855-1863.

[276] Koza J.R. (1991): *Genetic Programming*, The MIT Press, Cambridge, MA.

[277] Koza J.R. (1994): *Genetic Programming II. Automatic Discovery of Reusable Programms*, The MIT Press.

[278] Koza J.R. and Rice J.P. (1991): *Genetic generation of both the weights and architecture for a neural network*, Proceedings of the International Joint Conference on Neural Networks, Seatle, WA, USA, pp. 397-404.

[279] Krishnamraju K.V., Buckley J.J., Reilly K.D., and Hayashi Y. (1994): *Genetic learning algorithms for fuzzy neural nets*, Proceedings of the 3rd IEEE International Conference on Fuzzy Systems (FUZZ-IEEE'94), Orlando, FL, USA, Vol. 3, pp. 1969-1974.

[280] Kropp K. and Baitinger U.G. (1993): *Optimization of fuzzy logic controller inference rules using a genetic algorithm*, Proceedings of the European Congress on Intelligent Techniques and Soft Computing (EUFIT'93), Aachen, Germany, pp. 1090-1096.

[281] Kruse R., Gebhardt J., and Klawonn F. (1994): *Foundations of Fuzzy Systems*, John Wiley & Sons, Chichester, New York.

[282] Kruse R., Schwecke E., and Heinsohn J. (1991): *Uncertainty and Vagueness in Knowledge-Based Systems: Numerical Methods*, Springer-Verlag, Berlin.

[283] Krzyzak A., Linder T., and Lugosi G. (1994): *Nonparametric classification using radial basis function nets and empirical risk minimization*, Proceedings of the 12th Internatational Conference on Pattern Recognition, Jerusalem, Israel, pp. 72-76.

[284] Kuncheva L.I. (1996): *On the equivalence between fuzzy and statistical classifiers*, International Journal of Uncertainty, Fuzziness and Knowledge-Based Systems, Vol. 4, No. 3, pp. 245-253.

[285] Kuncheva L.I. (2000): *Fuzzy Classifier Design*, Physica-Verlag, A Springer-Verlag Company, Heidelberg, New York.

[286] Kung S.Y. (1993): *Digital Neural Networks*, PTR Prentice Hall, Englewood Cliffs, New Jersey.

[287] Lakoff G. (1973): *Hedges: a study in meaning criteria and the logic of fuzzy concepts*, Journal of Philosophical Logic, Vol. 2, pp. 458-508.

[288] Larsen P.M. (1980): *Industrial applications of fuzzy logic control*, International Journal of Man-Machine Studies, Vol. 12, No. 1, pp. 3-10.

[289] Lee C.C. (1990): *Fuzzy logic in control systems: fuzzy logic controller. Part I, Part II*, IEEE Transactions on Systems, Man and Cybernetics, Vol. SMC-20, No. 2, pp. 404-418, 419-435.

[290] Lee K.-M., Kwak D.-H, and Lee-Kwang H. (1994): *A fuzzy neural network model for fuzzy inference and rule tuning*, International Journal of Uncertainty, Fuzziness and Knowledge-Based Systems, Vol. 2, No. 3, pp. 265-277.

[291] Lee K.-M., Kwak D.-H, and Lee-Kwang H. (1996): *Fuzzy inference neural network for fuzzy model tuning*, IEEE Transactions on Systems, Man, and Cybernetics. Part B., Vol. 26, No. 4, pp. 637-645.

[292] Lee S.C. and Lee E.T. (1970): *Fuzzy neurons and automata*, Proceedings of the 4th Princeton Conference on Information Science Systems, pp. 381-385.

[293] Lee S.C. and Lee E.T. (1974): *Fuzzy sets and neural networks*, Journal of Cybernetics, Vol. 4, pp. 83-103.

[294] Lee S.C. and Lee E.T. (1975): *Fuzzy neural networks*, Mathematical Bioscienses, Vol. 23, pp. 151-177.

[295] Lee S. and Kil R. (1988): *Multilayer feedforward potential function network*, Proceedings of the IEEE 2nd International Conference on Neural Networks, Vol. 1, San Diego, CA, USA, pp. 161-171.

[296] Lee M.A. and Takagi H. (1993): *Integrated design stages of fuzzy systems using genetic algorithms*, Proceedings of the 2nd International Conference on Fuzzy Systems (FUZZ-IEEE'93), San Francisco, CA, USA, Vol. 1., pp. 612-617.

[297] Lee M.A. and Takagi H. (1993): *Dynamic control of genetic algorithms using fuzzy logic techniques*, Proceedings of the Fifth International Conference on Genetic Algorithms (ICGA'93), San Mateo, CA, USA, pp. 76-83.

[298] Liang Q and J.M. Mendel (1999): *An introduction to type-2 TSK fuzzy logic systems*, Proceedings of 1999 IEEE International Fuzzy Systems Conference, Seul, Korea, Vol. 3, pp. 1534-1539.

[299] Liang Q and J.M. Mendel (2000): *Interval type 2 fuzzy logic systems*, Proceedings of the IEEE International Conference on Fuzzy Systems (FUZZ-IEEE 2000), San Antonio, TX, USA.

[300] Lin C.T. (1994): *Neural Fuzzy Control Systems with Structure and Parameter Learning*, World Scientific, Singapore.

[301] Lin C.T. and Lee G.C.S. (1994): *Supervised and unsupervised learning with fuzzy similarity for neural network-based fuzzy logic control systems*, In: Yager R.R., Zadeh L.A. (Eds.), Van Nostrand Reinhold, New York, pp. 85-125.

[302] Lin C.T. and Lee G.C.S. (1996): *Neural Fuzzy Systems. A Neuro-Fuzzy Synergism to Intelligent Systems*, Prentice-Hall, Inc.

[303] Linkens D.A. and Nyongesa H.O. (1996): *Learning systems in intelligent control: an appraisal of fuzzy, neural and genetic algorithm control applications*, Proceedings IEE - Control Theory Applications, Vol. 143, No. 4, pp. 367-386.

[304] Lippmann R.P. (1987): *An introduction to computing with neural nets*, IEEE ASSP Magazine, pp. 4-22.

[305] Lippmann R.P. (1989): *Pattern classification using neural networks*, IEEE Communications Magazine, Vol. 27, pp. 47-64.

[306] Liska J. and Melsheimer S.S. (1994): *Complete design of fuzzy logic systems using genetic algorithms*, Proceedings of the 3rd IEEE International Conference on Fuzzy Systems (FUZZ-IEEE'94), Orlando, FL, USA, pp. 1377-1382.

[307] Löwen R. (1978): *On fuzzy complement*, Information Sciences, Vol. 14, pp. 107-113.

[308] Maeda Y. and De Figulerido J.P. (1997): *Learning rule for neuro-controller via simultaneous perturbation*, IEEE Transactions on Neural Networks, Vol. 8, pp. 1119-1130.

[309] Mamdani E.H. (1974): *Applications of fuzzy algorithm for simple dynamic plant*, Proceedings IEE, Vol. 121, No. 12, pp. 1585-1588.

[310] Mamdani E.H. and Assilian S. (1975): *An experiment in linguistic synthesis with a fuzzy logic controller*, International Journal of Man-Machine Studies, Vol. 7, pp. 1-13.

[311] Magrez P. and Smets P. (1989): *Fuzzy modus ponens: a new model suitable for applications in knowledge-based systems*, International Journal of Intelligent Systems, Vol. 4, pp. 181-200.

[312] Maren A., Harston C., and Pap R. (1990): *Handbook of Neural Computing Applications*, Academic Press, San Diego, CA, USA.

[313] Marko K.A., James J., Dosdall J, and Murphy J. (1989): *Automotive control system diagnostics using neural nets for rapid pattern classification of large data sets*, Proceedings of the 2nd International IEEE Joint Conference on Neural Networks, Washington, D.C., pp. 13-17.

[314] Marks R. (1993): *Computational versus artificial*, IEEE Transactions on Neural Networks, Vol. 4, No. 5, pp. 737-739.

[315] Martinez T.M., Ritter H.J., and Schulten K.J. (1990): *Three-dimensional neural net for learning visuomotor coordination of a robot arm*, IEEE Transactions on Neural Networks, Vol. 1, pp. 131-136.

[316] McCarthy J. (1997): *Epistemological problems of artificial intelligence*, Proceedings of the 5th International Joint Conference of Artificial Intelligence, Cambridge, MA, USA, pp. 1038-1044.

[317] McCulloch W.S. and Pitts W. (1943): *A logical calculus of ideas immanent in nervous activity*, Bulletin of Mathematical Biophysics, Vol. 5, pp. 115-133.

[318] Medgassy P. (1961): *Decomposition of Superposition of Distributed Functions*, Hungarian Academy of Science, Budapest.

[319] Medsker L.R. (1994): *Hybrid Neural Network and Expert Systems*, Kluwer Academic Publishers.

[320] Medsker L.R. (1995): *Hybrid Intelligent Systems*, Kluwer Academic Publishers.

[321] Medsker L.R. (1997): *Neuro-expert architecture and applications in diagnostic / classification domains*, In: Jain L.C. and Jain R.K. (Eds.), Hybrid Intelligent Engineering Systems, World Scientific, Singapore.

[322] Memmi D. (1989): *Connectionism and artificial intelligence*, Neuro-Nimes'89 International Workshop on Neural Networks and Their Applications, Nimes, France, pp. 17-34.

[323] Mendel J.M. (1999): *Computing with words, when words can mean different things to different people*, Proceedings of the International ICSC Congress on Computational Intelligence: Methods and Applications, Third International ICSC Symposium on Fuzzy Logic and Applications, Rochester Institute of Technology, Rochester, NY.

[324] Mertz C.J. and Murphy P.M., *UCI repository of machine learning databases*, http://www.ics.uci.edu/pub/machine-learning-databases.

[325] Michalewicz Z. (1992): *Genetic Algorithms + Data Structures = Evolution Programs*, Springer-Verlag, Berlin, Heidelberg, New York.

[326] Miller G.F., Todd P.M., and Hagde S.U. (1989): *Designing neural networks using genetic algorithms*, In: Schaffer J.D. (Ed.), Proceedings of the Third International Conference on Genetic Algorithms and Their Applications, Morgan Kaufmann Publishers, San Mateo, CA, USA, pp. 379-384.

[327] Minski M. (1967): *Computation: Finite and Infinite Machines*, Prentice-Hall, New York.

[328] Minsky M. and Papert S. (1969): *Perceptrons*, The MIT Press, Cambridge, MA.

[329] Mitra S. and Hayashi Y. (2000): *Neuro-fuzzy rule generation: survey in soft computing framework*, IEEE Transactions on Neural Networks, Vol. 11, No. 3, pp. 748-768.

[330] Mitra S. and Kuncheva L. (1995): *Improving classification performance using fuzzy MLP and two-level selective partitioning of the feature space*, Fuzzy Sets and Systems, Vol. 70, pp. 1-13.

[331] Mitra S. and Pal. S.K. (1994): *Neuro-fuzzy expert systems: overview with a case study*, In: Tzafestas S. and Venetsanopoulos A.N. (Eds.), Fuzzy Reasoning in Information, Decision and Control Systems, Kluwer Academic Publishers, Boston/Dordrecht, pp. 121-143.

[332] Mitra S. and Pal. S.K. (1994): *Self-organizing neural network as a fuzzy classifier*, IEEE Transactions on Systems, Man, and Cybernetics, Vol. 24, No. 3, pp. 385-399.

[333] Mitra S. and Pal. S.K. (1995): *Fuzzy multi-layer perceptron, inferencing and rule generation*, IEEE Transactions on Neural Networks, Vol. 6, No. 1, pp. 51-63.

[334] Mizumoto M. and Tanaka K. (1976): *Some properties of fuzzy sets of type 2*, Information and Control, Vol. 31, pp. 312-340.

[335] Mizumoto M. and Tanaka K. (1981): *Fuzzy sets of type 2 under algebraic product and algebraic sum*, Fuzzy Sets and Systems, Vol. 5, pp. 277-290.

[336] Mizumoto M. and Zimmerman H.J. (1982): *Comparison of fuzzy reasoning methods*, Fuzzy Sets ans Systems, Vol. 8, pp. 253-283.

[337] Montana D.J. (1992): *A weighted probabilistic neural network*, Advances in Neural Information Processing Systems, Vol. 4, pp. 1110-1117.

[338] Montana D.J. (1995): *Neural network weight selection using genetic algorithms*, In: Goonatilake S. and Khebbal S. (Eds.), Intelligent Hybrid Systems, John Wiley & Sons, pp. 85-104.

[339] Montana D.J. and Davis L. (1989): *Training feedforward neural networks using genetic algorithms*, Proceedings of Eleventh International Joint Conference on Artificial Intelligence, Morgan Kaufmann Publishers, San Mateo, CA, USA, pp. 762-767.

[340] Moody J. and Darken C. (1989): *Learning with localized receptive fields*, In: Touretzky D., Hinton G., and Sejnowski T. (Eds.), 1988 Connectionist Models Summer School, Pittsburgh, Morgan Kaufmann Publishers, San Mateo, CA, USA, pp. 133-143.

[341] Moody J. and Darken C. (1989): *Fast learning in networks of locally-tuned processing units*, Neural Computation, Vol. 1, No. 2, pp. 281-294.

[342] Mouzouris G.C. and Mendel J.M. (1997): *Nonsingleton fuzzy logic systems: Theory and application*, IEEE Transactions on Fuzzy Systems, Vol. 5, No. 1, pp. 56-71.

[343] Musílek P. and Gupta M.M. (2000): *Fuzzy neural networks*, In: Sinha N.K. and Gupta M.M. (Eds.), Soft Computing and Intelligent Systems: Theory and Applications, Academic Press, San Diego, pp. 161-184.

[344] Nagy G. (1968): *State of the art in pattern recognition*, Proceedings IEE, Vol. 56, pp. 836-862.

[345] Nauck D. (1994): *A fuzzy perceptron as a generic model for neuro-fuzzy approaches*, Proceedings of the Conference: Fuzzy-Systeme'94, Munich.

[346] Nauck D. (1994): *Building neural fuzzy controllers with NEFCON-1*, In: Kruse R., Gebhardt J., and Palm R. (Eds.), Fuzzy Systems in Computer Science, Vieweg, Braunschweig, pp. 141-151.

[347] Nauck D., Klawonn F., and Kruse R. (1997): *Foundations of Neuro-Fuzzy Systems*, John Wiley & Sons.

[348] Nauck D. and Kruse R. (1993): *A fuzzy neural network learning fuzzy control rules and membership functions by fuzzy error backpropagation*, Proceedings of the IEEE International Conference on Neural Networks (ICNN'93), San Francisco, CA, USA, pp. 1022-1027.

[349] Nauck D. and Kruse R. (1994): *NEFCON-1: An X-window based simulator for neural fuzzy controllers*, Proceedings of the IEEE International Conference on Neural Networks, Orlando, FL, USA, pp. 1638-1643.

[350] Nauck D. and Kruse R. (1995): *NEFCLASS - A neuro-fuzzy approach for the classification of data*, In: George K., Carrol J.H., Deaton E., Oppenheim D., and Hightower J. (Eds.), Applied Computing 1995, ACM Symposium on Applied Computing, Nashville, TN, USA, ACM Press, New York, pp. 461-465.

[351] Nauck D. and Kruse R. (1996): *Designing neuro-fuzzy systems through backpropagation*, In: Pedrycz W. (Ed.), Fuzzy Modelling: Paradigms and Practice, Kluwer Academic Publishers, Boston, pp. 203-228.

[352] Nauck D. and Kruse R. (1996): *Neuro-fuzzy classification with NEFCLASS*, In: Kleinschmidt P., Bachem A., Derigs U., Fischer D., Leopold-Wildburger U., and Möhring R. (Eds.), Operation Research Proceedings 1995, Springer-Verlag, Berlin, pp. 294-299.

[353] Negoita C.V. and Ralescu D.A. (1975): *Applications of Fuzzy Sets to System Analysis*, Birkhäuser Verlag, Stuttgart.

[354] Nelles O. (1996): *FUREGA – fuzzy rule extraction by a genetic algorithm*, Proceedings of the 4th European Congress on Intelligent Techniques and Soft Computing (EUFIT'96), Aachen, Germany, pp. 489-493.

[355] Nelson M.M. and Illingworth W.T. (1991): *A Practical Guide to Neural Nets*, Addison-Wesley.

[356] Nguyen H.T., Sugeno M., Tong R., and Yager R.R. (Eds.) (1995): *Theoretical Aspects of Fuzzy Control*, John Wiley & Sons, New York.

[357] Nguyen H.T. and Sugeno M. (Eds.) (1998): *Fuzzy Systems. Modeling and Control*, Kluwer Academic Publishers, Boston, London, Dordrecht.

[358] Nguyen H.T. and Walker E.A. (2000): *A First Course in Fuzzy Logic*, Second Edition, Chapman & Hall/CRC, Boca Raton, FL.

[359] Nguyen D. and Widrow B. (1989): *The truck backer-upper: an example of self-learning in neural networks*, Proceedings of the International Joint Conference on Neural Networks (IJCNN-89), Vol. II, pp. 357-363.

[360] Nguyen D. and Widrow B. (1990): *The truck backer-upper: an example of self-learning in neural network*, IEEE Control System Magazine, Vol. 10, No. 3, pp. 18-23.

[361] Nie J. and Linkens D. (1995): *Fuzzy-Neural Control. Principles, algorithms and applications*, Prentice Hall, New York, London.

[362] Niranjan M. and Fallside F. (1988): *Neural Networks and Radial Basis Functions in Classifying Static Speech Patterns*, Technical Report, CUEDIF-INFENG17R22, Engineering Department, Cambridge University.

270   References

[363] Nomura H., Hayashi I., and Wakami N. (1991): *A self-tuning method of fuzzy control by descent method*, Proceedings of the 4th International Fuzzy Systems Association World Congress (IFSA'91), Brussels, Belgium, pp. 155-158.

[364] Nomura H., Hayashi I., and Wakami N. (1992): *A self-tuning method of fuzzy reasoning by genetic algorithm*, Proceedings of the 1992 International Fuzzy Systems and Intelligent Control Conference, Louisville, KY, USA, pp. 236-245.

[365] Nozaki K., Ishibuchi H., and Tanaka H. (1996): *Adaptive fuzzy rule-based classification systems*, IEEE Transactions on Fuzzy Systems, Vol. 4, No. 3, pp. 238-249.

[366] Nowicki R. (1999): *Neuro-Fuzzy Systems Performing Different Types of Fuzzy Inference*, Ph.D.Thesis, Technical University of Czestochowa, Poland (in Polish).

[367] Nowicki R. and Rutkowska D. (2000): *New neuro-fuzzy architectures*, Proceedings of the International Conference on Artificial and Computational Intelligence for Decision, Control and Automation in Engineering and Industrial Applications (ACIDCA'2000), Intelligent Methods, Monastir, Tunisia, pp. 82-87.

[368] Oja E. (1982): *A simplified neuron model as a principal component analyzer*, Journal of Mathematical Biolology, Vol. 15, pp. 267-273.

[369] Oja E. (1992): *Self-organizing maps and computer vision*, In: Wechsler H. (Ed.), Neural Networks for Perception, Vol. 1, Academic Press, San Diego, CA, USA, pp. 368-385.

[370] Oliver I.M., Smith D.J., and Holland J.R.C. (1987): *A study of permutation crossover operators on the Traveling Salesman Problem*, In: Grafenstette J.J. (Ed.), Proceedings of the Second International Conference on Genetic Algorithms, Hawrence Erlbaum Associates, Hillsdale, N.J., pp. 224-230.

[371] Orckinnikov S.V. (1983): *General negation in fuzzy set theory*, Journal of Mathematical Analysis and Applications, Vol. 92, pp. 234-239.

[372] Pal S. and Mitra S. (1992): *Multi-layer perceptron, fuzzy sets and classification*, IEEE Transactions on Neural Networks, Vol. 3, pp. 683-697.

[373] Park D, Kandel A., and Langholz G. (1994): *Genetic-based new fuzzy reasoning models with application to fuzzy control*, IEEE Transactions on Systems, Man, and Cybernetics, Vol. 24, pp. 39-47.

[374] Park J. and Sandberg I.W. (1991): *Universal approximation using radial-basis function networks*, Neural Computation, Vol. 3, pp. 246-257.

[375] Parker D.B. (1982): *Learning Logic*, Invention Report S81-64, File 1, Office of Technology Licensing, Stanford University.

[376] Parzen E. (1962): *On estimation of a probability density function and mode*, Annals of Mathematics and Statistics, Vol. 33, pp. 1065-1076.

[377] Passino K.M. (1996): *Toward bridging the perceived gap between conventional and intelligent control*, In: Gupta M.M. and Sinha N.K. (Eds.), Intelligent Control Systems: Theory and Applications, IEEE Press, New York, pp. 3-27.

[378] Passino K.M. and Yurkovich S. (1998): *Fuzzy Control*, Addison-Wesley.

[379] Patterson D.W. (1996): *Artificial Neural Networks. Therory and Applications*, Prentice Hall, Singapore

[380] Pawlak Z. (1982): *Rough sets*, International Journal of Computer and Information Science, Vol. 11, pp. 341-356.

[381] Pawlak Z. (1991): *Rough Sets. Theoretical Aspects of Reasoning about Data*, Kluwer Academic Publishers, Dordrecht.

[382] Pedrycz W. (1991): *Neurocomputations in relational systems*, IEEE Transactions on Pattern Analysis and Machine Intelligence, Vol. 13, pp. 289-296.

[383] Pedrycz W. (1993): *Fuzzy Control and Fuzzy Systems*, John Wiley & Sons, New York.

[384] Pedrycz W. (1993): *Fuzzy neural networks and neurocomputations*, Fuzzy Sets and Systems, Vol. 56, pp. 1-28.

[385] Pedrycz W. (1993): *Fuzzy-set based models of neurons and knowledge-based networks*, IEEE Transactions on Fuzzy Systems, Vol. 1, No. 4, pp. 254-266.

[386] Pedrycz W. (1995): *Fuzzy Sets Engineering*, CRC Press, Boca Raton, Ann Arbor, London, Tokyo.

[387] Pedrycz W. (1998): *Computational Intelligence: An Introduction*, CRC Press, Boca Raton, New York.

[388] Pedrycz W. (2000): *Neural networks in the framework of granular computing*, International Journal of Applied Mathematics and Computer Science, Vol. 10, No. 4, pp. 723-745.

[389] Pedrycz W. and Card H.C. (1992): *Linguistic interpretation of self-organizing maps*, Proceedings of the 1st IEEE International Conference on Fuzzy Systems (FUZZ-IEEE'92), San Diego, CA, USA, pp. 371-378.

[390] Pedrycz W. and Reformat M. (1996): *Genetic optimization with fuzzy coding*, In: Herrera F. and Verdegay J. (Eds.), Genetic Algorithms and Soft Computing, Physica Verlag, pp. 51-67.

[391] Perneel C., Themlin J.M., Renders J.M., and Acheroy M. (1995): *Optimization of fuzzy expert systems using genetic algorithms and neural networks*, IEEE Transactions on Fuzzy Systems, Vol. 3, No. 3, pp. 300-312.

[392] Pétieau A.M., Moreau A., and Willaeys D. (1990): *Tools for approximate reasoning in expert systems*, Proceedings of the TIMS/ORSA Conference, Las Vegas, NE, USA.

[393] Piegat A. (1999): *Modeling and Fuzzy Control*, EXIT Academic Publishing House, Warsaw, Poland (in Polish).

[394] Piliński M. (1996): *Universal Network Trainer*, Proceedings of the Second Conference on Neural Networks and Their Applications, Szczyrk, Poland, pp. 383-391.

[395] Piliński M. (1997): *FLiNN – User Mannual*, Polish Neural Network Society, Czestochowa, Poland (in Polish).

[396] Piliński M. (1997): *Methodology of Automatic Learning of Fuzzy Controllers Using Neural Networks*, Ph.D. Thesis, Technical University of Czestochowa, Poland (in Polish).

[397] Plaut D., Nowlan S., and Hinton G. (1986): *Experiments on Learning by Back Propagation*, Technical Report CMU-CS-86-126, Department of Computer Science, Carnegie Mellon University, Pittsburgh, PA.

[398] Poggio T. and Girosi F. (1989): *A Theory of Networks for Approximation and Learning*, A.I. Memo 1140, MIT, Cambridge, MA.

[399] Pople H. (1977): *The formation of composite hypotheses in diagnostic problem solving: An exercise in synthetic reasoning*, Proceedings of the International Joint Conference on Artificial Intelligence, Vol. 5, pp. 1030-1037.

[400] Pople H. (1982): *Heuristic methods for imposing structure on ill-structured problems: The structuring of medical diagnostics*, In: Szolovits P. (Ed.), Artificial Intelligence in Medicine, Westview Press, Boulder, CO, USA, pp. 119-190.

[401] Pople H., Myers J., and Miller R. (1975): *DIALOG: A model of diagnostic logic for internal medicine*, Proceedings of the International Joint Conference on Artificial Intelligence, Vol. 4, pp. 848-855.

[402] Powell M.J.D. (1987): *Radial basis functions for multivariable interpolation: A review*, In: Mason J.C. and Cox M.G. (Eds.), Algorithm for Approximation of Functions and Data, Oxford University Press, pp. 143-167.

[403] Procyk T.J. and Mamdani E.H. (1979): *A linguistic self-organising process controller*, Automatica, Vol. 15, pp. 15-39.

[404] Radecki T. (1977): *Level fuzzy sets*, Journal of Cybernetics, Vol. 7, pp. 189-198.

[405] Reilly K.D., Buckley J.J., and Krishnamraju K.V. (1996): *Joint back-propagation and genetic algorithms for training fuzzy neural nets with applications to the "Robokid" problem*, Proceedings of the Conference: IPMU'96 , Granada, Spain, Vol. 1, pp. 187-192.

[406] Renals S. and Rohwer R. (1989): *Phoneme classification experiments using radial basis functions*, Proceedings of the International Joint Conference on Neural Networks, Washington, D.C., pp. 461-467.

[407] Riplay B.D. (1996): *Pattern Recognition and Neural Network*, Cambridge University Press.

[408] Rocha A.F. (1981): *Neural fuzzy point processes*, Fuzzy Sets and Systems, Vol. 5, No. 2, pp. 127-140.

[409] Rosenblatt F. (1957): *The Perceptron: A Perceiving and Recognizing Automaton*, Project PARA, Cornell Aeronaut. Lab. Rep. 85-460-1, Cornell University, Ithaca, NY, USA.

[410] Rosenblatt F. (1958): *The perceptron: a probabilistic model for information storage and organization in the brain*, Psychological Review, Vol. 65, pp. 386-408.

[411] Rosenblatt F. (1959): *Principles of Neurodynamics*, Spartan Books, New York.

[412] Rovatti R. and Guerrieri (1996): *Fuzzy sets of rules for system identification*, IEEE Transactions on Fuzzy Systems, Vol. 4, pp. 89-102.

[413] Rumelhart D.E., Hinton G.E., and Williams R.J. (1986): *Learning internal representations by error propagation*, In: Parallel Distributed Processing: Foundations, Vol. 1, The MIT Press, Cambridge, MA, pp. 318-362.

[414] Ruspini E.H. (1969): *A new approach to clustering*, Information and Control, Vol. 15, No. 1, pp. 22-32.

[415] Ruspini E.H. (1970): *Numerical methods for fuzzy clustering*, Information Sciences, Vol. 2, pp. 319-350.

[416] Ruspini E.H. (1972): *Optimization in sample descriptions – Data reduction and pattern recognition using fuzzy clustering*, IEEE Transactions on Systems, Man, and Cybernetics, Vol. SMC-2, p. 541.

[417] Ruspini E.H. (1973): *New experimental results in fuzzy clustering*, Information Sciences, Vol. 6, pp. 273-284.

[418] Ruspini E.H. (1977): *A theory of fuzzy clustering*, Proceedings of the 1977 IEEE Conference on Decisions and Control, New Orleans, pp. 1378-1383.

[419] Russo M. (1998): *FuGeNeSys – a fuzzy genetic neural system for fuzzy modeling*, IEEE Transactions on Fuzzy Systems, Vol. 6, No. 3, pp. 373-388.

[420] Rutkowska D. (1997): *Intelligent Computational Systems. Genetic Algorithms and Neural Networks in Fuzzy Systems*, PLJ Academic Publishing House, Warsaw, Poland (in Polish).

[421] Rutkowska D. (1997): *Neural structures of fuzzy systems*, Proceedings of the IEEE International Symposium on Circuits and Systems (ISCAS'97), Hong Kong, pp. 601-604.

[422] Rutkowska D. (1997): *Fuzzy inference systems with neural networks-based defuzzification*, Archives of Theoretical and Applied Computer Science, Vol. 9, pp. 109-129.

[423] Rutkowska D. (1998): *On generating fuzzy rules by an evolutionary approach*, Cybernetics and Systems: An International Journal, Vol. 29, No. 4, pp. 391-407.

[424] Rutkowska D. (1998): *Non-singleton fuzzy models*, Applied Mathematics and Computer Science, Vol. 8, No. 2, pp. 435-444.

[425] Rutkowska D. (1999): *Neural-fuzzy-genetic systems with RBFN defuzzifier*, In.: M. Mohammadian (Ed.), Computational Intelligence for Modelling, Control, and Automation (CIMCA'99), IOS Press, pp. 184-189.

[426] Rutkowska D. (2000): *Neural network architectures of fuzzy systems*, In: Hampel R., Wagenknecht M., and Chaker N. (Eds.), Fuzzy Control Theory and Practice, Physica-Verlag, A Springer-Verlag Company, Heidelberg.

[427] Rutkowska D. and Hayashi Y. (1999): *Neuro-fuzzy systems approaches*, Journal of Advanced Computational Intelligence, Vol. 3, No. 3, pp. 177-185.

[428] Rutkowska D. and Nowicki R. (1999): *Fuzzy inference neural networks based on destructive and constructive approaches and their application to classification*, Proceedings of the 4th Conference on Neural Networks and Their Applications, Zakopane, Poland, pp. 294-301.

[429] Rutkowska D. and Nowicki R. (2000): *Neuro-fuzzy architectures based on Fodor implication*, Proceedings of the 8th Zittau Fuzzy Colloquium, Zittau, Germany, pp. 230-237.

[430] Rutkowska D. and Nowicki R. (2000): *Implication-based neuro-fuzzy architectures*, International Journal of Applied Mathematics and Computer Science, Vol. 10, No. 4, pp. 675-701.

[431] Rutkowska D. and Nowicki R. (2001): *Neuro-fuzzy systems: Destructive approach*, In: Chojcan J. and Leski J. (Eds.), Fuzzy Sets and Their Applications, Silesian University Press, Gliwice, Poland, pp. 285-292.

[432] Rutkowska D., Nowicki R., and Rutkowski L. (1999): *Singleton and non-singleton fuzzy systems with nonparametric defuzzification*, In: Szczepaniak P. (Ed.), Computational Intelligence and Applications, Physica-Verlag, A Springer-Verlag Company, Heidelberg, New York, pp. 292-301.

[433] Rutkowska D., Nowicki R., and Rutkowski L. (2000): *Neuro-fuzzy architectures with various implication operators*, In: Sincák P., Vascak J., Kvasnicka V., and Mesiar R. (Eds.), The State of the Art in Computational Intelligence, Physica-Verlag, A Springer-Verlag Company, Heidelberg, New York, pp. 214-219.

[434] Rutkowska D., Piliński M., and Rutkowski L. (1997): *Neural Networks, Genetic Algorithms, and Fuzzy Systems*, PWN Scientific Publishers, Warsaw, Poland (in Polish).

[435] Rutkowska D. and Rutkowski L. (1999): *Neural-fuzzy-genetic parallel computing system as a tool for various applications*, Proceedings of the Third International Conference on Parallel Processing & Applied Mathematics, Kazimierz Dolny, Poland, pp. 489-498.

[436] Rutkowska D., Rutkowski L., and Nowicki R. (1999): *On processing of noisy data by fuzzy inference neural networks*, Proceedings of the IASTED International Conference Signal and Image Processing (SIP'99), Nassau, Bahamas, pp. 314-318.

[437] Rutkowska D., Rutkowski L., and Nowicki R. (2001): *Neuro-fuzzy system with inference based on bounded product*, In: Mastorakis N. (Ed.), Advances in Neural Networks and Applications, World Scientific and Engineering Society Press, pp. 104-109.

[438] Rutkowska D. and Starczewski A. (1999): *Two-stage clustering algorithm*, Proceedings of the 4th Conference on Neural Networks and Their Applications, Zakopane, Poland, pp. 220-225.

[439] Rutkowska D. and Starczewski A. (1999): *Parallel computing in application to medical diagnosis*, Proceedings of the 5th International Conference: Computers in Medicine, Łodz, Poland, Vol. II, pp. 71-76.

[440] Rutkowska D. and Starczewski A. (2000): *Fuzzy inference neural networks and their applications to medical diagnosis*, In: Szczepaniak P.S., Lisboa P.J.G., and Kacprzyk J. (Eds.), Fuzzy Systems in Medicine, Physica-Verlag, A Springer-Verlag Company, Heidelberg - New York, pp. 503-518.

[441] Rutkowska D. and Starczewski A. (2001): *A neuro-fuzzy classifier that can learn from mistakes*, Proceedings of the 10th International Conference on System-Modelling-Control, Zakopane, Poland, Vol. 2, pp. 189-194.

[442] Rutkowska D. and Wiaderek K. (2000): *Fuzzy classification of colour patterns*, Proceedings of the 5th Conference on Neural Networks and Soft Computing, Zakopane, Poland, pp. 368-373.

[443] Rutkowska D. and Zadeh L.A. (Eds.) (2000): *Neuro-Fuzzy and Soft Computing*, special issue of the International Journal of Applied Mathematics and Computer Science, Vol. 10, No. 4.

[444] Rutkowski L. and Gałkowski T. (1994): *On pattern classification and system identification by probabilistic neural networks*, Applied Mathematics and Computer Science, Vol. 4, No. 3, pp. 413-422.

[445] Rutkowski L. and Starczewski J. (2000): *From type-1 to type-2 fuzzy inference systems. Part 1, Part 2*, Proceedings of the Fifth Conference on Neural Networks and Soft Computing, Zakopane, Poland, pp. 46-51, 52-64.

[446] Sadler D.R. (1975): *Numerical Methods for Nonlinear Regression*, St. Lucia, University of Queensland Press.

[447] Sage A.P. (Ed.) (1990): *Concise Encyclopedia of Information Processing in Systems and Organization*, Pergamon Press, New York.

[448] Saito K. and Nakano R. (1988): *Medical diagnostic expert system based on PDP model*, Proceedings of the 2nd IEEE International Conference on Neural Networks, San Diego, CA, USA, pp. 255-262.

[449] Sanchez E. (1993): *Fuzzy genetic algorithms in soft computing environment*, Proceedings of the 5th International Fuzzy Systems Association World Congress (IFSA'93), Seul, Korea, pp. 1-13.

[450] Satyadas A. and Krishnakumar K. (1994): *GA-optimized fuzzy controller for spacecraft altitude control*, Proceedings of the 3rd IEEE International Conference on Fuzzy Systems (FUZZ-IEEE'94), Orlando, FL, USA, pp. 1979-1984.

[451] Sbarbaro-Hofer D., Neumerkel D., and Hunt K. (1992): *Neural control of a steel rolling mill*, Proceedings of the IEEE International Symposium on Intelligent Control, Glasgow, pp. 122-127.

[452] Schaffer J.D. (1994): *Combinations of genetic algorithms with neural networks or fuzzy systems*, In: Zurada J.M., Marks II R.J., and Robinson C.J. (Eds.), Computational Intelligence and Imitating Life, IEEE Press, New York, pp. 371-382.

[453] Schaffer J.D., Whitley L., and Eshelman J. (1992): *Combinations of genetic algorithms and neural networks. A survey of the state of art*, Proceedings of the International Workshop on Combinations of Genetic Algorithms and Neural Networks (COGANN-92), Baltimore, MD, USA, pp. 1-37.

[454] Schizas C.N., Pattichis C.S., and Middleton L.T. (1992): *Neural networks, genetic algorithms, and k-means algorithm: In search of data classification*, Proceedings of the International Workshop on Combinations of Genetic Algorithms and Neural Networks (COGANN-92), pp. 201-222.

[455] Schneider M., Kandel A., Langholz G., and Chew G. (1996): *Fuzzy Expert System Tools*, John Wiley & Sons, London.

[456] Schwefel H.-P. (1965): *Kybernetische Evolution als Strategie der Experimentellen Forschung in der Strömungstechnik*, Diploma Thesis, Technical University of Berlin, Germany.

[457] Schwefel H.-P. (1984): *Evolution strategies: A family of non-linear optimization techniques based on imitating some principles of organic evolution*, Annals of Operating Research, Vol. 1, pp. 165-167.

[458] Schweizer B. and Sklar A. (1961): *Associative functions and statistical triangle inequalities*, Publicationes Mathematicae, Debrecen, Vol. 8, pp. 169-186.

[459] Schweizer B. and Sklar A. (1963): *Associative functions and abstract semi-groups*, Publicationes Mathematicae, Debrecen, Vol. 10, pp. 69-81.

[460] Sejnowski T.J. and Rosenberg C.R. (1986): *NETtalk: a Parallel Network that Learns to Read Aloud*, John Hopkins University Electrical Engineering and Computer Science Technical Report, JHU/EECS-86/01.

[461] Sejnowski T.J. and Rosenberg C.R. (1987): *Parallel networks that learn to pronounce English text*, Complex Systems, Vol. 1, p. 145.

[462] Setonio R. (1997): *Extracting rules from neural networks by pruning and hidden-unit splitting*, Neural Computation, Vol. 9, pp. 205-225.

[463] Shafer G. (1976): *A Mathematical Theory of Evidence*, Princeton University Press, Princeton, N.J.

[464] Shannon C.E. (1950): *Automatic chess player*, Scientific American, Vol. 182.

[465] Shi Y., Eberhart R., and Chen Y. (1999): *Implementation of evolutionary fuzzy systems*, IEEE Transactions on Fuzzy Systems, Vol. 7, No. 2, pp. 109-119.

[466] Shimojima K., Fukuda T., and Hasegawa Y. (1995): *Self-tuning fuzzy modeling with adaptive membership function, rules, and hierarchical structure based on genetic algorithm*, Fuzzy Sets and Systems, Vol. 71, pp. 295-309.

[467] Shortliffe E.H. (1976): *Computer-Based Medical Consultations: MYCIN*, Elsevier, New York.

[468] Shonkwiler R. and Miller K.R. (1992): *Genetic algorithm, neural network synergy for nonlinearity constrained optimization problems*, Proceedings of the International Workshop on Combinations of Genetic Algorithms and Neural Networks (COGANN-92), pp. 248-257.

[469] Sincak P., Hric M., Sarnovsky J., and Kopco N. (2000): *Fuzzy cluster identification in the feature space using neural networks*, Proccedings of the 6th International Conference on Soft Computing (IIZUKA 2000), Iizuka, Japan, pp. 849-854.

[470] Sincak P., Kopcik M., Kopco N., and Jaksa R. (1997): *Intelligent control of single inverted pendulum*, Proceedings of the Biannual IFAC Workshop of Automation and Control, Smolenice, Slovakia, pp. 375-380.

[471] Simpson P.K. (1990): *Artificial Neural Systems. Foundations, Paradigms, Applications, and Implementations*, Pergamon Press, New York.

[472] Skinner B.F. (1953): *Science and Human Behavior*, The Free Press, New York.

[473] Smith S.F. (1980): *A Learning System Based on Genetic Adaptive Algorithms*, Ph.D. Thesis, University of Pittsburgh.

[474] Song Q. and Bartolan G. (1993): *Some properties of defuzzification neural networks*, Fuzzy Sets and Systems, Vol. 61, pp. 83-89.

[475] Song Q. and Smith R.E. (1992): *Neural network representations of defuzzification*, Proceedings of the Conference on Artificial Neural Networks in Engineering, St. Luis, MO, USA.

[476] Specht D. (1988): *Probabilistic neural networks for classification, mapping or associative memory*, Proceedings of the 2nd IEEE International Conference on Neural Networks, San Diego, CA, USA, Vol. 1, pp. 523-532.

[477] Specht D. (1990): *Probabilistic neural networks*, Neural Networks, Vol. 3, No. 1, pp. 109-118.

[478] Srikanth R., George R., Warsi N., Prabhu D., Petry F.E., and Buckles B.P. (1995): *A variable-length genetic algorithm for clustering and classification*, Pattern Recognition Letters, Vol. 16, pp. 789-800.

[479] Starczewski A. (1999): *Hybrid Learning of Neuro-Fuzzy Systems Using Clustering Algorithms*, Ph.D. Thesis, Technical University of Czestochowa, Poland (in Polish).

[480] Starczewski A. and Rutkowska D. (2000): *New hierarchical structure of neuro-fuzzy systems*, Proceedings of the 5th Conference on Neural Networks and Soft Computing, Zakopane, Poland, pp. 383-388.

[481] Starczewski A. and Rutkowska D. (2000): *Multi-segment neuro-fuzzy system in medical diagnosis*, National Conference on Telemedicine, Łodz, Poland, pp. 29-33 (in Polish).

[482] Straszecka E. (1998): *On an application of Dempster-Shafer theory to medical diagnosis support*, Proceedings of the 6th European Congress on Intelligent Techniques and Soft Computing (EUFIT'98), Aachen, Germany, Vol. 3, pp. 1848-1852.

[483] Straszecka E. and Straszecka J. (1999): *Dempster-Shafer theory and basic probability assignment in diagnosis support*, Proceedings of the EUROFUSE-SIC'99 Conference, Budapest, Hungary, pp. 395-398.

[484] Sugeno M. (1985): *An introductory survey of fuzzy control*, Information Sciences, Vol. 36, pp. 59-83.

[485] Sugeno M. (Ed.) (1985): *Industrial Application of Fuzzy Control*, North Holland, Amsterdam, The Netherlands.

[486] Surmann H., Kanstein A., and Goser K. (1993): *Self-organizing and genetic algorithms for an authomatic design of fuzzy control and decision systems*, Proceedings of the European Congress on Intelligent Techniques and Soft Computing (EUFIT'93), Aachen, Germany, pp. 1097-1104.

[487] Sutton R. and Barto A. (1981): *Towards a modern theory of adaptive networks: expectation and prediction*, Psychological Review, Vol. 88, No. 2, pp. 135-170.

[488] Syswerda G. (1989): *Uniform crossover in genetic algorithms*, In: Schaffer J.D. (Ed.), Proceedings of the Third International Conference on Genetic Algorithms, Morgan Kaufmann Publishers, San Mateo, CA, USA, pp. 2-9.

[489] Syswerda G. (1991): *Schedule optimization using genetic algorithms*, In: Davis L. (Ed.), Handbook of Genetic Algorithms, Van Nostrand Reinhold, New York.

[490] Tadeusiewicz R. (1993): *Neural Networks*, RM Academic Publishing House, Warsaw (in Polish)

[491] Takagi H. (1990): *Fusion technology of fuzzy theory and neural networks – survey and future directions*, Proceedings of the International Conference on Fuzzy Logic & Neural Networks (IIZUKA'90), Iizuka, Japan, pp. 13-26.

[492] Takagi H. (1995): *Cooperative systems of neural networks and fuzzy logic and their application to consumer products*, In: Yen J. and Langari R. (Eds.), Industrial Applications of Fuzzy Control and Intelligent Systems, IEEE Press, pp. 89-101.

[493] Takagi H. (2000): *Fusion technology of neural networks and fuzzy systems: A chronicled progression from the laboratory to our daily lives*, International Journal of Applied Mathematics and Computer Science, Vol. 10, No. 4, pp. 647-673.

[494] Takagi T. and Sugeno M. (1985): *Fuzzy identification of systems and its applications to modeling and control*, IEEE Transactions on Systems, Man and Cybernetics, Vol. 15, pp. 116-132.

[495] Tan A.H. (1997): *Cascade ARTMAP integrating neural computation and symbolic knowledge processing*, IEEE Transactions on Neural Networks, Vol. 8, pp. 237-250.

[496] Teodorescu H.-N., Kandel A., and Jain L.C. (Eds.) (1999): *Fuzzy and Neuro-Fuzzy Systems in Medicine*, CRC Press, Boca Raton, London, New York.

[497] Terano T., Asai K., and Sugeno M. (1992): *Fuzzy Systems Theory and Its Applications*, Academic Press.

[498] Thimm G. and Fiesler E. (1997): *Higher order and multilayer perceptron initialization*, IEEE Transactions on Neural Networks, Vol. 8, pp. 349-359.

[499] Thrift P. (1991): *Fuzzy logic synthesis with genetic algorithms*, Proceedings of the 4th International Conference on Genetic Algorithms (ICGA), San Diego, CA, USA, pp. 509-513.

[500] Tou J.T. and Gonzalez R.C. (1974): *Pattern Recognition Principles*, Addison-Wesley, Reading, MA.

[501] Trillas E. and Valverde L. (1985): *On implication and indistinguishability in the setting of fuzzy logic*, In: Kacprzyk J. and Yager R.R. (Eds.), Management Decision Support Systems Using Fuzzy Sets and Possibility Theory, Verlag TÜV Rheinland, Köln, pp. 198-212.

[502] Tryon R.C. and Bailey D.E. (1970): *Cluster Analysis*, McGraw-Hill, New York.

[503] Tsoukalas L.H. and Uhrig R.E. (1996): *Fuzzy and Neural Approaches in Engineering*, John Wiley & Sons, New York.

[504] Turing A.M. (1963): *Computing machinery and intelligence*, In: Feigenbaum E. and Feldman J. (Eds.), Computers and Thought, McGraw-Hill, New York, pp. 1-35.

[505] Türksen I.B. (1995): *Type I and "interval-valued" type II fuzzy sets and logics*, In: Wang P. (Ed.), Advances in Fuzzy Theory and Technology.

[506] Türksen I.B. (1999): *Type I and type II fuzzy system modeling*, Fuzzy Sets and Systems, Vol. 106, pp. 11-34.

[507] Türksen I.B. (2001): *Type 2 fuzziness in the new millennium*, In: Mastorakis N. (Ed.), Advances in Fuzzy Systems and Evolutionary Computation, World Scientific and Engineering Society Press, pp. 150-155.

[508] Verbruggen H.B., Zimmerman H.-J., and Babuska R. (Eds.) (1999): *Fuzzy Algorithms for Control*, Kluwer Academic Publishers, Boston, Dordrecht, London.

[509] Verhagen C.J.D.M. (1975): *Some general remarks about pattern recognition; Its definiton; Its relation with other disciplines; A literature survey*, Journal of Pattern Recognition, Vol. 83, pp. 109-116.

[510] von der Malsburg C. (1973): *Self-organization of orientation sensitive cells in the striate cortex*, Kybernetik, Vol. 14, pp. 85-100.

[511] Wagenknecht M. and Hartmann K. (1988): *Application of fuzzy sets of type 2 to the solution of fuzzy equation systems*, Fuzzy Sets and Systems, Vol. 25, pp. 183-190.

[512] Wang L.-X. (1992): *Fuzzy systems are universal approximators*, IEEE Transactions on Systems, Man and Cybernetics, Vol. SMC-7, No. 10, pp. 1163-1170.

[513] Wang L.-X. (1994): *Adaptive Fuzzy Systems and Control*, PTR Prentice Hall, Englewood Cliffs, New Jersey.

[514] Wang L.-X. and Mendel J.M. (1992): *Generating fuzzy rules from numerical data, with applications*, USC-SIPI Report 169, University of Southern California, CA, USA.

[515] Wang L.-X. and Mendel J.M. (1992): *Generating fuzzy rules by learning from examples*, IEEE Transactions on Systems, Man and Cybernetics, Vol. 22, No. 6, pp. 1414-1427.

[516] Wang L. and Yen J. (1999): *Extracting fuzzy rules for system modeling using a hybrid of genetic algorithms and Kalman filter*, Fuzzy Sets and Systems, Vol. 101, No. 3, pp. 353-362.

[517] Wasserman P.D. (1989): *Neural Computing. Theory and Practice*, Van Nostrand Reinhold, New York.

[518] Waterman D. (1986): *A Guide to Expert Systems*, Addison-Wesley.

[519] Weber S. (1983): *A general concept of fuzzy connectives, negations and implications based on t-norms and t-co-norms*, Fuzzy Sets and Systems, Vol. 11, pp. 115-134.

[520] Werbos P. (1974): *Beyond Regression: New Tools for Predictions and Analysis in the Behavioral Sciences*, Ph.D. Thesis, Harvard University, Cambridge, MA.

[521] Weiss G. (1994): *Neural networks and evolutionary computation. Part I: Hybrid approaches in artificial intelligence*, Proceedings of the First IEEE Conference on Evolutionary Computation, pp. 268-272.

[522] Weiss G. (Ed.) (1999): *Multiagent Systems. A Modern Approach to Distributed Artificial Intelligence*, The MIT Press, Cambridge, MA.

[523] Werntges H.W. (1993): *Partitions of unity improve neural function approximators*, Proceedings of the IEEE International Conference on Neural Networks, San Francisco, CA, USA, pp. 914-918.

[524] Wettschereck D. and Dietterich T. (1992): *Improving the performance of radial basis fuction networks by learning center locations*, In: Moody J.E., Hanson S.J., and Lippmann R.P. (Eds.), Advances in Neural Information Processing Systems, Vol. 4, Morgan Kaufmann Publishers, San Mateo, CA, USA.

[525] Whitley D. (1988): *GENITOR: a different genetic algorithm*, Proceedings of the Rocky Mountain Conference on Artificial Intelligence, Denver, CO, USA.

[526] Whitley D. (1989): *Applying genetic algorithms to neural network learning*, Proceedings of the Seventh Conference of the Society of Artificial Intelligence and Simulation Behaviour, Sussex, England, Pitman Publishing, pp. 137-144.

[527] Whitley D., Starkweather T., and Bogart C. (1990): *Genetic algorithms and neural networks: Optimizing connections and connectivity*, Parallel Computing, No. 14, pp. 347-361.

[528] Whitley D., Starkweather T., and Fuquay D. (1989): *Scheduling problems and traveling salesman: the genetic edge recombination operator*, Proceedings of the Third International Conference on Genetic Algorithms and Their Applications, Morgan Kaufmann Publishers, San Mateo, CA, USA.

[529] Widrow B. (1959): *Adaptive sampled-data systems – A statistical theory of adaptation*, WESCON Convention Record: Part 4, pp. 74-85.

[530] Widrow B. (1960): *An Adaptive "Adaline" Neuron Using Chemical "Memistors"*, Standard Electronics Laboratory Technical Report 1553-2.

[531] Widrow B. and Hoff M. (1960): *Adaptive switching circuits*, IRE Western Electric Show and Convention Record, Part 4, pp. 96-104.

[532] Widrow B. and Stearns S.D. (1985): *Adaptive Signal Processing*, Prentice-Hall, Englewood Cliffs, New Jersey.

[533] Willmott R. (1980): *Two fuzzier implication operators in the theory of fuzzy power sets*, Fuzzy Sets and Systems, Vol. 4, pp. 31-36.

[534] Willshaw D.J. and von der Malsburg C. (1976): *How patterned neural connections can be set up by self-organization*, Proceedings of the Royal Society of London, Series B, Vol. 194, pp. 431-445.

[535] Winston H. (1984): *Artificial Intelligence*, Second Edition, Addison-Wesley, Reading, MA.

[536] Wolberg W.H., Mangasarian O.L. (1990): *Multisurface method of pattern separation for medical diagnosis applied to breast cytology*, Proceedings of the National Academy of Science of the USA, Vol. 87, pp. 9193-9196.

[537] Wong C.C., Su M.C., and Lin N.S. (1996): *Extraction of fuzzy control rules using genetic algorithms*, In: Chiang W. and Lee J. (Eds), Fuzzy Logic for the Applications to Complex Systems, World Scientific, Singapore, pp. 47-52.

[538] Yager R.R. (1980): *On the measure of fuzziness and negation. Part II: Lattices*, Information and Control, Vol. 44, pp. 236-260.

[539] Yager R.R. (1980): *An approach to inference in approximate reasoning*, International Journal of Man-Machine Studies, Vol. 13, pp. 323-338.

[540] Yager R.R. (1980): *Fuzzy subsets of type II in decisions*, Journal of Cybernetics, Vol. 10, pp. 137-159.

[541] Yager R.R. (1986): *A characterization of the extension principle*, Fuzzy Sets and Systems, Vol. 18 , pp. 205-217.

[542] Yager R.R. (1987): *On the aggregation of processing units in neural networks*, Proceedings of the 1st IEEE International Conference on Neural Networks, San Diego, CA, USA, pp. 327-333.

[543] Yager R.R. (1988): *On ordered weighted averaging aggregation operators in multi-criteria decision making*, IEEE Transactions on Systems, Man, and Cybernetics, Vol. SMC-18, pp.183-190.

[544] Yager R.R. (1991): *On a semantics for neural networks based on linguistic quantifiers*, Technical Report MII-1103, Machine Intelligence Institute, Iona College, New Rochelle, N. Y., USA.

[545] Yager R.R. (1992): *OWA Neurons: A New Class of Fuzzy Neurons*, Technical Report MII-1217, Machine Intelligence Institute, Iona College, New Rochelle, N. Y., USA.

[546] Yager R.R. (1997): *Fuzzy logics and artificial intelligence*, Fuzzy Sets and Systems, Vol. 90 , pp. 193-198.

[547] Yager R.R. and Filev D.P. (1994): *Essentials of Fuzzy Modeling and Control*, John Wiley & Sons.

[548] Yager R.R. and Kacprzyk J. (1997): *The Ordered Weithted Averaging Operators: Theory and Applications*, Kluwer Academic Publishers, Boston.

[549] Yager R.R. and Zadeh L.A. (Eds.) (1994): *Fuzzy Sets, Neural Networks, and Soft Computing*, Van Nostrand Reinhold, New York.

[550] Yamakawa T. (1990): *Pattern recognition hardware system emploing a fuzzy neuron*, Proceedings of the International Conference on Fuzzy Logic & Neural Networks (IIZUKA'90), Iizuka, Japan, pp. 943-948.

[551] Yamakawa T. and Furukawa M. (1992): *A design of membership functions for a fuzzy neuron using example-based learning*, Proceedings of the 1st IEEE International Conference on Fuzzy Systems (FUZZ-IEEE'92), San Diego, CA, USA, pp. 75-82.

[552] Yamakawa T. and Tomoda S. (1989): *A fuzzy neuron and Its application to pattern recognition*, Proceedings of the 3rd International Fuzzy Systems Association World Congress (IFSA'89), Seatle, WA, USA, pp. 30-38.

[553] Yamakawa T., Uchino E., Miki T., and Kusanagi H. (1992): *A neo fuzzy neuron and its application to system identification and prediction of the system behavior*, Proceedings of the 2nd International Conference on Fuzzy Logic & Neural Networks (IIZUKA'92), Iizuka, Japan, pp. 477-483.

[554] Yan J., Ryan M., and Power J. (1994): *Using Fuzzy Logic. Towards Intelligent Systems*, Prentice-Hall, New York.

[555] Yao X. (1993): *A review of evolutionary artificial neural networks*, International Journal of Intelligent Systems, pp. 539-567.

[556] Yoon B., Holmes D.J., Langholz G., and Kandel A. (1994): *Efficient genetic algorithms for training layered feedforward neural networks*, Information Sciences, Vol. 76, pp. 67-85.

[557] Yuan B., Klir G.J., and Swan-Stone J.F. (1995): *Evolutionary fuzzy c-means clustering algorithm*, Proceedings of the 4th IEEE International Conference on Fuzzy Systems (FUZZ-IEEE'95), Yokohama, Japan, pp. 2221-2226.

[558] Yuille A.L., Kammen D.M., and Cohen D.S. (1989): *Quadrature and the development of orientation selective cortical cells by Hebb rules*, Biological Cybernetics, Vol. 61, pp. 183-194.

[559] Zadeh L.A. (1965): *Fuzzy sets*, Information and Control, Vol. 8, No. 3, pp. 338-353.

[560] Zadeh L.A (1971): *Similarity relations and fuzzy orderings*, Information Science, Vol. 3, pp. 177-200.

[561] Zadeh L.A (1971): *Towards a theory of fuzzy systems*, In: Kalman R.E. and DeClaris N. (Eds.), Aspects of Network and System Theory, Holt, Rinehart and Winston, New York.

[562] Zadeh L.A (1972): *A fuzzy-set theoretic interpretation of linguistic hedges*, Journal of Cybernetics, Vol. 2, pp. 4-34.

[563] Zadeh L.A (1973): *Outline of a new approach to the analysis of complex systems and decision processes*, IEEE Transactions on Systems, Man, and Cybernetics, Vol. SMC-3, No. 1, pp. 28-44.

[564] Zadeh L.A (1974): *On the analysis of large scale systems*, In: Gottinger H. (Ed.), Systems Approaches and Environment Problems, Vandenhoeck and Ruprecht, pp. 23-37.

[565] Zadeh L.A (1974): *Fuzzy logic and its application to approximate reasoning*, Information Processing, Vol. 74, pp. 591-594.

[566] Zadeh L.A (1975): *Calculus of fuzzy restrictions*, In: Zadeh L.A., Fu K.-S., Tanaka K. and Shimura M. (Eds.), Fuzzy Sets and Their Applications to Cognitive and Decision Processes, Academic Press, New York, pp. 1-39.

[567] Zadeh L.A (1975): *The concept of a linguistic variable and its application to approximate reasoning*, Information Science, Part I, Vol. 8, pp. 199-249, Part II, Vol. 8, pp. 301-357, Part III, Vol. 9, pp. 43-80.

[568] Zadeh L.A. (1976): *A fuzzy-algorithmic approach to the definition of complex or imprecise concepts*, International Journal of Man-Machine Studies, Vol. 8, pp. 246-291.

[569] Zadeh L.A (1979): *Fuzzy sets and information granularity*, In: Gupta M., Ragade R., and Yager R. (Eds.), Advances in Fuzzy Set Theory and Applications, North Holland, Amsterdam, pp. 3-18.

[570] Zadeh L.A. (1981): *Test-score semantics for natural languages and meaning representation via PRUF*, In: Rieger B. (Ed.), Empirical Semantics, Germany, pp. 281-349.

[571] Zadeh L.A. (1983): *The role of fuzzy logic in the management of uncertainty in expert systems*, Fuzzy Sets and Systems, Vol. 11, pp. 199-227.

[572] Zadeh L.A. (1986): *Outline of a computational approach to meaning and knowledge representation based on a concept of a generalized assignment statement*, In: Thoma M. and Wyner A. (Eds.), Proceedings of the International Seminar on Artificial Inteligence and Man-Machine Systems, Springer-Verlag, Heidelberg, pp. 198-211.

[573] Zadeh L.A (1994): *Fuzzy logic, neural networks and soft computing*, Communications of the ACM, Vol. 37, No. 3, pp. 77-84.

[574] Zadeh L.A (1996): *Fuzzy logic and the calculi of fuzzy rules and fuzzy graphs: a precis*, Multiple Valued Logic, Vol. 1, pp. 1-38.

[575] Zadeh L.A (1996): *Fuzzy logic = computing with words*, IEEE Transactions on Fuzzy Systems, Vol. 4, pp. 103-111.

[576] Zadeh L.A (1997): *Toward a theory of fuzzy information granulation and its centrality in human reasoning and fuzzy logic*, Fuzzy Sets and Systems, Vol. 90, pp. 111-127.

[577] Zadeh L.A (1999): *From computing with numbers to computing with words – from manipulation of measurements to manipulation of perceptions*, IEEE Transactions on Circuits and Systems - I: Fundamental Theory and Applications, Vol. 45, No. 1, pp. 105-119.

[578] Zadeh L.A (2000): *Outline of a computational theory of perceptions based on computing with words*, In: Sinha N.K. and Gupta M.M. (Eds.), Soft Computing and Intelligent Systems: Theory and Applications, Academic Press, San Diego, New York, Tokio, pp. 3-22.

[579] Zadeh L.A. (2001): *A new direction in AI. Toward a computational theory of perceptions*, AI Magazine, Vol. 22, No. 1, pp. 73-84.

[580] Zhang L., Wang L., Zang Y., Seki H., and Itoh H. (1995): *On rule checking and learning in an acupuncture diagnosis fuzzy expert system by genetic algorithm*, Proceedings of the 4th IEEE International Conference on Fuzzy Systems (FUZZ-IEEE'95), Yokohama, Japan, pp. 455-460.

[581] Zhang X., Hang C.-C., Tan S., and Wang P.-Z. (1996): *The min-max function differentiation and training of fuzzy neural networks*, IEEE Transactions on Neural Networks, Vol. 7, pp. 1139-1150.

[582] Zhang Y. and Kandel A. (1998): *Compensatory Genetic Fuzzy Neural Networks and Their Applications*, World Scientific, Singapore.

[583] Zimmermann H.-J. (1991): *Fuzzy Set Theory and Its Applications*, Kluwer Academic Publishers, London.

[584] Żurada J.M. (1992): *Introduction to Artificial Neural Systems*, West Publishing Company.

[585] Żurada J.M. and Lozowski A. (1996): *Generating linguistic rules from data using neuro-fuzzy framework*, Proccedings of the 4th International Conference on Soft Computing (IIZUKA'96), Iizuka, Japan, pp. 618-621.

[586] Żurada J.M., Marks II R.J., and Robinson C.J. (Eds.) (1994): *Computational Intelligence. Imitating Life*, IEEE Press, New York.

[587] FlexTool (GA) M2.1, Flexible Intelligence Group, L.L.C. Tuscauloosa, AL 35486-1477, USA

[588] Evolver – The Genetic Algorithm Problem Solver, Axcelis, Inc. 4668 Eastern Avenue N., Seatle, WA 98103, USA.

[589] BrainMaker, California Scientific Software, Nevada City, CA95959, USA.

[590] Genetic Training Option, California Scientific Software, Nevada City, CA95959, USA.

[591] Webster's New World Dictionary of Computer Terms, Third Edition, Prentice-Hall, Englewood Cliffs, New Jersey.